■ Learned Ignorance

Learned Ignorance

Intellectual Humility among Jews,
Christians, and Muslims

EDITED BY

James L. Heft, S.M.,
Reuven Firestone,

AND

Omid Safi

OXFORD
UNIVERSITY PRESS

OXFORD
UNIVERSITY PRESS

Oxford University Press, Inc., publishes works that further
Oxford University's objective of excellence
in research, scholarship, and education.

Oxford   New York
Auckland   Cape Town   Dar es Salaam   Hong Kong   Karachi
Kuala Lumpur   Madrid   Melbourne   Mexico City   Nairobi
New Delhi   Shanghai   Taipei   Toronto

With offices in
Argentina   Austria   Brazil   Chile   Czech Republic   France   Greece
Guatemala   Hungary   Italy   Japan   Poland   Portugal   Singapore
South Korea   Switzerland   Thailand   Turkey   Ukraine   Vietnam

Published by Oxford University Press, Inc.
198 Madison Avenue, New York, New York 10016

www.oup.com

Library of Congress Cataloging-in-Publication Data
Learned ignorance : intellectual humility among Jews, Christians, and Muslims
/ edited by James L. Heft, Reuven Firestone, and Omid Safi.
    p.   cm.
Proceedings of a conference held in June 2007 at the Tantur Ecumenical Institute
in Jerusalem. Includes index.
ISBN 978-0-19-976930-8; ISBN 978-0-19-976931-5 (pbk.);
ISBN 978-0-19-977306-0 (ebook)
1. Abrahamic religions—Congresses.   2. Religions—Relations—Congresses.
3. Catholic Church—Relations—Congresses.   I. Heft, James.
II. Firestone, Reuven, 1952–   III. Safi, Omid, 1970–
BL410.L43 2011
201'.5—dc22   2010030256

■ *Rabbi Dr. Michael Signer*
  (1945–2009)

■ *"Dialogue does not occur between religions but*
  between people who are profoundly committed to
  a life within their own community."

■ *We dedicate this volume to Michael Signer, deeply*
  grateful for his leadership, scholarship and personal
  commitment to interreligious dialogue.

CONTENTS

■ CONTRIBUTORS

Asma Afsaruddin is Professor of Islamic Studies in the Department of Near Eastern Languages & Cultures at Indiana University, Bloomington. She is the author and editor of four books, including *The First Muslims: History and Memory* (2008) and *Excellence and Precedence: Medieval Islamic Discourse on Legitimate Leadership* (1999). She has also published extensively on pluralism in Islamic thought; interfaith relations, reconciliation, and violence in Islamic sources; and gender issues in scholarly journals such as the *Journal of Religious Ethics*, the *Muslim World*, the *Journal of Ecumenical Studies*, and the *Journal of Church and State*, in addition to more popular venues such as the *Christian Science Monitor* and the *Review of Faith and International Affairs*. A recipient of research grants from the Guggenheim Foundation and the Carnegie Corporation, Afsaruddin is currently completing a manuscript on jihad and martyrdom in Islamic thought and practice, forthcoming from Oxford University Press.

David Burrell has been working since 1982 in comparative issues in philosophical theology in Judaism, Christianity, and Islam, as evidenced in *Knowing the Unknowable God: Ibn-Sina, Maimonides, Aquinas* (1986), *Freedom and Creation in Three Traditions*, (1993), and two translations of al-Ghazali: *Al-Ghazali on the Ninety-Nine Beautiful Names of God* (1993), and *Al-Ghazali on Faith in Divine Unity and Trust in Divine Providence* (2001). More recent books include collected essays outlining strategies in philosophical theology, *Faith and Freedom* (2003), a theological commentary on the book of Job, *Deconstructing Theodicy* (2008), and an appreciation of the life and work of John Zahm C.S.C. from his writings: *When Faith and Reason Meet* (Notre Dame, IN: Sorin Books, 2009). A visiting member of the Dominican Institute for Oriental Studies in Cairo, as well as the Tantur Ecumenical Institute in Jerusalem, he is currently professor of ethics and development at Uganda Martyrs University.

Elizabeth Groppe is associate professor of systematic theology at Xavier University in Cincinnati, Ohio and co-director of Xavier's Ethics/Religion and Society Program. She earned her doctorate at the University of Notre Dame and is the author of *Yves Congar's Theology of the Holy Spirit* (Oxford, 2004) and *Eating and Drinking* (Fortress, forthcoming) a volume in a series on Christian faith and the practices of everyday life. Her articles on trinitarian theology, pneumatology, and Christian-Jewish relations have been published in *Theological Studies, Modern Theology, Horizons, Worship,* and the annual volume of the College Theology Society. Her interests in constructive theology include garnering the resources of the Christian tradition to respond to the crises of ecological degradation, failed economic systems, and war. Her work in Christian-Jewish dialogue has origins in a trip to the Center for Dialogue and Prayer near Auschwitz led by Rabbi Michael and Betty Signer in 2000.

Rabbi Reuven Firestone is professor of medieval Judaism and Islam at Hebrew Union College in Los Angeles and founding co-director of the Center for Muslim-Jewish Engagement (www.usc.edu/cmje). His books include *Journeys in Holy Lands: The Evolution of the Abraham-Ishmael Legends in Islamic Exegesis* (SUNY Press), *Jihad: The Origin of Holy War in Islam* (Oxford University Press), *Children of Abraham: An Introduction to Judaism for Muslims* (Ktav), *Jews, Christians, Muslims in Dialogue: A Practical Handbook*, with Leonard Swidler and Khalid Duran. *New London, CT: Twenty-Third Publications, 2006, An Introduction to Islam for Jews* (JPS, 2008), and *The Revival of Holy War in Modern Judaism* (forthcoming), and he has written over eighty articles and book chapters on Judaism, Islam, and comparative studies between Judaism, Christianity and Islam that appear in a variety of journals, encyclopedias and scholarly compilations.

James L. Heft, a member of the Society of Mary (Marianists), did doctoral studies in historical theology at the University of Toronto. In 2006, after thirty years at the University of Dayton, he joined the faculty of the University of Southern California where he is the president of the Institute for Advanced Catholic Studies. Along with three other leaders in Catholic higher education, he founded, in 1996, *Catholic Education: A Journal of Inquiry and Practice*. He has published and edited eight books and written over 160 articles and book chapters. He has also been a nationally recognized leader in cross-disciplinary faculty development work and is the recipient of four honorary degrees.

Afra Jalabi is a Montreal-based writer. She was raised in Syria, Germany, and Saudi Arabia before immigrating to Canada. She has a BA in anthropology and political science from McGill University, an MA in journalism from Carleton University, and has worked as a columnist for the Arab press for the last ten years. She is a member of the editorial board of the *Journal of Law and Religion*. Her interests lie in the theory of nonviolence, early Islamic history and texts, Quranic exegesis, and feminist theory. Jalabi has also been a research assistant and editor for her uncle, Jawdat Said. She is a PhD candidate in the Department of Religion at Concordia, University in Montreal.

Stanislaw Krajewski obtained a PhD in mathematics at the Institute of Mathematics of the Polish Academy of Sciences. Currently a professor at the Institute of Philosophy of the University of Warsaw, he has worked in logic and philosophy of mathematics as well as philosophy of religion and interfaith dialogue. He is co-founder of the Polish Council of Christians and Jews, of which he has been the Jewish co-chairman since its inception in 1989. From 1997 to 2006, he was on the board of the Union of Jewish Religious Communities in Poland, and, from its beginning in 1990 until 2006, he was a member of the International Council of the Auschwitz Camp Museum and Memorial. Krajewski is the author of papers in the field of logic, as well as publications on Judaism, Jewish experience, and Christian-Jewish dialogue, and, most recently, he has published *The Mystery of Israel and the Mystery of the Church* (in Polish); *Poland and the Jews: Reflections of a Polish Polish Jew* (in English, Krakow:

Austeria, 2005). He co-edited *Abraham Joshua Heschel: Philosophy, Theology and Interreligious Dialogue* (in English, Wiesbaden: Harrassowitz Verlag, 2009).

Rabbi Shira Lander is a visiting assistant professor of religious studies at Rice University. She earned her BA, cum laude, in Mathematics and Philosophy from Yale University, her MA in Jewish Studies and rabbinic ordination from the Hebrew Union College-Jewish Institute of Religion, and her PhD in Greco-Roman period Judaism and Christianity from the University of Pennsylvania. Her dissertation examined the social uses and effects of Christian martyr cult rituals in late Roman North Africa. Lander has taught at the Ecumenical Institute of St. Mary's Seminary and University in Baltimore, where she was awarded a Dunning Distinguished Lectureship Chair; Johns Hopkins University; Princeton University; the University of Maryland-Baltimore County; Baltimore Hebrew University; and the University of Delaware. She has published on a variety of topics ranging from Jewish studies to Roman period interreligious relations. Most recently, she wrote for Oxford University Press a commentary on 1 Corinthians (forthcoming *Jewish Annotated New Testament*). Her current research project, Spatial Relations, explores the interaction of Christians, Jews, and polytheists in sacred spaces of the late antique Mediterranean.

Daniel Madigan is an Australian Jesuit who has also studied and taught in India, Pakistan, Egypt, Turkey, Italy, and the United States. From 2000 to 2007 he was the founding director of the Institute for the Study of Religions and Cultures at the Pontifical Gregorian University, Rome. He currently directs a PhD program in religious pluralism at Georgetown University, where he is Jeanette W. and Otto J. Ruesch Family Associate Professor in the Department of Theology, as well as a senior fellow in the Al-Waleed Center for Muslim-Christian Understanding and also in the Woodstock Theological Center, where he directs a program on Christian Theologies Responsive to Islam.

Fr. Michael B. McGarry, originally from Los Angeles, studied for the Catholic priesthood for the Paulist Fathers in Baltimore and Washington, DC, and did his graduate work in theology at University of St. Michael's College in the University of Toronto. He has also taken courses in Jewish Studies at the Hebrew University of Jerusalem. For many years, he has been involved in Jewish-Christian relations, speaking on a variety of topics including Christology, preaching, and Shoah education. He has written *Christology after Auschwitz* and (with Yehezkel Landau) *Pope John Paul II in the Holy Land*. For a number of years, he served on the advisory committee to the United States Conference of Catholic Bishops on Catholic-Jewish Relations. He has served in many pastoral and academic settings, including rector of St. Paul's College in Washington DC, and pastor of Newman Hall, the Catholic Parish at the University of California, Berkeley. From 1999 to 2010, he served as Rector of the Tantur Ecumenical Institute in Jerusalem. In 2009, he was elected president of the Paulist Fathers, where he serves today.

Omid Safi is the Chair for the Study of Islam at the American Academy of Religion. A leading Muslim public intellectual in America, he is a professor of religious studies at the University of North Carolina. His understanding of religion is shaped both by the pluralistic Sufi dimension of Islam as well as the teachings of Martin Luther King, Jr., Gandhi, and His Holiness the Dalai Lama. He is the editor of the volume *Progressive Muslims: On Justice, Gender, and Pluralism* (Oxford: Oneworld Publications, 2003). In this volume, he brought together fifteen Muslim scholars and activists to imagine a new understanding of Islam that is rooted in social justice, gender equality, and religious/ethnic pluralism. His work *The Politics of Knowledge Premodern Islam* was published by UNC Press in 2000. His latest work is *Memories of Muhammad: Why the Prophet Matters*, published by HarperOne in 2009.

Rabbi Michael A. Signer was the Abrams Professor of Jewish Thought and Culture in the Department of Theology at the University of Notre Dame and the Director of the Notre Dame Holocaust Project. He held degrees from Hebrew Union College and the University of Toronto, and he was the author and editor of over fifty articles and six books on topics that range from Medieval Latin biblical commentaries to contemporary Jewish-Christian relations. His works include *Humanity at the Limit: The Impact of the Holocaust Experience on Jews and Christians* (Bloomington: Indiana University Press, 2000); *Memory and History in Christianity and Judaism* (Notre Dame, IN: University of Notre Dame Press, 2001); *Jews and Christians in Twelfth-Century Europe* (Notre Dame, IN: University of Notre Dame Press, 2001); and *Coming Together for the Sake of God* (Collegeville, MN: Liturgical Press, 2007). From 1998 to 2009, he has served Judaism's Reform movement as co-chair of the Joint Commission on Interreligious Affairs. He was one of four authors of *Dabru Emet: A Jewish Statement on Christians and Christianity*. John Cavadini, chair of Notre Dame's theology department, remembers him as someone who "created opportunities for spiritual exchange of great depth." He died in 2009; this volume is dedicated to him.

Mustafa Abu Sway is Professor of Philosophy and Islamic Studies at Al-Quds University in Jerusalem, Palestine, which he joined in 1996. Dr. Abu Sway earned his BA (1984) from Bethlehem University and his MA (1985) and PhD (1993) from Boston College. He has taught at the International Islamic University-Malaysia (1993–1996), and was a visiting Fulbright Scholar-in-Residence at the Wilkes Honors College at Florida Atlantic University (2003–2004), as well as a visiting professor of Islamic Studies at Bard College, NY (Fall, 2008). Among his works are two books: *Islamic Epistemology: The Case of Al-Ghazzali* (English), and *The Religious Rulings (Fatawa) of Al-Ghazzali* (Arabic). Dr. Abu Sway is very active in interfaith dialogue and, for many years has advocated *convivencia* and a "theology of soft-otherness." He published numerous papers on contemporary issues involving Islam and Muslims, including the "Palestinian Issue." Dr. Abu Sway has appeared on TV shows on Al-Jazeera, BBC, CNN, and others.

Pim (W.G.B.M.) Valkenberg studied theology at the Utrecht State University and the Catholic Theological University of Utrecht in the Netherlands. After the public defense of his dissertation on Thomas Aquinas and the use of Scripture in his theology, he worked as assistant and associate professor of dogmatic theology and the theology of religions at the Catholic University of Nijmegen (1987–2007). Since September 2006, he has worked as a theologian with special interest in Christian-Muslim dialogue at Loyola University Maryland. His recent research has concentrated on Christian-Muslim dialogue in the context of Abrahamic partnership, both in the present and in the past. His publications include a dissertation on St. Thomas Aquinas (*Words of the Living God*, Leuven: 2000), on Abrahamic dialogue in the Middle Ages (*The Three Rings*, Leuven: 2005) and on interreligious dialogue (*The Polemical Dialogue*, Saarbrücken: 1997). His most recent book publication is *Sharing Lights on the Way to God: Muslim Christian Dialogue and Theology in the Context of Abrahamic Partnership* (Amsterdam / New York: Editions Rodopi, 2006), containing reflections on Muslim-Christian dialogue in the Netherlands and readings of texts by al Ghazali, Said Nursi, and Fethullah Gülen from the perspective of a comparative Muslim-Christian theology.

Olivier-Thomas Venard, a Dominican priest, is professor of New Testament at the École Biblique et Archéologique Française de Jérusalem. He has published numerous articles and edited collections. He is the author of a trilogy on literature, scripture, and theology: *Thomas d'Aquin, poète-théologien:* vol. 1: *Théologie et littérature: une saison en enfer* (2003); vol. 2: *La langue de l'ineffable. Le fondement théologique de la métaphysique* (2004) ; vol.3 : *Pagina sacra : le passage de l'Écriture sainte à l'écriture théologique* (2009). A member of the Jewish-Christian committee of the Latin Patriarchate, a regular guest of the interreligious conference of the Shalom Hartmann Institute, a co-organizer of the joint seminar of the École Biblique and the Hebrew University on The New Testament as Second Temple Jewish Literature, in Jerusalem, he also contributes regularly in the field of interreligious studies.

■ Learned Ignorance

Learned Ignorance

An Introduction

James L. Heft

Charles Dickens famously remarked that it is the best and the worst of times.[1] The turmoil of the French Revolution and the upending of a thousand-year social order in Europe have startling parallels today on the global level. The attack on the World Trade Center Towers in New York City, the devastating tsunami that took nearly a quarter of a million lives, the Iraq war, a global economic crisis, and the abject poverty of a sixth of the population of our planet, taken together, certainly qualify our times as the worst of times. On the other hand, the battle against AIDS, the gradual spread of the human rights movement, the targeting of curable diseases by major philanthropic organizations, and the efforts of some of the religious leaders of the world to work toward greater understanding and respect for others who believe differently than they do, again taken together, certainly help us to speak of our own time in history as the best of times. In our current times, both at their best and worst, something profound on the global scale is struggling to be born. The purpose of this volume is to demonstrate one facet of what might be described as one of the best things of our own time: serious and sustained interreligious dialogue.

The papers bound in this volume represent the ongoing effort of the Institute for Advanced Catholic Studies at the University of Southern California to break new ground in interreligious dialogue. They are actually the fruit of the third interreligious conference organized by the Institute. In 2003, the Institute organized its first such international conference in order to explore how deeply religious people—Jews, Christians, and Muslims—can and should be moved, precisely because of their religious commitments, to work for justice and peace. Key papers from that conference were published in 2004 under the title, *Beyond Violence: Religious Sources of Social Transformation in Judaism, Christianity and Islam* (New York: Fordham University Press). The media focuses regularly on how religion can be a source of violence and terrorism, but that volume, now translated into French, told a different, very important and underreported part of the human experience: deeply religious and politically engaged people who work for justice and peace. This important conference anticipated by several years Pope Benedict XVI's plea to religious leaders to embrace reason and avoid violence—a plea he made in a lecture he gave at the University of Regensburg on September 12, 2006.

So challenging and fruitful was the experience of that first interreligious dialogue for the Institute that we followed it with a second, this time focusing on a serious problem that the followers of the same three religions face in the secularized and pluralistic west: how to pass their faith traditions on to the next generation. Key papers from that international conference, also held at the University of

Southern California, were published in 2006 under the title, *Passing on the Faith: Transforming Traditions for the Next Generation of Jews, Christians and Muslims* (New York: Fordham University).

Both of these experiences of interreligious dialogue and the very positive reception of the books that came out of them made it clear that such dialogues not only had to be continued but needed to go even deeper. The theme of this, our third venture, was conceived one afternoon at the University of Notre Dame when Fr. David Burrell, the Emeritus Hesburgh Professor of Philosophy and Theology and I met in the office of the late Rabbi Michael Signer, Professor of Jewish Thought and Culture. The three of us were searching for a topic for the third "trialogue," as we called it then. After talking about a number of possible themes, we hit upon the theme of "learned ignorance," and knew immediately that this theme could be the basis of a very challenging and fruitful trialogue. We immediately set about identifying and then inviting an international group of scholars—Jews, Catholics, and Muslims—who were not only excellent scholars, but also genuinely religious believers. We also wanted this group to include established as well as junior scholars, men as well as women. We desired to bring some new but no less articulate voices to the table. We also wanted the representatives of the three religions to be roughly equal in number—though, once the dialogue had strated, unforeseen circumstances on the part of several Jewish and Muslim participants prevented that goal from being realized. Over the next six months, we pulled together an international group of religious scholars who promised to provide both seasoned and fresh insight into our unusual theme.

■ LEARNED IGNORANCE

The phrase *learned ignorance* comes from the title of the first and most important book written by the fifteenth century Cardinal of the Roman Catholic Church, Nicholas of Cusa (1401-1464) *De docta ignorantia* (1440). Nicholas actually took the term from Augustine, who likely borrowed the idea from Socrates. It is best to let Nicholas himself explain what he meant by "learned ignorance":

> ...Socrates believed he knew nothing except that he did not know. The very wise Solomon declared that all things are difficult and cannot be explained in words (Eccl. 1), and another thinker of the divine spirit says that wisdom and the seat of understanding lie hidden "from the eyes of all the living" (Job 28). Likewise, the very profound Aristotle, in the First Philosophy, asserts that with things most evident by nature we encounter the same difficulty as a night owl trying to look at the sun. If all this is true, since the desire in us for knowledge is not in vain, surely then it is our desire to know that we do not know. If we can attain this completely, we will attain learned ignorance. For nothing more perfect comes to a person, even the learned, the more one knows that one is ignorant. It is toward this end that I have undertaken the task of writing a few words on learned ignorance.[2]

How should we understand this paragraph from Nicholas? Why is this theme important? Couldn't a stress on "not knowing" run the risk of leading to relativism, to an inability to come to any reliable conclusions about the nature of reality?

Could it also not lead to despair about ever arriving at the truth? Wouldn't some people, believing that they will never know anything fully become intellectually lazy, or think that any knowledge claims are pretentious or even vain? These are not idle questions.

Nevertheless, as many of the papers in this volume will show, the inability to understand something fully does not necessarily mean understanding nothing at all, nor does a limitation of knowledge give grounds for intellectual laziness. The sacred writings of all three religious traditions certainly make statements that claim to speak truthfully about God; they also exhort believers to seek true knowledge. David Burrell opens the way to understanding how our inescapably limited knowledge does not lead to relativism when he writes:

> In assessing the truth of statements of faith, we ought not to approach them as though they offer explanation, but rather for what they are: convictions. Convictions that there is a sense to it all; not that *we* can make sense of it all. What fuels that conviction is one's growing capacity to use a language which helps us progressively gain our bearings in the midst of a journey.[3]

If we follow Burrell's suggestion about how to think of statements of faith, we might then say, in the context of Catholic theology, that dogmas, the most authoritative statements of the faith for Catholics, are not primarily explanations but are rather affirmations or, in Burrell's words, convictions. Those convictions, it should be added, are not just emotional statements or personal feelings; they are believed to have real cognitive content. That is, these convictions actually say something about reality—but they are statements, nonetheless, which capture only inadequately the reality they attempt to express.

Perhaps the literary skill of a gifted novelist more than the expository writing of the academic can make clearer how limited words are when used to express the richness of the human experience of God. Marilynne Robinson, Pulitzer Prize winner and author of the novels *Housekeeping, Gilead*, and most recently *Home*,[4] describes how words are strained and stretched when describing the experience of God. She notes that St. Paul, a verbally eloquent person, does not hesitate to say, when speaking of "deeply interior encounters with the inexpressible," that he has "thoughts too deep for words," that he knows of "things that cannot be told, which man may not utter." She writes that "language, lovely as it is, is the merest scrim on reality, never by any means sufficiently descriptive and entirely capable of going off on its own and making apparent meaning and logic where none exists." Not only is our experience of God mysterious, our experience of ourselves leaves us inarticulate: "This primary intuition of the strangeness of it all, of our single selves as unspeakably fragile and brilliant observers of a grandeur for which we have tried through all our generations to find words, this is the experience that seems to me to underlie religion."[5]

Besides a gifted novelist commending reverence before the inexpressible, other authors, some included in this volume, use the phrase "intellectual humility" to underscore our limited ability to describe our religious experience. Although intellectual humility is sometimes difficult to find in the academic world, it is an especially appropriate quality of the scholarly religious believer. Yet, the idea of intellectual humility does not quite get at the deeper meaning of learned ignorance, at least as we are using the term in this book. Intellectual humility describes the attitude of a thinker. Learned ignorance, on the other hand, is the acknowledgment of religious believers that what they try to understand—namely, God, and the ways of God—constantly transcends their ability to grasp fully and articulate adequately what they have experienced. In other words, learned ignorance has more to do with a realization arrived at after thinking carefully about the focus of one's intellectual efforts—God—than it is a description of an attitude, appropriate as it is, of persons who know that their knowledge is limited. Cusa tells us that at "the root of learned ignorance" is the realization that "God is not able to be known as God is."[6]

An emphasis on learned ignorance, or the realization among learned people that their grasp of reality is inescapably limited, prevents all forms of fundamentalism, which assumes that believers are in perfect possession of ultimate reality. Once that illusion is fixed in believers' minds, all that remains is to force their belief on others. But Judaism, Christianity, and Islam all affirm that God alone is absolute and that all affirmations about God and God's revelation are inescapably limited.

■ PREPARING FOR THIS TRIALOGUE

In beginning preparations for our trialogue to be held at the Tantur Ecumenical Institute in Jerusalem in June of 2007, we realized that our chosen theme was not the easiest to grasp. We were not aware of any interreligious dialogue that had ever set out to explore this theme. Few religious leaders, to say nothing of the typical academic, have the habit of stressing how little they are able to grasp of God. The planning committee, which included Michael Signer, David Burrell, Omid Safi, Reuven Firestone, Michael McGarry and myself, decided that it would, therefore, be very useful to have a preliminary meeting of all the participants for two reasons: (1) so that they could get to know each other; and (2) so that they would have some time to think together about how each of them might understand and approach the theme. We, therefore, gathered for several days in Cambridge, Massachusetts, in June of 2006.

A month before we met, we asked all the participants to make available to each other autobiographical essays about interreligious dialogue. Those essays proved to be both revealing and fascinating. Each participant had been asked to address in his or her essay the following questions: How did you get interested in interreligious dialogue? What have you learned from other religions? What do you think now are the big issues in interreligious dialogue? The answers to these essays were so interesting and illuminating that we have included edited versions of them at the beginning of each chapter as a personal introduction for each author.

After spending some time learning about each other, we then turned our attention to the theme. This initial exploration of the theme helped not only to clarify the idea of "learned ignorance," but also allowed the participants to figure out what aspect of the theme they thought they might be able to write about. The planning committee asked each participant to write and submit a month after the Harvard meeting a single page description of their proposed approach to the theme. The planning committee then discussed their topics, made suggestions about their development and focus, and then sent back to the participants some comments aimed to help them in their research and writing. All the participants had drafts of their papers ready by May 1 of 2007. These papers were then circulated electronically among all the participants in preparation for our meeting at Tantur in Jerusalem the following month.

We decided to hold our trialogue at Tantur, an international ecumenical institute situated on the main road between Jerusalem and Bethlehem. In October of 1963, Orthodox, Anglican, and Protestant observers at the Second Vatican Council told Pope Paul VI of their dream of an international ecumenical institute for theological research and pastoral studies. After the pope's 1964 pilgrimage to the Holy Land, the Vatican purchased Tantur (Arabic for "hilltop") and then leased it to the University of Notre Dame for fifty years. By 1971, the University, led then by Fr. Theodore Hesburgh, had built a beautiful and spacious institute that began welcoming scholars and religious leaders from all over the world. Besides ecumenism, Tantur also sponsors programs that explore the relationships between Christians and people of other world faiths, especially Jews and Muslims. Given the fact that our trialogue involved the three Abrahamic religions, and that all three religions have holy places in the ancient city of Jerusalem, Tantur became the natural place for us to meet and discuss "learned ignorance."

At Tantur,[7] the fifteen of us gathered for three solid days around an oblong table and followed a strict regimen for dialogue. Each author was allowed to present key points of his or her paper for eight minutes. A member of another religious tradition was asked beforehand to respond with a critique of the paper and pose several discussion questions, and to do so in five minutes. Then for nearly an hour, all the participants joined in a discussion of the paper. Typically four or five of the participants wanted to speak at once. The moderator took down their names and they followed one after the other—except if someone wanted to intervene immediately. To indicate that the person wanted to respond immediately to something that was said, that person pointed his or her index finger down on the surface of the table. The process worked very well. The discussions on the final day were just as intense and exciting as they were on the first day. The energy of the group never flagged.

We also took time during the week to visit together those places sacred to all three religious traditions. Visits to the Church of the Holy Sepulcher, the Western Wall, and the Dome of the Rock were made possible for all the members of the trialogue. We also made pilgrimages through parts of the ancient city and shared our thoughts as we did. Holding the trialogue in Jerusalem turned out to be a very good idea!

■ TRIALOGUES IN CONTEXT

Interreligious dialogue is not new. One prominent form over the centuries has been the religious disputation, in which religious thinkers aimed to prove their opponents wrong and convince them to convert to the "winner's" religion. Carefully structured arguments between Jews and Christians, Christians and Muslims, and Muslims and Jews aimed to discredit the religious claims of the opponent. It is only in the last century, and at that mainly in the west, that interreligious dialogues began to try to understand the beliefs of other persons and to respect their religious freedom.

In the late nineteenth and early twentieth centuries, Protestants took the lead in calling for dialogues among Christians; they were called ecumenical dialogues—that is, dialogues focused on mutual understanding and greater collaboration and unity among Christians. Catholics, with a few exceptions, stayed clear of these conversations until the mid-twentieth century. It was not until then that respectful interreligious dialogues were organized. No doubt, the massive tragedy of the *Shoah* that wiped out one-third of the Jewish people in the world made it painfully evident to religious leaders that something had to be done to create mutual understanding and respect. In our own day, interreligious dialogues in the west have typically been structured to make respectful conversation and mutual understanding possible. These dialogues have been called *bilateral* conversations. When such dialogues include representatives of a third religious tradition, they have been called *trilateral* conversations. Some interreligious dialogues have included more than three religions, and they have had several names, most often being called *multi-lateral* dialogues.

In a slim volume published in 2005,[8] Bradford Hinze provides a helpful survey of the trialogues among Jews, Christians, and Muslims that have been held in the recent past. They differ in focus from *bilateral* dialogues. For example, when Jews and Muslims talk, they often focus on their shared commitment to radical monotheism. Or when Jews and Christians talk, they speak about their common spiritual roots, the importance of the Hebrew Scriptures to both communities, and how to deal with anti-Semitism that has infected Christianity. Or when Christians and Muslims speak, they often focus on the importance of key figures in their traditions, such as Jesus and Muhammad, and the importance of witnessing to their faith and meeting the challenges that come from both traditions given their strong missionary commitments. The focus of trialogues has typically been to foster cooperation in facing common ethical challenges; were they to have taken up explicitly theological issues, they would have found convergence more difficult to achieve.[9]

Quite aware of this important history, the planners of this trialogue decided to take up an explicitly theological issue, one that would explore the understanding and expression of the core beliefs of three traditions. Serious theological conversations among the three Abrahamic religions have been rare.[10] We fully realized that the theme of "learned ignorance" would present its own challenges, but decided nonetheless to try to meet them. We were not disappointed.

■ POPES AND POLITICAL TENSIONS

In the meantime, a lot has been going on in the world that has advanced serious interreligious dialogue. In the Catholic world, and referring to the leadership of only the two most recent popes, extraordinary initiatives have been taken, especially by John Paul II. The geopolitical situation in the mid 1980s was ominous; Cold War tensions between the United States and the Soviet Union reached new heights. In response to these growing tension, Pope John Paul II invited Christian, Jewish, Muslim, Buddhist, Hindu, and other religious leaders to come together and be with him in Assisi on October 27th, 1986, to pray for peace. Moved by the terrible tragedies of the war in the Balkans, he did this again in 1993, and then once again in January 2002, after the terrorist attacks on the United States on September 11th, 2001.

Vatican II opened the Catholic Church to interreligious dialogue. At that time, however, the Church's actual participation in interreligious dialogue was very limited. In fact, Vatican II's document about the Church's relation to nonChristian religions was the shortest of the Council's sixteen documents. That being said, however, there can be little doubt that the Council wanted to promote interreligious dialogue. From the fourth to the nineteenth centuries, none of the twenty general councils of the Church even used the word *dialogue*. Vatican II used that word in six of its sixteen documents, and in all the rest of the documents, the word is implied.[11] Late in his long papacy, in preparing the Catholic Church for the beginning of the third millennium, John Paul II wrote:

> In the climate of increased cultural and religious pluralism that is expected to mark the society of the new millennium, it is obvious that this (interreligious) dialogue will be especially important in establishing a sure basis for peace and warding off the dread specter of those wars of religion that have so often bloodied human history.[12]

At the 2002 Assisi meeting, all the leaders representing most of the world's religions affirmed together ten statements that committed them to work to end violence and create the conditions for peace. Four of those statements explicitly called for more interreligious dialogue.[13]

The ongoing violence in the Middle East and the wars in Afghanistan and Iraq led the newly elected Pope Benedict XVI to state in clear and unintentionally provocative terms the need for religions to be instruments of peace. On September 12, 2006 at the University of Regensburg, where he had been a professor before being appointed in 1981 by John Paul II to be the head of the Congregation for the Doctrine of the Faith, Benedict gave an address aimed to disassociate religion and violence. Ironically, a quotation in that speech evoked a violent response from a few Muslims. Benedict quoted a statement by a certain Manuel Palaeologus, a late medieval Byzantine emperor, who had written: "Show me just what Muhammad brought that was new, and there you will find things only evil and inhuman, such as his command to spread by the sword the faith he preached." Less noticed but just as unfortunate was his reference to the thought of the eleventh-century Muslim scholar, Ibn Hazm, who claimed that God was not bound by human notions of rationality. Perhaps because he was new at being pope, or perhaps because he was speaking to his former colleagues at his old university, he did not have his speech vetted by any of the groups in the Vatican officially concerned with interreligious dialogue. If he had, it is likely that they would have suggested that he not cite the Palaeologus quotation nor refer to ideas of the nonmainstream Muslim scholar Ibn Hazm. Understandably, the Muslim reaction was immediate and sharp. One of the papers in this volume treats at length this papal address and the reactions to it, as well as the pope's visit to Turkey two months later.

■ NEW MUSLIM INITIATIVES FOR DIALOGUE

It sometimes happens that very positive things follow tragic events. There can be little doubt, for example, that the Shoah made many Christians aware of the danger and consequences of anti-Semitism and led them to work seriously at purging their teachings, texts, and hearts of that poisonous prejudice. A similar thing might be said about Benedict's Regensburg address. Although the reaction of some Muslims was violent, most took the more productive step of insisting on the importance of interreligious dialogue. Thus, on October 6, 2006, not a month after Benedict's lecture, thirty-eight Muslim scholars sent an open letter to Benedict correcting several of his statements, condemning as "unIslamic" the violence among Muslims that the pope's speech had provoked, and quoted John Paul II on the importance of interreligious dialogue. These scholars asked for further dialogue with the pope, but that open letter received no formal response from the Holy See.

On October 13, 2007, a much more substantive letter, "A Common Word Between Us and You,"[14] signed by 138 Muslim scholars and religious leaders from all over the world and representing different branches of Islam, was sent to the pope and other leaders of the Christian religion. This time, the pope, in the person of his secretary of state, responded on November 29 by welcoming a dialogue with a small group selected by the organizers of the "Common Word" statement. The focus of that statement is explicitly theological. Drawing upon the Scriptures of the three religions—that is, from the Qur'an, and the Hebrew Scriptures (more specifically on the Book of Deuteronomy) and several texts of the New Testament, it develops a "common word" about the importance of loving God and loving one's neighbor. It stresses that what is at stake is not only peaceful relations between adherents to the three religions, but also their eternal salvation. It concludes by referring to a Qur'anic text often repeated by Muslims in interreligious dialogues that God ensured the existence of many religions so that the followers of them can compete with each other in doing good works (Q. 5:48).

Catholic scholar of Islam and Jesuit Thomas Michel, a veteran of the Catholic/ Muslim dialogue, stated that this 2007 Muslim document represents a watershed moment in the dialogue between Muslims and Christians for three reasons: (1) it was signed by a very broad spectrum of Muslim leaders from forty countries who had to put aside intra-Muslim conflicts; (2) it moves the conversation off geopolitical conflicts and firmly onto theological grounds; and (3) it comes not from westernized Muslims, but from the heart of Arab Muslim countries.[15]

More recent trialogues have taken place: in Qatar in May of 2008 and in Madrid in July of 2008. The trialogue held in Qatar, known as the Doha Conference on Interfaith Dialogue, issued a common statement that called for tolerance among religions and a respect for all human life, and stressed that the participants not only discussed values they held in common, but also "some of the difficult and tragic issues which disfigure our world and create violence and injustice in so many countries."[16] The Madrid conference was sponsored by the Guardian of the Holy Sites Abdullah of Saudi Arabia. The participants in that conference issued a three-page statement that underscores the "value of dialogue as the best way for mutual understanding and cooperation," and condemns terrorism as "one of the most serious obstacles to dialogue and coexistence."[17] Representatives of all three religions, including representatives of the Vatican, attended both of these trialogues. What fruit these important initiatives will bear remains to be seen. Nevertheless, there is surely now more active engagement and positive dialogue among these three religious traditions than ever before. Our trialogue on "learned ignorance" parallels these important conferences, but explores more explicitly than any of them fundamental theological issues.

■ THE CHAPTERS OF THIS VOLUME

We have organized the chapters of this book so that they fall under four headings: (1) Learned Ignorance and the Need for Dialogue; (2) Particularity or Exclusiveness; (3) Violence, Apology, and Oppression; and (4) The Promise and Meanings of Religious Pluralism. We conclude the book with an Epilogue written by the three editors of this volume.

Introducing the Theme and the Meaning of Dialogue

Introducing the history and importance of interreligious dialogue, David Burrell's chapter sketches the historical interactions, political and theological, of Jews, Christians, and Muslims. He asks how today the adherents of the Abrahamic faiths can move beyond the certitudes that have led to conflict in the past. He does not stop there. He also asks how they can move beyond the more recent political appeals for mutual tolerance, in order to arrive at the genuine welcome of each other. Certainly these religions must make stronger commitments to human rights and issues of justice. Those commitments will, however, come at a price: although humility can be acquired without humiliation, humiliation is unfortunately the usual road to humility. Burrell knows well that discovering one's own prejudices and critiquing honestly and fairly one's own religious traditions is humbling.

Burrell stated that our June 2007 Tantur Trialogue was especially effective in leading the participants, despite differences in faith commitments, to an even stronger common bond, "for as we acknowledge the failing of our community in the face of other believers, we cannot help but acknowledge the failing of our community before God." In the last analysis, progress in interreligious dialogue depends less on documentable advances than it does on fidelity and friendship.

Pim Valkenberg explores the meaning of "learned ignorance" as understood by the unusual fifteenth-century scholar and Cardinal of the Catholic Church, Nicholas of Cusa. Building on the writings of ancient authors and Thomas Aquinas, Valkenberg explains the meaning of Nicholas' statement that we do not know how God is, but only how God is not. Nicholas wrote not only at a time when the Latin Church was especially interested in reestablishing a better relationship with the Greek Church, but also when it feared the advance of Muslim armies along its eastern borders. With regard to Islam, Nicholas studied the Qur'an to which he applied a *pia interpretatio*, that is, a faithful interpretation of Islam's sacred book—an interpretation that he believed would help Christians purify incorrect thinking about the Trinity and the Incarnation. Skilled not only in philosophy and theology but also in mathematics, Nicholas emphasized that not-knowing actually resulted in a valuable kind of knowing: "the more we are instructed in this ignorance, the closer we approach the truth."

The chapter contributed by the late Michael Signer, to whom this volume is dedicated, sheds further light on often unexplored dimensions of interreligious dialogue, and in doing so, draws explicitly on the thought of Nicholas of Cusa. In a chapter entitled "Seeing the Sounds," Signer explores those aspects of dialogue that transcend the merely verbal exchanges, even though verbal exchanges remain an important part of any dialogue. Signer sifts through parts of the Jewish tradition and finds that, without surrendering any integrity, that tradition both affirms the value of humility and goes beyond the particularity of Israel. The Bible exhorts the Israelites to make "themselves as ownerless as the desert," in order to be prepared to receive divine revelation. Only through humble withdrawal and becoming ownerless, Signer claims, can the Jewish people acquire the gift of God's word. Through successful conversation about religious texts, Jews, Christians and Muslims can arrive at something that resembles the ascetic act of becoming ownerless. Thus, without surrendering their religious integrity, they can affirm themselves as "owners" of their own religious tradition while hearing and learning about the religious traditions of others. The process does not relativize, but rather conforms to the notion that to be human is to use our senses and then to process our perceptions into speech, thereby engaging in conversation with our interlocutors and receiving another gift—in essence—another revelation. Signer crosses religious boundaries when he draws upon Nicholas of Cusa's treatise on "learned ignorance" as a resource for people committed to interreligious dialogue. He places Nicholas's thought in conversation with the rabbinic perception of the Sinai experience of revelation.

And finally, in this introductory section of the book, Asma Afsaruddin, drawing upon the Qur'an, describes the conditions for fruitful interreligious dialogue. She stresses two key concepts: (1) the knowledge of one another based on respect for diversity and difference; and (2) "moderation" as a defining characteristic of righteous believers. To support the first concept, she builds on the well-known Qur'anic verse, "O humankind! We have created you from a male and a female, and made you into nations and tribes, that you might get to know one another. The noblest of you in God's sight is the one who is most righteous" (Qur'an 49:13). The commentary tradition, traced back to the Prophet, identifies piety and consciousness of God as taking precedence over lineage and genealogy.

To support her second point, about moderation, Asma connects two verses of the Qur'an. First, she quotes the often cited text: "We have made you [believers] into a middle community, so that you may bear witness [to the truth] before others and so that the Messenger may bear witness [to it] before you." She links this text to a lesser known one in which righteous Jews and Christians are also described as constituting a "balanced" or "moderate" community (Qur'an 5:66). Toward the end of her chapter, she contrasts the generous readings of these verses with the "supersessionist" reading of the Qur'an that depicts Islam as having trumped all the earlier revelations. She concludes her call for genuine dialogue by referring to the Hebrew notion of hospitality for the stranger, the Christian's notion of loving one's neighbor as oneself, and the Qur'anic concept of the importance of the knowledge of the other.

This first part of the book, then, features chapters that provide an overview of interreligious dialogue, explore the theme of "learned ignorance," and offer a series of reflections on attitudes and dispositions needed for entering fruitfully into such dialogue.

Must Particularity Be Exclusive?

Can there be fruitful dialogue if participants in the dialogue make absolutist claims? Such claims are usually based on the idea that one group has all the truth and the other group or groups possess none. Are all claims of "particularity" or uniqueness the same as absolute claims? Is it possible to be faithful to one's own particularity without falling into absolutism? These issues are explored in this second part of this book.

Few claims have sounded more absolutist, indeed more arrogant, to non-Catholics and adherents of other religions than the Catholic dogma of papal infallibility. In a historical and theological study, I locate the dogma in its context (nineteenth-century Europe and Vatican Council I, 1869–1870), and then trace the ways in which subsequent historical developments and official Church teachings address at least some of the most widespread misunderstandings of the dogma. I suggest that the meaning of the dogma becomes clearer when one understands that dogmas do not explain God and revelation so much as they affirm and protect those truths. The rabbis speak about "putting a fence around the Law," so that the Law itself is protected. Even the word *mystery*, quite capable of inducing intellectual laziness ("You'll just have to accept it; it's a mystery!") must be understood in ways that both encourage critical thinking but still recognize the limits of all intellectual efforts to understand God.

The bishops of the Second Vatican Council (1962–1965) added further clarifications of the meaning of infallibility. They called for a greater use of Scripture and a greater awareness of history than had been true of official Church teaching in the previous centuries. Scripture is not systematic theology. Scripture does not elaborate a philosophical system. Rather, it is a collection of books of different genres from different periods of history, addressed to different people facing different situations. It likes to relate history, tell stories, use poetic images, and metaphors. Jesus makes great use of parables. Encouraging a greater awareness of history makes it clearer that, over time, understandings, presuppositions, and the expressive power of language have changed. Ecumenical and interreligious dialogues are based on forthright affirmations of belief, but also on an increased awareness of the limitations of these affirmations, to say nothing of the difficulties those who make those affirmations have in actually living them. I conclude by underscoring the need to "take seriously the historical conditioning of official Church teaching, of dogmatic statements, and of even the inspired Word of God," and to do so without falling into agnosticism and relativism.

Jewish "chosenness" may be similar to Catholic infallibility in its potential for exclusiveness and absolutism. Taking a phenomenological approach, Reuven

Firestone tackles the Jewish idea of "chosenness" (or election) that seems to be deeply imbedded, not just in Judaism, but in all major monotheistic faiths. What, he asks, might be the origin of this notion? What might it have meant to be "chosen" in the ancient world? Assuming that the competing religious truth claims made in past history and now jutting into our own day are linked to ancient concepts of chosenness, Firestone sets out to explore its origins from the perspective of both historical and social-scientific approaches to the study of religion.

Firestone notes that ancient Israel shared in an idea of chosenness that seemed to be an essential part of Near Eastern tribal religions, and which appears to be associated with the idea of a tribal god who is in exclusive and intimate relation with its own religious people. Yet Israel's tribal God differed from neighboring tribal religions. Israel affirmed a universal creator-God of Genesis as the one and only god of the universe, without losing a sense of intimacy with this transcendent God. When the religion of Israel became known in the later Greco-Roman antiquity as the ancient and authoritative expression of monotheism, some of its most basic notions were absorbed by newly developing monotheistic religions. Such sharing actually encouraged competition and antagonism between monotheistic religions. Firestone shows how understanding historical context and historicizing monotheism can soften the harshness of absolutist claims for exclusive truth without relativizing faith. He concludes that understanding the social processes affecting religion and religious argument can help those engaged in religious dialogue reduce or even eliminate off-putting forms of absolutism.

At the core of the differences between the monotheisms of Judaism and Islam on the one hand, and of Christianity on the other, is the Christian doctrine of the Trinity, rooted as it is in the doctrine of the Incarnation, or the word made flesh. Affirming Jesus as Lord is the key particularist claim of Christianity. Olivier-Thomas Venard explains that the doctrine of the Incarnation can lead Christians to humility or to pride. Venard notes that in recent years interreligious dialogues have avoided theological issues, like the Incarnation, and concentrated instead on issues of ethics. Even though it took Christians nearly five centuries to formulate the dogma of the Trinity, they should not assume today that there is no need for improvement or further clarifications of that dogma. New questions have arisen. Competent theologians are aware that when they speak about God, they know that *what* they utter may be true, but they do not know *how* their utterance is true: "Thus, the meditation about Christ results not in an answer silencing all questions," writes Venard, "but in an ultimate question putting an end to all answers."

Interreligious dialogue is still another reason for humility. Why? Because meeting a faithful person from another monotheistic faith is a religious experience in itself. From the time of Aquinas on, it becomes clear that faith is not something through which believers can grasp reality as much as it is something that grasps believers. Venard suggests that it helps to think of interreligious dialogue as a "lovers' quarrel": it is never simply solved except in and through love, and is never solved by walking away or by silence and shutting out the other. Rather, the way of interreligious dialogue is always more profitable when it is characterized by loving relationship than by rupture in relationship.

Rabbi Shira Lander returns to the problem of how Jews seem arrogant. Her approach is different than that of Rabbi Reuven Firestone who explored "chosenness" as a concept affecting all monotheisms. Instead, she explores how certain vectors of interpretation and thought in Jewish tradition have led to a kind of pious arrogance deeply imbedded in the Jewish self-concept. The association of certain supernatural traits with Judaism—such as eternality, moral and perhaps intellectual superiority, and oneness—shapes much of Judaism's communal self-understanding. Corporate identity is fundamental to Judaism's theological structure.

Lander takes the reader through references from the Hebrew Bible, rabbinic literature, scholarly commentaries, mystical works, and traditional and modern Jewish philosophers, to identify the trends of arrogance. She considers the ontological assumptions that are associated with these trends. Benefiting from the writings of Michael Wyschograd and David Novak, two modern Jewish thinkers who grapple with these issues in terms that confront both the demands of tradition and the responsibilities of modernity, she ends her chapter by pointing out a pathway for developing a corrective, a Jewish theology of humility.

The final chapter in this section also deals with the dangers of arrogance and the need for humility—but this time from a Muslim perspective. Afra Jalabi explores two major terms used in the Qur'an to refer to arrogance: "*istikbar*," which means to perceive oneself as bigger than one is, and "*uluw*," which means to perceive oneself as higher than one is. These two attitudes describe persons whose minds have become delusional. They no longer know their proper size or embrace proper attitudes toward themselves. Jalabi develops these two ideas through a close reading of two key Qur'anic narratives: that of Adam, Eve, and Satan on the one hand, and that of Moses and Pharaoh on the other.

God drives Satan out of Paradise because of his primal arrogance toward God and God's new creations, Adam and Eve. Satan became smaller by belittling Adam and Eve. Moses is portrayed in the Qur'an as a prophet, even as an intellectual, who speaks truth to Pharaoh's arrogant power. After analyzing these two stories, Jalabi reflects on the Qur'anic teaching that while our knowledge is limited, God is not. There is no end to what is beyond our knowing and no end to God's greatness. Jalabi concludes by drawing our attention to a text in the Qur'an that challenges all static worldviews with a powerful poetic image:

> And if all the trees
> On earth were pens,
> And the ocean were ink,
> With seven oceans behind it
> To add to its supply,
> Yet would not the Words of God be exhausted... (Qur'an 31:27)

In summary then, the second set of chapters argues that particular claims need not be absolutistic claims. That is to say, making unique claims for one's own religious tradition need not exclude the possibility that other religious traditions may also have valid reasons for unique claims. Moreover, avoiding absolutist claims need not lead to relativism.

Violence, Apologies, and Conflict

In the third section of this book, three authors address directly the realities that make mutual understanding so difficult—violence committed against the other, not only in the past, but also in the present. Elizabeth Groppe weaves together a close reading of Augustine's *Confessions*, a painful review of religious persecutions, especially of Jews by Christians, and her experience of visiting the holy sites of Jerusalem during the visit of all the participants in this trialogue to the Holy Land. She does all this in order to show how humility purifies religious believers and creates a greater capacity for dialogue. She recalls how early in his life Augustine, as a student of rhetoric, admired men who were more embarrassed by a lapse in grammar than they were by their elaborately crafted paeans to lust. Neo-Platonism helped Augustine escape the Manichaeism of his youth, but did not provide him the affective power he needed for his conversion. That power he finally found in the humility and human suffering of the Word Incarnate.

That humility, Groppe argues, must also purify theologies of the cross that have legitimated vengeance. That humility should allay the religious insecurities that arise in believers when they encounter people of other religions. She concludes that "we are truly in need of the *medicus humilis*, the balm of the Incarnate Word...." Nothing prevents us from coming to know God more than pride; nothing will help us to understand God better than a genuine humility, which for Christians, is found in the suffering of Christ.

Earlier in this introduction, I mentioned the uproar caused by a quotation in Pope Benedict's Regensburg address. Michael McGarry, then the director of Tantur, analyzes that lecture, and especially the subsequent calls by Muslims for an apology that the pope never offered. McGarry asks whether the pope should have apologized to the Muslim world. Drawing upon the Vatican's International Theological Commission's 1999 document, "Memory and Reconciliation: the Church and the Faults of the Past," McGarry distinguishes between *apology* and *regret*. He then explores the place of apology in interreligious dialogue.

McGarry asks three key questions: (1) is requiring an apology from the other a way of humiliating, or at least "taming" the other; (2) is "going only so far,"—that is, protecting the Church itself while blaming only the acts of individual Christians—a way of not truly expressing an apology; and (3) is apology possible or desirable when, because of cultural differences, it is seen as a weakness rather than a strength? Having lived for nearly a decade in Jerusalem, McGarry stresses the importance of cultural differences between the west and the Middle East, and concludes with six observations, one of which addresses directly the question of whether Benedict was right in not apologizing to the Muslim world.

Finally, Mustafa Abu Sway, a Palestinian Muslim, writes about the difficulties of carrying on interreligious dialogue in what he and other Palestinians in Israel experience as living under occupation. Abu Sway describes himself as simultaneously a faithful Muslim who is committed to living in a pluralistic relationship with other Abrahamic believers, and a Palestinian who is deeply committed to the cause of mutual co-existence. He focuses on a number of historical precedents, including that of the Prophet Muhammad himself and the famed Pact of Umar, and from them makes an argument for mutual co-existence among Muslims, Jews, and Christians. Abu Sway argues that the term *dhimmi* offers useful resources for this *convivencia*.

Drawing upon the Qur'an, Abu Sway builds on both theological and social permissions for interactions, ranging from "there is no compulsion in religion" (Qur'an 2:256) to permissions for intermarriage and sharing the food of and with the People of the Book. He also quotes Qur'an 29:46: "And argue not with the People of the Scripture unless it be in [a way] that is better, save with such of them as do wrong; and say: We believe in that which has been revealed unto us and revealed unto you; our Allah is One, and unto Him we surrender." Toward the end of his paper, Abu Sway connects the notion of intellectual humility with that of innate human knowledge (*fitrah*), as articulated by classical Islamic scholars like al-Ghazali. For Abu Sway, the fact that there is more than one religion evokes humility. Indeed, he suggests, religious plurality may itself be a part of God's design for humanity: "And if your Lord had willed, He truly would have made all peoples one nation, yet they cease not differing" (Qur'an 11:118).

Taken together, these chapters touch upon the pain associated with how religious people commit violence against others, and what can and should be done when that happens. If at the root of such violence are absolutist religious claims, there are ways, as these chapters demonstrate, to deal with such claims without falling into relativism. What should be done to avoid the history of violence that has blighted all three Abrahamic religions?

Religious Pluralism

Picking up on Abu Sway's concluding comments about religious pluralism, this final section of the book deals mainly with ways to think respectfully about the reality of different religions. Professor Stanislaw Krajewski, mathematician, philosopher, and theologian, reflects on the merits of pluralism by developing the idea of intellectual humility. He begins with reflections on the biblical Moses. Drawing upon the Torah, Krajewski describes Moses' leadership not as courageous or wise but rather as only very humble. He moves next to an examination of a sense of the truth as universal, or absolute or relative. Each of these perceptions of the truth brings in their wake problems when they confront claims of competing truth. How should one think about the source of such claims, which is to say, how should one think about God? Deeply familiar with both mathematics and philosophy, Krajewski notes that even though mathematicians are not necessarily sure that they believe in the existence of mathematical objects, they still are able to, and indeed must, construct a universe mathematically based on exactly that assumption. In a similar way, Krajewski argues, we construct our theological worlds, and are supported in this work by traditions that exude a sense of certainty. In Jewish contexts, this certainty is defined through the covenant, but even that certainty is valorized through humility. The finest traditional representation of that covenantal humility is "Beit Hillel," the famous school of Jewish thought that takes a position on truth that nevertheless cites even opposing views with respect.[18]

Krajewski then turns directly to the topic of religious pluralism in both its sub-jectivist and objectivist forms. The subjectivist approach, by which he understands an approach from within a religious tradition itself, is particularly interesting for religious dialogue. Jewish mysticism (Kabbalah) can, in this regard, be instructive, as well as some contemporary explorations by both Jewish and non-Jewish thinkers. Ultimately, an instability may in fact be desirable for dialogue to be suc-cessful. Krajewski uses the notion of oscillation, and applies it to the objectivist and subjectivist approaches to religious claims. Finally, he returns to the problem-atic meaning of Israel as "chosen." He believes that true dialogue allows for total respect for all sides involved through a combined awareness of both epistemic ignorance and convenantal certainty.

I had suggested in my own chapter on "Humble Infallibility" that it was one of the most misunderstood teachings of the Catholic Church. In his chapter, Daniel Madigan, a Roman Catholic theologian and Islamicist, closely analyzes the document published by the Congregation for the Doctrine of the Faith (CDF) in 2000, *Dominus Iesus* (*DI*)—a document, Madigan believes, which caused more controversy within the Catholic Church than any papal docu-ment since Pope Paul VI's 1968 encyclical, *Humanae vitae*, which condemned the use of artificial birth control. The CDF is the group within the Vatican responsible for maintaining orthodoxy in belief and theology. *DI* opposed what it perceived as relativism and indifference among many of the current theologies of religion, some of which have been developed through experi-ences of interreligious dialogue. The 2000 CDF document argued vigorously for the objective truth of Christianity, and more specifically of Catholicism, and asserted that the followers of others religions are, objectively speaking, in a "gravely deficient situation."

Working with distinctions between inside and outside, inclusive and exclusive, certainty and doubt, and paying further attention to insider and outsider lan-guage, Madigan rephrases the core truth of the CDF doctrine so that it might be better understood, even if not more widely accepted. In his analysis, he criticizes the approach to other religions that presume that it is possible to be purely objective, to stand outside of history and above any religious tradition. He also warns against the use of "proprietary language," that is, language that makes it sound as though believers possess the truth and own salvation, and that non-believers have to get it from those who "own it," that is, from believers, or go without it. He argues that even though Christianity is more theocentric than Christocentric, it is nonetheless Christomorphic, and the emphasis on that Christic particularity should never be abandoned by the Church. He concludes by suggesting that evangelization is never simply telling the Good News to others; it is also, and even more importantly, being and embodying for them that Good News, however inadequately.

The final chapter of this section on "Religious Pluralism," and of this book, is Omid Safi's chapter, entitled "Between Tradition and Reform," which recognizes a connection, a resonance, between the world of premodern Muslim mystics (Sufis) and those of contemporary Islamic reformers in Iran. As the heart of his paper he develops the notion of various stages of certainty (and doubt) that the premodern

Sufis write about, moving from knowledge to vision to reality. In the case of the modern Iranian reformers, he finds the constant affirmation that any religious articulation is inescapably time defined, human, and thus circumscribed by all the limitations of our own understanding and social location.

Safi gives succinct summaries of modern Iranian thinkers. He finds it unfortunate that many modern Muslims have great difficulty believing that premodern Muslims were so willing to recognize innovation and what he calls the "hybridity" of their own selves. Safi wants modern Muslims to embrace this great premodern tradition by focusing on the concept of *Ijtihad*, that is, the assertion that independent principled reasoning is able to come up with new answers to new problems. In the premodern case, there is the notion of moving beyond the "conventions" to arrive at a fresh understanding of God, an understanding that is dynamic and powerful. Safi concludes his chapter with a passionate call for greater mutual understanding among believers of different religious traditions, finding in the affirmation of religious pluralism a more faithful way to remain faithful to one's own religious tradition.

■ CONCLUSION

In the epilogue to this book, the three editors reflect together on one further question: what is the purpose of interreligious dialogue? At the very end of the intense conversations of these papers in the Tantur meeting in Jerusalem, one of the participants raised an obvious but difficult question. He asked, "What does your religious tradition give as reasons for interreligious dialogue?" We offered a variety of responses, but it was evident that we struggled to find words to describe what we had been doing for several days, and why we were engaging in these intense conversations. That question requires a more developed response, and the editors of this volume, quite aware of their own limitations and learned ignorance, nonetheless offer in the Epilogue their thoughts on what might be an adequate response to this important question.

■ Notes

1. Charles Dickens, *A Tale of Two Cities* (in *Three Novels* (Spring Books; 1977), p. 379. "It was the best of times, it was the worst of times, it was the age of wisdom, it was the age of foolishness, it was the epoch of belief, it was the epoch of incredulity, it was the season of Light, it was the season of Darkness, it was the spring of hope, it was the winter of despair, we had everything before us, we had nothing before us, we were all going direct to Heaven, we were all going direct the other way—in short, the period was so far like the present period, that some of its noisiest authorities insisted on its being received, for good and for evil, in the superlative degree of comparison only."

2. Nicholas of Cusa, *De docta ignorantia*, I, 1, par. 4 (English translation by H. Lawrence Bond in *Nicholas of Cusa: Selected Spiritual Writings* [NewYork: Paulist Press, 1997]), pp. 88–89. Bond notes that Cusa has over the centuries been subject to widely varying descriptions: "He has been characterized simultaneously as a humanist and a counter-Renaissance figure; as a heretic and a conservative; as a Gnostic and an agnostic; as a scientist and a pseudo-scientist; as a papal monarchist and a conciliarist; as a reformer and an opportunist in need of reforming; as a peacemaker and a belligerent; as a politician and a pastor; and as

a philosopher and a theologian" (p. 15). Though Bond suggests that these different appraisals "often reveal more about the measurers than the measured," he also describes that while there was a fundamental continuity in Cusa's writings, ecclesial and political circumstances changed significantly during his life and contributed to different emphases in his writings.

3. David Burrell, *Faith and Freedom: An Interfaith Perspective* (Blackwell, 2004), p. 245.

4. *Housekeeping* (Farrar, Straus and Giroux, 1981), *Gilead* (Farrar, Straus and Giroux, 2004), and *Home* (Farrar, Straus and Giroux, 2008).

5. Marilynne Robinson, "Credo: Reverence First and Then Belief," in *Harvard Divinity Bulletin*, Vol. 36, No. 2, Spring 2008, p. 29.

6. Bond, "Introduction," p. 31. It should be remembered that Cusa did not rest in the *Via negativa*; that is, he did not think it sufficient to stress only what cannot be grasped about God. Especially in his later life, he emphasized that one had to pass beyond the *via negativa* and say more. And for Cusa, the condition that allows the Christian theologian to "say more" is the reality of Jesus Christ (again, see Bond, pp. 33–34).

7. Ideally, we wanted to meet in Jerusalem because of the sites which are sacred to all three religions. We realized that it might be most difficult for our Muslim participants to enter the country. As a backup plan, we kept open the possibility of meeting in southern Spain where once, in the middle ages, all three traditions lived for a short time in peace together. Fortunately, we did not have to make use of our backup plan.

8. Bradford E. Hinze and Irfan A. Omar, eds., *Heirs of Abraham: the Future of Muslim, Jewish and Christian Relations* (Orbis Books, 2005).

9. Hinze describes the many trialogues from the 1970s to the beginning of the new millennium (see pp. 7–15), in which individuals (such as Leonard Swidler, the editor of the *Journal of Ecumenical Studies*, and Eugene Fisher, long time staff member of the United States Conference of Bishops, now retired), as well as universities and organizations (especially Georgetown University and the American Academy of Religion) have fostered interreligious dialogue among Jews, Christians and Muslims.

10. No doubt, part of the pessimism concerning the possibility of theologically focused interreligious dialogue derives from views of those religious believers who overstate their differences with believers of in other religions. Even John Paul II, who did so much to promote peace and understanding between religions, wrote in 1994 in his *Crossing the Threshold of Hope* that "some of the most beautiful names in the human language are given to the God of the Koran, but He is ultimately a God outside of the world, a God who is only Majesty, never Emmanuel, God with us. Islam is not a religion of redemption. There is no room for the Cross and the Resurrection. Jesus is mentioned, but only as a prophet who prepares for the last prophet, Muhammad. There is also mention of Mary, His Virgin Mother, but the tragedy of redemption is completely absent. For this reason not only the theology but also the anthropology of Islam are very distant from Christianity" (*Crossing the Threshold of Hope* [Knopf, 1994], pp. 92–93).

11. John Borelli, "University Students and the Mandate of Interreligious Dialogue," in *Origins*, Vol. 36, No. 14, September 14, 2006, p. 220.

12. Apostolic Letter, *Novo Millennio Inuente*, in *Origins*, Vol. 30, No. 31, January 18, 2001, p. 506.

13. See Michael L. Fitzgerald and John Borelli, *Interfaith Dialogue: A Catholic View* (Orbis Books, 2006), p. 150.

14. The Muslim letter is at www.acommonword.com.

15. Reported by John L. Allen in his column, "All Things Catholic," February 1, 2008, (Vol. 7, No. 21), p. 3.

16. See "Signs of the Times," *America*, June 9–16, 2008, p. 6.

17. See Robert Mickens, "Mixed Reaction to Saudi Olive Branch," in *The Tablet*, July 26, 2008, p. 36.

18. Nobel laureate Amartya Sen's book, *The Argumentative Indian: Writings on Indian History, Culture and Identity* (Farrar, Straus and Giroux, 2005), describes the same "Beit Hillel" kind of respect for opposing views in Indian religious culture and identity, citing examples from the *Bhagawad Gita* (Krishna and Arjuna debating whether to participate in a certain war) and a debate in the *Rig Veda* (on the existence of God and whether to participate in a certain war) where the arguments of the "losing" side are preserved and respected. I am indebted to my colleague David Herrelko for pointing this out to me.

PART I

Learned Ignorance and Interreligious Dialogue

1 Some Requisites for Interfaith Dialogue

David B. Burrell

My story begins where so many western stories do, with ecumenical exchange among Christians. My father married a Catholic woman of British Catholic ancestry, with nothing "immigrant" about her, so quite sure of her pedigree. His own Christian faith was beyond dispute, yet he never worshiped with us, but rather cooked for us a splendid Sunday brunch, which became our meal of predilection for the week! So tolerance and mutual respect, as well as service, were part of our home. After completing a B.A. in Liberal Studies at Notre Dame in 1954, I took my chances with the Congregation of Holy Cross, which had founded the university, and have found it a stimulating and supportive milieu ever since. Four years of theology in Rome (1956–1960) gave me a foretaste of the theology disseminated in Vatican II—*via* Bernard Lonergan and *nouvelle theologie*—and opened me to European languages, while philosophy study at Yale honed my logical and analytic skills. Soon asked to chair the Department of Theology at Notre Dame, I was charged with developing an ecumenical faculty during the seventies. With the help of colleagues like Joseph Blenkinsopp, Stanley Hauerwas, Robert Wilken, and John Howard Yoder, ours proved to be an exciting venture: to show, in the spirit of Vatican II, how a Catholic university could host an ecumenical faculty and allow it to flourish so as to enrich our shared catholic tradition. It was that experience of "mutual illumination" that has expanded analogously into an interfaith environment for me, as it has for many others.

In my own case, it began with gift of a Judaica position (to Theodore Hesburgh, C.S.C., as president the University) by the Bronfmann family. So we were charged with integrating this position into a faculty of Theology, and the group of faculty just mentioned came up with a Solomonic solution. Not wishing simply to engage a rabbi to teach rabbinics, as could so easily happen in a religious studies department, we decided to bring together our faculty in Hebrew scriptures, New Testament, and early church to create an umbrella sector entitled Judaism and Christianity in Antiquity. (In our next external review, we were praised for this imaginative strategy.) As chair, I had to oversee these maneuvers, so I learned how internally related Judaism and Christianity have been from the outset, despite the parting of the ways. During this period I was asked by my religious congregation to inaugurate an exchange with our primary mission in Bangladesh, so I taught philosophy in the seminary in Dhaka during the fall of 1975. During the summer of 1975, I was asked to participate in a Jewish-Christian-Muslim encounter session at Tantur Ecumenical Institute in Jerusalem, sponsored by the Lilly

Endowment in a grant to Sister Marie Goldstein RSHM, a doctoral graduate of Notre Dame. A serendipitous invitation, as it turned out, because I knew nothing of Islam, and anyone familiar with interfaith exchange knows how rare it was to include Muslims in those early days. So after a summer learning how adherents of each of the Abrahamic faiths tried to live out their traditions, I spent four months in a 92 percent Muslim country. If my Jewish friends had helped me to realize the deeply religious and therapeutic role of the *shabbat,* friends in Bangladesh introduced me to that palpable Muslim sense of the presence of God: "see you tomorrow; in sh'Allah!" Returning to Notre Dame, I was preoccupied with executing our strategies regarding Judaica studies as well as developing my own appreciation of Judaism, but Islam had touched my heart. So when asked to direct Tantur for a year (1980–1981) at the end of my term as chair of theology at Notre Dame, it occured to me that I needed to expand my interfaith understanding to include Islam, so I began two years in Jerusalem with an *ulpan* to learn enough Hebrew to negotiate the streets, to begin the following year a study of Arabic. Yet that decision was also to include an intimation that is especially relevant to this account.

Two years in Jerusalem and subsequent summers in Cairo opened me intellectually to interfaith patterns for learning, and the past six years living each spring at Tantur, on the seam between Israel and Palestine, have rendered those patterns actual and painfully acute. For the fact is that Christians are a minority in the land where Jesus lived, and this minority is wedged between two majorities. So Tantur, founded in1967 as an ecumenical institute by Pope Paul VI, was immediately thrust into an interfaith milieu, as is any Christian living in this Holy Land.

I hope that a fresh engagement in interfaith adventure can help to surmount our current impasses. If our religious traditions, taken singly, have proven ineffectual in responding to violence committed in their name, whether the state powers concerned be explicitly or implicitly linked with one of these religious traditions, could it be that fellow other-believers may empower us to be critical of the distortions of our own traditions, as well as help us discover our respective resources for peace and justice? In short, what we have not learned from our own we may well learn from one another. And is not that the positive face of the contentious world in which we live?

How do the adherents of each Abrahamic faith move beyond the certitudes that have led to contention, as well as beyond more recent political appeals for mutual tolerance, to discover how to welcome one another? A bevy of cultural factors have coalesced, to be sure, to make us more acutely aware of our need for one another, yet nothing short of personal encounter can demonstrate how the other's presence can deepen, even confirm, appreciation of our own faith. The trick becomes incorporating the receptive posture such encounters evoke into an intellectual humility able to animate new forms of mutual inquiry. This chapter explores that challenge.

My life has been particularly blessed, from an ecumenical family to a range of interfaith encounters, to living and working among Jews and Muslims, notably in Jerusalem. It was the milieu of the Holy Land that effectively worked a transformation in my scholarship as well, employing the languages of this environment to trace the exchange among philosophical theologians—notably, Ibn Sina and al-Ghazali, Maimonides and Aquinas—from the twelfth and thirteenth centuries. Many have noted that the presence of a pervasive philosophical tradition—Aristotle in a neo-Platonic key—helped to facilitate an intellectual exchange among Muslims, Jews, and Christians (in that order) in that epoch, yet we face even more formidable obstacles than the absence of such an overarching framework in trying to emulate that interaction today. We shall trace some of these difficulties, yet we also enjoy far more sophisticated access to sources and a vast range of secondary reflections in each tradition. What we may lack, however, for a host of cultural reasons, is the requisite intellectual humility to engage one another fruitfully. Indeed, that is hardly an anticipated concomitant result of graduate study in the west today! Nevertheless, a recent comprehensive study of "the impossibility of interreligious dialogue" by Catherine Cornille lists humility, and especially "doctrinal humility," as the prime requisite for fruitful dialogue. Writing from a Christian perspective, she notes the rich Christian tradition of spiritual humility, proceeds to offer three telling reasons for doctrinal humility: historical consciousness, eschatology, and apophatic theology. She briefly traces the way other religions praise humility, insisting, in the face of a creator God, that their adherents develop it.[1]

We shall focus on intellectual humility as it has been displayed (or not) in Jewish, Christian, and Muslim exchange over the centuries, to uncover pointers toward what might facilitate as well as block current exchanges, then delineate some crippling sociocultural obstacles to exercising dialogue in today's situation, to close with suggested ways to step beyond our current impasses. Genuine interreligious dialogue constitutes a formidable task, indeed, calling for humility on the part of believers from each Abrahamic faith as they find themselves having to acknowledge responsibility for exacerbating the problem more than contributing to the solution.

■ HISTORICAL INTERACTIONS

John of Damascus stands as a key figure in the earliest exchanges between a settled Orthodox Christianity and the Muslims, arriving from the Arabian peninsula, who were animated by a vigorous revelation. His father served in the new Islamic government, which sought the services of many Syriac Christian translators to render Greek philosophical writings into Arabic. Moreover, the Byzantine hegemony was hardly uniform, as many eastern Christians doubtless preferred unknown and untested rulers to the often oppressive ecclesiastical-political regime of Byzantium. Given that the only available hegemonies were religious, it was largely a question of which one granted more tolerance to local custom and beliefs. Moreover, Muslims would have little stake in engaging differences among Christians in doctrine, though they were mightily impressed with Byzantine imperial structures, seeking quickly to mimic their splendor in Damascus, first in Umayyad and then in Abbasid polities, and through them to the farthest reaches of the Mediterranean world. In his critical comment on this cultural assimilation, Seyyed Muhammad Khatami, onetime president of Iran, offers a Shi'ite perspective, which helps to explain what had long been a conundrum for me: the apparent propensity in Islam for a strong ruler when the religion itself is anything but hierarchical.[2] It is Khatami's simple contention that I have just noted: Coming as they did from the Arabian peninsula, the Muslims who invaded the stately Byzantine empire were utterly impressed with imperial splendor, and quickly sought to adopt it. Thenceforth, and, indeed, as much for Shi'ites as for Sunnis, the history of Islam has been punctuated by imperial regimes: Abbasid, Ottoman, and Moghul among the Sunnis, and Savafid among the Shi'a—to name but a few. Much as Christians not only acquiesced to Constantine's granting their religion an imperial status but also came to enjoy the attendant privileges, learning to read their revelation through the lens of power, so would Islam adapt the Qur'an and the *sunna* tradition to subserving imperial ambitions.

Yet an imperial polity could also make room for differences; indeed, relegating intrareligious disputes to the courts of each religious community allowed imperial regimes to concentrate on larger issues, as well as fostered a political climate of tolerance. Making room for such differences thereby aligned the prevailing Islamic hegemony with those Qur'anic verses that fostered co-existence. This climate came to favor a form of interreligious exchange known as *disputation*. Often taking the form of Muslim commentary discourse on revelation, these public disputations proposed to lay out the religion's tenets of each group for the other to hear, with an eye to showing the superiority of one over the other.[3] Similar exchanges were undertaken in Christian lands with Jews, notably in the Iberian peninsula and in Provence, where the atmosphere of the Islamicate had made itself felt. In these exchanges, Talmudic forms of reason were in evidence. Indeed, George Makdisi has argued that such disputations formed the matrix for the early scholastic form of instruction via "disputed questions."[4] We cannot forget, however, that Christians in the Islamicate, and Jews in Christendom, had to comport themselves as a minority group, because, no matter how much tolerance the political structures may (or may not) have permitted, societal norms prevailed. Moreover, the very structure of such disputations, as we have suggested, set up a win/lose scenario, so more thoughtful exchange would have to await another modality. Such a shift would also require sociopolitical structures more favorable for reflection.

These emerged in the west in the form of religious communities, first as monasteries and then, also, by friaries (notably Franciscan and Dominican), which enjoyed a degree of freedom from both secular and ecclesiastical authority, though, in fact, secular authority in the west was decidedly less structured than in the Islamicate, however fractured it was there. The result was a flourishing of intellectual life from the twelfth century on, especially as translations of Greek philosophy began to emanate from the Islamicate in the thirteenth century. For if Islamic thinkers, like al-Farabi ("the second Aristotle") and Ibn Sina (Avicenna), had to depend on the goodwill of patrons whose position was subject to political vicissitudes, monks and friars enjoyed a sustaining community that could provide, not only a secure milieu for intellectual inquiry, but teams of secretaries to assist their intellectually endowed confreres. Moreover, the philosophically minded of each Abrahamic community encountered the potentially totalizing intellectual milieu of neo-Platonism, whereby everything emanated elegantly from the One, yet compromising the freedom of creation. So they turned for assistance, when they could, to those from other faiths, seeking ways to explicate the way their sources of revelation announced the free creation of the universe by an intentional creator. In the face of a philosophical scheme which articulated the source of the universe in terms of an intellect emanation that need not be free, this required substantial philosophical elaboration. Evidently, those who came later were able to interact with their predecessors, which is precisely what we find in Moses Maimonides's use of Ibn Sina, as well as his presumed inspiration by al-Ghazali, while Aquinas's employ of Maimonides (and of his assimilation of Ibn Sina) is clear from citations in his work.[5] Therefore, despite and indirectly because of the ongoing crusades, the Mediterranean milieu fostered such exchange among intellectual inquirers of different Abrahamic faiths, intent as they were on finding philosophical ways to elucidate their shared belief in a free creator. Even though the "exchange" was often one way, given circumstances and generational differences, the results were quite spectacular, testifying to the fruitfulness of an overarching philosophy as well as the shared conviction that truth sought could be found where it was recognized. Where differences in faith may have seemed irreconcilable, employing a philosophical tradition to bolster those verities of revelation that were shared proved a powerful incentive to learn from one another.

■ SOME IMPLICATIONS FOR TODAY

Several centuries separate us from this medieval arena of exchange, carried out amidst hostilities among the Abrahamic faiths, as history has conspired to enlarge the arena to encompass the globe and to redistribute power relations so as to transmute differences into clashes, often fueled by resentment at the profound shift in power. Now, it is the lack of analogies among the three Abrahamic faiths that are instructive: Even those Christians who believed that the "new testament" had effectively replaced the "old" had to tolerate the presence of Jews in their societies, for they could never utterly deny their own spiritual ancestry. Yet Jews seldom posed a threat, as social arrangements reinforced the conviction that Judaism is for Jews. However, a revelation expressly destined for the entire human race, whose very claims proved oxymoronic for Christians, had to be on a potential collision course with Jesus's command to "preach the gospel to all nations," even though Islam, coming along last, had expressly provided privileged niches for Jews and for Christians as possessors of a divine revelation.

Therefore, as the Muslim world gained territory and power, it was destined to be a geographic as well as a spiritual other, for Christendom could hardly find room for so potent an adversary in its midst—not even the grudging space granted to Jews. Yet a burgeoning medieval and early modern Europe could hardly resist the charms and allurements of the renowned Islamic civilization, especially as their elites sought elegant accessories from India and China, which passed through the heart of the Islamicate on their way to Europe across the fabled "silk road." Indeed, the desire to find a tax-free route to those very accessories would spell the end of such fated interaction between Christendom and the Islam world, as Columbus's voyage opened up far more than the Indies: two continents to exploit. So, after arresting the Ottoman imperial forces at the gates of Vienna in 1565, western Europe could confidently turn its back on Islam to pursue the mercantile missionizing of north and south America, the result of which was an extraordinary development on all levels, culminating in Napoleon's landing in Alexandria in 1799, to initiate western colonization of both Ottoman and Moghul empires—the once-glorious Islamic world.

In breathlessly short compass, such is our Christian history with Islam, once marked by fruitful philosophical and theological exchanges in medieval times, as well as an enduring fascination for, if not seduction by, the "marvels of the East." Yet the technological gulf stimulated by European exploitation of America, and marked by Napoleon's conquest soon consolidated by British imperial forces, led inescapably (via the introduction of the secular, socialist, utopian movement of European—though not Islamic—Jewry called Zionism) to a simmering resentment in the Islamic world and the resurgence of a form of political Islam that might hope to recover some of their collective pride. All this remains powerfully present in that part of west Asia that looks like the Middle East from London, especially because Britain's presence of power had been replaced by that of the United States in this traditionally Islamic domain. Yet we cannot forget that "the Islamicate" traditionally provided room for Jews as well as for Christians, who were always to be found among Arabs, who themselves constitute only 20 percent of the Islamic world. So, just as there are religious differences among Arabs, ethnic differences abound among Muslims, thus reminding us that this rich panoply of taste and cultures should help to offset media stereotypes. Nothing can effect that better than mixing of peoples, so one of the most powerful incentives for learning about Islam among contemporary western Europeans or Americans is the fact that one's daughter's roommate in college turns out to be a Muslim! In a fashion quite opposite to Napoleon's landing in Alexandria, we can also say of these encounters that "the rest is history," which should open us to the theological potential of our times.

Yet the novel factor in today's three-body problem among Jews, Christians, and Muslims remains the success of Zionism in realizing a Jewish state in biblical Palestine, yet affecting the entire Levant. Here, the power imbalance between Palestinians and Israelis in the current sociopolitical environment palpably affects the discourse. How can discussion continue in such a climate? Only with exceptionally fair-minded discussants who can bring the rich resources of the Abrahamic faiths to the table, and do so in a milieu that has shown itself to be sensitive to the realities affecting each tradition. Such has indeed been our experience at Tantur, and here is where intellectual humility is especially demanded. It simply will not do to restrict ourelves to discussing only "religious issues," and so avoid the painful consequences of political power exercised by our respective communities, directly or indirectly. In fact, to try to do so can only exhibit "bad faith," that is, a pervasive denial of the negative effects of our religious traditions throughout history into today's world. My counselor for twenty-five years, Helen Luke, wrote the following on humility: "We might gain humility without humiliation, but that is not the normal way!" So intellectual humility will be tested in our response to those actions of our respective religious communities that anyone would find humiliating. As the course of history makes abundantly clear, each of our Abrahamic faiths can boast of exemplary persons who contributed positively to human flourishing, and did so as Jews, Christians, or Muslims; yet we must also decry co-religionists who have betrayed their faith, or even worse, distorted their tradition to attempt to justify the unjustifiable. The Qur'an labels such "believers" *hypocrites*, reserving special opprobrium for them, as Jesus did for a prominent group of religious leaders of his time, and as the Hebrew prophets never tire of doing. Yet it seems proper that such criticism come from within the community itself, painful as that must be. That is one of the earmarks of intellectual humility in this interreligious arena.

The alternative will lay the blame for any defilement of a religious tradition on the other-believer, and proceed to defend one's own faith by denigrating theirs. That is a common enough tactic, of course, illustrating a primary way in which people can employ religious convictions to exploit differences and foment violence. Yet it should be clear that *religion* here has become quite detached from its goal of returning everything to the One from whom we have received everything. So the ones whom Jesus and the Qur'an castigate as hypocrites are pretending to represent God while their actions only display God's absence from the transaction. Yet anyone who bears a religious role knows how easily that can be done, so once again, the need for humility! But this exercise also shows how humility hardly bespeaks weakness, but rather expresses a way of suffering for and with one's community. So Aquinas, in discussing martyrdom, reminds us how *enduring* always requires more courage than *lashing out*, for lashing out is a spontaneous *reaction*, whereas enduring is a reflective *response* to something ostensibly or potentially harmful. Developing the capacity to endure what is ostensibly or potentially harmful becomes the key to discerning whether what we fear is truly so or not; lashing out (by way of immediate reaction) can, of course, wreak even greater harm than the anticipated ostensible harm. Only what we have called intellectual humility can keep us from rash judgment in frightening situations.

It should be clear that we are backing into an account of human flourishing and degradation remarkably similar to the one Augustine came to through his arduous journey to discern the truth of such things. For whatever stands in the way of truth revealing itself to us is always a form of pride, insisting that we know it already! However, that is the very attitude that we characteristically associate with successful people, in Augustine's time as well as our own. So it seems that the path to humility will inevitably involve some kind of community, which can temper our need to "know it all or do it all," thereby allowing us to overcome the fear of falling or failing, so as to have better access to what is true and right. That is the kind of community we experienced in our deliberations at Tantur in June 2007, which also showed us how differences in faith commitment can forge even stronger communal bonds, for as we acknowledge the failings of our community in the face of other-believers, we cannot help but acknowledge the failing of our community before its God. In this way, we become prophets to one another, in a sense hallowed by both Jews and Muslims. As we fulfill that role among ourselves, no one of us can claim to be standing apart to bring the "word of the Lord," for the word is discovered in that very interaction. So the experience itself brings us to a fresh understanding of *prophecy*, and one inextricably linked to the way differences in faith can assist the participants to grow in their own faith. Yet it should become clear that the only way to this discovery lies through accepting blame ourselves for the failures of our traditions, and then turn to seek the help of other-believers to redress those failures. If that sounds like a novel posture for religious persons, must we not admit that it rather repristinates what we originally found attractive in the religious quest, and celebrate the fact that we have discovered it together with other-believers. In fact, we may find this so exhilarating that we begin to wonder if there can be any other way.

Let me assay an explanation why that may be the case. The quality of intellectual humility needed to counter religious arrogance must be potent indeed, for it reflects the age-old tug-of-war between faith in God and trust in idols. The Hebrew Scriptures, together with the Qur'an, remind us that this struggle is constantly taking place within us as it is within our communities; indeed, that idolatry represents the default pattern for human beings. It bespeaks our penchant to rely on ourselves, reserving the power of gods to keep disaster at bay. In this sense, the practice of idolatry does not parallel the covenantal relation of God with God's own people, but only mimics it. Indeed, as the Hebrew prophets constantly remind us, no authentic relationship is possible with an idol, because idols are but projections of our ambitions, of our ego, personal and collective. Similarly, a posture of intellectual arrogance represents the face of one who pretends to "go it alone," on the strength of "knowing it all," yet remains in fear of impending disaster, for we cannot help but realize no one can control everything. So what we see in purported self-sufficiency is a defensive brittleness. And when that is combined with religion, we can only sense the absence of God! The best example I can offer of this contrast is that in French between optimism and hope, or *espoir* and *espérance*.

It is a telling example in the context of Abrahamic faiths, because it expresses the transition that a quarter century in Israel/Palestine (or "the Holy Land") has worked in me. Just as I had to realize fifty years ago, when I arrived in Rome to study theology for the Catholic priesthood, how uptight and Protestant I was as an American Catholic in the face of everything Italian, so twenty-five years of experience with the Holy Land was to challenge my native American optimism. It was not until I returned to the United States after my initial two years in Jerusalem (1980–1982), however, that I began to sense what was happening. For the constant query, "When are they going to solve that problem over there?" suddenly struck me as banal and insensitive. I say "suddenly," to acknowledge that the attitude reminded me of what my own had been before living among the peoples of this land, for Americans invariably turn every situation into a problem so that it can be solved, and I am an American! Formed as I was in the linguistic analysis Wittgenstein taught us, I began to see how inextricably connected the two were—*problem* with *solution*—and how deeply that form of life and thinking is grounded in a naive optimism: Every problem must have a solution, or, in the words of the U.S. Navy's construction battalion [CB's] in World War II, "The impossible takes a little longer."

The attitude becomes endemic to immigrants finding a land of opportunity, and doubtless stems from the prospect of an apparently endless frontier, rolling over Native American humans and animals with relative insouciance. To acknowledge any givens, anything not plastic before human ingenuity, seems fatalistic, and so promises an end to untold human suffering. Indeed, the very notion of *suffering* will come to seem eliminable, as a progressively expanding economy brings prosperity in its wake. At root, *to suffer* means "to undergo" what cannot be altered to suit one's needs, and the very meaning of *progress* turns on that ability to cater to what we humans regard as our needs. Only when this penchant to make nature subservient to satisfying our needs begins to backfire, in what we have learned to call the ecological crisis, does the idolatry inherent in this approach to things become evident.

The world of nature presents itself as the most palpable evidence we have of a creator, especially when we experience its overwhelming beauty. Taking a small step toward intellectual humility helps us become aware of how destructive our penchant to manipulate nature to serve our purported needs can be. In other words, human self-sufficiency becomes self-destructive, turning an open universe into a prison created by our need to satisfy our palpable needs. Yet once we begin to realize how much a problem-solving attitude must make everything manipulable and plastic to our needs, the optimism native to Americans reveals its Janus-face as its sinister side emerges. What alternatives can we propose when we can no longer pretend to solve every problem? Within the parameters of optimism, of course, the sole alternative is pessimism! If the idol will not succeed in averting catastrophe, we are doomed! However, there is another path, but from the perspective of *optimism* we cannot even name it properly, for if we are told it is hope, the only way we can understand *hope* is as a form of optimism! But that is like saying that, among the idols, there is a most powerful one that people call God, which, of course, is often what religion offers, and what critics of religion want to reduce it to.

How can we find a way out of such a mindset? In my case, it came through the witness of people who had learned to suffer, yet they were not at all fatalistic. They began to show me another path by the way they lived their lives. A literary example can be found in Raja Shehadeh's *Strangers in the House*, a memoir of his family's forced exodus from Jaffa in 1948, poignantly recounting the manner in which Israeli dominance of the land had taken its toll, yet doing so without rancor![6] What shines through these lives is a salutary sense of suffering which may involve pain, but more fundamentally means living through a situation in which much lies beyond one's control. Yet whether it lies in the control of those who think they are controlling things remains doubtful. The result is doubtless oppression, but not without a sense of humor.

Now, the most palpable contrast between Israel and Palestine is not so much a Jewish *versus* a Christian/Muslim one, but rather one of a society dominated by *optimism versus* one discovering *hope* (as an alternative to despair). The trajectory adopted by Jews in Israel, in reacting to the unspeakable tragedy of the Shoah, has largely been an American one of "make do." Much of its development has, of course, been funded by the Americas, North and South, but the attitudes are distinctively those we have been identifying with "American," that is, the United States. Lacking the open frontier to make that come naturally, however, a nationalist, socialist, utopian ideology, European and nineteenth-century in origin, took its place, offering an alternative vision of society designed to give all Jews a nation-state in which to live and to flourish. Those Jews who willingly cast their lot and their lives with this venture also had a stake in shaping its future, and so developed from the outset a critical eye toward what a Jewish state should be. Indeed, the amount of auto-criticism that has characterized Israel from the days of early settlements in Palestine (*yishuv*) through the formation of the state, offers an exemplary instance of a vision-directed society—another similarity with the early United States. Yet by restricting the vision to Jewish society, and then to a Jewish state, Zionist ideology indirectly contributed to denying the presence of others in their midst, so that the spectacular victory of 1967 resulted in the vision's unraveling, as the logical move of returning the land conquered to those whom the Jewish state could not admit to their polity (and remain demographically Jewish) gave way to an irresistible strategy of exploitation.[7] Predictably, a vocal minority in Israel continues to decry this devolution of the vision, though its replacement by the current dominant outlook of "economic liberalism" has also proven irresistible. So Israeli society today is haunted by the poignant words of the native American chief: "without a vision the people die."

Here again, intellectual humility can show a way forward. If the secular vision of Zionism has proved unable to withstand its own undoing, so, it appears, has the original American vision, which was given fresh expression after World War II in the Marshall Plan of aid to a devastated Europe, then recalled to its unfinished domestic agenda by the dream of Martin Luther King, Jr., and, more recently, has been obscured by a decisive turn toward unilateral protection of its own interests as well as imposing those interests on the rest of the world. Here, once more, whether it be Israel or the United States, the dominant religious groups have failed to offer an alternative vision to renew and restore the original vision as it vanishes, however different those visions were for the early United States and for Israel. Therefore, to thinking people there remains a simple alternative: Either work to mine the rich resources in each society for a humanistic vision, or bring all religious groups together in a concerted fashion to help generate a fresh version of the vision for Israeli or American society.

In his recent stirring call to fellow Muslims, *Western Muslims and the Future of Islam*, Tariq Ramadan reminds them that Islam has adapted to one society after another, from Arabia to Iberia, from Iran to South Asia, China, and Indonesia, and is now given the chance to adapt to the west.[8] His call, which has certainly been heard in America, and differently in various parts of Europe, involves Muslims interacting with others in so adapting, yet doing so in a way that offers a distinctive contribution as well. For him, the Islamic strictures against usury mean that Muslims cannot simply adopt "economic liberalism" as it seems to have captured the west. In this, of course, Ramadan is one with Catholic social teaching. Muslims may prod Catholics to recover that vision, critical of economic liberalism, by insisting that another way must be found to organize the societies to which Ramadan directs his attention, and, as we recently piloted at Tantur, he may well provide the impetus needed to project a concerted religious vision for these societies. There remains a vigorous humanistic alternative, of course, but if both groups can collaborate in projects on the ground, these alternatives need not be stark; they can offer salutary competition in the doing of good works, especially as religious groups act out of faith, rather than comport themselves as one more interest group in society, and thus they can reverse the stereotype that could easily impede cooperation.

The key to such collaboration, as I have insisted, can only be a healthy dose of intellectual humility. Indeed, the purpose of the extensive illustration from Israeli/Palestinian society is to show that one practical correlate of such humility can be a newfound hope—a hope that need not fail when optimism disappoints or when truncated vision self-destructs. Christians are taught that hope, like faith and charity, is a theological virtue, which means that it can only be sustained by a living relationship to the free creator. However, to insist that it is *theological* is not to demand that it be explicitly *religious*, for any effective humanist vision can only be sustained, I would contend, by something more than the evidence history affords of the human. Placing the emphasis on *faith* rather than *religion* may help us move beyond the religious/secular dichotomy, much as we have tried to overcome the polarity of optimism/pessimism, to call attention to a dimension that sustains human activity, which need not calculate results. This will involve a way of life that facilitates the transition from optimism to hope, and so can begin to teach us the difference. Our fledgling conversations at Tantur certainly did something of that for our small group, accomplishing it in an interfaith setting. Yet an unmistakable humanist element was present as well. We can, I believe, read a pledge of hope in that encounter, especially if these notably Christian reflections on intellectual humility as a door to genuine hope can be complemented by Jewish and Muslim reflections on their traditions in a similar vein, to see if we can reinforce one another in this way.

■ Notes

1. Catherine Cornille, *The Impossibility of Inter-religious Dialogue* (New York: Continuum, Herder and Herder, 2008).

2. Seyyed Muhammad Khatami, *La religion et la pensee prises ou piege d'autocratie*, (Cahiers de MIDEO 4; Louvain/Paris: Peeters, 2005).

3. Gabriel Said Reynolds, *Muslim Theologian in a Sectarian Milieu: Abd al-Jabbār and the Critique of Christian Origins* (Boston: Brill, 2004).

4. George Makdisi, *The Rise of Colleges: Institutions of learning in Islam and the West* (*Edinburgh: Edinburgh University Press, 1981*).

5. David Burrell, *Knowing the Unknowable God* (Notre Dame, IN: Notre Dame Press, 1986).

6. Raja Shehadeh, *Strangers in the House* (South Royalton, VT: Steerforth Press, 2002).

7. Yeshayahu Leiibowitz, *Judaism, Human Values, and the Jewish State*, ed.Eliezer Goldman, trans. Raphael Levy. (Cambridge, MA: Harvard University Press, 1992).

8. Tariq Ramadan, *Western Muslims and the Future of Islam* (Oxford: Oxford University Press, 2005).

2 Learned Ignorance and Faithful Interpretation of the Qur'an in Nicholas of Cusa (1401–1464)

Pim Valkenberg

My engagement in interreligious dialogue might have been with me for a longer time than I often think because, during my MA in theology, I studied systematic theology (Thomas Aquinas) together with phenomenology of religions (esp. Islam)—not a very common combination. However, my engagement really began shortly after my PhD in 1990 when I was asked to develop the theological principles behind a new MA program at the Department of Theology of the Catholic University in Nijmegen, the Netherlands. This program had interreligious dialogue as its primal focus, and I found out that current systematic theological or missiological approaches to this dialogue could be summarized as the theology of religions. From the very beginning, I have tried to combine the scholarly study of interreligious dialogue with the grassroots work of organizing dialogues, not only to let my students know about the relevance of their studies, but also because I think that a theology of religions should be nourished by actual dialogues. I have elaborated this connection between interreligious dialogue and theology in my *Sharing Lights on the Way to God: Muslim-Christian Dialogue and Theology in the Context of Abrahamic Partnership* (Amsterdam/New York: 2006).

I do think that dialogue between religions is important, not only because of world peace or intercultural collaboration, but mainly because differences matter. In some forms of theology of religions, the religions of the world are seen as slightly different variations on a common theme. I do not agree with such an approach, mainly because I think that the specifics of a religion are often the most important issues for the adherents of the religion. Most Christians would not agree with the thesis that Christ is just one of the revelations of God. My research has shown me that Judaism, Christianity, and Islam are often so opposed to one another precisely because they have both common sources and different traditions of interpretation, the differences being more germane to religious identities than the commonalities.

Finally, for me as a theologian, the ultimate goal of an interreligious dialogue cannot be but a theological one: to learn about God. The process of dialogue, however, shows in the first place that we learn about God by learning about the other, and second that we learn about ourselves through knowledge of the other. It is my conviction that the Christian tradition contains many important references to learning from the stranger as a way to learn about Christ. Of course, I realize that such a theological dialogue is certainly not the only form of interreligious dialogue. In most contexts, theological dialogue is actually less important than dialogues about social matters or about spiritual experiences; nevertheless, it has its own place.

As a teacher of theology, I always try to convince my students that every new insight leads to a couple of fresh questions, so that the quest for knowledge never stops. Although I think that this may be the case in every academic field, it is especially true in theology, because the subject matter in this field infinitely surpasses the limits of human comprehension. I often sense that some of my students do not like this idea of infinite questioning, because they want to have definite boundaries, straightforward doctrines and, most of all, clear guidelines for their assignments.

Nevertheless, it must also be admitted that theology as "faith seeking understanding" (*fides quaerens intellectum*) often unfortunately gratified this longing for immediate and comprehensive answers. Many companions in the tradition of neo-Scholasticism proceeded *more geometrico*, as if the basic data were as clear as glass and as measurable as cubes. The method of questions and answers used in many catechetical texts seemed to satisfy the thirst for knowledge, because most students would think that the answers contained the truth, the whole truth and nothing but the truth. However, there is another tradition of theology in which understanding implies the awareness that we know nothing yet, that every answer evokes a dozen new questions.[1] Significantly, the greatest theologians realized in the final analysis that they knew nothing about the essence of the subject matter of their discipline, whereas their less gifted colleagues seemed to be quite confident about their grasp of the subject. In this respect, theologians do not differ from most other students and scholars.

This contribution to the volume on "learned ignorance" in the Abrahamic faiths concentrates on Nicholas of Cusa (1401–1464). He wrote in an exemplary way about the paradox of "knowing not to know."[2] Even more importantly, he may have been the first theologian to make this insight fruitful in the context of what is now termed interreligious dialogue. I will show how Nicholas applied his insight in the paradoxical nature of our knowledge of God—often described by scholars as his "perspectivism," "conjectural universe" or "coincident theology"[3]—to the possibility of being taught by religious others, that is, by those who believe in another religion. After having discussed his *De docta ignorantia*, I will give an interpretation of some important texts from his *De pace fidei* and his *Cribratio alcorani*. However, in order to show what is new in Cusanus and what continues an already established tradition of negative theology and religious hermeneutics, I want to begin with Dionysius the Areopagite and Thomas Aquinas.

■ DIONYSIUS THE AREOPAGITE AND THOMAS AQUINAS

The tradition of not knowing in theology has been named negative or apophatic theology. Its ancestor is Dionysius, nicknamed the Areopagite, because he tried to pass himself off as the Dionysius who converted to Christianity after hearing St. Paul's famous speech at the Areopagus in Athens (Acts 17:34). As Bernard McGinn states, "[t]his pious fiction gave the writings a quasi-apostolic reputation that made them *the* authority in matters mystical for most writers in East and West down to modern times…"[4] In fact, Dionysius was probably a monastic writer from fifth century Syria who used neo-Platonist philosophical traditions to deepen his Christian mysticism. The God whose names he tried to enumerate in the work that became known in the West as *De divinis nominibus* is a God who may be worshiped as "an unknown God," just as did the Athenians according to Paul (Acts 17:23); yet, Dionysius would agree with Paul that Christians have the duty to proclaim the identity of this God in words derived from the Scriptures. At the same time, questions about what exactly are the authoritative Scriptures and who has the right to explain them may be hotly debated.

In the first paragraph of his treatise *On the Divine Names*, Dionysius shows that Scripture serves as guideline for our language about God, yet God transcends our possibilities of naming so endlessly that our knowing is an unknowing:

> […] Here too let us hold on to the scriptural rule that when we say anything about God, we should set down the truth "not in the plausible words of human wisdom, but in demonstration of the power granted by the Spirit" to the scripture writers, a power by which, in a manner surpassing speech and knowledge, we reach a union superior to anything available to us by way of our own abilities or activities in the realm of discourse or of intellect. This is why we must not dare to resort to words or conceptions concerning that hidden divinity which transcends being, apart from what the sacred scriptures have divinely revealed. Since the unknowing of what is beyond being is something above and beyond speech, mind, or being itself, one should ascribe to it an understanding beyond being. Let us therefore look as far upward as the light of sacred scripture will allow, and, in our reverent awe of what is divine, let us be drawn together toward the divine splendor.[5]

The name that Dionysius gives to God indicates that his unknowing is caused by God's eminence: God is the "divinity which transcends being" or, in the stately translation by C.E. Rolt, the "Super-Essential Godhead," a rendering of the Greek *hyperousios thearchia*.[6] At the beginning of his shorter treatise on mystical theology, he even addresses God as the Super-Essential, Supra-Divine, Super-Excellent Trinity, and prays:

> Lead us up beyond unknowing and light, up to the farthest, highest peak of mystic scripture, where the mysteries of God's Word lie simple, absolute and unchangeable in the brilliant darkness of a hidden silence. Amid the deepest shadow they pour overwhelming light on what is most manifest. Amid the wholly unsensed and unseen they completely fill our sightless minds with treasures beyond all beauty.[7]

Thomas Aquinas was influenced by Dionysius, even though the sober and precise language of the great Scholastic contrasts sharply with the "language of superabundance" that is so characteristic of Dionysius.[8] Thomas quotes him fairly often in his systematic theological works and wrote a commentary on Dionysius's treatise on the divine names. In this commentary, he interprets Dionysius's paradoxical utterances on "the unknowing of what is beyond being" and "brilliant darkness" by developing a threefold pattern for our knowing and naming God. He takes his cue from a lapidary formulation in Dionysius: "we ascend to God through the removal and excess of all things and in the cause of all things."[9] In the question on knowing God from his *Summa theologiae*, Thomas spells this out more clearly:

> Our natural knowledge begins from the senses. Therefore our natural knowledge can go as far as it can be led by perceptible things. But our mind cannot be led by perceptible things so far as to see the essence of God, because perceptible creatures do not equal the power of God as their cause. Therefore from the knowledge of perceptible things the whole power of God cannot be known, and neither, consequently, can his essence be seen.

We can, however, know something about God, for instance, that God exists and that God is the cause of creatures. Thomas concludes:

> Therefore we know of his relationship with creatures, that he is cause of them all; also that creatures differ from him, namely, that he is not in any way part of what is caused by him; and that being uncaused is attributed to him not on account of any defect on his part, but because he exceeds all things.[10]

This threefold pattern in our knowing God—affirming because of God's creation of all things, removing because of the infinite distance between God and creatures, and being aware of God exceeding all created things—has been interpreted differently in the history of Thomism. Although traditional interpretations underscore the possibility of an affirmative doctrinal basis, a group of theologians associated with the Thomas Institute at Utrecht, in the Netherlands, gives a more linguistic reading of Aquinas's God-talk, stressing his words that "we have no means for considering how God is, but rather how He is not."[11] Meanwhile, some other members of the same group try to balance somewhat more the negative and positive sides of Aquinas's *triplex via*.[12]

One of the consequences of Thomas's stress on the fact that we do not know how God is but rather know only how God is not is that he is keenly aware of the peculiar nature of our knowledge of God as a form of knowledge that is utterly dependant on God's will to reveal Godself. Therefore, Aquinas characterizes theology as *sacra doctrina*, holy teaching in which we receive our teaching from God—or Christ as God incarnate—through Scripture, and transmit this teaching to others. This explains why Thomas may use *sacra doctrina* and *sacra Scriptura* as synonyms, and why Scripture and the tradition of the Church are so important as sources of theological reasoning.[13]

Once again, when he writes about the reasons for metaphorical language in Scripture, Thomas discusses in the first question of his *Summa theologiae* the nature of *sacra doctrina* and refers to Dionysius and his "negative theology." He quotes Dionysius saying that "it is more fitting that divine matters should be conveyed under the figure of lowly bodies than of noble bodies." Thomas Aquinas explains that

> this is more appropriate to the knowledge of God that we have in this life; for what God is not is clearer to us than what God is. Therefore likenesses drawn from things farthest

away from God form within us a truer estimate that God is above whatever we may say or think of God.[14]

As Michel Corbin notes in one of his Christological studies on Thomas, the divine descent into human form, "taking the form of a slave" (Phil. 2:7), forms the Christological warrant for recognizing God in "the least ones" (Mt. 25:45).[15]

Finally, Thomas quotes Dionysius once again when he deals with the basic hermeneutical question of interpreting theological authorities. As we read before, Dionysius said that we should not dare to speak about the hidden eminent Deity otherwise than in language revealed to us in Holy Scripture. In his commentary on this text from *De divinis nominibus*, Thomas points to the Latin translation that says: "we should not dare to say or think differently from the divinely revealed expressions *from* the sacred writings,"[16] noting that Dionysius writes, "*from (ex)* the sacred writings," not "*in (in)* the sacred writings," Therefore, Aquinas concludes. "everything that may—according to the rule of faith—be derived from the text of Scripture, may be used in our God-talk even though it is not literally contained in Scripture." In this manner, Thomas formulates a hermeneutical rule that creates space for theological language not directly contained in Scripture and yet remains faithful to Scripture.

It is this notion of faithfulness to Scripture while using different phrases than are used in Scripture that will return in Nicolas of Cusa; both authors, Aquinas and Cusanus, used this notion when confronted with ecumenical issues. In the case of Thomas, Pope Urban IV, while preparing for the Council of Lyons in 1274, asked him to write an assessment of Greek theology. In the prologue to the work he wrote, Thomas shows his awareness of the fact that the sayings of the Greek Fathers of the Church have to be explained carefully because of their historical distance from his own time and the development of doctrine. Therefore, some of their sayings do not sound exactly the way he would phrase them in the thirteenth century; in those cases, he said, we should not reject those formulations, nor should we stretch them any further, but we should explain them with reverence.[17] It is my contention that this hermeneutical idea of *reverenter exponere* or of *pie exponere* as Thomas writes elsewhere,[18] is very important in an ecumenical context. This rule of "faithful interpretation" shows that, although we are aware of the differences, partly caused by historical, cultural, and linguistic factors, partly by doctrinal differences, we are still willing to interpret others as our brothers and sisters in faith: we begin our interpretation not with an hermeneutics of suspicion but with an hermeneutics of a shared faith, because we realize that, in talking about God, the Greeks in this instance intend to approach the same reality as we do in our faith.[19] It goes without saying that such an attitude is of the utmost importance in trialogues among adherents of the three monotheistic religions. Although Jews and Muslims may be reminded once again that the Christian affirmation of a Trinitarian God is not meant to derogate from the Oneness of God, Christians should remind themselves that Jews and Muslims refer to the God of Jesus Christ, even if they do not wish to refer to Christ when speaking about God.

As far as I know, Thomas did not extend his own ecumenical rule to interfaith relations, although he was aware that some of the major sources for his approach to God were Jewish and Muslim sources.[20] However, there are some indications that Nicholas of Cusa did extend his awareness of our learned ignorance of God to its interfaith implications.

■ NICHOLAS OF CUSA AND THE LEARNED IGNORANCE OF GOD

The remainder of this chapter concentrates on Nicholas of Cusa, because in his work the awareness of the limits of our knowledge of God is connected to an awareness of the limits of our judgment on those of other religions.

Living two centuries later than Thomas Aquinas, Nicholas of Cusa (1401–1464) was directly involved in attempts to reunite the Western (Latin) and Eastern (Greek) churches. He wrote his book *De docta ignorantia* in 1440 just after the Council of Ferrara and Florence (1438–1439). Although Nicholas probably did not attend the Council, he was sent as a delegate by the pope to Constantinople to facilitate its organization. The fall of Constantinople in 1453 led Nicholas to write his work on interfaith harmony, *De pace fidei*. In both cases, political events seemed to influence Cusanus's thinking on religious plurality as an advantage rather than as a hindrance to Christian truth.[21]

Earlier, I mentioned proceeding *more geometrico* as a mistaken way to evade the uncertainty that characterizes human knowledge of God. Nevertheless, Cusanus himself proceeds in the manner of a geometrician when talking about *docta ignorantia* or learned ignorance.[22] After all, he was not only a philosopher and a theologian, a Cardinal of the Roman Catholic Church and a specialist in Canon Law; he was a mathematician as well.[23] In the beginning of his book on learned ignorance, he takes Anselm's well-known formula *id quo maius cogitari nequit* ("that than which nothing greater can be thought") as a point of departure to characterize God as the Maximum that coincides with the Minimum because nothing is opposed to it.[24] The three books of the *docta ignorantia* describe three ways of looking at this Maximum. First, the Maximum exists in itself in Oneness as the Absolute Maximum; second, it exists in the universe as a contracted Maximum that does not exist independently of the plurality in which it is present; and third, it exists in Christ as the absolute and contracted Maximum at the same time. It is interesting to note that, according to Nicholas, all nations worship God and believe Him to be the absolute Maximum.[25] Although I cannot do justice to the dialectical subtlety that Cusanus applies in describing these three ways of looking at the Maximum, I will try to give at least an idea of their relevance for interreligious dialogue and relations.

We begin by asking, What does Nicholas mean by "learned ignorance"?[26] On the one hand, he seems to think that one who knows that he does not know is wiser than one who thinks that he knows; on the other hand, he seems to imply that not knowing bestows a certain kind of knowledge as well, so that something can be learned by not knowing. This is suggested by the final lines of chapter three: "the more deeply we are instructed in this ignorance, the closer we approach to truth."[27] This insight has interesting anthropological implications, which are useful for our approach to interreligious dialogue as well: because *docta ignorantia* implies that we are aware of our human condition, it is connected with a certain conjectural understanding of truth.[28] In the field of interreligious dialogue, this insight suggests that through differences we learn about ourselves and about God—and about the connection between the two.[29]

Toward the end of the first book, Nicholas distinguishes between affirmative theology, according to which the many nations give names to God in which they variously relate God to creatures, and negative theology, which critiques these creature-related names of God. For instance, he remarks that the name "the One" for God transcends all understanding. Therefore,

> [...] not "oneness" but "oneness to which neither otherness nor plurality nor multi-plicity is opposed" befits God. This is the maximum name, which enfolds all things in its simplicity of oneness; this is the name which is ineffable and above all understanding.[30]

Although affirmative theology relates God to God's creatures in diverse ways, neg-ative theology is needed to refrain from thinking about God as if God were a creature. Cusanus notes that worshipping God must be based on affirmative the-ology. Therefore, through affirmative theology, religion "worships God as one and three, as most wise and most gracious, as inaccessible Light, as Life, as Truth and so on. And it always directs its worship by faith, which it attains more truly through learned ignorance."[31] On the other hand, "the theology of negation is so necessary for the theology of affirmation that without it God would not be worshipped as the Infinite God but, rather, as a creature. And such worship is idolatry; it ascribes to the image that which befits only the reality itself." Cusanus applies the "anti-idolatrous" function of negative theology to the traditional (affirmative) language of the Christian religion as follows:

> Sacred ignorance has taught us that God is ineffable. He is so because He is infinitely greater than all nameable things. And by virtue of the fact that [this] is most true, we speak of God more truly through removal and negation—as [teaches] the great Dionysius, who did not believe that God is either Truth or Understanding or Light or anything which can be spoken of (Rabbi Solomon and all the wise follow Dionysius). Hence, in accordance with this negative theology, according to which [God] is only infi-nite, He is neither Father nor Son nor Holy Spirit.

Positive theology is necessary in order to be able to relate to God and speak to God in worship; but negative theology is necessary in order to critique our human language about God and to realize that God is above all names, including the names of Father, Son, and Spirit. Just like Thomas Aquinas, Nicholas refers not only to Dionysius as his main source, but also to Maimonides, although he con-fuses Rambam (Rabbi Moyses ben Maimon) with Rashi (Rabbi Solomon ben Jitzhak).[32] Just like Maimonides and Aquinas, Cusanus distinguishes between a mode of knowing God that is accessible to us in this human life and a mode of knowing God which will be reality for us in Paradise. All of them quote Zechariah 14:9 as an important source text: "On that day, the LORD shall be one and His name shall be one."[33]

Several times, Cusanus refers to another biblical source for a more explicit knowledge of God: "[A]ccording to the testimony of that most unique preacher of truth, Paul, who in a rapture was illuminated from on high."[34] Paul refers to this experience of being caught up to the third heaven or to Paradise in II Corinthians 12:1–4. These words refer to Paul as the preacher of Christ, and thus refer to the Christological climax of Cusanus's observations on learned ignorance: because Christ is humanity united to the Word of God, He is the *maximum simul contractum et absolutum*; that is, He is the contracted maximum human nature united with the absolute maximum in the hypostatic union. When writing about the mysteries of faith in God incarnate, the language Nicholas uses becomes as ecstatic as that of his predecessor Dionysius:

> But soundest faith-in-Christ, made steadfastly firm in simplicity, can, in accordance with previously given instruction in ignorance, be increased and unfolded in ascending degrees. For although hidden from the wise, the very great and very deep mysteries of God are revealed through faith in Jesus, to the small and humble inhabitants of the world [...] Since God is not knowable in this world (where by reason and by opinion or by doctrine we are led, with symbols, through the more known to the unknown), He is apprehended only where persuasive considerations cease and faith appears. Through faith we are caught up, in simplicity, so that being in a body incorporeally (because in spirit) and in the world not mundanely but celestially we may incomprehensibly contemplate Christ above all reason and intelligence, in the third heaven of most simple intellectuality. Thus, we see even the following: viz., that because of the immensity of His excellence God cannot be comprehended. And this is that learned ignorance through which most blessed Paul, in ascending, saw that when he was being elevated more highly to Christ, he did not know Christ, though at one time he had known only Christ.[35]

In this text, Saint Paul becomes the paramount witness of *docta ignorantia* in his mystical journey to heaven, as described in II Corinthians 12:1–4. Although he knew Christ as a human being, he now comes to see that he did not know Christ in this new reality (see II Corinthians 5:16–17). The word *learned* in "learned ignorance" is, therefore, not just an adjective, but also a participle because it refers to our having been taught about ignorance by the One who is the teacher par excellence in Christianity, Christ. Christ teaches us that, although we thought we knew about him, in reality we do not really know who He is. The name of Christ remains a mystery to us.[36] This is—according to Thomas Aquinas—the meaning, after His resurrection, of his *noli me tangere* to Mary Magdalene (the *Apostola apostolorum*): "Stop holding on to me, for I have not yet ascended to the Father. But go to my brothers and tell them: 'I am going to my Father and your Father, my God and your God'" (John 20:17).[37]

In the sentences that follow the preceding quotation, Nicholas of Cusa describes the ascension of the believers to learned ignorance in images that may remind us of Paul and Mary Magdalene, but allude to Dionysian language of mist and darkness as well. The editors and translators of his work did not notice it,[38] yet I am convinced that these images allude to two famous ascents from the Hebrew Bible as well: Moses on Mount Sinai (Exodus 19) and Elijah on Mount Horeb (I Kings 19). In both cases, the ascent is a symbol for the believers on their way to meet God and to learn that God is not known the way they thought they knew God.

Therefore, we who are believers in Christ are led in learned ignorance unto the Mountain that is Christ and that we are forbidden to touch with the nature of our animality. And when we attempt to view this Mountain with our intellectual eye, we fall into an obscuring mist, knowing that within this mist is the Mountain on which, alone, all living beings possessed of an intellect are well pleased to dwell. If we approach this Mountain with greater steadfastness of faith, we will be snatched from the eyes of those who live sensually, so that with an inward hearing we will perceive the sounds and thunderings and frightening signs of its majesty. [...] At this point we [shall] hear, in the holy instruments and signs of the prophets and the saints, the voice not of mortal creatures but of God Himself; and we [shall] see God more clearly, as if through a more rarefied cloud.[39]

It is amazing how Cusanus is able to couple the analytical and dialectical language of philosophy with the symbolic and associative language of mysticism. Although he is mainly known as a philosopher, paragraphs such as the preceding one justify introducing a volume on Nicholas of Cusa in the series "the Classics of Western Spirituality."[40]

▪ NICHOLAS OF CUSA AND A FAITHFUL INTERPRETATION OF THE QUR'AN

Although Nicholas of Cusa wrote his three books on *Learned Ignorance* in the context of what we would now call "ecumenical conversations," his work on the *Peace of Faith* may be characterized as its application to what may anachronistically be named "interreligious dialogue."[41] Nicholas wrote this dialogue in 1453 as an immediate reaction to rumors about the fall of Constantinople to the Muslims. Again, the plurality of human approaches to God is his point of departure. At the very beginning of *De Pace Fidei*, he introduces this main theme as follows:

> There was a man who, having seen the sites in the vicinity of Constantinople in the past, was inflamed with zeal for God when he was told of the deeds which had been committed in Constantinople recently and the great cruelty inflicted by the King of the Turks. Consequently, groaning, he beseeched the Creator of All, appealing to His kindness, to restrain the persecution that was raging more fiercely than usual on account of the difference of rites between the religions.[42]

These last words allude to the wise man's conviction that this violence between religions can be overcome if one realizes that the various religious rites are, in fact, variations of a single adherence to God. This concept in Cusanus—*una religio in rituum varietate*—may sound like an axiom in the pluralist approach in contemporary theology of religions, according to which the several religions are just slightly different approaches to the same Reality. Whereas the words "one religion in a variety of rites" may almost be conceived as a translation of Wilfred Cantwell Smith's famous distinction between the one basic faith of humankind and the diversity of religious belief systems,[43] such an anachronistic reading would misjudge Cusanus's position as a Christian theologian for whom Christ as the Word of God is the only true Way to God. And yet it is significant that Nicholas of Cusa developed this very idea while reading Muslim sources, since a remark on "one faith – different rites" can be found in a marginal note by his own hand in Cusanus's personal copy of the so-called "Toledan Collection" that contained a number of Muslim works translated from Arabic into Latin.[44]

Toward the end of the first chapter of *De pace fidei*, Cusanus mentions in the form of a prayer the relation between the basic incomprehensibility of God and the plurality of human approaches to God. In this prayer, the representative of the religions beseeches God, the giver of life who is sought through different ways and in different rites and who is called by different names, to manifest Himself in a way in which He can be apprehended.

> If You will deign to do the foregoing, the sword will cease, as will also the malice of hatred and evils; and all men will know that there is only one religion in a variety of rites (*una religio in rituum varietate*). But this difference of rites cannot be eliminated; and perhaps it is not expedient that it be eliminated, for the diversity may make for an increase of devotion, since each region will devote more careful attention to making its ceremonies more favorable, as it were, to You, the King. If so, then at least let there be one religion – just as You are one – and one true worship of You as Sovereign.[45]

Let me try to reconstruct the argument in this prayer. Although there is an infinite distance between God and creatures, and human beings, therefore, cannot know God, God is able to make Godself manifest. Whereas Cusanus as a Christian Church leader and theologian would say that God *has* in fact become manifest in Christ, the representative of the religions who prays to God abstracts from this Christian revelation. He asks God to give such a revelation, so that the religions of the world may be united as God is one.

Cusanus, however, has enough experience in politics to realize that, in fact, the differences will remain because of the different human customs, and, therefore, it may make sense to live with diversity as an incitement to spiritual emulation.[46] One form of such spiritual emulation in which we learn from religious differences to enrich our own faith is shown in chapter nine where a Jew discusses the concept of Trinity with the Word—Christ functions as the major interlocutor in Nicholas's dialogue—and the Word points to the way in which the Arabs understand this concept:

> The Arabs, too, and all the wise will easily understand…that to deny the trinity is to deny the divine fecundity and creative power and that to profess the trinity is to deny a plurality and an association of gods. For the fecundity, which is also trinity, does not make it necessary that there be a plurality of gods who work together to create all things. The Arabs will be much better able to grasp the truth of the trinity in this manner than in the manner in which they speak of God as having an essence and a soul…Now in the manner in which Arabs and Jews deny the trinity, assuredly it ought to be denied by all. But in the manner in which the truth of trinity is explained above, of necessity it will be embraced by all.[47]

This text can be interpreted in two different fashions. It can be understood as part of the old Christian tradition of apologetics in which the truth of the Christian faith is defended against others, or it can also be understood as representative of a new interest in the arguments that other religions give for their own points of view. Thus, in his survey of the perception of Islam in the West, Norman Daniel interprets Cusanus as an heir of the apologetic tradition, whereas, in a similar survey, Rollin Armour interprets him as a notable innovator.[48]

More particularly, Jasper Hopkins and others have argued that this text should be read as a new hermeneutical approach to Islam in which Cusanus applies the concept of a *pia interpretatio,* which he will develop later in his Christian reading of the Qur'an.[49] According to their interpretation, Nicholas opens up possibilities for Christians to understand better their own faith in the Trinity by considering the Islamic perspective on this mystery of faith. If the Arabs deny a certain interpretation of the concept of the Trinity, this may help Christians to realize that they rightly reject interpretations that conceive of the Trinity in terms of family relationships or a heavenly association.[50] In this respect, Nicholas of Cusa seems to be able to show how interreligious dialogue may help us to expurgate our own religious tradition, or at least to prevent some of the most distorted and unhelpful interpretations of this tradition.

Historically speaking, it seems that Cusanus's hermeneutical insights ripened when he read the Qur'an with the intention of giving a Christian theological assessment of this book. He uses the term *pia interpretatio* four times in the second book of his *Sifting of the Qur'an,* a work that he wrote in 1460–1461 in order to provide Pope Pius II with some materials for a letter to Sultan Mehmet II, the conqueror of Constantinople.[51] In this work, Nicholas tries, like a prospector, to sift the materials of the Qur'an in hopes of finding in the bed of the river nuggets of gold in the silt. The image is striking insofar as Cusanus generally displays a negative attitude toward the contents of the Qur'an; for that reason, some scholars contrast the polemical nature of this work to the peaceful nature of *De pace fidei.*[52] In this respect, Cusanus's approach is not too different from Raymond Martin's approach to the Talmud two centuries before in which Martin spoke about pearls to be found in the dunghill.[53] However, as the prologue to the *Cribratio* tells us, Cusanus went to great length in order to obtain good copies and good translations of the "book-in-law of the Arabs," and in this way, his attitude was more like Thomas Aquinas in his search for documents on behalf of his assessment of Greek theology.[54] Cusanus describes the goal of his work as follows:

> I applied my mind to disclosing, even from the Koran, that the Gospel is true. And in order that this [disclosure] may readily be made, I will here set forth in a few words my overall conception.
>
> [...] Jesus, the son of the Virgin Mary and the Christ who was foretold by Moses and the Prophets to be coming, did come and did reveal most perfectly—according to the testimony even of Muhammad the oft-mentioned way, for He was ignorant of nothing. Therefore, it is certain that anyone who follows Christ and His way will attain unto an understanding of the desired Good. Hence, if Muhammad in any respect disagrees with Christ, then it follows either that he does so out of ignorance, because he did not know Christ and did not understand Him, or that there is perverse intent, because he did not intend to lead men to that goal-of-rest to which Christ showed the way but rather sought his own glory under the guise of that goal. A comparison of the law of Christ with the

law of Muhammad will teach [us] that both of these [alternatives] must be believed to be true.

Nicholas, it would seem, considers two possibilities: either Muhammad disagrees with Christ because of ignorance—and in this case he would not be so different from Christians—or he disagrees with him because of his wicked intentions. In the next section, Cusanus admits both possibilities, but he states that ignorance is the deeper cause, and that eventual malice follows from it.

> I believe that the following must be maintained: viz. that ignorance was the cause of [Muhammad's] error and malevolence. For no one who is acquainted with Christ disagrees with Him or detracts from Him. Now, my intention is as follows: having presupposed the Gospel of Christ, to scrutinize the book of Muhammad and to show that even in it there are contained those [teachings] through which the Gospel would be altogether confirmed, were it in need of confirmation, and that wherever [the Koran] disagrees [with Christ], this [disagreement] has resulted from Muhammad's ignorance and, following [thereupon], from his perverse intent. For whereas Christ sought not His own glory but the glory of God-the-Father and the salvation of men, Muhammad sought not the glory of God and the salvation of men but rather his own glory.[55]

The ambiguity of Nicholas's approach to the Qur'an is quite clear in this prologue. On the one hand, the old tradition that sees Muhammad as an imposter and his Qur'an as a falsification, lingers on.[56] On the other hand, Nicholas seems to incline toward a more benevolent interpretation that explains the divergences between Gospel and Qur'an and between Jesus and Muhammad not as the result of malevolence but as the result of ignorance. According to this *pia interpretatio,* the book of Muhammad can be seen as a form of learned ignorance: Muhammad did not know Christ, but nevertheless the Gospel may be confirmed by the contents of this book. One might be tempted to translate *pia interpretatio* as "benevolent interpretation" because it is an interpretation that tries to relate in a positive way the contents of the Qur'an to the Gospel of Jesus, not however neglecting the differences. This benevolent interpretation is possible because, not only did Muhammad not know Jesus, neither do Christians know Christ in the full sense of the word, as Nicholas made clear in the Christological chapters of his *docta ignorantia*. Although there is a clear difference between Christians who accepted Christ as the Truth revealed by God, and Muslims who only accept Christ as a prophet of God, still we all are human beings and, therefore, on our way to the full truth that will only be revealed to us if we meet Christ after this life.

Jasper Hopkins is correct when he suggests that translating *pia interpretatio* as "benevolent interpretation" does not do justice to the theological intention of Cusanus's book.[57] I do not agree, however, with his translation of *pia interpretatio* as "devout interpretation," because the word *pius* in Medieval Latin has different connotations than *pious* or *devout,* translations that smack of nineteenth-century pietism. *Pius* may mean "conscientious," "upright," "faithful," "respectful," "righteous," or "loyal," as well as pious or devoted, and the same holds true for the German word *fromm* or the Dutch *vroom,* which imply steadfastness in faith rather than abundant piety. I, therefore, propose to translate *pia interpretatio* as "faithful interpretation," which implies a loyalty to our own religious tradition in the first place, but also a presumption that it is possible to build bridges to other religious traditions. As Cusanus indicates both in *De pace fidei* and in *Cribratio alcorani*, Christians may learn from the Islamic tradition about their own faith.

A similar relation between learned ignorance and faithful interpretation is suggested once again by Cusanus at the beginning of the second book of the *Cribratio alcorani*, in a chapter that bears the title, "on mystical theology, according to which God is ineffable."

> Let me now turn to a clarification of [the doctrine of] the Trinity that we revere in the divinity. And let me show that on a devout interpretation the Koran does not contradict [the doctrine of] the Trinity in the sense in which we who adhere to the Gospel speak of trinity. [58]

After these words, Nicholas introduces an Arab who, using the words of the Qur'an argues that there should be no plurality in God. He replies:

> To the foregoing I reply that the Gospel not only condemns any [belief in a] plurality of Gods but also affirms a plurality of Gods to be impossible. For no one doubts that God is the Beginning and is that from which all things originate. [But] how would a plurality be the Beginning? For before plurality there is Oneness, or Singularity. And Oneness is, necessarily, eternal. For it is the unqualified Beginning, which must be eternal because it is the Beginning and is not anything originated. Now, this Beginning can be considered without respect to things originated, so that it is as much not-Beginning as Beginning. For this reason it is altogether infinite and boundless, incomprehensible and ineffable. Assuredly, then, since it surpasses all the senses and every intellect and every name and everything nameable, it is not said to be one or three or good or wise or Father or Son or Holy Spirit (and the case is similar as regards whatever can be spoken of or thought of) – even as Dionysius the Areopagite teaches that [God] infinitely excels and precedes all such names. [59]

The final part of this quotation, including the reference to Dionysius, is strikingly similar to the text on negative theology from *De docta ignorantia* I.26 as quoted earlier.[60] One may conclude, therefore, that Cusanus's teaching on learned ignorance helped him to understand the Qur'an as supporting the Gospel, and, at the same time, as a valid critique of certain misunderstandings in the Christian tradition.

There is a very interesting ambiguity in Cusanus's approach to the Qur'an. On the one hand he follows an old tradition of polemics and apologetics, but on the other he seems to be aware of the hermeneutical possibilities of a more faithful and benevolent interpretation of the Qur'an, based on the insight that Christians, being aware of the infinite distance between their God-talk and the One God who surpasses every name and concept, may learn from the *docta ignorantia* of others.

Jasper Hopkins has published several reflections on Cusanus's Christian theological approach to the Qur'an. I would like to summarize this approach as follows: A faithful interpretation of the Qur'an presumes that its basic intent is to give praise and glory to God without diminishing the honor and witness due to Christ. Although such a hermeneutical reflection originates in contemporary

Christian theological considerations concerning the nature of Christian-Muslim relations, it may be confirmed by a careful reading of the following text from the *Cribratio alcorani*:

> But suppose we admit—as the followers of the Koran claim ([a claim] whose denial all the wise and zealous believe, as was made evident above)—that the goal and intent of the book of the Koran is not only not to detract from God the Creator or from Christ or from God's prophets and envoys or from the divine books of the Testament, the Psalter, and the Gospel, but also to give glory to God the Creator, to praise and to bear witness to Christ (the son of the Virgin Mary) above all the prophets, and to confirm and to approve of the Testament and the Gospel. [If so,] then when one reads the Koran with this understanding, assuredly some fruit can be elicited [from it].[61]

Jasper Hopkins gives a similar interpretation of this text in the fourth of the five hermeneutical rules he borrowed from Cusanus:

1. Interpret the Qur'an in such a way that it is compatible with the Christian Scriptures;
2. Try to interpret the Qur'an in such a way as to render it self-consistent;
3. Where the Qur'an contradicts the Gospel, look for the human author's (i.e., Muhammad's) true intent;
4. Interpret the Qur'an as intending to give glory to God (*al-hamdu lillah*) without detracting from Christ;
5. Work, insofar as possible, with the interpretations that the wise among the Arabs assign to the Qur'an.[62]

The important contribution of Nicholas of Cusa and the relation between learned ignorance and a faithful interpretation of sacred writings from other religions can be seen especially in the fourth and fifth rules. Let me comment by way of conclusion on both rules, beginning with the fifth rule.

The fifth rule seems to open the possibility for a premodern Christian endorsement of contemporary practices of reading Scriptures together as Jews, Christians, and Muslims. Although reading groups that identify themselves as practicing "Scriptural Reasoning" suppose that each representative of a religion is the primary partner in explaining the sacred texts of this religion, the theoretical approach of comparative theology envisages practices in which Christians may give their own interpretations of non-Christian sacred texts.[63] In both cases, there is an interesting practice of interreligious reading that invites theologians to start hermeneutical reflections on such practices. Nicholas of Cusa, in applying his hermeneutical principle of faithful interpretation points to the commonalities between Christianity and Islam and, therefore, makes possible what amounts to one of the first deliberately Christian readings of the Qur'an. However, the fact that Christians know that God has revealed Godself to us in Christ implies that there are insurmountable differences as well. These differences would seem to suggest that Muslims have a hermeneutical privilege in interpreting the Qur'an just like Christians have a hermeneutical privilege in interpreting the Gospel.[64]

Meanwhile the fourth hermeneutical rule, as formulated by Jasper Hopkins, may have even greater theological consequences. It seems to suggest the possibility that

Christians may recognize God as author of the Qur'ān—in this instance a God who may sometimes disclose the truth of the Gospel even beyond the intent of its human author. This leads to the difficult question of the extent to which it is possible to see God as inspiring Christians in some extraordinary way through the Qur'ān. The textual basis for such a view in Cusanus is admittedly small, but here it is:

> Therefore, in the Koran the splendor of the Gospel shines forth to the wise, i.e., to those who are led by the spirit of Christ—[shines forth] even beyond the intent of the [Koran's] author.[65]

The quotation goes on later to excoriate Muhammad and others who prefer this world and their lusts more than the future world and the way of Christ. However, this one sentence of Nicholas of Cusa may be seen as one of the pearls trapped in the shackles of the old apologetic tradition—one of the pearls that may help us to find the truth in new ways, fully knowing that we will ultimately understand in the next life what we do not know in this life. Muslims have a very nice expression with which they end their theological works, one with which I wish to end this chapter. It serves as a reminder of the insufficiency of our theological language: *Allāhu a'lam*: God knows better.

■ Notes

1. In the trialogue meetings, I profited most of all from the learned yet inquisitive responses by Rabbi Dr. Shira Lander from Baltimore. Her questions prompted me to rethink much of what I wrote. I thank Professors Wilhelm Dupré from Nijmegen, Henk Schoot from Utrecht and, of course, David Burrell from Tantur and Notre Dame for their questions and their suggestions as well.

2. See, among others, Clyde Lee Miller, *Reading Cusanus: Metaphor and Dialectic in a Conjectural Universe* (Washington, D.C.: The Catholic University of America Press, 2003), and *Cusanus: the Legacy of Learned Ignorance*, ed. Peter J. Casarella (Washington, D.C.: the Catholic University of America Press, 2006).

3. See Louis Dupré, "The Question of Pantheism from Eckhart to Cusanus," and Bernard McGinn, "Seeing and Not Seeing: Nichlas of Cusa's *De visione Dei* in the History of Western Mysticism," in *Cusanus: the Legacy of Learned Ignorance*, pp. 74–88 and 26–53.

4. *The Essential Writings of Christian Mysticism*. ed. and intro. Bernard McGinn (New York: Modern Library, 2006), p. 283.

5. Pseudo-Dionysius the Areopagite, *The Divine Names*, in trans. C. Luibheid *The Complete Works, The Classics of Western Spirituality* (Mahwah NJ: Paulist Press, 1987), p. 49.

6. Dionysius the Areopagite, *On the Divine Names and the Mystical Theology*, trans.C.E. Rolt (London: SPCK, 1920), p. 51.

7. Pseudo-Dionysius the Areopagite, *The Mystical Theology*, in trans. C. Luibheid, *The Complete Works, The Classics of Western Spirituality* (Mahwah NJ: Paulist Press, 1987), p. 135.

8. See Michel Corbin, "Négation et transcendance dans l'oeuvre de Denys," *Revue des sciences philosophiques et théologiques* 69 (1985): 41–76.

9. Quotation as given by Rudi te Velde in his *Aquinas on God: The "Divine Science" of the Summa Theologiae* (Aldershot – Burlington VA: Ashgate, 2006), p. 76.

10. This and the previous quotation are taken from Thomas Aquinas, *Summa theologiae* I. 12. 12; Frederick Christian Bauerschmidt, trans., *Holy Teaching: Introducing the Summa Theologiae of St. Thomas Aquinas* (Grand Rapids MI: Brazos Press, 2005), p. 62.

11. Aquinas, *Summa theologiae* I. 3 intr. This "linguistic" and "negative" reading is based on the work of David B. Burrell, *Aquinas: God and Action* (London- Notre Dame: University of Notre Dame Press, 1979). For the "Utrecht hypothesis," see Herwi Rikhof, "Thomas at Utrecht," in *Contemplating Aquinas. On the Varieties of Interpretation*, ed. Fergus Kerr (London: SCM Press, 2003), pp. 105–136.

12. See Te Velde, *Aquinas on God*, pp. 72–77; also Pim Valkenberg, *Sharing Lights on the Way to God: Muslim-Christian Dialogue and Theology in the Context of Abrahamic Partnership* (Amsterdam – New York: Editions Rodopi, 2006), pp. 213–219.

13. See Wilhelmus G.B.M. Valkenberg, *Words of the Living God: Place and Function of Holy Scripture in the Theology of St. Thomas Aquinas* (Leuven: Peeters, 2000), pp. 8–18.

14. Thomas Aquinas, *Summa theologiae* I.1.9 ad 3. Bauerschmidt, trans., *Holy Teaching*, p. 41. In his famous commentary on Romans (München, 1924), Karl Barth makes a similar argument. He interprets Paul's words about the salvation of the non-Jews (Romans 11:11–24) as referring to nonbelievers, and adds that those who do not believe may be favored by God above those who believe religiously, because religious people claim to have some knowledge about God, while the unbelievers at least know that they do not know.

15. Michel Corbin, *L'inouï de Dieu: six etudes christologiques* (Paris: Desclée De Brouwer, 1980), p. 204.

16. Dionysius, *De divinis nominibus* 1,1, in Johannes Sarracenus, trans., *Igitur universaliter non est audendum dicere aliquid nec etiam cogitare de supersubstantiali et occulta deitate praeter ea quae divinitus nobis ex sanctis eloquiis sunt expressa.* Text in Thomas Aquinas, *Opera Omnia* (ed. Vivès) XXIX, 375.

17. Aquinas, *Contra errores Graecorum*, prologue: *Unde, si qua in dictis antiquorum doctorum inveniuntur quae cum tanta cautela non dicantur quanta a modernis servatur, non sunt contemnanda aut abiicienda, sed nec etiam ea extendere oportet, sed exponere reverenter* (text in *Opera Omnia*, ed. Busa, III, 501).

18. *Summa theologiae* I.31.4 ad 2um: *Unde non est extendenda talis locutio, sed pie exponenda, sicubi inveniatur in authentica scriptura.*

19. For "hermeneutics of suspicion" and "hermeneutics of faith" or "hermeneutics of recollection," see Paul Ricoeur, *Hermeneutics and the Human Sciences*, ed. and trans. John B. Thompson (Cambridge: Cambridge University Press/Paris: Editions de la Maison des Sciences de l'Homme, 1981), p. 34.

20. See Pim Valkenberg, "How to Talk to Strangers: Aquinas and Interreligious Dialogue in the Middle Ages," in *Jaarboek 1997 Thomas Instituut te Utrecht*, pp. 9–47; *Aquinas in Dialogue: Thomas for the Twenty-First Century*, eds. Jim Fodor and Frederick C. Bauerschmidt (Oxford – Malden MA: Blackwell, 2004). For Jewish and Muslim sources in Aquinas's God-talk, see David Burrell, *Knowing the Unknowable God: Ibn Sina, Maimonides, Aquinas* (Notre Dame IN: University of Notre Dame Press, 1986); Mercedes Rubio, *Aquinas and Maimonides on the Possibility of the Knowledge of God: An Examination of the* Quaestio de attributis, *Amsterdam Studies in Jewish Thought*, 11 (Dordrecht: Springer, 2006).

21. See Inigo Bocken, "Nicholas of Cusa and the Plurality of Religions," in eds. Barbara Roggema, Marcel Poorthuis, Pim Valkenberg, *The Three Rings. Textual Studies in the Historical Trialogue of Judaism, Christianity, and Islam*, (Leuven: Peeters, 2005), pp. 163–180.

22. I used Jasper Hopkins's introduction to and translation of this work: *Nicholas of Cusa on Learned Ignorance. A Translation and an Appraisal of De Docta Ignorantia* (Minneapolis: the Arthur J. Banning Press, 1981). For the Latin text, I used *Nikolaus von Kues, Philosophisch-theologische Schriften*, Herausgegeben und eingeführt von Leo Gabriel, übersetzt und kommentiert von Dietlind und Wilhelm Dupré (Wien: Herder, 1964), Band I, pp. 192–297. Other English translations may be found in *Of Learned Ignorance by Nicolas Cusanus*, trans.Fr. Germain Heron, intro.Dr. D. Hawkins (New Haven, CT: Yale University

Press, 1954) and *Nicholas of Cusa: selected spiritual writings*, trans. and intro., H. Lawrence Bond, preface by Morimichi Watanabe (The Classics of Western Spirituality, New York–Mahwah NJ: Paulist Press, 1997), pp. 87–206.

23. On Cusanus and the sciences, see Tamara Albertini, "Mathematics and Astronomy" in *Nicholas of Cusa: A Guide to a Renaissance Man*, eds. C.M. Bellitto, T.M. Izbicki, G. Christianson (New York – Mahwah NJ: Paulist Press, 2004), pp. 373–406; Karsten Harries, "On the Power and Poverty of Perspective: Cusanus and Alberti," in *Cusanus: The Legacy of Learned Ignorance*, pp. 105–126; Elizabeth Brient, "How Can the Infinite Be the Measure of the Finite? Three Mathematical Metaphors from *De docta ignorantia*," in *ibid*, pp. 210–225.

24. Cusanus, *De docta ignorantia* I.2, trans. Hopkins p. 51.

25. *De docta ignorantia* I.7. Cf. *In jedem Namen wird genannt was unnennbar bleibt. Wegmarken im Denken des Nikolaus von Kues 1401–1464*, ausgewählt und eingeleitet von Wilhelm Dupré (Maastricht: Shaker Publishing, 2001), pp. 100–101.

26. Hopkins discusses this question on pages 2–5 of his introduction.

27. *Quanto in hac ignorantia profundius docti fuerimus, tanto magis ipsam accedimus veritatem.* Latin text ed. Dupré I, 202; English trans. Hopkins p. 53.

28. Personal communication from Wilhelm Dupré; see also Inigo Bocken, *Waarheid en interpretatie. Perspectieven op het conjecturele denken van Nicolaus Cusanus* (Maastricht: Shaker Publishers, 2002), and Clyde Lee Miller, *Reading Cusanus*, pp. 23 (sacred ignorance as a gift) and 35 (sacred ignorance and *coincidentia oppositorum*).

29. This is one of the most important elements in Shira Lander's reply to my paper at the Trialogue conference in Tantur, June 2007.

30. Cusanus, *de docta ignorantia* I,24; trans. Jaspers, *On Learned Ignorance*, p. 80.

31. This and the following two quotations are taken from: Cusanus, *de docta ignorantia* I, 26., trans. Hopkins, p. 84.

32. See Hopkins, *Learned Ignorance*, p. 189 n. 87. The reference is to *Guide for the Perplexed*, I, 59 (Hopkins, p. 192) or I, 57 (Bond, *On Learned Ignorance*, p. 309).

33. Zechariah 14:9 is quoted by Cusanus together with Deuteronomy 6:4 in *De docta ignorantia* I,24 (ed. Dupré I, p. 280). On how Zechariah 14:9 is understood in Maimonides and Thomas Aquinas, see Rubio, *Aquinas and Maimonides on the Possibility of the Knowledge of God*, pp. 127–160.

34. Cusanus, *de docta ignorantia* III, 4., trans. Hopkins, p. 133.

35. Cusanus, *de docta ignorantia* III, 11., trans. Hopkins, , pp. 149–150 (no. 245).

36. See Henk J.M. Schoot, *Christ, the "Name" of God: Thomas Aquinas on Naming Christ* (Leuven: Peeters, 1993).

37. Thomas Aquinas, *Summa theologiae* III.55.6 ra.3; *Lectura in Ev. Ioan.* XX lect.3; cf. Valkenberg, *Words of the Living God*, pp. 115 and 173.

38. Dupré only refers to II Corinthians 12:2 and Romans 15:4; Hopkins refers to Hebrews 12:18–22, Romans 9:5, Romans 15:4, Psalm 32:6 and John 1:14; Bond refers to Romans 15:4, Psalm 32:6 and John 1:14.

39. Cusanus, *de docta ignorantia*, III.11., trans. Hopkins, p. 150 (no. 246).

40. *Nicholas of Cusa, Selected Spiritual Writings*, trans. and intro. H. Lawrence Bond New York – Mahwah NJ: Paulist Press, 1997) was published as volume 89 in the series *The Classics of Western Spirituality*. On the relevance of Cusanus for Western Spirituality, see Bond's introduction, pp. 13–19.

41. Inigo Bocken, "Nicholas of Cusa and the Plurality of Religions," in eds., Barbara Roggema, Marcel Poorthuis, Pim Valkenberg *The Three Rings. Textual Studies in the Historical Trialogue of Judaism, Christianity, and Islam*, (Leuven: Peeters, 2005), pp. 163–180, here 171.

42. Nicholas of Cusa, *De pace fidei* 1, trans. Bocken, "Nicholas of Cusa and the Plurality of Religions," p. 172.

43. See W.C. Smith, *The Meaning and End of Religion: A New Approach to the Religious Traditions of Mankind* (New York: The Macmillan Company, 1963); *Towards a World Theology: Faith and the Comparative History of Religion* (Basingstoke and London: the Macmillan Press, 1981).

44. See James E. Biechler, "Interreligious Dialogue," in eds. C.M. Bellitto, T.M. Izbicki, G. Christianson *Introducing Nicholas of Cusa: A Guide to a Renaissance Man,* (New York - Mahwah NJ: Paulist Press, 2004), pp. 270–296, here 279.

45. Nicholas of Cusa, *De pace fidei* chapter 1 (nos. 5–6), trans. Bocken, "Nicholas of Cusa and the Plurality of Religions," pp. 174–175. Correction adapted from Jasper Hopkins, *Nicholas of Cusa' De Pace Fidei and Cribratio Alkorani: Translation and Analysis,* 2nd ed. (Minneapolis: The Arthur J. Banning Press, 1994), p. 35.

46. Such a different form of pluralism may, in fact, be found in the Qur'an. See Pim Valkenberg, *Sharing Lights on the Way to God: Muslim-Christian Dialogue and Theology in the Context of Abrahamic Partnership* (Amsterdam – New York: Editions Rodopi, 2006), pp. 150–162.

47. Nicholas of Cusa, *De pace fidei,* chapter 9; trans. Bocken, "Nicholas of Cusa and the Plurality of Religions," p. 178.

48. Norman Daniel, *Islam and the West: The Making of an Image* (Edinburgh, 1960, repr. Oxford: Oneworld, 1993), p. 307; Rollin Armour, *Islam, Christianity and the West: A Troubled History* (Maryknoll NY: Orbis Books, 2002), p. 109. See also Neil Elliott, *From "The Heresy of the Saracens" to "The War against the Turks"* (Birmingham: Centre for the Study of Islam and Christian-Muslim Relations, occasional papers no. 9, September 2001).

49. See Jasper Hopkins, "The Role of *pia interpretatio* in Nicholas of Cusa's Hermeneutical Approach to the Koran," in id., *A Miscellany on Nicholas of Cusa* (Minneapolis: the Arthur J. Banning Press, 1994), pp. 39–55; Bocken, "Nicholas of Cusa and the Plurality of Religions," pp. 177–180.

50. The word *consocialitas* in Cusanus's text is a faithful rendering of the Qur'anic notion of *shirk* (giving God associates or partners, and, therefore, polytheism or idolatry).

51. The German historian of theology Ludwig Hagemann has edited the text of the *Cribratio Alkorani* as vol. VIII of *Nicolai de Cusa Opera Omnia* (Hamburg: F. Meiner Verlag, 1986). See also L. Hagemann, *Der Kur'an in Verständnis und Kritik bei Nikolaus von Kues* (Frankfurt a/M: Knecht, 1976); *Nikolaus von Kues im Gespräch mit dem Islam* (Altenberge: Oros Verlag, 1983); *Christentum contra Islam: eine Geschichte gescheiterter Beziehungen* (Darmstadt: Primus, 1999). For *pia interpretatio* in the *Cribratio alcorani*, see the literature mentioned in footnote 49 and Walter Andreas Euler, "An Italian Painting from the Late Fifteenth Century and the *Cribratio alkorani* of Nicholas of Cusa," in *Cusanus: the Legacy of Learned Ignorance*, ed. Peter J. Casarella (Washington, D.C.: Catholic University of America Press, 2006), pp. 127–142.

52. Armour, *Islam, Christianity, and the West*, p. 109; Euler, "An Italian Painting and the *Cribratio alkorani,*" p. 131.

53. For Raymond Martin and his approach to the Talmud, see Syds Wiersma, "Aquinas' Theory on Dialogue Put into Practice," in *Jaarboek 2005 Thomas Instituut te Utrecht 25* (2006), pp. 9–41.

54. Jasper Hopkins (see next footnote) mentions a number of works on Islam and the Qur'an by Dionysius the Carthusian, Ricoldo of Montecroce, and Peter the Venerable, and translations from Arabic texts (including the Qur'an) by Robert of Ketton, Herbert of Dalmatia, and Peter of Toledo that were in Cusanus's possession on pp. 194–195 of his English translation of the *cribratio alkorani*. Moreover, Norman Daniel, *Islam and the West,*

p. 307, mentions the correspondence between Cusanus and Juan de Segovia who translated some materials for him as well. For a comparison between Ricoldo and Nicholas, see Jasper Hopkins, "Islam and the West: Ricoldo of Montecroce and Nicholas of Cusa," in *A Miscellany on Nicholas of Cusa* (Minneapolis: the Arthur J. Banning Press, 1994), pp. 57–97.

55. This quotation and the previous one are taken from: Nicholas of Cusa, *Cribratio Alkorani*, prologue, nos. 4 and 9–10. Trans. in *Nicholas of Cusa's Scrutiny of the Koran (De Pace Fidei and Cribratio Alkorani), trans. and analysis by Jasper Hopkins* (Minneapolis: the Arthur J. Banning Press, 1994), pp. 76 and 78–79.

56. John of Damascus is, if not the founder, certainly the most important early proponent of this tradition. See "John of Damascus: The Heresy of the Ishmaelites," in Roggema, Poorthuis, & Valkenberg, *The Three Rings*, pp. 71–90.

57. Hopkins, "The Role of *pia interpretatio* in Nicholas of Cusa's Hermeneutical Approach to the Koran," p. 52–55.

58. Cusanus, *Cribratio Alcorani*, II, 1 (no. 86). Trans. Hopkins, p. 115.

59. Ibid. (no. 88), transl. p. 116.

60. See the text in translation quoted in the paragraph after footnote 31.

61. Cusanus, *Cribratio alcorani*, I, 9, no. 44 (ed. Wilpert, II, 447). Trans. Hopkins, p. 96.

62. See Hopkins, "The Role of *pia interpretatio*," pp. 45–50.

63. As introduction to Scriptural Reasoning, see David F. Ford/Chad C. Pecknold (eds.), *The Promise of Scriptural Reasoning* (Modern Theology 22/3, July 2006); Peter Ochs (ed.), *The Return to Scripture in Judaism and Christianity* (New York – Mahwah, NJ: Paulist Press, 1993; eds. Peter Ochs and Nancy Levine, *Textual Reasonings* (Grand Rapids, MI/Cambridge: Eerdmans, 2002). For Comparative Theology, see Francis Clooney, "Comparative Theology: A Review of Recent Books," *Theological Studies* 56 (1995): pp. 521–550, and, most recently, *Comparative Theology: Deep Learning Across Religious Borders*, Chichester: Wiley-Blackwell, 2010. For the series Christian Commentaries on Non-Christian Sacred Texts, see the next footnote.

64. See Catherine Cornille, "Introduction" to *Song Divine: Christian Commentaries on the Bhagavad Gita*, Christian Commentaries on Non-Christian Sacred Texts (Leuven: Peeters, 2006), pp. 1–8, here 4–5.

65. *Cribratio alcorani* I.6, no. 42. Trans. Hopkins, p. 95.

3   "Seeing the Sounds": Intellectual Humility and the Process of Dialogue

Michael A. Signer

It is my experience that dialogue does not occur among religions but among people who are profoundly committed to a life within their own communities. When they speak to one another or write for one another they have an opportunity to extend the blessing that the Creator has given to humanity: bringing the image of God and the word that gives life to another with no expectation other than the response, "Here I am. I am prepared to listen to you." Therefore, the life of the speaker or writer, for me, always constitutes an important part of the dialogue.

As a child growing up in Los Angeles, I suffered no religious intolerance or mockery from any of the non-Jews who lived on my street or in my schools. Jews were by no means a majority of the students, but every December there was both a Christmas and Hanukkah play. Our school trips took us to the California missions where we learned about the cooperation between the Franciscan friars and the native populations. These sentences seem so naive by contemporary standards, but they do reflect that doors to other religious traditions were opened in my early years.

The hours of study of religious texts started when I entered UCLA (and my future seminary: Hebrew Union College). During those four years I engaged in the historical study of Judaism, Islam, and Christianity. Professor Arnold J. Band taught in Modern Hebrew literature that the reader is in continuous "dialogue" with a text and that through a rigorous close reading of the text within its historical context, new and transformative readings are generated. Opportunities to meet and engage in dialogue were very limited.

After my ordination as a Rabbi at Hebrew Union College in Cincinnati, I entered doctoral studies at the Center for Medieval Studies in the University of Toronto. During my first year I encountered two mentors whose intellectual interests and personal traits would guide me into areas previously unexplored. Professor Haim Hillel Ben-Sasson, the senior medieval Jewish historian at Hebrew University was a visiting scholar. I had a weekly tutorial with him that focused on medieval Hebrew texts that described the encounter between Jews and Christians during that era. During the same semester, I met Fr. Leonard E. Boyle, OP who taught the introductory course in Paleography. Who would have thought that studying ancient handwritings could disclose the physical environment not only of the writer, but the worlds of those who copied the text? Fr. Boyle taught us that the text and its reception by copyists was not the work of drones, but a continuous dynamic act of reading and re-writing. The paths of these two mentors converged when Professor Ben-Sasson suggested that I write my dissertation on a twelfth-century canon of St. Victor in Paris, Andrew, whose commentaries on Hebrew Scripture included insights gained from conversations with Jewish contemporaries.

From 1974 to 1992 I taught and did research at Hebrew Union College in Los Angeles where I was deeply involved in interreligious dialogue. In 1992, I was invited to join the Department of Theology at the University of Notre Dame and move into a distinct minority position as the location for my dia-logic activity, very often now with laity. The University provided hospitality and remarkable new opportunities to develop my interests in historical research into the variety of medieval encounters and the continuing trans-formation of Jewish-Christian relations that happened in the years after the Vatican Council II. Tantur Ecumenical Institute, on the border between Jerusalem and Bethlehem, disclosed new insights into the need for dialogue and prayer among the Jewish, Christian, and Muslim populations in that area. Religions of the Word require the revealed word to be voiced in conversation and understanding rather than disputation and violence.

I continue to grow in my conviction that sincere and open heart in dia-logue gives birth to more dialogue.

■ PROLOGUE

A gathering of scholars whose task is to expound the theme of intellectual humility invites at the same time wry smiles and courage. Those who study develop their intellects in order to communicate with colleagues who are prepared to engage them in argument. However, as these arguments develop, we might ask to what extent we are called to disclose humility—the renunciation of pride—as part of the process. Is humility intrinsic to our subject matter, or does the substance of our subject control the tone of the arguments we present?

The subject is also complicated by a distinct lack of historical precedent for our endeavor. Jews, Christians, and Muslims have engaged in arguments in the past. However, the results have often been predetermined by intention of the author rather than by the merits of the arguments themselves. There are intima-tions of formal humility and politesse in the dialogues that were composed dur-ing the Middle Ages or even in the writings of eighteenth-century Western European apologists of the Enlightenment. However, these treatises do not raise the virtue of humility as a primary requisite for engaging the other traditions in discourse. It would be risible to think of Jewish authors suggesting that their reli-gious truth was linked to a lower order of either personal virtue or intellectual power than those demanded or disclosed by interlocutors from other religious traditions.

However, when these traditions turn away from one another and toward God or Allah who is Creator, Revealer, and Redeemer, another mode of discourse pre-vails. The engagement between the Revealer and the community that receives revelation is not a conversation among equals. It is, rather, a gift from a supernal Being. The response to the revelation is inquiry, questioning, interpretation—and not intellectual jousting. In some sense, the response to revelation or the tradition of interpretation that often acquires a status of revelation—in Judaism the Oral Torah—is one of *askesis,* of withdrawal, humility, or gratitude.

An example of this response from the Jewish tradition may be drawn from Numbers Rabbah:

> Why was Torah given in the desert? This teaches that anyone who does not make themselves like the desert (KeMidbar)—hefker (ownerless)—is not capable of acquiring Wisdom and Torah."[1]

Let us emphasize the importance of some phrases in the response to the query. First, we should note that the words for revelation are encompassed by *receive Torah*. In the rabbinic tradition, the encounter between Israel and God at Mount Sinai is called *Matan Torah*, the gift of Torah [or teaching].[2] In this way, the people of Israel—and, by extension, all humanity—was offered the gift of God's word at Sinai. To encounter God's word is to receive a gift.

The second phrase to be noted in this passage is the word *hefker* or ownerless. This concept is used in Jewish law to designate property that has not been claimed, so that people can then establish themselves and their right to it. We should also underscore the notion that the individual must take action by "making themselves as ownerless as the desert" in order to receive revelation. To acquire wisdom and divine instruction in Torah, one must perform an action of nonownership. This oscillation between declaring something ownerless and acquisition stands in the same path as the notion of "intellectual humility." In order to increase our intellectual gifts, and as I will argue, in order to transmit them to others, we must take the opposite action of declaring that our capacity to obtain the full measure of wisdom and Torah—the divine gift—is beyond our capacity. If we stipulate this claim at the beginning, we shall discern that all claims in interreligious conversations are not truths in themselves but claims made by those who live out their engagement with God through their communities. To become ownerless is not to renounce ownership but a specific form of *askesis* that forecloses our ability to identify our interpretation or our own lives with the will of God.

Through the course of this paper, I want to demonstrate that it is precisely in conversations between Jews, Christians, and Muslims about religious texts that we can make that ascetic act of becoming ownerless—and then, without surrendering any integrity, affirm ourselves as owners of our religious tradition. What happens in this process is that our horizons and the focal plane of our vision and thought are not relativized but actually conform themselves to the notion that to be human is to use our senses: listen and see, and then process these perceptions into speech. My claims about this process are modest: We shall not take the path of Schiller to equate the education of human beings as connected to mutual tolerance and understanding as an automatic process.[3] We will not reify the notion of dialogue as a blunt instrument whereby individuals reduce their prejudgment of the other and their religious truth claims. There is far too much historical experience of disruptive violence both in premodern time and modernity.

However, I do want to suggest that, in conversation across confessional tradi-tions, particularly when we read texts together, we do put a distance between our-selves and our words via the process of reading together first and then speaking. In these conversations we bring out thoughts into voice, but in the process of conversation itself we cannot guarantee how they are understood any more than we can make the claim that others actually hear us, until we have listened patiently.

We should, as a matter of humility, make one further renunciation. I have delib-erately used the term *conversation* because I believe it reduces the pressure on interreligious exchanges. In the past, the idea of dialogue had a venerable history, but such dialogues are scripted by an author. The conversations described in this paper are captured better by the word *transcript,* where the oral communications are transformed by writing.

Following this proposal about modest claims, I hope that this paper will speak to the theme of learned ignorance in the following way. The foundation of this paper is that the Jewish experience of the revealed word of God at Mt. Sinai is con-stituted by the senses of sight and hearing, which is disclosed in Exodus 20:15: "And all the people saw the sounds." The explanations of this verse by classical Jewish exegetes point toward interpretation and conversation in the presence of others as a way to affirm our human capacity for encountering the divine but the encounter itself demands that we admit to a learned ignorance analogous to the type described by Nicholas of Cusa. We proceed, then, first to describe the link between learned ignorance and interreligious conversation. Next, I will describe my own experience of an interreligious conversation between Jews, Christians, and Muslims that took place during a course at the Cardinal Bea Institute in Rome. Then, I will analyze that encounter on the basis of Jewish exegetical interpretations of the sensory experience of Israel at Mt. Sinai.

■ CUSA'S *ON LEARNED IGNORANCE* AND THE EXPERIENCE OF INTERRELIGIOUS CONVERSATION

Nicholas of Cusa's treatise *On Learned Ignorance* begins by setting forth the con-cept of absolute maximum, which is the God of all being (Bk 1), and then describes the "contracted maximum," which is the universe, the maximum effect of the abso-lute and the sum of all contracted (i.e., derived) things (Bk.2). Cusa then moves to the "absolute and contracted maximum"—for him, Jesus Christ—the maximum in the universe united with the absolute perfection of the universe and the center and circumference of all intellectual nature.[4] The entire study rests on the premise that absolute truth is humanly incomprehensible, and that the highest level of learning a human being can obtain is to know that one is ignorant.

The other notion, quite seductive at first, is the "coincidence of opposites." This notion implies that opposites are dissolved at infinity. If we stipulate that this is indeed the case, then theological method would call for the principle of logically setting opposites into a harmony and the principle of viewing opposites as recon-ciled. Although this may be the case within a single religious tradition, it would surely not serve as a guideline for interreligious conversation because it would—on first appearance—demand that all religious traditions dissolve themselves at either metaphysical or temporal infinity. Were this to be the case, our current meetings as Christians, Jews, and Muslims would be oriented toward preparing for an eschatological moment of homogeneity. However much this might be a *desideratum* among some believers, Cusanus's notion of learned ignorance would restrain us from making such a sweeping claim. It is necessary to recognize that we understand matters as we do because the relationship between our universe and the infinite follows from the notion that the universe is contracted because it is derived from the absolute maximum. All things are contracted within the universe, but because they are derived from God, they all had an antecedent existence enfolded in God. Therefore, the coincidence of opposites does not exist apart from the infinite where God is not the coincidence of opposites but the absolute maximum in which opposites antecedently coincide. Our human capacity extends to envisioning a deity who works coincidence in the historical experience of human beings. Whether it exists in nature or persons, the agent of coincidence can only be something that is both absolute and limited maximum. Cusanus argued that the final coincidence occurs in the reality of Jesus Christ who is both human and divine. However, as a Jew I would propose a different locus for the "coincidence that is available to Jews, Christians, and Muslims—namely, that the reverence for the word of God in revealed texts and their continuing interpretation by generations of religious communities becomes the ground for a coincidence. The "coincidence in the word" would resonate in Judaism, Christianity, and Islam because they may all be described, as Fr. Daniel Madigan has suggested, as *Logos* traditions—that is, communities who are born in the word and draw their continuity by interpreting it.[5] The link between Cusanus's coincidence works with these three traditions because coincidence unites one thing with another in a way that it does not exclude the other but rather includes all. This coincidence would necessitate a species occurring in the middle sharing the nature of the largest number of things. What I hope to describe and advocate in this paper *is that interreligious dialogue that should be focused on the reading and interpretation of religious texts in the presence of members of other religious communities.*

In support of the experience of intellectual humility that is gained through reading religious texts in the presence of the other, we can call upon the words of Abraham Joshua Heschel when he asked, "What is the purpose of *interreligious* cooperation?" His response was,

> It is neither to flatter nor to refute one another, but to help one another; to share insight and learning; to cooperate in academic ventures on the highest scholarly level, and *what is more important to search in the wilderness for the well-springs of devotion, for treasures of stillness, for the power of love and care for man. What is urgently needed are ways of helping one another in the terrible predicament of here and now by the courage to believe that the word of the Lord endures forever as well as here and now; to cooperate in trying to bring about a resurrection of sensitivity, a revival of conscience; to keep alive the divine sparks in our souls, to nurture openness to the spirit of the Psalms, reverence for the words of the prophets, and faithfulness to the living God*[6]

This eloquent description of what occurs in the process of interreligious cooperation echoes many aspects of Cusanus's appropriation of the notion of intellectual humility. Conversations across the divisions of religious convictions would seem to require both cognitive and affective dimensions. Without the predisposition to acknowledging that one's partners in conversation bring gifts to the table, there is little hope that more profound understanding of the divinity, which is at the ground of human existence, will ever be reached.

It is also important not to err in thinking that when people engage in reading texts together that a unity of interpretation or a consensus is the goal. Here Cusanus helps again as he developed a nuanced version of unity, which is important for interreligious discussion. If *unity* means "homogeneity" or "the loss of individual religious identities," one must reject it as damaging to communities as a surrender of principle, or if it means "the creation of a third entity," then it becomes syncretism. However, for Cusanus, not all unities constitute coincidence. There is a notion, for Cusanus, of convergence where we discover the unity of substance without mingling and without obliteration of either party or substance. Only God's unity is a unity to which "neither otherness nor plurality nor multiplicity is opposed. This unity is the maximum name enfolding all things in its simplicity of unity and this is the name which is ineffable and above all understanding."[7] In this way, coincidence formulates all religious statements in terms of their relation to infinity. Through coincidence we may say that the absolute maximum, which infinitely transcends all opposition, enfolds as well as unfolds all that is known but not comprehended. Therefore, learned ignorance sees and coincidence enunciates what otherwise fails the sciences, wisdom, and language. Therefore, it requires those who would engage in interreligious dialogue to recognize that language is used in a symbolic manner. This symbolic use is required because the reading of sacred texts in each religious community arises from a vision beyond what terms and names seem to be, and toward what they become with reference to absolutes. Therefore, a coincident logic requires elevating the intellect above the force of words rather than insisting that they possess only one dimensional meaning.

This elevated vision of language in the system of Cusanus would not deny the value of individual statements, but it would relativize the possibility that any statement would be predicated as absolute and adequate descriptions of ultimate reality. In the hermeneutical process of reading texts in the presence of the other, people have a visual and aural experience involved in the reenactment of these claims. They sit in the presence of texts, read them aloud, hear them, and explain them.

When these texts are read in the ancient languages, participants have a sense of distance or alienation that prevents them from easily withdrawing their immediate ability to understand the texts. We become dependent on the voices and the vision of those who sit before us and proclaim them as part of their community. However, when we voice our interpretations before people from other religious communities, our insights may disclose dimensions previously unseen and unheard by those with whom they have become so familiar, either through recitation or ritual or rote.

To return for a moment to Cusanus and learned ignorance: He makes it clear that learned ignorance is experiential as well as speculative. It is the *experience* of seeing the truth that precedes the telling of it. Its method of theological seeing and telling differs from other ways as "sight from hearing." "Those who through learned ignorance are transported from hearing to the seeing of the mind rejoice that they have attained the knowledge of ignorance by a more certain experience."[8] We can, therefore, conclude that learned ignorance is the experiential source of theology through which one is elevated to the vision of divine things. For Cusanus, knowing precedes theologizing, just as experience precedes understanding. The theologian's task is, in a figurative sense, "incarnational" because the task is to render the eternal or infinite truth into finite forms. Thus, the labor of developing coincidence is "iconographic" because it implies that theological interpretation requires picturing the divine work of coincidence *in* the Word, rather than directly in God who surpasses all language and knowing. Theological language should communicate God's uniting activity, the divine word contracted to the human word without confounding the integrity of either.

The reading of religious texts in the presence of the other provides this opportunity to share language about God from one of our three traditions with members of the other traditions. I do not suggest that this method of dialogue is a substitute for theological reflection within our own traditions. Jews, Muslims, and Christians have large theological agendas within their communities and often encounter difficulties of both method and substance in the intra-confessional situations. It is beyond the scope of this paper to advocate for the notion of learned ignorance beyond what I understand as its warrant in the Jewish tradition. However, I would like to describe two examples of my experience of "learned ignorance" in the context of interreligious settings.

■ THE CLASSROOM: A SITE OF INTERRELIGIOUS READING AND LEARNED IGNORANCE

Like so many others who have engaged in discussions across confessional lines, I often did not recognize the moment of insight until long after it was past. However, various experiences have indicated to me that it is possible to create a situation in which the possibilities for these insights can be more open. In the particular example I describe, it was not the content of the course but the framework for the discussions that provided the reality for the insights. In retrospect, the situation I describe was a continuing opportunity for all members of the group to make themselves as ownerless as the desert—and thereby to become more receptive to the Jewish tradition than their previous experiences had allowed them.

The group gathered at the Gregorian University in the winter semester 2005. The course was "Christianity in Jewish Terms" based on a book I had edited with four other Jewish colleagues.[9] Our primary goal in writing that book was to present the Christian tradition under rubrics that would help knowledgeable Jews understand both the similarities and differences of Christianity from Judaism. However, I also realized that the majority of the students were not native speakers of English. The written language of the book would thereby become a considerable challenge for them. The next surprise was in the composition of the students. There were eight Christian students, five Muslim students, and one Hindu. What I had thought would be bilateral discussion between Christians and Jews (or at least one Jew) had now become an interreligious conversation between members of the so-called Abrahamic communities and a member of the Hindu tradition. The students immediately sensed a disorientation when they entered a class taught by a

Rabbi, and the Muslims were, now, no longer the outsiders nor were they the problem (as they often had been in their classes in Christian theology). In order to make the classroom more amenable to conversations between all traditions, I prepared translations of texts from the Hebrew Bible and Rabbinic literature for each week. One student read the translation to the class, and then we commenced an interchange of ideas about the possible trajectories of ideas suggested in these texts. Wherever possible, I added most significant Hebrew terms (either biblical or rabbinic). As the students began to familiarize themselves with rabbinic methods of interpretation, they began to offer their own perspective fully within the spirit of rabbinic thinking. At times this occurred by a clever reinterpretation of a biblical verse. On other occasions, a student was able to expand the horizons of a rabbinic statement.

It also became clear that the rabbinic texts provided a basis for Christian and Muslim students to raise issues with one another. This is a process that I call triangulation wherein the Muslim or Christian says, "We have no problem with the Jewish tradition on this issue. Rather, it is the Christians [or Muslims] who are mistaken." When this happened I would always announce to the students, "We can continue this line of argument if you like. But, if we do so I would prefer to take out a polemical treatise from our medieval authors because we are now treading on that path and they could make arguments much more eloquently than we can. However, perhaps we can ask a new question or move in a new direction to interpret this text so that we can all be enriched." To this formulation I would often append the following statement, "We all have issues that are unsettled between us. When one of our communities is absent, we tend to project those difficulties upon them. Perhaps, when we engage in bilateral discussions between communities we should always keep the absent community in mind." With the act of imagining the third community when we engage in interreligious consultations, we are reminded of Emmanuel Levinas's formulation of the "third sphere" where justice "comes to mind."[10]

During moments of tension and strong disagreement, the text before us continued to act as the ground of discussion. New questions and insights arose out of our reading of the text. Disagreements were not resolved nor was there any consensus on the interpretation of the text. However, the notion of returning week after week to a set of Jewish texts acted as a bridge between all our communities. A consensus seemed to emerge that the word of God was behind the text, and our discussions permitted all of us to engage in continuing a search on the collective level that strengthened each member of the group in their quest to live in the presence of God within their own communities.

It has become clear to me that, when people of religious conviction gather together and read religious texts, they have a singular opportunity to experience what the Rabbis considered the process of becoming ownerless as the desert, and thereby open to receiving the gift of religious insight.

The process, as we shall see, resonates to the moment described in Exodus 20:15 as the people "seeing the sounds." The conditions for becoming ownerless are set by the free decision of all members of the group to sit in front of one another. Within such an assembly, there is an opportunity to create spatial distance and proximity to those who are different. By stipulating to read the religious text of another community—not to possess its meaning but simply to read it aloud together—each member of the assembly sets themselves the task of realizing how their prejudgments of the religious text can distort their hearing of both text and translation. If we consider the group that met in the Gregorianum, there was an immediate provision that the ground upon which we sat belonged to no member of the group. Yes, the Catholics who were present shared the religious tradition of the university, but most of them came from countries outside of Italy. Muslims had come to Rome to study another religious tradition and were, of their own free will, ready to live in a space that was alien to their culture (as they came from cultures as different as India, Turkey, and Pakistan). There was a sense of alienation from language as the majority of the class were not native speakers of English. These conditions created a conscious sense of estrangement from one another, whereas the proximity was presented by the text from a religious tradition that had some overlap with all members of the class but belonged only to me, their instructor.

My classroom at the Gregorian University reflects a method developed by Peter Ochs and Steven Kepnes which they have called "Scriptural Reasoning." In their book, *Reasoning after Revelation: Dialogues in Postmodern Jewish Philosophy* (Westview Press, 1998), the editors outline the patterns for setting out what they call "textual reasoning" as a dialogic approach to the texts of tradition. Robert Gibbs suggests that "I think our search will be most fruitful if we take as our model the reading of Jewish texts together. This spontaneous reading-together is a form of (Franz) Rosenzweig's 'speech-thinking' that can help us get to a cross-pollination of social reading and philosophical treatise. Rosenzweig suggests a model of reading where we hear all the voices at the same time."[11] Steven Kepnes then adds,

> Postmodern Jewish subjectivity involves a "decentering" of the modern, autonomous self through a hermeneutical enterprise of alternatively losing and finding that self through the interpretation of Jewish texts. In this hermeneutical and dialogic process the self is integrated into the community and the tradition. In decentering the self, this hermeneutical process recenters Jewish text, or Torah, as the fulcrum around which Jewish existence revolves.[12]

Although Kepnes refers specifically to the Jewish tradition, I would suggest that the same process of decentering the self by means of a text may be extended to the discussions between religious communities. In the moments of reading and inter-preting a text together, the group is joined as a community that is bonded by the process of reading and discussion. In this method, the senses become a primary source of knowledge and the oral becomes the primary mode of reliving the revealed text. I have witnessed the success of the method described by Ochs, Gibbs, and Kepnes over a three-year period at the Center for Theological Inquiry at Princeton School of Theology where Jews, Christians, and Muslims engaged in reading their sacred texts in the presence of one another. Our discussions vali-dated my impressions of what happened during the course of study at the Gregorian University in Rome. None of the Princeton group departed from our study sessions without gaining insight into his or her tradition, as well as learning about the nuance and sophistication of the participants from other traditions.

■ LEARNED IGNORANCE AT SINAI: HEARING, SEEING, TALKING

We turn now to address the issue of the basis for learned ignorance, the reading of texts in the presence of the other, as a moment of revelation. In the system described by Nicholas of Cusa, there is a clear emphasis on the connection between the affective and the cognitive aspects of learned ignorance. The theologian seeks the light of God who is *Simplex* and in whom all opposites coincide. We can find echoes of this notion of grasping at the light reflected in the created world in the narratives presented in the biblical book of Exodus when the Israelites arrived at Mt. Sinai and prepared themselves to receive God's gift of revelation. This climactic moment at Sinai has been enshrined in the festival cycle of the Jewish people since antiquity. From Egypt through the Sea of Reeds, the people newly liberated encountered God at the foot of the mountain. The book of Exodus employs sensory terms when disclosing the events. In this paper, which focuses on the experience of interreligious dialogue as a source of learned ignorance, we have attempted to draw the analogy between the experience of the revealed moment when studying together with active believers in other traditions and the theological notion of learned ignorance where experience of the word through others precedes the expression of the word through one's own epistemic journey toward a deeper experience of God in the language of the tradition of origin.

When reading about the children of Israel who emerged from Egypt, we observe that the book of Exodus makes consistent use of sensory language, especially "seeing" and "hearing":

> Thus shall you say to the house of Jacob and declare to the children of Israel: You **have seen** what I did to the Egyptians, how I **bore you on eagles' wings** and brought you to me. Now then, if you will obey me faithfully and keep my covenant, you shall be my treasured possession among all the peoples. Indeed the earth is mine (Ex. 19: 3–4).
>
> And the Lord said to Moses, "I will come to you in a **thick cloud**, in order that the people may **hear when I speak** with you and **trust** you thereafter" (Ex. 19: 9).
>
> Let them be ready for the third day, for on the third day the Lord will come down, in the **sight of all the people** on Mount Sinai (Ex. 19: 11).
>
> Now Mount Sinai **was all in smoke**, for the Lord had come down upon it **in fire; the smoke rose like the smoke of a kiln** and the whole mountain trembled violently. The **blare of the horn grew louder and louder**. As Moses spoke, God answered him in **thunder**. Then the Lord said to Moses, "Go down, warn the people not to break through to the Lord to **gaze**, (lir'ot) lest many of them perish" (Ex. 19: 18–21).

In these examples (emphasis is mine) the assembled community is called upon to use the visual and auditory senses to comprehend the reality of divine activity in the world. The gift of Torah is not only the content of the divine word but a clear witness to the activity of the divine within the created world. Theophany is not at all esoteric in these verses, but the divine becomes manifest in forms that people could see, feel, smell, and touch. Although the Jewish tradition may have emphasized an anti-iconic or iconoclastic way of imagining the deity, it is clear that the visible and audible were parts of the "immemorial past" and touchstones for a rabbinic approach to God that, as Elliot R. Wolfson has so ably demonstrated in his book, *Through A Speculum that Shines: Vision and Imagination in Medieval Jewish Mysticism*, emphasizes the visionary tradition.[13]

In the verse immediately following the Decalogue, Scripture turns to a most enigmatic verse. I present first the contemporary translation and then a paraphrase that corresponds more directly to the Hebrew words:

> All the people witnessed the thunder and lightening, the blare of the horn and the mountain smoking; and when the people saw it, they fell back and stood at a distance (Ex. 20: 14 [Heb] 15 [Eng]).

A more literal translation would be, "All the people saw the sounds, the flames of fire, the sound of the ram's horn, and the mountain of smoke, and the people were afraid and stood back."

Clearly, my own focus in this paper is on the mixture of sight and sound. By turning to the rabbinic tradition, a set of possible interpretations follows that extends my claim that the sight and sound are characterized by interpretation:

> Rabbi Ishmael: They saw what was visible and heard what was audible. Rabbi Akiba: They saw and heard that which was visible. They saw the fiery word coming out of the mouth of the Almighty as it was struck upon the tablets as Scripture states, "The sound of the Lord hewed out flames of fire" [Ps. 29.7][14]

The explanation offered by Rabbi Ishmael indicates that there is no mixture at all of sensory experience. The moment of revelation presents itself as an occasion in which each sense discerns the data appropriate to its strength. By contrast, Rabbi Akiba prefers to delineate a synesthesia, a mixture of sensory experiences, where two senses acted together at the same moment to receive the singular moment of divine revelation. His warrant for this opinion is the text from Ps. 29:7, which describes the power of the divine sound to hew out flames of fire. According to Rabbi Akiba, what determines the sensory experience of the people is the utterly singular mode of divine communication. Divine words are flames of fire that come from the supernal source. They require a decoding or translation that demands an extraordinary use of human sensory power. By the account of Rabbi Akiba, these verses demand a humble approach by the reader who will recognize the disharmony of the biblical sentence as an invitation to learned ignorance. To put it simply, the divine communication at Sinai was so unique that human sensory experience was altered. Subsequent approaches to revealed texts are, therefore, efforts to grasp that moment of origin.

However, there is another exegetical approach that may be apposite to our description of interreligious conversation as a site of reenacting the moment of revelation:

> Rabbi said, "This is to proclaim the excellence of the Israelites. For when they all stood to receive the Torah they interpreted the divine word as soon as they heard it." For Scripture said, "He compassed it, he understood it, and he kept it as the apple of his eye" [Deut. 32.10], meaning as soon as they heard it, they interpreted it.[15]

In this interpretation *to see* means "to interpret." The simultaneous act of seeing and sounds results in the act of interpretation. Rabbi's approach in this passage may be interpreted in connection with a passage ascribed to Rabbi Judah in Pirke d'Rabbi Eliezer: "A person speaks with his friend and hears the tone of his voice, but he does not see his light. [At Sinai] Israel heard the voice of the Holy One and they saw the voice from the mouth of the Almighty in lightening and thunder." Sinai is a singular moment when perceptions differ from other occasions. The warrant from Scripture, Deut. 32:10 in this passage, also frames the reality of Israel at Sinai as a moment of divine solicitude: "He found him in a desert region, in an empty howling waste. He engirded him, watched over him, guarded him like the apple of his eye." It is the word *yevoneneyhu* that is crucial for Rabbi Judah's interpretation because it encompasses understanding as part of the process that occurred at Sinai. God encompassed Israel and gave them the capacity to understand, because they were the "apple of his eye." This ocular figure indicates the resonance between the people seeing the sound, and the divine sound that is seen. What joins the seeing and the seen is the process of interpretation or understanding.

We have not exhausted the possibilities for interpretation of this passage, but I believe that there is sufficient evidence to indicate that receiving the gift of Torah includes all the senses. Furthermore, to capture the meaning of the divine word demands the sensory as well as the intellectual processes.

It must also be stated that we have bracketed the notion of the Jews as a singular people who were chosen to receive revelation, and we have deliberately focused on the idea of how the revelation was received. Israel and the nations are part of the cosmos created by the Almighty. The possibility for all to receive the gift of divine instruction is certainly implicit in the rabbinic interpretations of all these passages. The interpretations of Sinai call upon all readers of the passage to note the combination of visual and auditory vocabulary that were present. The response of Israel, "All that the Lord has said we shall do and we shall hearken" (Exodus 19:8), also puts the sense of hearing in conjunction with action. We could speculate that, in the communities of Christianity and Islam, the call to discipleship or the piercing word of Allah in the Qur'an is a call that requires human action and obedience rather than propositional truth as an authentic response. The notion of revelation's gift as call and response also moves our argument back to the notion that learned ignorance (hearkening) also implies action (responsibility).

■ CONCLUDING THOUGHTS

Nicholas of Cusa's formulation of learned ignorance would seem, then, to suggest that conversations between Jews, Christians, and Muslims ought to focus on process rather than argument. If God is beyond knowledge and description, then the revealed texts are endowed with a superfluity of meaning. Mountains of written words in each of our traditions attest to the search to uncover the extension of these texts for the community of each era.

In this paper we have argued that reading religious texts in the presence of others has the potential to complement the work of interpretation and appropriation that has been at the heart of our communities. At the core of these conversations is the idea that to arrive at the interpretation of a religious text is a gift.

The preparation for receiving the gift is to make oneself as ownerless as the desert. To interpret in the face of the Other is to admit from the outset that at the foundation of all religious life is a human choice to renounce absolute control of all possible interpretations. To confront the revealed text of another religious community and its interpretation is to admit the impossibility of controlling the meaning of the texts for the other. To welcome others into a community of readers is also to open the possibility that insights based on their observations may open new dimensions to texts that were familiar to us.

In the third section of the paper we suggested that the moment of revelation at Sinai—the moment that constituted Israel as a people covenanted with their God—emphasized the senses of sight and hearing. Although philosophical traditions of antiquity adopted an approach of skepticism toward knowledge gained through the senses, the Hebrew Scriptures and the Rabbis emphasized these human endowments as avenues to truth. The God of Israel approached biblical people with words transmitted through nature as well as in the words spoken to Moses. To "see the voices" was to perceive these visual stimuli and to interpret them. In the hermeneutical process of seeing, hearing, and talking, the divine message was transmitted to the people.

Our daily reality as human beings who express themselves within the framework of religious traditions indicates that conversation across religious communities is far from self-understood or even praiseworthy. Many people in our communities assert that conversation or dialogue leads to weakness and relativism rather than insight. It would be my speculation that they understand their religious obligation as one of ownership rather than to become ownerless. However, in the past twenty years we have observed the stark reality of those who advocate that religious traditions are possessions and who make exclusive claims to ownership of the majesty of God. Words and interpretations can and often do lead to acts of violence and the diminution of other humans who are created in the image of God. However, the reality presented to our eyes and ears also evokes revulsion to these acts of destruction.

It is our witness to the use of religious texts as warrants for destruction that animates those of us who gather for interreligious dialogue. Talk alone, talk unbridled by discipline, cannot lead to respect. However, patience and humility trained by reading texts slowly, seeing the face of the others and hearing their insights may be a first step toward recognizing the potential of study across religious lines as a step toward restoring the image of God in the world.

■ Notes

1. Bamidbar Rabbah, Vilna ed., ch. 1, paragraph 7. The translation is mine.
2. This phrase occurs once in the Mishnah, *Taanit* 4:8, and is the standard term for the Theophany at Sinai in the *Mekhilta d'Rabbi Ishmael*.
3. Friedrich Schiller, *On the Aesthetic Education of Man: In a Series of Letters* (Oxford, England: The Clarendon Press, 1967).
4. For purposes of this discussion I have relied upon *Nicholas of Cusa: Selected Spiritual Writings*, trans. H. Lawrence Bond, Preface by Morimichi Watanabe (New York, Mahwah, NJ: Paulist Press, 1997).

5. Fr. Madigan made this suggestion during the meeting of a course held at the Cardinal Bea Institute for Judaic Studies in the Gregorian University (Rome), 2005.

6. Emphasis mine. Abraham Joshua Heschel, *Moral Grandeur and Spiritual Audacity: Essays,* ed. Susannah Heschel (New York; Farrar Straus Giroux, 1996), p. 300.

7. *Nicholas Cusanus: Selected Writings.* "On Learned Ignorance," p. 121.

8. Nicholas Cusanus, *Apologia docta ignorantia* II.3.

9. Tikva Frymer-Kensky, David Novak, Peter Ochs, David Fox Sandmel and Michael Signer, eds., *Christianity in Jewish Terms* (Boulder, CO: Westview Press, 2000).

10. Robert Bernasconi, "The Third Party: Levinas on the Intersection of the Ethical and the Political," *Journal of the British Society for Phenomenology*, 30, 1 (January 1999).

11. Peter Ochs and Robert Gibbs, *Reasoning after Revelation: Dialogues in Postmodern Jewish Philosophy* (Boulder, CO: Westview Press, 1998), p. 16.

12. Ibid., p. 24.

13. (Princeton, NJ: Princeton University Press, 1994).

14. *Mekhilta d'Rabbi Ishmael*, translated by Jacob Lauterbach (Philadelphia: Jewish Publication Society of America, 1949) Tractate *BaHodesh*, ch. 9, p. 266.

15. Ibid.

4

Finding Common Ground: "Mutual Knowing," Moderation, and the Fostering of Religious Pluralism

Asma Afsaruddin

It is possible to say that I have been engaging in interreligious dialogue for a long time, sometimes without my consciously being aware of it. Being a Muslim in largely Christian America means one is frequently being asked to explain at least the basic tenets of Islam by non-Muslim friends, acquaintances, and colleagues of various sorts. As a religious person myself, I am interested in other people's faith backgrounds and formation, their constellation of cherished beliefs and values, and possible congruence with Islamic values. These cross-religious encounters have been primarily with friends and colleagues from Christian backgrounds and to a lesser extent from Jewish backgrounds, and have been very valuable. In my native Bangladesh, where I lived until my teens, I grew up in a very homogeneous Muslim environment. But starting in college (Oberlin College in Ohio) and thereafter, many of my comfortable and easy assumptions about Islam have been interrogated and nuanced on account of my interreligious encounters over the years.

My current strong interest in interreligious dialogue was sparked in the aftermath of the September 11 attacks. As someone who teaches and does research in Islamic thought and intellectual history, I began to be invited to various public forums and interviewed by the media on a host of issues pertaining to Islamic doctrine, law, and ethics. I am repeatedly asked to explain the rudiments of Islam and the potential relationship between traditional Islamic thought and current events. In the past nine years, I have taken part, for example, in interfaith dialogue with the Blackfriars at Oxford University, with certain members of the Fuller Theological Seminary in California, an evangelical Protestant institution representing a denomination whose influential leaders have expressed strident hostility toward Islam and Muslims, and with Christian participants in the "Common Word" project initiated by Muslim scholars from all over the world in 2007. I have also spoken at a number of churches and civic associations, such as the Rotary Club, all of which have provided precious opportunities to engage potentially divisive religious and political issues. In recent years, I have regularly taken part in the current Archbishop of Canterbury Rowan Williams's "Building Bridges" seminar which brings select Muslim and Christian scholars together annually to explore commonalities and interrogate their differences in various locales.

These experiences have been mutually illuminating, enriching, and humbling at the same time.

Through interaction with practitioners of the Abrahamic faiths in particular, I have learned that there is indeed much common ground between committed believers. This is not a mere pious truism. My most intense interactions have been with Christians and, in recent years, specifically with Catholics, because of my previous academic position at the University of Notre Dame. In the area of social teachings, there are a significant number of values in common between Muslims and Christians, particularly with the advent of post-Vatican II Catholic social teaching. For example, justice is a particularly prominent social and moral concept in Islam and Christianity (and in Judaism) and there is a common concern for respecting people's intrinsic human dignity as God's loving creation. It is fair—and imperative—to say that the time for triumphalist and exclusivist attitudes is past. I strongly believe that dialogue must focus strenuously on finding—and in many cases retrieving—common ground based on shared moral and ethical values and to move beyond theological controversies. Respectful dialogue allows practitioners to speak for themselves, their own faith, and communities, and not to have themselves refracted through someone else's ideological prism and somehow found wanting or made to be a deformed version of the other. Polemicists and propagandists resort to this method. Interfaith conversations must develop instead a shared, universal idiom to express and embrace both the similarities and differences among faith communities and avoid the pitfalls of particularism.

In the aftermath of September 11, the necessity of interfaith dialogue and fostering religious pluralism has loomed large for those who are concerned about the much-touted "clash of civilizations" between "Islam and the West," fomented apparently by irreconcilable religious and cultural values.[1] To counter such notions, it has become imperative for people of faith and good will to reclaim the common ground that has historically existed among the Abrahamic faith communities and to further build upon it to respond to the specific challenges of post-September 11 global realities.[2] The opportunities for both increasing polarization and rapprochement currently exist. Which trend will gain ground depends on which side is the more credible in presenting their case. The success of dialogic encounters and pluralist initiatives depends to a considerable extent on how credibly we are able to marshal scriptural warrants and historical examples from within our own religious traditions to create and nurture universal principles of co-existence and moderate, civil behavior toward one another. The greatest challenge in creating these religiously inspired counternarratives is to account for the natural differences that exist among humankind and to regard them as a divinely mandated feature which, through our respectful acceptance of and engagement with them, enrich our earthly lives.

In this paper I focus on three Qur'anic concepts from which universal ethical principles may be derived to promote harmonious relationships between diverse peoples and faith communities in full recognition, even in celebration, of our differences. These concepts are: (1) knowledge of one another (Ar. *al-ta'aruf*), based on respect for diversity and difference; (2) the commonality of human beings based on righteousness and ethical conduct rather than on religious labels and denominations;[3] and (3) moderation as a defining characteristic of righteous believers. These concepts and their bearing on interfaith dialogue and peaceful co-existence are discussed in greater detail later, particularly through the prism of exegeses of critical Qur'anic verses that deal with these concepts. It will become apparent later that, although a number of premodern Muslim exegetes showed appreciation for the Qur'anic valorization of diversity, their own social and histor-ical circumstances limited their conceptualization of the extent of diversity and its impact on interfaith relations. It is, therefore, suggested that in our contemporary, increasingly cosmopolitan world, we may read these texts with fresh eyes today and uncover exegetical possibilities that will help reconfigure relations among reli-gious communities from a more pluralist *and intellectually humble* perspective.

■ KNOWLEDGE OF ONE ANOTHER

The concept of *al-ta'aruf* or "knowledge of one another" derives from Qur'an 49:13, which states: "O humankind! We have created you from a male and a female, and made you into nations and tribes, that you might get to know one another. The noblest of you in God's sight is the one who is most righteous." The medieval Muslim exegete Muhammad ibn Jarir al-Tabari (d. 923) explains this verse as emphasizing that only on the basis of piety may we distinguish between human beings, not on the basis of lineage and descent. He quotes a *hadith* or a saying of the Prophet Muhammad in this context in which he relates that all humans were descended from Adam and Eve. "Indeed," the Prophet asserts, "God will not question you regarding your pedigree and tribal affiliation on the Day of Judgment, for only the most righteous is the noblest before God."[4]

Another well-known medieval exegete Isma'il ibn Kathir (d. 1353), cites the following *hadith* in exegesis of this verse, "The Muslims (Ar. *al-muslimun*) are brothers. No one among them has any superiority over another, except on the basis of piety/godliness (Ar. *taqwa*)."[5] Here Ibn Kathir apparently understands the term *al-muslimun* in its general confessional sense and thus restricts the notion of the equality of believers as applying to Muslims alone. This is in contrast to the *hadith* given earlier cited by the earlier exegete al-Tabari, which clearly propounds the equality of all human beings, recognizing distinction among them only on the basis of personal righteousness. But it would also be possible for us to translate *al-muslimun* as occurs in the *hadith* cited by Ibn Kathir in its basic sense of "those who submit [to God]," thus extending the purview of this *hadith* to include all believers who are united by their common faith in God and differentiated only on the basis of their piety. This inclusive understanding, after all, is more in accor-dance with the predominantly nonconfessional Qur'anic usage of this term, as in Qur'an 3:67; 3:84; 5:44; and others.[6]

In our contemporary period, the significance of Qur'an 49:13 lies precisely in the fact that it offers us a clear scriptural mandate for embracing the existing diver-sity among peoples and to respect the pluralism in beliefs that we encounter—a moral desideratum for many of us. The verse transparently exhorts the believer to accept differences in ethnic and cultural backgrounds as divinely ordained and to be concerned only with the larger, common issues of morality and ethics. A related verse, Qur'an 5:48, further underscores this notion. It states,

> For every one of you We have appointed a law and way of life. And if God had so willed, He could surely have made you all one single community, but (He willed it otherwise) in order to test you by means of what He has given you. So hasten to do good works! To God you all must return; and then He will make you truly understand all that on which you were inclined to differ.

These two verses (49:13 and 5:48) are crucial proof-texts invoked particularly by modernist and liberal Muslims today to indicate divine sanction of religious pluralism. Modernist and liberal Muslims, in my usage, refer to observant Muslims who, starting roughly in the eighteenth century, began to emphasize the inherent adaptability of Islamic principles and thought to modernity.[7] Many classical as well as modern commentators on the Qur'an have taken serious note of these verses and commented on how this affects the relationship of Muslims to practitioners of other faiths.[8] Possibly the most significant part of this verse is the statement, "For every one of you We have appointed a law and way of life." Every community— religious or religiocultural community—is thus regarded as having its own law and its own way of life and capable of attaining spiritual growth in keeping with this law and way of life. According to the Qur'anic view of prophecy, various prophets were sent over time to different communities to give them specific laws and to indicate a way of life to their people in keeping with their genius and in a manner that would ensure their spiritual and societal development. This is further emphasized in the next part of verse 5:48, which states, "And if God had so willed, He could surely have made you all one single community." It would not be difficult for God, after all, to fashion a single community out of humankind. But the Qur'anic view is that pluralism is a divinely mandated feature that adds richness and variety to human existence. Each community's laws or way of life should be such as to ensure growth and the enrichment of life, without causing harm to others. Beyond this proviso, a wide variety of local customs and cultural variations has traditionally been tolerated in many Islamic societies through time.

The last part of this Qur'anic verse states that everyone will return to God and it is He who "will make you truly understand all that on which you were accustomed to differ." A parallel verse (6:108) drives home this message more forcefully. It states, "Do not revile those [idols] they call upon beside God in case they revile God out of hostility." Both verses stress that it is not for human beings to pronounce on the rectitude of religious doctrines since that leads to dissension and strife in this world. The Prophet Muhammad himself is clearly warned that it is not among his duties to chastise people for their beliefs contrary to Islam, including idolatry, which represents the polar opposite of cherished Islamic tenets of monotheism and iconoclasm. Denigrating someone's deeply held religious beliefs is very likely to invite a retaliatory response, as Qur'an 6:108 points out. The initial act of denigration is one of supreme ungraciousness that has no place in Qur'anic ethics, and, increasingly, in global ethics today.[9] Humans themselves should only be concerned with the performance of good deeds and refrain from pronouncing on the salvific nature of others' religious affiliations. This is a powerful Qur'anic principle that is in perfect accord with the spirit of our own pluralist age.

Historically, this Qur'anic principle found reflection in the principle of *irja'* which evolved in roughly the eighth century of the Common Era in the Muslim world. The root of the Arabic term *irja'* connotes both "hope" and "deferment." Because of a number of doctrinal schisms that developed in the early period, some Muslim theologians [wisely] saw immense virtue in postponing or deferring to God any definitive judgment on the correctness of a particular dogma that was not explicitly referred to in the Qur'an or *hadith*. This principle was specifically formulated in contradistinction to the notion of *takfir* ("accusation of unbelief"), resorted to by the seventh century schismatic group, the Khawarij. The Khawarij had mutinied against 'Ali ibn Abi Talib, the fourth caliph, when the latter agreed to human arbitration to resolve the dispute between him and Mu'awiya, the governor of Syria, over issues of leadership. The Khawarij (literally, "the seceders") claimed that arbitration was the prerogative of God alone and human arbitration was unwarranted in this case. Their slogan was "Judgment/arbitration belongs to God alone" (Ar. *La hukma illa lillah*; cf. Qur'an 12:67), which they appear to have understood to mean that an issue as momentous as political leadership could be determined only by direct divine intercession (it is not clear what form they might have expected this to take). The Khawarij considered those Muslims (the overwhelming majority) who disagreed with them to have lapsed from the faith and thus to be fought against until they capitulated—a chilling harbinger of today's minoritarian extremist views.

In contrast to the fissiparous doctrine of *takfir*, the principle of *irja'* stated that any Muslim who proclaimed his or her belief in the one God and the prophetic mission of Muhammad (that is, affirmed the basic creedal statement of Islam) remained a Muslim, regardless of the commission of even gravely sinful actions, thereby holding out the hope and promise of moral rehabilitation in this world and of forgiveness in the next. A sinning Muslim was liable for punishment for criminal wrong-doing but could not be labeled an unbeliever by his co-religionists. Those who subscribed to such views were known as the Murji'a.[10]

The specific Qur'anic proof-text (9:106) invoked to sanction this position (and from which the Murji'a get their name) is as follows: "There are those who are deferred (*murjawna*) to God's commandment—and He may chastise them or turn toward them [sc. in mercy]." The verse was interpreted by the Murji'a and those inclined to agree with them to refer to God's exclusive prerogative in judging human faith and conduct in the hereafter and to restrict human interventionist judgment in this regard. This liberal attitude was key in shaping the doctrinal positions of the majoritarian Sunni Muslim community. Its full appellation—*ahl al-sunna wa-'l-jama'a* ("the people of prophetic custom [sc. those who follow the practices of Muhammad] and communal unity")—underscores its basic accommodationist outlook, which strove to contain dissension in order to preserve the unity of the Muslim community.

Modernist and liberal Muslims have begun to re-emphasize the Qur'anic principle of human nonjudgment and noninterference in matters of faith, hoping to convince the skeptics among their co-religionists of a genuine regard for religious pluralism within Islam on the basis of these scriptural warrants.[11] Extremist Muslims today, however, have resurrected the doctrine of *takfir* and, like the seventh century Khawarij, attempt to wield it as a powerful cudgel to browbeat other Muslims into adopting their Manichaean world-view.

The verses cited earlier and their exegeses thus remain of critical importance in our time as humanity engages in a quest for genuine understanding between individuals, faith communities, cultures, and nations. As part of this quest, traditions of tolerance within the Islamic heritage that historically have been accommodating of a diversity of perspectives and helped keep extremism at bay for lengthy periods of time clearly need to be foregrounded by Muslims today as they battle the forces of intolerance and illiberalism in their midst. It is noteworthy that Qur'an 49:13 goes beyond simple toleration of our diversity of background; it further advocates that one should proactively get to know one another (Ar. *li-ta 'arafu*) so as to inspire in us affection for the other and to appreciate *in genuine humility* the diverse gifts and richness that we bring, in accordance with God's plan, to one another.

Because of the more parochial circumstances of their own time, medieval exegetes tended to gloss the verb *ta'arafu* to mean learning about each other's tribal and similar affiliational backgrounds in order to establish bonds of kinship and affection. In explanation of *ta'arafu*, the exegete al-Tabari, for example, glosses it as commanding people to get to know one another so that they may discover their bonds of kinship. He warns that knowledge of such kinship is not meant to induce any sense of superiority but rather "to bring you closer to God, for indeed only the most pious among you is the most honorable."[12] Ibn Kathir, in his exegesis of this term, cites a *hadith* in which the Prophet states, "Learn about each other's pedigrees so as to establish your blood-ties, for it is such ties which lead to love among people."[13]

In our globalizing world, we can expand the exegetical purview of this verb to extend to not just our blood relatives but all the co-residents of the global village we are now beginning to regard as our shared home, thus realizing more fully the pluralist potential of this verse. In our vastly expanded contemporary circumstances, Qur'an 49:13 may be understood as goading us into learning about each other as inhabitants of different countries, cultures, and faith communities, so as to discover our ultimate commonalities as human beings. Like knowledge of the ties of blood kinship, knowledge of one another as fellow humans is also conducive to affection and good will among diverse peoples. Appropriately, it is this commonality that we proceed to focus on in the next section.

■ THE COMMONALITY OF HUMAN BEINGS IN THE MIDST OF DIFFERENCE

The commonality of humans based on righteousness and faith in God is a belief that may be regarded as naturally proceeding out of the Qur'anic regard for pluralism and diversity based on religion, ethnic background, etc., as briefly discussed earlier. The Qur'an asserts that all righteous believers will receive their reward from God, as in verse 2:62, which states unambiguously, "Those who believe, those who are Jews and Christians and Sabeans, whoever believes in God and the Last

Day and does right, surely their reward is with their Lord, and there shall no fear come upon them, neither shall they grieve." Another verse (29:46) counsels Muslims to say to the People of the Book, as Jews and Christians are known, "We believe in the revelation that has come down to us and in that which came down to you; our God and your God is one, and it is to Him that we submit."

According to this Qur'anic vision, believers are to come to the aid of one another, whether they be Jews, Christians, or Muslims, and they are to work with one another in enjoining what is right and preventing what is wrong, a basic moral and ethical principle in Islam. This joint venture is stressed clearly in verse (22:40), which declares, "If God had not restrained some people by means of others, monasteries, churches, synagogues and mosques, where God's name is mentioned frequently, would have been destroyed." An early Qur'an commentator Muqatil b. Sulayman (d. 767) stresses that without this sense of religious solidarity for the sake of God, the monasteries of the monks, the churches of the Christians, the synagogues of the Jews, and the mosques of the Muslims would all have been destroyed. All these religious groups (al-milal), he says, mention the name of God profusely in their places of worship and God defends these places of worship through the Muslims.[14]

The Qur'an commentary known as Tanwir al-Miqbas, traditionally attributed to the Prophet's Companion Ibn 'Abbas, refers to the monasteries (sawami') of Christian monks, the synagogues (biya') of the Jews, and the fire-temples of the Zoroastrians as being entrusted to Muslims for their protection (kulla ha'ula'i fi ma'man al-muslimin).[15] What is noteworthy—and unusual—about this exegesis is that it also includes non-Abrahamic houses of worship—the Zoroastrian fire-temples—as deserving of protection by Muslims against those who seek to destroy them.[16] Because it is widely believed that this was the first verse to be revealed to Muslims allowing fighting in self-defense against injustice, this verse assumes critical importance today in reminding us of the original purpose of undertaking the combative jihad. The Qur'anic ecumenical call to action in defense of all houses of worship contained in this verse underscores that the struggle to achieve a moral and just world order today, in which we all equally have a stake, must be a multifaith and multicultural one. In particular, this verse should remind certain Muslims today who practice exclusivism in the name of Islam that our fellowship, according to the Qur'an itself, does not extend only to members of our own faith tradition but to all believers of diverse faith communities.

The theme of the oneness of humankind is repeated several times in the Qur'an. We are told that all human beings have been "created of a single soul" (4:1) and that they are all descended from the same parents (49:13). At the same time, the Qur'an also recognizes and accepts the physical diversity of God's creation. This is not a contradiction; the Islamic world view has often been described as based on diversity within unity, or "the integration of multiplicity into Unity."[17] Within the global community of human beings who are equal before the Divine Being, linguistic, ethnic, and cultural differences are embraced as part of God's mercy. These differences are also projected as signs or miracles of God. "And of His signs," the Qur'an says, "is the creation of the heavens and the earth and the diversity of your tongues and colors. Surely there are signs in this for the learned." (30:22)

Diversity in physical appearance, ethnic and cultural traits, and so forth, is thus to be respected and celebrated as a desired feature of the divine design.

In a significant Qur'anic verse (2:117), we are given a definition of a truly righteous person that is revealing of the qualities of such an individual. This verse states,

> It is not righteousness (or virtue) that you turn your faces toward the East and the West, but righteousness belongs to the one who believes in God, and the Last Day, and the angels and the Book and the prophets, and who gives away wealth out of love for Him to the near of kin and to the orphans, to the needy, the traveler and to those who ask and in order to set slaves free. These are they who keep up prayer and pay the obligatory alms, who keep their promise when they make one, and are patient in distress and affliction and in times of conflict—these are they who fulfil their duty.

This verse may be understood to support the basic premise of religious pluralism by de-emphasizing adherence to a particular creed or belief as a litmus test for righteousness. It stresses rather the importance of compassionate behavior, sensitivity to others' sufferings and needs, and one's own steadfastness in the face of calamities and afflictions. Only such persons are deemed truly righteous.

The Arabic word used in Qur'an 2:117 to refer to righteousness is al-birr and here it is equated with faith. In exegesis of this verse, Ibn Kathir records a hadith in which the Prophet, when asked to define faith by one of his Companions replied, "When you perform a good deed, your heart loves it, and when you perform a bad deed, your heart hates it."[18] According to this report, righteousness is predicated on its active manifestation in acts of charity toward others, which the believer's heart recognizes as intrinsically good. To phrase it differently, we may say that the properly formed conscience of the faithful allows them to recognize what is inherently right or bad and encourages them to enact or practice goodness. This is a nonsectarian approach to gauging the moral valence of actions. Of course, like any other faith tradition, Islam has its own truth claims and requires of its adherents (as do other religions) allegiance to a core set of confessional/creedal principles and practices. Beyond such core beliefs and at the level of deeds, we are able to move into the realm of recognized commonalities among many faith traditions, based on universal, shared notions of human dignity, charity, and justice, for example. Interfaith dialogue is premised on the discovery of such common ground among different religious groups and the formulation of a shared religious idiom.

Throughout time, Muslims of good will have understood these inclusive verses to sanction the coexistence of diverse peoples and nations. One may retrieve valuable examples from the early history of Muslims to document that this Qur'anic ideal was often translated into reality. When the Prophet emigrated from Mecca to Medina (two cities in what is Saudi Arabia today), he found himself in a pluralist situation. There was religious as well as tribal diversity in Medina. He not only accepted this diversity but legitimized it by drawing up an agreement with different religious and tribal groups and accorded them specific rights on the basis of this agreement. This agreement is known as the Pact or Constitution of Medina, and it represented the foundation of a revolutionary new political and religious culture. What is noteworthy in this agreement is that all together—Muslims of

Quraysh from Mecca, Muslims of Medina belonging to various tribes, and the Jews of Medina belonging to different tribes—were understood to constitute a unified community (Ar. *umma*).[19]

Although Muslims would later arrogate the term *umma* to refer only to the Muslim community, it is noteworthy that the Qur'an uses this term, not only in reference to the community of Muslims, but to the communities of Jews and Christians as well, and specifically to refer to the righteous contingent within distinctive religious communities. Thus righteous Muslims constitute an *umma wasa-tan* ("a middle community;" Qur'an 2:143), whereas righteous Jews and Christians constitute an *umma muqtasida* ("a balanced community;" 5:66) and *umma qa'ima* ("an upright community;" Qur'an 3:13). (The principle of moderation as a defining characteristic of the faithful is further discussed later). The Constitution's emphasis on righteousness and upright behavior rather than on religious affiliation as constituting the principal requirements for membership within the first Muslim polity in Medina is thus shaped by this Qur'anic perspective on *umma*.[20] Historians of Islam and other scholars have pointed to the Constitution of Medina as the earliest documentary evidence of the pluralist impulse within Islam.[21]

After the death of the Prophet, when Islam expanded out of the Arabian peninsula into Syria, Palestine, and Egypt, it encountered the earlier largely Christian populations of these areas. In return for the payment of a poll tax (*jizya*) from which the poor, the elderly, and religious functionaries were generally exempt, these Christian populations were granted protection of life and property and the right to practice their religion. Popular anecdotes recount how Coptic Christians in Egypt, weary of being persecuted as heretics by the Byzantines, celebrated the arrival of the Muslim Arabs on their shores in the seventh century.[22] For at least two centuries after the early Muslim conquests, until roughly the middle of the tenth century, the majority of the population in these regions remained Christian.[23] This fact clearly establishes that they were not coerced en masse into accepting the faith of their rulers. This is as it should be; the Qur'an after all categorically declares that there is no compulsion in religion (Qur'an 2:256).

Our historical sources point to the active participation of many Christians and Jews in the flourishing intellectual life of the Islamic world from the eighth century on. In the eighth and ninth centuries, Syriac-speaking Christians, funded by their Muslim patrons, translated the classics of the ancient world written in Greek and Old Persian, for example, into first their native tongue and then into Arabic. Their inclusion in the intellectual life of medieval Islam helped preserve the wisdom of the ancient world and allowed for its later transmission to medieval Europe.[24] Individual Christians and Jews sometimes obtained high positions in Muslim administrations throughout the premodern period. Two Christian physicians, for example, attended to Harun al-Rashid, the celebrated ruler in Baghdad of *Arabian Nights* fame; and Saladin, during the period of the Crusades, had in his employ a Jewish physician, the famous Maimonides or Ibn Maymun, as he was called in Arabic. In medieval Muslim Spain, Jews and Christians were active participants in the cultural and intellectual life that flourished under the Moors. The mutually beneficial interactions among Muslims and Jews, in particular in Muslim Spain, led to the creation of what may be called Judeo-Arabic or Judeo-Islamic culture. In the fourteenth century, Jews forced to flee from the atrocities of the Spanish Reconquista in the fifteenth century found refuge in Muslim Ottoman lands and established thriving, religiously autonomous communities there. Clearly, the Qur'an's decree of noncompulsion in religion, and its injunction to show kindness toward Jews and Christians in particular, were often taken quite seriously by those who revered it as sacred scripture.

Muslim receptivity to people from the Abrahamic faith traditions, who are fellow monotheists and share to a considerable extent a similar scriptural and prophetic tradition, is understandable. It is worthy of note that, as Muslims encountered over time those outside the monotheistic Abrahamic tradition, the Qur'anic principle of noncoercion in faith was also generally extended to them. Thus the Zoroastrians of Persia and the Hindus of India also came to be accorded the status of "protected people" by their Muslim rulers, a status traditionally reserved for Jews and Christians.[25] This meant that, in return for their loyalty to the state and payment of their taxes, they, too, could continue to practice their religion and their traditional way of life.

A disclaimer is appropriate here: by no means am I implying here that this was a halcyon age completely free of discrimination and persecution of religious minorities. Non-Muslims generally did not enjoy the full rights of Muslims in the premodern period when membership in the community was primarily determined on the basis of faith. However, by the standards of the premodern age, the elastic concept of the "People of the Book" allowed multiple religious communities to coexist, often peacefully, for stretches of time under various Muslim rulers. The rubric "Islamic civilization" masks the fact that at its zenith, it was, in fact, quite a hybrid and cosmopolitan civilization, whose members were of different ethnic, religious, and cultural backgrounds

The idea of pluralism is considered dangerous by many today, and it was so considered by many in the past, on the grounds that it promotes relativism and contributes to a watering down of one's religious identity. A number of medieval exegetes by the tenth century began to propagate the daring and self-serving idea that Qur'an 2:256, with its injunction against coercion in religious matters, had been abrogated by verses that allow fighting against non-Muslims (such as Qur'an 9:5 and 9:29) under specific conditions.[26] Some of them were also of the opinion that Qur'an 5:48, which we have pointed to as the quintessential pluralist verse, was to be understood as referring only to those communities that had predated the rise of historical Islam. Non-Muslim religious communities after the time of Islam were not to be regarded as following an equally valid law and way of life.[27]

Such illiberal interpretations (magnified by today's extremists), which considerably undermined the Qur'anic ethos, was by no means accepted by all scholars in the premodern period. Thus two of the best known Qur'an commentators mentioned before, al-Tabari (d. 923)[28] and Ibn Kathir (d. 1373)[29] resolutely maintained that Qur'an 2:256 had not been abrogated and its injunction remained valid for all time. A later work on the Qur'anic sciences by the Mamluk scholar al-Suyuti (d. 1505) does not refer to Qur'an 2:256 as an abrogated verse.[30] It is, therefore, obvious that, as late as the fifteenth century, there was by no means a scholarly consensus on the abrogation of Qur'an 2:256 and that the most influential commentators of the classical and medieval periods continued to maintain the normative applicability of this verse. The controversial principle of abrogation (Ar. *naskh*) and the frequently skewed and intolerant understandings of the text that it generated are being revisited by a number of Muslim scholars today in a highly critical vein.

Examples of such exegetical dialectics in the premodern period reveal to us competing and complex trends in communal identity formation, particularly in relation to non-Muslims. Muslim supersessionists, who eventually came to form the predominant school of thought, subscribed to the superiority of Islam over other revealed religions (although not necessarily always denying their validity). This happened despite the fact that no explicit principle of supersession may be adduced from the Qur'anic text. The Qur'an instead usually refers to itself as confirming prior revelations. One such verse is the first part of Qur'an 5:48 which states, "And to you [O Muhammad] we have sent down the Book [the Qur'an] in truth confirming (*musaddiq*) the Books [i.e., prior revelations] that have come before it and as a protector over them." But a certain degree of Muslim triumphalism vis-à-vis their non-Muslim subjects came to color the exegetes' readings of scripture, subverting the overall Qur'anic message of religious pluralism. Thus, most exegetes privileged Qur'an 3:85 over 5:48; the former verse states, "Whoso desires another religion than Islam, it shall not be accepted of him; in the next world he shall be among the losers," preferring to understand Islam in the narrow, confessional sense.[31] Such reductive understandings ensued from atomistic readings of Qur'anic verses. A holistic approach to the text would have instead allowed these exegetes to read, for example Qur'an 3:85, within a discursive, comparative relationship to other verses, such as Qur'an 3:67,[32] which posit a universal, ecumenical understanding of *Islam* and *Muslims*.

The rise of extremism in most faith communities today has rendered *pluralism* an urgent global shibboleth today. Inclusivist readings of foundational religious texts that promote a pluralist world-view are thus imperative for people of faith who wish to combat intolerance in their midst. A good sense of the history of the reception of these historical texts in variegated circumstances is also crucial. In regard to Muslims, it is essential, as Fazlur Rahman has observed, that they see beyond the historical formulations of their faith and return to the wellsprings of the Qur'an for moral and spiritual renewal today. In this manner, Muslims will be able "to distinguish clearly between normative Islam and historical Islam."[33] Those who are doing precisely that have been rewarded by being able to retrieve a Qur'anic world view that is accepting of diversity and peaceful co-existence, a world view that was often mirrored in the praxis of particularly the early Muslim community and that is especially relevant to our own times.[34] Putting it in today's terms, the Qur'anic verses 49:13 and 30:22, in particular, may be understood to contain a ringing endorsement of religious, cultural, and ethnic pluralism that is not only tolerated but embraced as being a part of the overall divine plan.

▪ MODERATION AS A DEFINING CHARACTERISTIC OF THE FAITHFUL

The Qur'anic definition of righteous Muslims as constituting a middle or moderate nation/community (Ar. *umma wasat*) in Qur'an 2:143 is well known among Muslims and has been enthusiastically adopted by them as a self-designation and as a divine mandate to avoid extremes in one's beliefs and conduct. This verse states, "We have made you [believers] into a middle community, so that you may bear witness [to the truth] before others and so that the Messenger may bear witness [to it] before you." What is less well known, however, is that this verse has its parallel in Qur'an 5:66 in which righteous Jews and Christians are also described as constituting a balanced or moderate" community (Ar. *umma muqtasida*). This verse states, "If they [sc. The People of the Book] had upheld the Torah and the Gospel and what was sent down to them from their Lord, they would have been given abundance from above and from below. Some of them constitute a balanced community, but many of them are prone to wrong-doing." In these two verses taken together, the Qur'an thus suggests that it is subscription to a common standard of righteousness and upright conduct that determines the salvific nature of a religious community, and not the denominational label it chooses to wear. Such a view transcends sectarianism and offers the possibility of formulating universal principles of ethical and moral conduct that help contribute to the formation of a moderate and tolerant global community today.[35]

A brief comparison of early and late Qur'an commentaries on the meanings of the epithets *wasat* and *muqtasida* as they occur in these two verses are illuminating of changing Muslim self-understanding of the nature of their community and its relation with Jews and Muslims. With regard to Qur'an 2:143, the well-known exegete al-Tarbari glosses *wasat* as "just" (*'adl*). He cites relevant *hadiths* going back to the Companion Abu Sa'id al-Khudri and in one instance to another Companion Abu Hurayra, which equate "a middle nation" (*umma wasat*) with "a just people" (*'udul*). According to one report, Muslims have been called a middle nation because "they mediate between the Prophet, peace and blessings be upon him, and [the rest of] the nations."[36]

Al-Tabari refers to another common signification of *wasat*: the part that is between two extremes. This allows him to understand *wasat* in relation to Muslims in a more confessional vein. He remarks that God chose to describe Muslims as "middle" because of their moderation in religion (*li-tawassutihim fi'l-din*). This is in contrast to Christians on the one hand who are regarded as being excessive in their veneration of Christ and in their practice of asceticism and, on the other, in contrast to Jews who are regarded as being too legalistic in their religious practices and prone to rejecting their prophets. In contrast, asserts al-Tabari, Muslims are people of moderation and balance (*ahl tawassut wa-i'tidal*) in the practice of their religion.[37] The verse, according to al-Tabari, may, therefore, also be parsed to mean that Muslims are the best of all religious communities. The term *wasat*, he remarks, commonly refers in Arabic to the best (*al-khiyar*). Thus, a common Arabic expression that states "Someone is of middle rank in his clan," is intended to underscore the greatly elevated status of that person. Clearly al-Tabari here understands this phrase to confer singular distinction on Muslims to the exception of any other religious group.[38]

Other exegetes similarly emphasized "justness" as being an important component of "middleness" or "moderation." Thus the thirteenth century Andalusian exegete Muhammad b. Ahmad al-Qurtubi (d. 1273) was of the opinion that "middle" is equal to "just," because the most praiseworthy part of a thing is its middle. He cites a *hadith* to this effect in which the Prophet glosses "middle" as "just."[39] The middle of a valley, al-Qurtubi continues, is its best spot, where water and grass are the most plentiful. Because the middle naturally avoids excess and deficiency, it is praiseworthy as is this community (sc. Muslims). 'Ali b. Abi Talib, the prominent Companion and the fourth caliph (and the first imam of the Shi'a) is known to have recommended always adopting the middle way, for that is where the mighty and the lowly meet.[40] Al-Qurtubi derives further significance from the continuation of the verse "so that you may be witnesses over the people." He understands it to affirm the essential justness of Muslims as a community and entrusting them with being witnesses over other communities on the basis of this attribute.[41]

In more recent times, Muhammad 'Abduh (d. 1905), the famous reformist thinker who served as the rector of al-Azhar University concurred with earlier exegetes that "middle" (*wasat*) as occurs in Qur'an 2:143 means "just" and "the best." Anything that goes beyond the golden mean is excessive whereas that which falls short of it veers toward the other extreme and is deficient, he says. Both extremes represent deviations from "the upright way" and, therefore, are wrong and blameworthy. The "best" (*al-khiyar*) is the middle between two extremes of a matter. 'Abduh maintains that by virtue of being a middle community, the Muslims are just and the best, because, in their beliefs, character, and deeds, they avoid the extremism (*al-ghuluw*) of those who are immoderate in their religion and the shortcomings of those who are remiss in their religious practices. Before the rise of Islam, he says, people were either focused exclusively on the physical and mechanical observance of religion or were given over totally to asceticism and withdrawal from the world. Islam chooses the mean between these two extremes by acknowledging both the otherworldly and worldly aspects of religion.[42]

With regard to commentaries on Qur'an 5:66, we see a clear tension between early inclusive Muslim views of the People of the Book based on shared values and later, more exclusive views of them. Thus in the *Tanwir al-miqbas*, the Qur'an commentary attributed to Ibn 'Abbas, *umma muqtasida* is glossed as referring to a just and upright group from among the People of the Book This group, according to the author, included 'Abd Allah b. Salam and his companions; Buhayra the monk and his companions; the Negus, the king of Abyssinia; and Salman al-Farisi and his companions.[43] In this possibly quite early exegesis (if its first/seventh century provenance is accepted), *umma muqtasida* in particular includes Christians who are popularly known to have been exceptionally well disposed toward Islam, some of whom had actively aided Muslims in their time of dire need, as did the Negus of Abyssinia, and who recognized their scriptural kinship to Muslims without converting to Islam, like Buhayra the monk.[44]

In al-Tabari's important commentary on this verse, we find an interesting and significant collection of exegetical reports attributed to early exegetes from the first and second centuries of Islam, which allow us to re-create a historically shifting trajectory of meanings ascribed to the term *umma muqtasida* over time. One such report is from the well-known Companion Qatada who explains "a moderate community" as referring to those from among the People of the Book who "abide by His book and His command," whereas the rest who do not are criticized in the Qur'an for their wrongdoing. A very early exegete al-Suddi (d. 745) is quoted by al-Tabari as equating *umma muqtasida* with "a believing (*mu'mina*) community."

Ibn Zayd, another early authority, says that umma muqtasida referred to people who were known for their obedience to God (ahl ta'at allah), "and these are the People of the Book." Finally, the Successor al-Rabi'b. Anas (d. 756) is cited as saying that umma muqtasida referred broadly to "those who are neither harsh nor excessive in their religion."[45] These specific glosses going back to early authorities, as recorded by al-Tabari, recognize and praise moderation among observant Jews and Christians who are true to their own scripture and laws and who are thus obedient to God. Furthermore, these moderate scriptuaries are distinguished by their temperateness and kindliness in the practice of their religious duties.

Al-Tabari himself, however, in the late ninth century, understands the term umma muqtasida in a more partisan vein. He glosses this phrase as a reference to those People of the Book who are "moderate in their speech regarding Jesus, son of Mary, speaking the truth about him that he is the Messenger of God and His word which He cast into Mary and a spirit from Him," and not exceeding the bounds by saying that he was divine nor being remiss in saying that he lacked divine guidance.[46] Al-Tabari's exegesis indicates to us that, by his time, Muslim self-definition in relation to Jews and Christians had become markedly more confessional, focusing more on doctrinal issues rather than on shared values of righteous conduct.

The well-known fourteenth-century exegete Fakhr al-Din al-Razi (d. 1209) documented these historical attitudinal changes. In his exegesis of Qur'an 5:66, al-Razi defines iqtisad, which is related to the adjective muqtasida, as "moderation" or "judicious balance" (al-i'tidal) in ones's deeds that avoids both excess (ghuluw) and a falling short of something (taqsir). With regard to the term al-umma al-muqtasida, al-Razi points to two schools of thought on this issue. One of them regards only those who believed [sc. embraced Islam] from among the People of the Book, such as 'Abd Allah b. Salam from among the Jews and the Negus[47] from among the Christians, as belonging to the umma muqtasida. The other school, however, was of the opinion that umma muqtasida referred to practicing Jews and Christians in general who are just and upright in their religion and not harsh in their behavior. Al-Razi points out that praise for upright scriptuaries is found elsewhere in the Qur'an, as in 3:75, which states, "There are those among the People of the Book who, if you were to give them a coin for safekeeping, they would return it to you."[48] Jews and Christians, according to this verse, are, thus, equally capable of being just and honest, and such a trustworthy contingent among them also deserves the epithet muqtasida, according to this school of thought.

Al-Qurtubi in his brief commentary on the meaning of muqtasida, echoes the views of many of his predecessors. Like al-Razi, he too identifies two strands of thinking on this issue. One, to which al-Qurtubi himself subscribes, was of the opinion that this phrase refers to those formerly Jews and Christians who embraced Islam, such as the Negus, Salman al-Farisi, and 'Abd Allah b. Salam for "they were temperate (iqtasadu) and only said what was appropriate in regard to Jesus and Muhammad, upon them be blessings and peace." Al-Qurtubi continues that other exegetes, however, have understood this phrase to refer to those among the People of the Book who did not convert to Islam but who, nevertheless, "did not cause any harm nor did they jeer [sc. at Muslims]—and God knows best."[49]

The twentieth century exegete, Muhammad ʿAbduh, echoes many of his pre-modern predecessors in his explanation of *umma muqtasida* but also breaks new ground by foregrounding the criterion of righteous and just conduct as under-girding the Qurʾanic discourse on moderation. He says that the phrase refers to a "contingent of people who are moderate and upright in matters of religion" (*jamaʿa muʿtadila fi amr al-din*), who are neither extreme nor deficient in the practice of their faith." Some believed that this moderate contingent referred to upright Jews and Christians whereas others thought that it referred to those from among the People of the Book who had embraced Islam (*aslamu*). ʿAbduh comments that no community or nation has ever lacked a righteous contingent of people, usually a minority, who strive to better and elevate their community. Nations are headed for disaster because of the larger numbers of people who resort to wrongdoing and wreak havoc on earth and the fewer numbers of those who do good.[50]

From among this contingent of upright people from various communities who hasten to do good and effect reform, continues ʿAbduh, arise prophets and sages who revive religion at different times in history. When the Islamic reform was ini-tiated through the speech of the Prophet Muhammad, the upright and moderate contingent from among the People of the Book and others besides them were receptive to it (*qabbalahu*).[51] They, "along with their Arab brothers," he comments, are thus the revivers of monotheism, virtue, and decency, of the sciences, the arts, and of civilization."

Interestingly, unlike any premodern exegete, ʿAbduh furthermore turns Qurʾanic criticism of lax Jews and Christians against lax Muslims of his time, who con-tribute to corruption on earth "all the while taking pride in their religion, despite the fact that they fail to live up to the precepts of its sacred book and boast of the virtues of their prophet while they abandon his practice and customs." Lax Muslims have also abandoned the task divinely entrusted to them "of returning to the Qurʾan and establishing its precepts, by being receptive to wisdom (*hikma*) wher-ever it may be found, and by supporting reform wherever they may encounter it." Thus ʿAbduh clearly indicates that Muslims do not earn the designation of "a mid-dle or moderate community" by virtue of being Muslims in name or by cultural ascription, but rather, as is the case of Jews and Christians, by living up to the moral and ethical standards enjoined by their own scripture.

In summary of this section, we note that many premodern exegetes in their exegesis of Qurʾan 2:143 drew a parallel between the Arabic terms *wasat* and *khi-yar*, which allowed them to postulate the theological syllogism that Muslims as the "middle nation" must also be the "best nation." "Middleness" or "moderation" was accordingly construed as the most excellent theological midpoint between Christian and Jewish doctrines and praxis, thus avoiding the excessive other-worldliness of Christianity and the excessive legalism of Judaism, for example. Muslims, it was confidently asserted, situate themselves squarely in the middle and avoid the extremes of these two groups. Moderation was, therefore, invoked by many premodern exegetes as a quality inhering in the salvific Muslim community, denied to the People of the Book who, by virtue of their doctrinal tenets and reli-gious practices, were prone to immoderation.

The same exegetes had to take note of Qur'an 5:66, however, which describes a righteous contingent of Christians and Jews as constituting a "moderate/balanced nation" (*umma muqtasida*). How to reconcile potentially conflicting constructions of moderation and the salvific faith communities signified thereby? The doctrine of supersession effectively resolved this dilemma for many scholars. Only those Jews and Christians who had gone on to embrace Islam were included by them under the rubric of *umma muqtasida*. More punctilious scholars noted, however, that Qur'an 3:75, for example, praised certain People of the Book as being righteous and honorable in their words. The conclusion that the attribute of *iqtisad* ("moderation;" "fairness") inhered in these upright Jews and Christians because of their righteous actions and was not contingent on their doctrinal beliefs could logically be reached on the basis of these verses. *Umma muqtasida* just as conceivably, if not with better cause, could thus be understood as a reference to practicing Jews and Christians who were upright and righteous in their conduct. Thus the ecumenical exegetes recognized moderation in all righteous practitioners of the Abrahamic faith communities, before and after the advent of Islam, who furthermore recognized their common spiritual kinship and came to the aid of one another. On the basis of the evidence provided by al-Tabari, this seems to have been the more prevalent view in the first two centuries of Islam.

Over time, however, the supersessionist view became the more dominant one in the later medieval period. As mentioned earlier, this happened despite the fact that the nonsupersessionist view is more in accordance with the Qur'anic perspective on the relations between the Abrahamic communities than the supersessionist one. The competing supersessionist and ecumenical or irenic readings of these two critical verses highlight for us the complex ways in which Muslims related to non-Muslims in changing historical and sociopolitical circumstances, details of which we cannot fully engage in at this time. It also drives home for us that textual hermeneutics is frequently contingent on the reader's individual circumstances, including personal, intellectual, and ideological proclivities, as well as the specific social and political circumstances in which the reader finds himself or herself.

Thus, Islamists of the twentieth century read their vision of a highly politicized Islam into Qur'an 2:143 and 5:66, for example. For example, in the conceptualization of the fiery Egyptian activist of the twentieth century Sayyid Qutb (d. 1966), the "middle/moderate community" referred to in Qur'an 2:143 becomes an eschatological polity which "has ended the previous era of humanity's infancy, and oversees the subsequent age of intellectual maturity."[52] In his exegesis of Qur'an 5:66, Qutb dwells only briefly on the term *umma muqtasida*, observing that it refers to a minority among the People of the Book "who do not commit excesses against themselves" (*ghayr musrifa 'ala nafsiha*). He uses this observation as a point of departure, however, for discoursing at length on a single prescribed "Islamic way of life" (*al-minhaj al-islami*), which is all-encompassing and predicated on the intrinsic relation "between this world and the next, faith and reason, the physical and the spiritual." This is the original Way of God mandated for all people, according to Qutb, but only true Muslims (namely Islamists like himself) follow and implement it. This Way dictates the ordering of every aspect of human life, including political governance, which, as we know from his other writings, was a main concern of Qutb's.[53] Such an understanding derived from Qur'an 5:66 is uniquely Qutb's and reflects the Islamist's anxiety chafing under political suppression in the twentieth century to posit a counterutopian world that would empower him in every way and compensate for his current state of disenfranchisement.

Historically speaking, the concept of "moderation" served Muslims well in the past, allowing them to realize, among other things, toleration of different religious communities in their midst to a considerable extent, according to premodern legal conceptions of faith-based citizenship and social status. In our contemporary period, re-emphasis on what has always been a highly important and traditional value for Muslims has begun to lead to significant amplifications and rearticulations of the concept of moderation. Moderation defined primarily as just and temperate behavior in various spheres of life allows its application and endorsement as a universal norm. Invoking universal understandings of what constitutes justice and temperateness—among them, a lack of partisanship in assigning moral value to individual actions regardless of that person's religious or other ideological affiliation and avoidance of injury to another—moderation can be deployed as a universal socioethical organizational principle in pursuit of the common good of humanity (termed *maslaha* in Arabic). Thus, already in the nineteenth century, the reformist scholar 'Abduh would articulate the position that because of the foundational concern of Islam with justice and tolerance, Muslim-majority societies, in order to realize the Qur'anic principle of moderation, must enshrine equal rights for all citizens, with no distinction between "the Muslim and non-Muslim, the pious and the impious, the rich and the poor."[54] 'Abduh's more expansive and ecumenical view, reflecting an important if relatively downplayed strand of premodern Islamic thought, is more in keeping with the spirit of our own times and of our globalizing world, in which finding common ground and a common idiom to express our mutual concerns has never been more important. These new and aggrandized aspects of moderation, shorn of their theological and partisan implications, find universal resonance today.

▦ CONCLUSION

In my final remarks, I would like to point to parallels between the Hebrew Bible's notion of hospitality to "the other" (*ger*), the Christian Bible's notion of loving one's neighbor as oneself, and the previously discussed Qur'anic concept of *ta'aruf.* Positive interaction with the other, which *hospitality, neighborliness,* and *ta'aruf* all signify, takes us considerably beyond mere coexistence. The valorization of difference as a necessary, divinely mandated positive feature of earthly existence allows us to relate to "the other" on the basis of mutual respect, equality, *and humility.* Finally, the adoption of moderation as a religious and ethical precept has a particular resonance in our fractious world today threatened by the extremism of religious and cultural supremacists in all the Abrahamic communities. In an age beset with strife and hate-mongering fomented by a minority—albeit a powerful, lethal minority—putting into practice these notions of hospitality and "mutual knowing" and the recognition of shared religious values, such as moderation, derived from our respective scriptural traditions will prove to be (and is already proving to be) a powerful antidote to religious exclusivism and the violence it often breeds.

■ Notes

1. For Huntington's views, see his "The Clash of Civilizations?" *Foreign Affairs* 72 (1993):22–49 and *The Clash of Civilizations and the Remaking of World Order* (New York: Simon and Schuster, 1996). For a detailed rebuttal of Huntington's arguments, see Roy Mottahedeh, "The Clash of Civilizations: An Islamicist's Critique," *Harvard Middle Eastern and Islamic Review* 2 (1995):1–26.

2. For a historical recounting of such common ground particularly between Islam and Christianity, see Richard Bulliet, *The Case for Islamo-Christian Civilization* (New York: Columbia University Press, 2006); for all three Abrahamic faiths, see, for example, Maria Rosa Menocal, *The Ornament of the World: How Muslims, Jews, and Christians Created a Culture of Tolerance in Medieval Spain* (New York: Little, Brown, and Company, 2002).

3. The discussion of these first two concepts is largely based on my earlier article, "Celebrating Pluralism and Dialogue: Qur'anic Perspectives," *Journal of Ecumenical Studies* 42 (2007): 389–406.

4. Al-Tabari, *Jami' al-bayan fi tafsir al-Qur'an* ("The Compendium of Eloquence in Exegesis of the Qur'an") (Beirut: Dar al-Kutub al-'Ilmiyya, 1997), 11:399.

5. Ibn Kathir, *Tafsir al-Qur'an al-'azim* ("Exegesis of the Glorious Qur'an") (Beirut: Dar al-Jil, 1990), 4:219.

6. This verse states, "Say: 'We believe in God, and that which has been sent down to us, and sent down on Abraham and Ishmael, Isaac and Jacob, and the Tribes, and in that which was given to Moses and Jesus, and the Prophets, of their Lord; we make no distinction between any of them, and to Him we surrender (*muslimun*).'" For a discussion of inclusivist and exclusivist understandings of this verse and of the term Islam itself, see Abdulaziz Sachedina, *The Islamic Roots of Democratic Pluralism* (Oxford: Oxford University Press, 2001), 38–40.

7. For examples of such Muslim scholars and thinkers, see the two anthologies edited by Charles Kurzman, *Liberal Islam: a source book* (New York: Oxford University Press, 1998); and *Modernist Islam, 1840–1940: a sourcebook* (Oxford: Oxford University Press, 2002). See also my recent book *The First Muslims: History and Memory* (Oxford: Oneworld Publications, 2008), 148–95.

8. Sachedina, *Islamic Roots*, 40; also the comprehensive survey by Sohail Hashmi, "The Qur'an and Tolerance: An Interpretive Essay on Verse 5:48," *Journal of Human Rights* 2 (2003): 81–103, and references therein.

9. This is worth remembering in the context of the alleged episodes of Qur'an desecration reported in connection with the treatment of Muslim prisoners by American security guards at Guantanomo Bay in 2005.

10. For a useful overview of these broad historical trends, see W. Montgomery Watt, *Islamic Political Thought* (Edinburgh: Edinburgh University Press, 1968), 54–63.

11. See, for example, Sachedina, *Islamic Roots*, 94–96.

12. Al-Tabari, *Jami'al-bayan*, 11:398.

13. Ibn Kathir, *Tafsir*, 4:218.

14. Muqatil b. Sulayman al-Balkhi, *Tafsir Muqatil b. Sulayman*, ed. 'Abd Allah Mahmud Shihata (Cairo: Mu'assasat al-halabi, 1969), 3:130.

15. *Tanwir al-miqbas min tafsir Ibn 'Abbas* (Beirut:Dar al-fikr, 1992), 353.

16. How different is this perspective from that of the Taliban, who destroyed the Buddhist temples in Afghanistan because they were "pagan!"

17. Syed Hossein Nasr, *The Heart of Islam* (New York: HarperSanFrancisco, 2002), 6.

18. Ibn Kathir, *Tafsir*, 1:196.

19. See Ibn Hisham, *al-Sira al-nabawiyya* ("The Prophet's Biography"), ed. Suhayl Zakkar (Beirut: Dar al-fikr, 1992), 1:351 ff. For an accessible biography of the Prophet in English, see Martin Lings, *Muhammad: his life based on the earliest sources* (New York: Inner Traditions International, 1983).

20. For an English translation of the full text of the Constitution and an analysis of its main tenets, see Montgomery Watt, *Muhammad at Medina* (Oxford: Oxford University Press, 1956), 221–25; and R. B. Serjeant, "The Constitution of Medina," *The Islamic Quarterly* 8 (1964), 3–16.

21. For example, Ali Bulac, "The Medina Document," in *Liberal Islam: A Sourcebook*, ed. Charles Kurzman (Oxford: Oxford University Press, 1998), 169–84; Muqtedar Khan, "The Primacy of Political Philosophy," in Khaled Abou El Fadl, *Islam and the Challenge of Democracy* (Princeton: Princeton University Press, 2004), 66–67.

22. Al-Baladhuri, *Kitab futuh al-buldan* ("The Book of the Conquests of the Lands"), tr. by Philip Hitti as *The Origins of the Islamic State* (New York, 1916), 211; and T. W. Arnold, *The Preaching of Islam* (New York, 1913), 54.

23. For example, Robert Schick, *The Christian Communities of Palestine from Byzantine to Islamic Rule* (Princeton, 1995), 77–80, 96–97; Michael Morony, *Iraq after the Muslim Conquest* (Princeton, 1984), 332–83.

24. For an extensive discussion of this translation movement, see Dimitri Gutas, *Greek thought, Arabic culture: the Graeco-Arabic translation movement in Baghdad and early 'Abbasid society (2nd-4th/8th-10th centuries)* (London and New York: Routledge, 1998).

25. Cf. Richard Bulliet, *Case for Islamo-Christian Civilization*, 18.

26. These verses have been referred to as "the sword verses." For a criticism of the views of certain medieval jurists who gave precedence to these verses over more conciliatory ones and who read them divorced from their historical contexts, see my article "Competing Perspectives on *Jihad* and Martyrdom in Early Islamic Sources," in *Witnesses for the Faith: Christian and Muslim Perspectives on Martyrdom*, ed. Brian Wicker (Aldershot: Ashgate, 2006), 20–23. For a brief account of how militants today privilege these intolerant interpretations, see Khaled Abou El Fadl, *The Great Theft: Wrestling Islam from the Extremists* (New York: Harper, San Francisco, 2005), 217–19.

27. For a nuanced, insightful discussion of these competing hermeneutics, see Khaled Abou El Fadl, *The Place of Tolerance in Islam* (Boston: Beacon Press, 2002), 3–23.

28. Al-Tabari, *Jami'al-bayan*, 3:25.

29. Ibn Kathir, *Tafsir*, 1:416–17.

30. Al-Suyuti, *al-Itqan fi 'ulum al-qur'an* ("Certainty regarding the Qur'anic Sciences"), ed. Mustafa Dib al-Bugha (Damascus:Dar Ibn Kathir, 1993), 2:706–12.

31. For this important discussion, see Sachedina, *Islamic Roots*, 31 ff.; Tariq Ramadan, *Western Muslims and the Future of Islam* (Oxford: Oxford University Press, 2004), 206–207.

32. This verse states, "Abraham was neither a Jew nor a Christian, but an upright monotheist (*hanif*), one who had surrendered to God (*muslim*), and he was not one of the associationists."

33. Fazlur Rahman, *Islam and Modernity: Transformation of an Intellectual Tradition* (Chicago: University of Chicago Press, 1982), 141.

34. See, for example, the selection of writings by various modern liberal authors in the previously mentioned anthology *Liberal Islam: A Sourcebook*.

35. For a more extensive treatment of the concept of moderation in the Qur'an, see my article "The Hermeneutics of Inter-Faith Relations: Retrieving Moderation and Pluralism as Universal Principles in Qur'anic Exegeses," *Journal of Religious Ethics* 37 (2009): 331–54. This section draws upon relevant portions of this article.

36. Al-Tabari, *Jami'al-bayan*, 2:9–10.

37. Ibid., 2:8–9.

38. Ibid., 2:8.

39. Ibid.

40. Ibid., 2:149–50.

41. Ibid., 2:152.

42. Rashid Rida, *Tafsir al-Qur'an al-Hakim*, ed. Ibrahim Shams al-Din (Beirut: Dar al-kutub al-'ilmiyya, 1999), 2:4–5. This commentary is commonly known as *Tafsir al-Manar*, and is attributed to Muhammad 'Abduh, even though his devoted student Rida was responsible for its final compilation. The commentary, however, was never completed.

43. *Tanwir al-miqbas*, 128.

44. Some of the later exegetes tried to get around this by maintaining that both the Negus and Buhayra had accepted Islam.

45. Al-Tabari, *Jami'al-bayan*, 4:645–46.

46. Ibid.

47. Here, the Negus is clearly assumed to have formally accepted Islam.

48. Al-Razi, *al-Tafsir al-kabir* (Beirut: Dar ihya' al-turath al-'arabi, 1999), 4:399.

49. Al-Qurtubi, *al-Jami'li-ahkam al-qur'an*, ed. 'Abd al-Razzaq al-Mahdi (Beirut: Dar al-kitab al-'arabi, 2001) 6:228.

50. Rida, *Tafsir*, 6:381.

51. Being receptive to Islam, in this case, does not connote conversion to it. In his usage of the Arabic verb *qabbala* here, 'Abduh is rather highlighting the receptivity of righteous people to shared human values and recognition of their commonality on this basis without abandoning their own religions.

52. Sayyid Qutb, *Fi Zilal al-Qur'an* ("In the Shade of the Qur'an") (Cairo: Dar al-shuruq, 2001), 1:131–32.

53. Ibid., 2:930–31.

54. Muhammad 'Abduh, *Tafsir al-manar* (Cairo: Matba'at al-manar, 1931), 10:71.

PART II

Must Particularity Be Exclusive?

5 Humble Infallibility

James L. Heft

Though I am hardly a Freudian, I do find that as I get older many of the experiences I had growing up in Cleveland Ohio after World War II have had a profound formative influence on me. My parents were both farmers from central Ohio—my dad a Methodist and my mother a Roman Catholic. No one from my father's family, as I later learned, attended their wedding, and the Catholic priest held the wedding ceremony not in the Church but in the rectory—such was the way in which "mixed marriages" were handled then. I was very close to both my parents, especially my father.

When I was in the second grade, I remember vividly sitting in the back of the classroom and the teacher announcing that "if you are not Catholic, you will not go to heaven." I stood up, slammed my fist into the desk, and yelled, "That's not true!" I repeated that statement even louder, "That's not true! My daddy's going to heaven!" As vivid as that memory remains for me, I can not recall what happened immediately afterwards—whether I was ordered to the cloak room or told to shut up or what. But I do know now that this second-grade experience actually relativized authority figures in my Catholic Church (the teacher was a sister) whenever what they said contradicted my own experience.

I grew up in a Slovenian neighborhood on Cleveland's east side. The only Jews I knew as a boy were Mr. Friedman, for whom my father worked, and Mr. Figowitz, who sold burlap bags to my father. Mr. Friedman owned Cook Coffee Company and my father was the manager of its major warehouse and roasting plant; Mr. Figowitz called regularly on my father, who was one of his major customers. About both Mr. Friedman and Mr. Figowitz I have only positive memories, because my father liked and respected his employer for his fairness and generosity, and because our family received gifts, usually baskets of fruit, at Thanksgiving and Christmas from both Mr. Friedman and Mr. Figowitz. I don't recall my parents ever speaking of "kikes" or of "jewing someone down," but I do remember wondering in grade school why the Jews killed Jesus.

After joining the Marianists, a Catholic religious order, and going through college, I began teaching in 1965 in a Catholic high school in Cincinnati. With a neighboring public school and several nearby Protestant congregations, I launched a series of co-ed ecumenical retreats for high school students. I thought it important to increase mutual understanding, despite some hesitations on the part of some school administrators and parents.

In graduate school (University of Toronto) a few years later, I got to know Emil Fackenheim, Rosemary Reuther, and Gregory Baum. I read their stuff and got involved in the Jewish-Christian dialogue in Toronto. Not long after I arrived at the University of Dayton, I organized a trialogue at which a Jewish scholar, Protestant professor, and I held a number of evenings open to the public (the turnout was extraordinary) during which we discussed difficult issues. Dayton was one of the first cities in the United States to launch a Jewish-Christian dialogue, which has continued to this day.

Most recently, especially since 2001, I have been learning about Islam. Fordham University Press published a book I edited and introduced, *Beyond Violence: Religious Sources of Social Transformation in Judaism, Christianity and Islam* (2003); it is now in its second printing, and in 2006, I edited another book: *Passing the Faith on to the Next Generation: Jews, Christians and Muslims.*

What are some of the things I have learned? First, any form of absolutism (one religion has all the truth and the others are false) or relativism (all the religions are basically the same) will not prove helpful if religions are to come to understand and respect each other as they really are. Second, I believe that the affirmation of one's faith with an openness to learn from people of other religions is a very good form for interreligious dialogue. It is surely better than professing one's faith and then assuming that without too much work you can then figure out the "strengths" and "weaknesses" of the other religion. And third, I think interreligious dialogue is most rewarding when the participants become friends and live their faith as genuinely as possible. At heart, religion is interpersonal and transformative.

■ INTRODUCTION

On the morning of the of July 18, 1870, during a three-hour ceremony in St. Peter's Basilica in Rome, encircled by a severe lightning and thunderstorm, Pope Pius IX promulgated the doctrine of papal infallibility. Perhaps no dogma of the Catholic Church has raised more questions and caused more misunderstandings than the claim that the pope can define a matter of faith and morals infallibly. In fact, some bishops concluded wrongly after that council that there would not be any need for future councils, since the pope, on his own, would be able, they assumed, to determine what the truth of the faith is. Perpetuating this misunderstanding, a number of religious leaders in Israel stated, shortly after Pope Benedict XVI gave his address on September 12, 2006 on religion and violence in Regensburg Germany, that the pope would not be able to apologize for his remarks about Mohammed because he is infallible.

The great English religious thinker, John Henry Newman (1801–1890), to whose thought I will return later in this chapter, wrote in 1875 that, although he believed that the pope could, under very restricted conditions, express the faith infallibly, he nonetheless hoped that a future council would be convened to "trim" and "balance" the teaching so that extreme interpretations of it would be more clearly ruled out. That same year, in response to a memo sent out by Prince von Bismarck, the German Chancellor, that claimed that the pope at Vatican I had, in effect, usurped all the powers of local bishops, the German bishops issued a statement that underscored their own teaching authority. The bishops made it clear that when he (Bismarck) assumed that the pope henceforth determined by himself what is true teaching and could exercise direct jurisdiction in every diocese of the Church—that Bismarck was simply wrong.[1]

Bismarck only reflected what a lot of people still mistakenly believe about papal authority. A few years ago, I introduced a talk on the relationship between pope and bishops with the following paragraph:

> A bishop with a doctorate in ecclesiology recently gave a presentation on the nature of the Church to an ecumenical group. He explained to the group the difference between the church as a worldwide corporation with a central headquarters in Rome and the church as a communion of dioceses. The next day a local paper misquoted him as saying that "The Pope is the Pope of Rome, not the Pope of the World." Catholics who read the newspaper had a variety of reactions: the theologically informed thought it was a misquote, ordinary Catholics were confused, and militant conservatives were indignant. The bishop wrote a correction which the newspaper published. It read: "The Pope is the Bishop of Rome, not the bishop of the world as though the world were all one diocese." Catholics who read the correction had, according to the bishop, a variety to reactions: "Those familiar with theology had their puzzle solved, average Catholics remained confused, and militant conservatives remained indignant." The bishop then drew the conclusion that "for most Catholics the correct statement was as much of a problem as the incorrect one."[2]

The confusion mentioned here has to do primarily with the authority of the pope and bishops to govern. Theologians distinguish between papal primacy and papal infallibility. Both were given precise definition at Vatican I. Primacy has to do with governing authority; infallibility has to do with teaching authority. To focus on the governing authority of the pope and other bishops will only add to our confusion, because the principal focus in this paper is not their governing authority but their teaching authority, and primarily on that of the pope. Our theme, "learned ignorance," has to do primarily with teaching authority or, more specifically, with how much anyone, including the pope, the bishops and all believers, actually can understand and can affirm accurately about God and what God has revealed.

The phrase, *learned ignorance*, can be traced in the west to Nicholas of Cusa (1401–1464), who wrote about *docta ignorantia*. Philosophers employ this phrase to underscore "the ineffability of God, and the implication that those who think they have affirmative knowledge of God are truly ignorant, the knowledgeable ones being those who are aware that they are ignorant of him."[3] Other papers in this volume will explain in more depth Cusa's arguments for a more modest epistemology…epistemology necessary for those who attempt to understand God. needed by those who attempt to understand God. Suffice it to say here that *learned ignorance* has to do with both the inexpressible character of certain realities and the inescapable limitations of our own ways of understanding such realities—those realities being, in the context of the Catholic tradition, divine revelation and the very nature of God.

At the outset, it is helpful to recall the paradoxical nature of revelation. Revelation not only reveals, but it also conceals. The New Testament presents Jesus as a master storyteller and teacher who speaks to people in parables. Sometimes, especially in the Gospel of Mark, Jesus seems to want his identity and teaching to remain hidden from those not sufficiently prepared and properly disposed to receive and hear him.[4] Toward the end of the Gospel of John, the evangelist confides to the reader that though he "witnessed" all the things he has written about, "there are still many other things that Jesus did; yet if they were written about in detail, I doubt that there would be enough in the entire world to hold the books to record them" (John 21: 25). Centuries later, Thomas Aquinas, commenting on this passage, observed that the evangelist was referring to a "depth issue," not a "space issue." It other words, it wasn't because authors would not be able to find enough parchment to record all that they would write, but rather because the message of Jesus was so deep that they would never be able to express it adequately, however much they wrote.[5] At another point in the *Summa*, Thomas reminds believers that in making an affirmation of faith, the words that are used do not in themselves reach the reality affirmed: "The act of the believer does not reach its end in the proposition, but in the revealed reality itself."[6] In other words, the object of faith, God, can never be adequately contained or described in words. Our encounter with God and revelation always transcends our ability to articulate that encounter adequately.

In view of these biblical and theological reminders of our "learned ignorance" before the mystery of God, we can ask whether the Catholic dogma of papal infallibility ignores those reminders. To answer that question, we need to examine carefully just what is and is not affirmed by the dogma of papal infallibility. Fortunately, there have been official clarifications and interpretations of that dogma both at the Council itself and since 1870 that make it clearer what that dogma actually affirms. But is it really possible to speak of humble infallibility? And if the answer is yes, what might that mean for interfaith dialogue and a religious commitment to peacemaking?

■ THE TEACHING OF VATICAN COUNCIL I (1869–1870) IN CONTEXT

There are two important sources for examining the teaching of the Vatican Council I on papal infallibility: the text of the dogmatic definition itself, and the official commentary, or *relationes,* provided by the Council's theological commission headed by bishop Vincent Gasser who on July 11, one week before the actual promulgation of the dogma, gave a famous four-hour presentation in which he explained what the dogma would and would not be affirming.[7] For example, Gasser told some bishops, who had asked whether the pope's infallibility could be considered "absolute," that in no way (*nullo modo*) was it "absolute," for absolute infallibility belongs to God alone. Every other form of "infallibility," Gasser explained, has its limits and conditions.

The first such limit has to do with what can be taught infallibly—namely, matters of "faith and morals," a phrase commonly used to indicate that being a Christian has to do not only with what one believes, but also with how one acts. However, the phrase does not lend itself to exact definition.[8] The Council fathers distinguished between faith and morals on the one hand, and matters that pertain to Church government and discipline on the other. The latter were not part of the object of infallibility. Moreover, Gasser explained that infallibility has a direct and an indirect object: the direct object is revealed truth (what then is commonly referred to, in somewhat reified terms, as "the deposit of faith"), while the indirect objects are those truths not directly revealed but that are necessarily connected to revelation.

Just what are those indirect objects? Neither Vatican I nor Vatican II actually clarified this matter. Francis Sullivan, an eminent ecclesiologist (a theologian who studies the nature of the church), wrote in 1983 that, although most Catholic theologians affirm that there is a secondary object of infallibility, they are not of one mind about just what is contained in that object.[9] For example, some theologians have argued that the Church, in its capacity to define infallibly, should be able to condemn any argument that claims that only empirically verifiable knowledge is a trustworthy basis for truth. Others argue either that only the general norms of natural law (e.g., do good and avoid evil) can be defined infallibly, or that it is only a specific application of natural law (e.g., the condemnation of artificial birth control) that can be defined infallibly. Few theologians doubt that the Church has a right to speak about such matters with authority, but many differ on whether speaking about such matters with authority requires that the bishops also speak on them infallibly.[10]

It should be evident, then, that many questions remain about the indirect object of infallibility. I have already indicated that, even with the direct object of infallibility, that is, God and God's self-revelation in Jesus Christ, Catholic theology acknowledges only a limited ability to express these truths.

Gasser also explained that papal infallibility is neither a personal possession of the pope nor something the pope can exercise when he is separated from the rest of the Church. To try to avoid giving the impression that the pope himself as a private person is the primary source on infallible teachings, the bishops chose in the official texts of Vatican I not to speak of papal infallibility. Instead, they wrote about "the infallible teaching authority" of the pope. Moreover, Gasser explained that the source of infallibility was the Holy Spirit who *assisted* the pope.[11] This *assistance* was contrasted with *inspiration,* which properly applied only to revelation. Only the Scriptures are said to be *inspired*; the pope is not *inspired*. If he were *inspired,* he could promulgate new truths that constitute revelation. But he is only *assisted.* In other words, the pope is not a source of revelation, the only source of which is God alone. Rather, the pope is someone who always somewhat inadequately expresses in human language clarifications of what the revelation given by God is, and how it should be understood. The pope does not add to God's revelation his own new truths, but only clarifies the truth that has already been revealed.

To say that the infallible teaching authority of the pope is not separate from the rest of the Church means that it is fundamentally "relational."[12] In preparing for a definition of dogma, the pope is obligated, according to Vatican I, to use all the means available to search out the meaning of the truth, even though he does not have a checklist of specific means that he has to go through one after the other to discern that meaning. In other words, as the actual definition makes clear, the infallibility with which the pope is blessed is that same infallibility that Jesus first gave to the entire Church. The infallibility of the entire Church grounds papal infallibility.

Perhaps now, after making several official clarifications about the doctrine, it will be useful to look at Vatican I's actual dogmatic definition of the infallible teaching authority of the pope:

It is a dogma divinely revealed: that the Roman Pontiff when he speaks *ex cathedra,* that is, *when acting* in his office of shepherd and teacher of *all Christians,* he defines, by virtue of his supreme apostolic authority, doctrines concerning *faith and morals,* to be held by the universal Church, possesses through the divine *assistance* promised to him in the person of St. Peter, the infallibility with which the divine Redeemer *willed his Church to be endowed* in defining doctrine concerning *faith and morals*; and that such definitions are therefore *irreformable* of themselves, and *not from the consent of the Church.*

My commentary on the definition already sheds some light on this definition. Note also, however, the phrase "when acting." The quality of infallibility is not a permanent possession of the pope who may use it whenever he wants; it is, rather, the result of acting only in a certain strictly defined capacity—when he is, for example, acting as teacher of all Christians.[13] We have also noted that infallibility is strictly limited to matters of faith and morals, and that there is no consensus yet today on what might be included as the secondary object of infallibility.[14] Again, the infallible teaching authority of the pope is that which the Lord granted to the Church as a whole. That infallibility of the whole Church becomes the rule of faith for papal teaching.

However, there is that one infamous phrase that some of the bishops added on at the last minute to the end of the proposed definition. That phrase has contributed to the consistent misunderstanding of the pope's relationship with the rest of the Church. The end of the official definition states that the pope's definitions are *irreformabiles, ex sese non ex consensu ecclesiae* ("of themselves, and not from the consent of the Church"). What could be a more obvious statement of papal absolutism! Actually, a little historical background will save us from that obvious conclusion.[15] Some of the fathers of the Council remained concerned about a belief, which has the name of "Gallicanism," common since the seventeenth century among French bishops. That belief, affirmed by the French bishops in 1682, claimed that, in questions of faith, the judgment of the pope is not irreformable, "unless the consensus of the Church is present within it."[16] These bishops were convinced that the consensus of the whole teaching Church represented the genuine tradition of the Church, and that concentrating only on the teaching authority of the pope, without the full collaboration of consent of the bishops, was wrong. Vatican I explained that infallible teachings had to bear within them both the consent of the bishops and the infallibility with which the Church as a whole had been blessed. Though not expressed as clearly as a number of bishops at the Council wished, the final definition did make it possible to understand that the irreformability of papal definitions stemmed from the pope having first discerned the faith of the Church before defining it.[17] However, questions about the inescapable historical conditioning of any dogmatic definition did not arise as an issue for official Church teaching until Vatican II and specific debates subsequent to 1970.

In summary, then, the actual definition of Vatican I carefully circumscribed in a number of important ways the infallible teaching authority of the pope. These limitations disappointed some of the bishops at the Council who had been hoping for a maximalist definition. But even further precisions and limitations were to be added by the next Council of the Church, to which we now turn.

■ THE CONTRIBUTION OF VATICAN II (1962–1965)

If Vatican Council I had not been interrupted by the Franco-Prussian war, the bishops would have continued their meeting, and then, after defining the infallibility of the pope, proceeded to take up the issue of the nature of the whole Church. Had they done so, it is likely that their teaching on the authority of the pope would have found itself situated in the context of a broader teaching about the nature of the Church as a whole. Instead, Vatican I never reconvened, and the Church had to wait until an 80-year-old pope announced on January 25th, 1959 that he would convene another Council, Vatican II (1962–1965). Then, at this new Council, there would be extended treatment of the nature of the Church itself, from which the bishops of Vatican I knew papal teaching authority should never be separated.

Vatican II produced sixteen documents, two of them referred to as "Dogmatic Constitutions": the document on revelation (*Dei verbum,* or "The Word of God") and the document on the Church (*Lumen gentium,* or the "Light of the Nations").[18] Although the Council did not formally promulgate any infallible definitions, it brought about extensive changes. It dealt with two subjects that had fundamental theological content: the nature of revelation and the nature and mission of the Church. For the purposes of our theme, a few of the major emphases of the Council documents on the Church are most significant. The very sequence of the eight chapters of *Lumen gentium* is significant: it begins with a theological reflection on the Church as a mystery (rather than with a visible institution that has a hierarchy with levels of governance). The next chapter is about the members of the Church, the "people of God," all of whom (not just religious brothers, nuns or priests) are called by their baptism to holiness. Moreover, through the guidance of the Holy Spirit, they have a *Sensus fidei,* an instinct for sensing what is an authentic articulation of the faith. Only after these two chapters does the document begin, in chapter 3, to discuss the hierarchy.

The document also makes an important clarification by stating that the Church of Christ "subsists" in the Roman Catholic Church.[19] In the past, the official teaching stated that the Church of Christ is the Catholic Church. Since the Council, theologians have debated just what "*subsistit*" means, some stressing that *only* in the Catholic Church is the fullness of the Church of Christ to be found, whereas others argue that the Council never intended to modify "*subsistit*" with adverbs such as *only* and *fully.*[20]

The bishops of Vatican II extended respect not only to other Christian Churches, but also to other religions. In an important set of statements in several of the sixteen documents, the Council stated that the Jews remain the chosen people of God, and quoting Paul's letter to the Romans (9:4–5), stated that the covenants, the law, the worship, and the promises belong to the Jews. In a speech given in Mainz Germany on November 17, 1980, John Paul II interpreted *Nostra aetate*'s statement to mean that the covenant that God made with the Jews was not annulled by the revelation of Jesus Christ.[21] Moreover, it stated that "neither all Jews indiscriminately at that time, nor Jews today, can be charged with the crimes committed during [Christ's] passion."[22] Concerning the Muslim people, the same document affirms that "the plan of salvation "also includes those who acknowledge the Creator." First among them are Muslims, "who professing to hold the faith of Abraham, along with us adore the one and merciful God, who on the last day will judge mankind."[23] Vatican II makes it clear that God is mysteriously active in other religions. That acknowledgment not only requires the Church to respect these religions, but also suggests that Catholics should be characterized by a humility born from the realization that means of salvation exist outside of the Catholic Church.

Returning now to the issue of teaching authority and infallibility in the Catholic Church, the document on the Church, *Lumen gentium*, stated in paragraph twenty-five a number of important things for our topic. Most importantly, it stated that the infallibility with which the Lord endowed his whole Church "extends as far as extends the deposit of divine revelation" when it defines matters of faith and morals. But how far does that extend? Again, the extent of revelation is a matter for the Church to determine over time through its debates and dialogues. Not everything that is written in Scripture is to be understood as infallibly true or meant for our salvation. Not everything that has been officially taught in the past should continue to be officially taught. Some teachings are infallible, and their truth is irreformable; other teachings, though official, are not infallible and, therefore, may be found to be false or in need of revision so as to express the truth more adequately.

What, then, did Vatican II's teaching about the Church add to the theme of this volume? Did it go beyond those limitations outlined by Vatican I and, thereby, make it more credible to speak of "humble infallibility"? One of the most helpful summaries of the ways in which the texts of Vatican II provide a more "relational" context for the infallible teaching authority of the pope defined by Vatican I grew out of the extended conversation in the United States between Roman Catholic and Lutheran theologians.[24] The ordinary published text of these discussions followed a common format: theologians and historians from both churches wrote research papers on a selected topic, in this instance *Teaching Authority and Infallibility in the Church* (Volume 6). They then discussed and debated their papers at several meetings and afterwards hammered out a common statement with which they could all agree. Then they singled out those points on which they were still unable to agree. Finally, the participants then described how they perceived each others' disagreements, and sometimes they suggested ways they might be able to lessen or overcome them.

The Catholic participants in the discussions on papal infallibility agreed on seven ways in which the Vatican Council II helped make clearer what I have referred to as the relational meaning of papal teaching authority.[25] In quick summary, these seven ways include: (1) a clearer statement of how the teaching of the pope and bishops needs to pay attention to the "sense of the faith" possessed by the entire people of God; (2) a clearer statement of how the pope's teaching authority is to be connected with that of all the bishops; (3) a clearer explanation of how the faith of the entire Church needs to be embodied in all papal definitions; (4) a reminder that the entire Church is a pilgrim Church, always on its way and never arriving fully or perfectly in this life at its final goal; (5) a recognition that the Church is inescapably "affected by human finitude and sinfulness"; (6) a realization of the need for ecumenical sensitivity to the concerns of other Christians who either misunderstand papal teaching authority or might provide clarifications about its authentic nature; and (7) a recognition that there is a "hierarchy of truths," some truths being more central and easier to grasp than others. The Catholic participants in this dialogue noted that even with these helpful contextualizing qualifications, no last word has been given on the infallible teaching authority of the pope.[26] The conclusions of an official dialogue carried on by Lutheran and Catholic theologians in one nation do not constitute the official teachings of the universal Church. However, it is evident, as we shall see later, that these U.S. dialogues have influenced official Church teaching on the doctrine of justification.

It is interesting to speculate whether Vatican I, had it not been interrupted in 1870, would have produced a document on the Church that included the multifaceted "contextualization" of its teaching on the infallible teaching authority of the pope provided some ninety years later by Vatican II. But during the nineteenth century, Europe had not yet gone through two horrific world wars and the near decimation of the Jewish people. Nor would it have been able to draw on a rich vein of theological research beginning in the 1920s produced by scholars who returned to the writings of the early Church theologians. Nor, finally, would it have been enriched by the new biblical research encouraged by Pope Pius XII (1939–1958), who in his 1943 encyclical, *Divino afflante spiritu*, emphasized the importance of historical studies attentive to different cultures, languages and biblical genres, in contrast to the previous reliance on an ahistorical Thomistic philosophy.

New times raise new questions, or at least new questions about matters of continuing concern. The concerns of historians, who became more adept at documenting historical changes, became, in the twentieth century, a major preoccupation in a Church that characteristically prides itself on its continuity. These issues are hardly resolved today.

■ *MYSTERIUM ECCLESIAE* (1973)

The Catholic philosopher Alisdair MacIntyre suggests that a tradition, if it is to be alive, embodies continuity but also supports arguments. Although there is more to a tradition than arguments over what is good and true and beautiful, all vital traditions, according to MacIntyre, are characterized by debates, differences, and conflicts aimed at reaching a clearer understanding of what is worthwhile.[27] On the 100th anniversary of the definition of the infallible teaching authority of the pope, the prominent Catholic Swiss theologian Hans Küng published a provocative book on papal infallibility, *Unfehlbarkeit? Eine Anfrage.*[28] Perhaps the most important consequence of the book (which was not well received by most Catholic theologians and especially historians), was that it provoked an important clarification from the Vatican's Congregation for the Doctrine of the Faith (CDF), headed then by Cardinal Franjo Seper.[29]

The 1973 CDF document explained that dogmatic definitions, or infallible definitions, can be seen at one and the same time as true and still, at a later date, in need of reformulation—something the bishops gathered at Vatican I never explicitly addressed. *Mysterium ecclesiae* (*ME*) described an inescapable fourfold historical conditioning of every dogmatic definition due to (1) the limited state of human knowledge at the time of the original definition; (2) the changeable conceptions and thought patterns that belong to a certain period of time; (3) the specific concerns that motivated the definition; and (4) the limited expressive power of the language used at the time of definition. In the light of these limitations, it can be said that the words of the definition are not what is "irreformable," because they are capable of being improved, so that their meaning might be more easily understood. How to distinguish clearly between words and meaning is no simple matter, and beyond the scope of this paper. However, in the light of these four inescapable limitations of dogmatic definitions, the CDF recognizes at least one way in which a doctrine may be said to "develop."[30] It explains that "it sometimes happens that some dogmatic truth is first expressed incompletely (but not falsely), and at a later date, when considered in a broader context of faith or human knowledge, it receives a fuller and more perfect expression."[31]

ME quotes Vatican I which explained that one of the difficulties the Church encounters in handing on divine revelation is the mysterious character of revelation. It recognizes that such difficulties

> arise from the fact that the hidden mysteries of God [now quoting Vatican I] "by their nature so far transcend the human intellect that even if they are revealed to us and accepted by faith, they remain concealed by the veil of faith itself and are as it were wrapped in darkness."

ME affirms at one and the same time a continuity in truth but a necessary change in its expression. It cites John XXIII's speech at the opening of Vatican II: "This certain and unchangeable doctrine, to which faithful obedience is due, has to be explored and presented in a way that is demanded by our times. One thing is the deposit of faith, which consists of truths contained in sacred doctrine, another thing is the manner of presentation, always, however, with the same meaning and signification."[32]

It might be helpful to provide an example of how even an "irreformable" dogmatic statement might be reformulated for good reasons. Since the Council of Trent (1543–1565), a seeming intractable difference has been entrenched in how Lutherans and Roman Catholics believe a person is saved—the so-called doctrine of justification. Lutherans believed that a person was saved not through works, but through "faith alone." Catholics believed that a person was saved through both faith and works, but never explained precisely the relationship between faith and works—at least they never explained it in a way that would satisfy Lutherans. On the other hand, neither did the Lutherans make sufficient accommodation to the Catholic concern for good deeds performed meritoriously by grace. For hundreds of years, this difference was thought to be a Church-dividing issue that would never be overcome.

To the surprise of many Lutherans and Roman Catholics, that very difference was overcome in a Joint Declaration on the doctrine of justification issued on October 31, 1999 by the Lutheran World Federation and the Vatican. What happened? Did the "deposit of faith" change? Was a statement once thought to be true forever no longer true, or no longer accepted as an adequate formulation? Or did lengthy conversation between Lutheran and Catholic theologians, trying to overcome stereotypes, working to transcend the polemical history they shared, and committed to turn again and again to the Scriptures and the person of Jesus as their starting point—did these efforts eventually pay off by finding a new way of formulating the doctrine that allows both of them to see their understanding of justification expressed more adequately in a new way?

In the words of the Jesuit Cardinal Avery Dulles, the Joint Declaration was made possible by the "ecumenical method" currently endorsed by the Catholic Church. That method, picking up on John XXIII's distinction between the content of faith and its expression (also repeated in Vatican II's *Gaudium et spes*, par. 62), stresses the importance of taking into account different ways of thinking about the same mystery of the faith and the historical experiences of the dialogue partner. Consequently, the participants in the dialogue become aware that they are at home with forms of thought that are different than those with which their dialogue partners are familiar. As Dulles explains, "The Catholic thought-form, as expressed at Trent, is Scholastic, and heavily indebted to Greek metaphysics. The Lutheran thought-form is more existential, personalistic, or, as some prefer to say, relational." Added to his recognition of different thought forms is the desire to find language that can make traditional doctrines, such as that of justification, more meaningful and accessible to people today. As a result of their dialogue, and despite some continuing disagreements that are considered "tolerable" by both Lutheran and Catholics, they were able to affirm a Joint Declaration that reads as follows:

> Together we confess: by grace alone, in faith in Christ's saving work and not because of any merit on our part, we are accepted by God and receive the Holy Spirit, who renews our hearts while equipping and calling us to good works.[33]

This Joint Declaration is, in my view, an extraordinary achievement. In order to achieve unity, neither the Catholics nor the Lutherans "sold out." They both revisited their own polemically ridden historical formulations, tried to get closer to the reality of God's saving activity that stood behind those formulations, worked hard to return to the "sources" (the New Testament texts, and even more radically, to the saving activity of Jesus Christ expressed in those texts, which, though inspired, still never adequately express revealed truth), to see if it is possible to restate the meaning of justification in a fresh way, unencumbered (or at least less encumbered) by a history of conflict.

■ THEOLOGICAL FOUNDATIONS OF "LEARNED IGNORANCE"

The process that led up to the 1999 Joint Declaration calls for further reflection. There are other examples in the Catholic tradition as well, such as Vatican II's declaration on religious freedom and its condemnation of slavery. The statement of these newly understood teachings are achieved, it seems, through a sustained effort that helps scholars and pastors push through traditional formulations that did not pay sufficient attention to the deeper dimensions of revelation. Take for example that unfortunate moment in Pius IX's (1846–1878) papacy when, in 1864, he published the *Syllabus of Errors*. He condemned the separation of Church and state, the freedom of the press, of religion, and freedom of conscience. In the European historical context at that time, though not in the then-American-historical context, the separation of Church and state was understood by European Church leaders to mean the opposition of the state to the Church; the freedom of the press meant the freedom to attack the Church and usurp its property; the freedom of religion meant that people could choose to believe whatever they wanted, regardless of the truthfulness of their chosen beliefs; and the freedom of conscience meant that individuals were not obligated to discern and act on the truth. Most theologians in the nineteenth century (Newman was an outstanding exception) did not help the leadership of the Church understand how the separation of Church and state could be helpful to both, how a free press will serve the public better than propaganda machines, how freedom of religion need not mean people believing whatever they wanted to believe, and finally how freedom of conscience did not mean indifference to the truth, but rather the freedom to seek it without external coercion.[34]

Nor are all these difficult matters of thought-forms and adequate language resolved today. A major part of the challenge that believers face in finding more or less adequate language to express religious realities is that the realities themselves, and especially the reality of God, is—for Jews, Christians, and Muslims—at one and the same time revealed and hidden. Moreover, even the best of human intellects are limited in their capacity to grasp such revealed mysteries. I almost said "revealed truths," but saying that what is revealed is first a truth might lead a person to think that as a truth it can be adequately formulated or defined for all time.[35] For the Christian, what in the last analysis is revealed is a person, actually three persons: Father, Son, and Holy Spirit. Again, the human vehicle of Christian revelation is not first a set of teachings, but a person who loves, lays down his life for others, and is raised from the dead only to return to the Father so as to send forth the Holy Spirit.

■ REFOCUSING ON THE THEME OF "LEARNED IGNORANCE"

Both the Second Vatican Council (1962–1965) and the 1973 Vatican document *Mysterium ecclesiae,* distinguish between the truth itself and the manner of its expression, affirming that the truth could remain the same even if its manner of expression changes. It is difficult to look at the Lutheran-Catholic Joint Declaration without coming to the conclusion that the truth it expresses is not exactly the same as that which either the Lutherans or the Catholics of the sixteenth century defended. It can be hoped that the Joint Declaration expresses more adequately, indeed more truthfully, the meaning of justification than did the formulations that Reformation polemics produced.

I suggested earlier, without elaborating, that Cardinal Newman made a great theological contribution to the theme of learned ignorance. He did it in several ways. First, he did it by criticizing sharply the excesses of rationalism—the tendency to think that conceptualizations can adequately capture reality. Although still a member of the Anglican Church, he defined rationalism in *Tract* 73 as an abuse of reason, that is, "a use of it for purposes for which it was never intended, and is unfitted":

> To rationalize in matters of Revelation is to make our reason the standard and measure of the doctrines revealed; to stipulate that those doctrines should be such as to carry with them their own justification; to reject them, if they come in collision with our existing opinions or habits of thought, or with difficulty harmonized with our existing stock of knowledge.[36]

Newman also stressed the importance of consulting the laity who, Vatican II made clear, are blessed with a sense of the faith, a *sensus fidei*, not to be equated with theological sophistication, but with an ability to discern what is true and orthodox in official teaching.[37] As both Vatican I and Vatican II made clear, the pope and the bishops are required to discern the faith of the people before they attempt any definition of a dogma.[38] That discernment is not based on a Harris Poll, or a quantitative measurement such as counting votes. Rather, it is a qualitative estimate that seeks to discern prayerfully what resonates with the foundational mysteries of revelation. Finally, to mention only one more contribution of Newman to the theme of learned ignorance, he described three distinct groups in the Church: theologians, administrators, and the faithful; that is, professional writers, professional overseers (bishops), and people of faith (among whom, of course, one would hope to find theologians and bishops). But without all three interacting and learning from each other, theologians become rationalists, overseers dominate, and the people fall into superstition.[39]

■ CONCLUSION

The purpose of this chapter is to make a little clearer how, within the Catholic Church, authoritative teaching, which includes but is not limited to papal teaching authority, has learned how to take seriously the historical conditioning of official teaching, of dogmatic statements, and even of the inspired Word of God. These matters are, of course, complex, and no definitive formulations or resolutions can be expected. After all, the reality involved is how the divine and the human interact, a reality to be approached on one's knees, indeed, with humility.[40] On the other hand, the Church rightly affirms the legitimacy of formulating propositions, that is, statements, which, though always inadequate, are essential in the life of the Church's worship and identity. For many Christians, and especially for Catholics, not professing the Creed is unthinkable.

If it took more than thirty years of painstaking prayer, research, dialogue, friendship, and trust for two groups of Christian believers who share the broad tradition of western Christianity—Lutherans and Roman Catholics—to come to a common affirmation of the meaning of the doctrine of justification, what efforts, what humility, and what deep listening, prayer, and study will it take for different religions—such as Judaism, Christianity, and Islam—to come to understand each other better, to transcend existing stereotypes, turn to the mystery of God in each other's presence, and learn from each other while remaining faithful to their own religious traditions?

Appendix A Catholic Reflections on Vatican II and Papal Infallibility

1. Vatican II made it clearer than had Vatican I that the infallibility of the pastors (pope and bishops) must be related to the *sensus fidelium* or the "sense of faith" possessed by the entire people of God. The popes and bishops are infallible insofar as they are assisted in giving official expression and formulation to what is already the faith of the Church as a whole. This theme of Vatican II underscores what is implicit in the assertion of Vatican I that the pope has no other infallibility than that which Christ conferred upon the Church.

2. Vatican II saw the infallibility of the pope as closely connected with that of the college of bishops. Indeed, when it described the infallibility of the Roman pontiff, it referred to him as "head of the college of bishops," a phrase not used in the constitution *Pastor aeternus* of Vatican I. This suggests that normally, when he defines a matter of faith and morals, the pope should be expected to consult his fellow bishops and proceed in a collegial manner (*Lumen gentium* 25, with footnote referring to Gasser in M 52: 1213 AC).

3. Vatican II points out that although no antecedent or subsequent *juridical* approval by the Church is necessary for the exercise of infallibility, the assent of the Church can never be wanting to an authentic definition "on account of the activity of that same Holy Spirit, whereby the whole flock of Christ is preserved and progresses in unity of faith" (*LG* 25). This observation, together with Vatican II's emphasis on the *sensus fidelium,* puts in proper context the assertion of Vatican I that papal definitions are irreformable *ex sese, non autem ex consensu ecclesiae* (DS 3074).

4. Vatican II placed the teaching of the pope in the context of a pilgrim Church. His definitions of faith will reflect the situation of a Church whose task is "to show forth the mystery of the Lord in a faithful though shadowed way, until at last it will be revealed in total splendor" (*LG* 8). In other words, such definitions will inevitably suffer from a certain obscurity.

5. Vatican II recognized that the Church, insofar as it is an institution on earth, is always affected by human finitude and sinfulness (*UR* 6), failings that may leave their mark even on the most solemn acts of the highest *magisterium.* Even while true in the technical sense, a dogmatic statement may be ambiguous, untimely, overbearing, offensive, or otherwise deficient.

6. By its ecumenical orientation, Vatican II gave rise to the question: Will infallibility be able to serve the purpose for which it is intended without far more consultation with Christian communities not in full union with Rome?

7. Vatican II called attention to the fact that "in Catholic teaching there exists an order or 'hierarchy' of truths, since they vary in their relationship to the foundation of the Christian faith" (*UR* 11). This important principle suggests the possibility that authentic faith in the basic Christian message may exist without explicit belief in all defined dogmas—a question to be discussed below (Section V).[41]

■ Notes

1. F. Donald Logan, "The 1875 Statement of the German Bishops on Episcopal Powers," *The Jurist* XXI, 3, (July 1961).

2. James L. Heft, S.M., "From the Pope to the Bishops: Episcopal Authority from Vatican I to Vatican II," in *The Papacy and the Church in the United States,* ed. Bernard Cooke (Mahwah, NJ: Paulist Press, 1989), p. 57.

3. Ted Honderich, ed., *Oxford Companion to Philosophy,* (New York: Oxford University Press, 1995), p. 619. Of course, the traditions of "learned ignorance" arose long before Cusa. To take but one example, Augustine frequently made statements that convey our limited ability to understand God: "Man can say nothing of what he is incapable of feeling, but he can feel what he is incapable of putting into words"; or "You can know something which you are not aware that you know"; or again, "It is better to find God by not finding him than by finding not to find him" (all quotations from Henry Chadwick, *Augustine* (New York: Oxford University Press, 1986), pp. 48, 49, and 50, respectively.

4. See Mark's Gospel: "Now when he was away from the crowd, those present with the Twelve questioned him about the parables. He told them: 'To you the mystery of the reign of God has been confided. To the others outside it is all presented in parables so that they will look intently and not see, listen carefully and not understand, lest perhaps they repent and be forgiven' "(4: 10–12). Even though the mysteries had been confided to his apostles, Jesus makes clear in the very next verse what is obvious: that they still don't understand: "He said to them: 'You do not understand this parable? How then are you going to understand other figures like it?' " (4: 13). Scripture scholars write about Mark's "messianic secret," that is, about how Jesus repeatedly tells his followers not to tell others about what he confides to them, since others, without accompanying Jesus on the way to Gethsemane and suffering with him his passion, are bound to misunderstand him and make him into a divine wonder-worker rather than someone made obedient through suffering.

5. *Summa theologiae* III, Q. 42, Art. 4, "Should Christ have written down his teaching?"

6. *Summa theologiae,* II–II, Q. 2, Art. 2.

7. Bishop Gasser's official commentary on the proposed definition may be found in Mansi, IV (52). For an excellent summary of Gasser's presentation, see Dom. Cuthbert Butler's *The Vatican Council: 1869–1870* (Maryland: Newman Press, 1962—first, published in 1930 by Wesminster England: Longmans, Green and Co.). In what follows, I am drawing freely on my own work, James L. Heft, S.M., *John XXII (1316–1334) and Papal Teaching Authority* (Lewiston New York: Edwin Mellen Press, 1986), especially pages 207 ff.

8. Two Jewish participants in our trialogue, Reuven Firestone and Stanislaw Krajewski, raised questions about, and made comments on, the difficulty of drawing clear lines between acceptable and unacceptable interpretations. For example, they asked "What are the precise boundaries for orthodoxy?" and "What are the limits beyond which an exegete may not go?" Professor Krajewski reminded everyone that quoting texts from other religions is dangerous because people who do so rarely have a sense of the fluidity they enjoy within that tradition. Although Alisdair MacIntyre's (see note 23) description of a tradition as a socially embodied and historically extended argument helps underscore such fluidity, that fluidity should lead neither to relativism nor to silence. Assertions, though always inadequate, are necessary. After all, creation began with God speaking and revelation began with God's Word.

9. Francis A. Sullivan, S.J., *Magisterium: Teaching Authority in the Catholic Church* (Mahwah, NJ: Paulist Press, 1983), pp. 131–136.

10. On natural law, see Sullivan, pp. 138–152.

11. Ibid., p. 104.

12. Hans Urs von Balthasar, *Le complex antiromain: essai sur les structures ecclesiale* (Apostolat des Editions, 1976), p. 227 (originally published as *Der antiroemishe Affekt* (Freiburg in Bresgau: Herder, 1974).

13. Keep in mind that this 1870 definition was promulgated long before the Catholic Church ever committed itself to serious ecumenical dialogue. The 1870 formulation raises the question today of the extent to which the pope, if he is to teach all Christians, should first consult *all Christians* and not just Catholic Christians.

14. Again, it should be pointed out that Vatican II explained that the Scriptures are to be considered utterly reliable in everything in them that God intended for our salvation (*Dei verbum*, par. 11). It is the work of theologians, bishops and believers to determine just what in Scripture is and is not intended for salvation. Few theologians would argue that 1 Timothy 2:11–14 is utterly reliable and meant for salvation: "A woman must listen in silence and be completely submissive. I do not permit a woman to be a teacher, or in any way to have authority over a man; she must be quiet. For Adam was created first, Eve afterward; moreover, it was not Adam who was deceived but the woman. It was she who was led astray and fell into sin."

15. One of the lessons I was taught in graduate school is that the obvious meaning of a text from another historical period is almost never the actual meaning.

16. See Sullivan, p. 93.

17. Vatican II clarified further the relationship between Episcopal consent and papal definition by stating in an official commentary on the Council's statement on the nature of the Church, *Lumen gentium* (paragraph 25), that the papal definitions "do not require the approbation of the people, but they carry with them and express the consensus of the whole community." Bishop Butler explained in 1977 that "the assent of the Church (to *ex cathedra* definitions and dogmas defined by ecumenical councils) can never be wanting on account of the same Holy Spirit who assists council or pope in the exercise of the Church's infallibility, where the whole flock of Christ is preserved and progresses in unity of faith" (see B. C. Butler, "Authority in the Church," *The Tablet*, May 21, 1977, p. 479); also Heft, *John XXII and Papal Teaching Authority*, pp. 215–216.

18. The American bishops had the greatest influence on shaping two other documents as well, the ones on religious freedom and ecumenism.

19. See *Lumen gentium*, par. 8. Also see *Unitatis redintegratio*, par. 4. Neither of these Council documents, when referring to the relation of the Catholic Church to the one Church of Christ, states that only in the Catholic Church does the fullness of the means of salvation exist.

20. On June 29, 2007, the Vatican returned to the question of the meaning of *subsistit*. Again, the document itself, in the form of short responses to five questions, repeats some of the points established by a previous document, *Dominus Iesus*. Although it states that Vatican II's teaching that the Catholic Church enjoys the fullest means of salvation is consistent with what the Church has always taught, it also makes clear that the *subsistit* formulation "brings out more clearly the fact that there are 'numerous elements of sanctification and of truth' which are found outside her [the Catholic Church's] structure, but which 'as gifts properly belonging to the Church of Christ, impel toward Catholic unity.'" There have been many criticisms by theologians to the effect that in the last decade statements from the Vatican have been going beyond what the Vatican II bishops intended (see especially Francis Sullivan, S.J., "The Meaning of *Subsistit in* as Explained by the Congregation of the Doctrine of the Faith," *Theological Studies*, 69, 1 (March 2008):. 116–124.

21. See http://www.vatican.va/holy_father/john_paul_ii/speeches/1980/november/documents/hf_jp…, accessed December 7, 2009.

22. See *Nostra aetate*, par. 4 in *Vatican Council II*, ed. Austin Flannery (Northport, NY: Costello Publishing, 1996). In the words of paragraph 16 of *Lumen gentium*, "On account of their fathers, this people [the Jews] remains most dear to God, for God does not repent of the gifts He makes nor of the calls He issues." One of the Jewish participants in the Tantur meeting asked whether these statements of Vatican II about the Jews contradict the obvious meaning of the Christian Scripture. There can be no doubt that throughout Christian history many writers and theologians produced anti-semitic and anti-Judiac works, rooted in their interpretations of certain passages of the New Testament. Although official teaching in the Church today claims that all such interpretations of the NT are incorrect, it has not said that the texts of the NT themselves bear the unfortunate and bigoted marks of the controversies between the early Church and the synagogue.

23. Also, par. 16 of *Lumen gentium*.

24. One of the surprising discoveries for many of the Lutheran theologians in this dialogue was that the need for infallible teaching authority was not an exclusively Catholic preoccupation. As one Lutheran remarked, "No Lutheran pastor climbs to the pulpit on any given Sunday and proclaims, 'Jesus is Lord, in my opinion!'" But given that the Lord has granted Christian pastors the capacity to preach and teach with authority, indeed infallible authority, there is all the more reason to be very attentive to the limitations of that authority, lest it be regularly abused.

25. See Appendix A of this paper for the full text of the seven points, to be found in "Roman Catholic Reflections." In *Teaching Authority and Infallibility in the Church: Lutherans and Catholics in Dialogue VI*, eds. Paul C. Empie, T. Austin Murphy, and Joseph A. Burgess (Minneapolis, MN: Augsburg Publishing House, 1978), pp. 44–45.

26. Volume 6, paragraph 20, p. 45. See Appendix A.

27. Alisdair MacIntyre, *After Virtue* (Notre Dame, IN: University of Notre Dame Press, 1981) and *Three Rival Versions of Moral Enquiry* (Notre Dame, IN: University of Notre Dame Press, 1990), chapter 10, "Reconcieving the University as an Institution and the Lecture as a Genre," for an application of his understanding of tradition as a socially embodied and historically extended debate.

28. Published in Zurich in 1970, and translated into English by E. Quinn, *Infallible: An Inquiry* (New York: Doubleday, 1971).

29. The CDF has the responsibility to make sure that Catholic teaching is not heretical. That congregation was led by Cardinal Joseph Ratzinger from 1981 to 2005, at which time he was elected to the papacy, taking the name of Benedict XVI. Cardinal William Levada, an American, now heads the CDF.

30. In 1845, the year he converted from the Anglican to the Roman Catholic Church, John Henry Newman published groundbreaking *An Essay on the Development of Christian Doctrine* (New York: Pelican Classic Paperback, 1974). A more recent and very helpful description of the ways in which doctrine might develop may be found in John Theil's *Senses of Tradition: Continuity and Development in Catholic Faith* (New York: Oxford University Press, 2000).

31. From Section 5 of the document.

32. *ME* follows this statement of John XXIII with the clarification that "…it is clear that he (John XXIII) admits that we can know the clear and unchanging meaning of dogmas. What is new and what he recommends in view of the needs of the times pertains only to the modes of studying, expounding and presenting that doctrine while keeping its permanent meaning."

33. Avery Cardinal Dulles, "Two Languages of Salvation: the Lutheran-Catholic Joint Declaration," in *First Things*, 98 (December 1999): 25–30.

34. Attention to the different historical contexts of the Church in Europe in the nineteenth century and of Church in America in the twentieth century permitted Jesuit

John Courtney Murray to argue in a 1949 article that a change needed to be made in the Church's official teaching on the relationship between Church and State. In the twentieth century, he saw (1) the de-Christianization of society; (2) the threat of totalitarianism; and (3) centrality of the human person. In Murray's analysis, these three changes required the Church (1) to work from "the bottom up," that is, no longer to require that the state and hierarchy of the Church control from the top down; and (2) to recognize that the totalitarian states makes all citizens rightly more suspicious of any authority claiming absolute authority; and (3) that the dignity of the human person requires that the rights of conscience and freedom from coercion be affirmed. Hence the official teaching of the Church, he argued, needed to be changed. John Courtney Murray, "On Religious Freedom," *Theological Studies*, 10, no.3, (September 1949): 423.

35. If, however, more theologians spoke of "truth" the way that Newman did, one would not be as concerned about the tendency to reduce it to verbal formulas mistakenly thought to be always adequate. Listen to Newman, again from his 1845 *Essay*: "...that the mind is below the truth, not above it, and is bound, not to descant upon it, but to venerate it...." (p. 357). One is also reminded of Vatican II's striking statement (Par. 10 of *Dei verbum*, the document on revelation), echoing Newman, that affirmed that "The teaching office is not above the word of God, but serves it, teaching only what has been handed on, listening to it devoutly, guarding it scrupulously and explaining it faithfully...."

36. See Ian Ker, *John Henry Newman: A Biography* (New York: Oxford University Press, 1988), p. 121.

37. See *Lumen gentium*, par. 12.

38. See my article about the special cases of the so-called Marian Dogmas: James L. Heft, S.M. "'*Sensus fidelium*' and the Marian Dogmas," in *One in Christ*, 28, no.2 (1992): 106–125.

39. Newman wrote: "Christianity, then, is at once a philosophy, a political power, and a religious rite: as a religion, it is Holy; as a philosophy, it is Apostolic; as a political power, it is One and Catholic. As a religion, its centre of action is pastor and flock; as a philosophy, the Schools; as a rule, the Papacy and the Curia" (*Via Media and the Anglican Church*, Preface to the third edition, 1877).

40. There are many different forms of thought that today are grouped under the general label of "postmodernism." I have not immersed myself in this literature. Perhaps if I had, I would find even better grounds to recommend a moderation of claims made by people who believe they can understand reality "objectively." Those forms of postmodernism that reject any meta-narrative will not be helpful, I believe, for us who wish to affirm a learned ignorance. The ignorance we speak of is, after all, "learned." Therefore, I believe our challenge is to acknowledge the many ways our understanding of reality is limited, without in that acknowledgment concluding that we can make no affirmations about reality at all. I leave it to wiser heads to describe how best we are able to do that.

41. Part II, Roman Catholic Reflections, "The Catholic Understanding of Papal Infallibility," in *Teaching Authority and Infallibility in the Church: Lutherans and Catholics in Dialogue VI*, eds. Empie, Murphy and Burgess (Minneapolis, MN: Augsburg Publishing House, 1978), pp. 44–45.

6 Chosenness and the Exclusivity of Truth[1]

Reuven Firestone

I grew up in a religiously liberal Jewish American home in which respect for the "other" was always held as an important value, and I believe that it was articulated in both religious and secular humanist language. On the other hand, I lived in a larger community that was considerably more conservative and largely homogeneously white, English-speaking, and middle class. I experienced no overt anti-Semitism as a child and felt completely at home in my white, middle-class environment. When I had just turned eighteen, with enough units to graduate from high school one semester before the end of the academic year, I earned some money and then flew in the early spring of 1970 to Europe to "see the world." My travels were a mind-opening experience through which I learned, among many other things, that I was not nearly as independent and daring as I had hoped. I became quite lonely traveling by myself; so after a month or two, I headed for Israel in order to connect with some acquaintances there. I had never visited Israel and knew very little about the country.

Although unaware at the time, I realize in retrospect that I had a firm expectation that the Jewish Israelis would be happy heroes, while the Arabs would be untrustworthy and quite less civilized. These were expectations that I had picked up from the larger environment in which I was raised. They clearly did not originate from my family. To my surprise, however, my first experiences in Israel turned these expectations on their heads. I observed unhappy Jewish Israelis acting quite unheroically—sometimes violently and barbarically—and I became fast friends with two elegant and cosmopolitan young Palestinian Muslim men two years my senior, who lived in a village on the West Bank and worked in the Old City of Jerusalem.

The story of these unfolding experiences will someday be written because it is both entertaining and, I think, emotionally touching, and perhaps even enlightening, but this is not the place for that. I ended up living for some months that spring and summer in the Muslim Quarter of Old Jerusalem, and then on a Jewish border kibbutz. I was blessed with a wonderful set of experiences and friendships in both communities that taught me to appreciate and respect (even if I didn't understand) the cultural, religious, and national traditions that so deeply informed the collective world views of these peoples.

As I piece together the issues that have moved me down the particular path of my adult life, I realize that those spring and summer months were pivotal experiences for me. Much of my professional and personal energy has since been devoted to the quest to understand the intricacies of the relationship between Jew and Muslim, Israeli and Palestinian, and "self" and "other."

One important lesson I have learned from my study of other religions is greater understanding of my own. This goes beyond the simple given that one tends to learn about oneself by knowing who one is not. I have learned how to apply more honesty to the study of my own religion (and self) by forcing myself to use the same methodologies that are far easier—and personally safer—to apply to religions of the other. Honest dialogue between religions must include the problem of making sense of a personal and particularist religious truth while allowing space for a different and perhaps even contrary truth in relation to others. To put it differently, I struggle with how to reconcile the particularity of religion with the universal of God. This is the largest arena of the problematic, but it is reflected in human relations at all levels. I believe a breakthrough is necessary on this point if our world will survive in any kind of meaningful way, not only theologically but also physically.

■ WHAT DOES IT MEAN TO "BE CHOSEN?"[2]

To choose is to limit in some way. It is an act of identifying, of distinguishing, of separating. Although it is possible to choose a few rather than only one, choosing is generally understood as singling out. The act of choosing immediately establishes a preference. The chosen is different than the others. Usually, that difference represents a higher location on the scale, but it can also mean choosing a loser—unintentionally, of course, because one hopes to choose a winner. Being chosen, at its most basic, therefore, would appear to be a special and positive status that places the chosen over and above the nonchosen.

If being chosen is generally a good thing, consider being chosen by God.

This nature of chosenness—its implied superiority—has been glorified by religious civilizations when in positions of imperial power, just as it has sustained religious communities suffering persecution. It has also made some religionists uncomfortable at times, even ancient times, but particularly in periods and places where democracy, equality, and freedom are considered defining categories. In our generation, the Enlightenment project hastened to remove religion from the political arena by relegating it to the personal sphere. However, that project is now being thoroughly re-examined. As a consequence, the "problematic" of chosenness takes on particular importance.

Theological approaches to the issue can be significantly enhanced by other disciplines in the academic study of religion, and particularly the discipline called the "history of religions," which examines religious phenomena from a historical, social-science perspective. The classical discipline of the history of religions (*Religiongeschichteschule*) studied religion strictly as a human, nontranscendent social-cultural phenomenon and assumed a Hegelian progression from simple to more complex societies and from "primitive" polytheism to more advanced monotheisms. Although this simplistic, Euro- and Christian-centered perspective has rightly become discredited, subjecting religious phenomena to critical inquiry based on social-science disciplines can be enlightening, and it is this method that is presented here. From such a perspective, what might be the origin of the notion of chosenness? What might it have meant to be chosen in the ancient world? Might the history of competing religious truth claims jutting into our own day be linked to ancient concepts of chosenness?

As just noted, being chosen is a sign of privilege. This privileged position would apply even for sacrifice, although in the case of sacrifice, chosenness takes on an awesome ambivalence. Take the biblical scapegoat offering, for example, in Leviticus 16:5–22. In this text, lots are drawn against two goats. One will be chosen through the casting of lots to become a *hatat*, a sin-offering, and sacrificed on the altar. The other will be presented alive before God as a *kapparah*, an atonement offering, and then sent off, alive into the desert, to a place called *azazeyl*. Both are chosen, but for different fates.

In some ancient cultures, not only special animals were chosen for sacrifice, but special humans were also chosen as sacrifices to the deity. It is difficult for us to even imagine the meaning of chosenness in such cases. From where I stand, it would seem to include a sense of great honor, but a greater sense of terror.

There is a famous story in Islamic tradition about a fateful choice for human sacrifice.[3] The story begins with Abd al-Muttalib, the grandfather of the greatest prophet in Islamic tradition, Prophet Muhammad. Abd al-Muttalib was an important personage among the tribe of Quraysh that populated the ancient Arabian settlement of Mecca. A structure known as the Ka`ba was already standing in Mecca during his lifetime. According to Islamic tradition, the Ka`ba was in Mecca from time immemorial, established originally by Adam, then taken up miraculously to heaven to avoid damage during the great Noahide Flood, and finally rebuilt on its original foundations by Abraham and his first-born son, Ishmael. One evening, many, many generations after Abraham and Ishmael, one of their progeny named Abd al-Muttalib fell asleep very close to the Ka`ba, at a place called al-Hijr, a location that is said to contain the graves of Ishmael and his mother, Hagar. Abd al-Muttalib received a vision that night commanding him to dig the Zam-zam well.

Wells, as sources of life-giving water in the hot and dry desert climate of Arabia, are often named. The Zam-zam is particularly important in Islamic tradition because it was the well that had saved Hagar and Ishmael in the desert.[4] Although the Zam-zam well was already famous at the time of Abd al-Muttalib, no one knew any longer where it was located! Its loss was a direct result of the decline of the original monotheism in Arabia, first established by the primordial Adam and then reinvigorated by Abraham when he brought Hagar and Ishmael to live in Mecca. Belief and loyalty to the one great God began to decay in Arabia after Ishmael. Every generation of Ishmael's offspring became increasingly steeped in the ignorance of idolatry. They became so deeply sunk in the mire of idol-worship that the sacred well that had sustained Hagar and Ishmael in the desert finally disappeared.

Quite unexpectedly, then, Abd al-Muttalib, one of Ishmael's descendents, received a vision instructing him to find and re-dig that sacred well. Before the emergence of Islamic monotheism, one was never sure in Arabia whether one received a vision from a god or from a demon. So Abd al-Muttalib went to his tribe and told them about his dream. When they asked him where the vision told him to dig the well, Abd al-Muttalib replied that he was not informed of its location.

He was advised, therefore, to go back and sleep again at the same place. If the vision really came from God, then its location would be made clear to him. But because demons were notoriously unreliable, if it were a demon he would not receive clarification. So when Abd al-Muttalib went back to his bed, he received the following message, given in a form of poetic prose called *saj'* that is similar to the rhetorical style found in the Qur'an:

> Dig Zam-zam, for if you dig it you will not regret,
> It is an inheritance from your mighty ancestors.
> It will never fail nor run dry,
> It will provide water to the great [number of] pilgrims.
> Like an ostrich flock, undivided,
> Giving oath to the Beneficent.
> It will be a legacy and a pact decided,
> Nothing like it, could you [possibly] consider.
> And it is between the scattered dung and the blood.[5]

In the days of Abd al-Muttalib, Mecca was a cultic center for the worship of many deities, and he had received his vision within the area in which were located most of the representations of the gods. So Abd al-Muttalib began to dig in that central area of Mecca. He chose a location between two blasphemous idols representing the gods, Isaf and Na'ila, where the Quraysh used to slaughter their sacrifices. This location was "between the dung and the blood." And lo and behold, he found the ancient well. But then his tribe demanded a share in it.

Water was a scarce commodity in those days in Arabia, as it is today, and whoever controlled the water source could accrue great power and wealth. The dispute thus became quite harsh and Abd al-Muttalib's tribe threatened him with physical harm. It was finally arbitrated through augury—the casting of lots—which in those days was done in the form of arrows. When the arrows were cast, they settled in Abd al-Muttalib's favor. The Quraysh were forced to comply with the results.

In the midst of the conflict, Abd al-Muttalib vowed that if ten sons would be born to him to protect him from such trauma in the future, he would sacrifice one of them to Hubal, the powerful god of the Ka'ba. He did eventually have ten sons, and when they grew up he remained true to his vow. He told them the story of the Zam-zam, the tribal argument and his vow, and he called on them to keep faith with his integrity and with his promise. When they agreed, he told each son to write his name on an arrow. When they were cast, the lot fell on Abdullah, his youngest and favorite son. Straightaway, he took him to the two idols where animals were sacrificed and took out a knife to slaughter his beloved son.

Some members of his tribe hurried over to him and said: "If you do this, there will be no stopping men from sacrificing their sons, and what will become of the people then?" He was told to visit a powerful sorceress who consulted a *tabi'*, a familiar spirit. If, after consulting her spirit, she told him to sacrifice his son, then he must do so. But she might have another solution to his problematic vow, and he had nothing to lose by seeing her.

After consulting her familiar spirit, the sorceress told him to return home with the boy and instructed him: "Take ten camels and cast lots against them and against the boy. If the lot falls against the boy, then add another ten camels until your lord, the god to whom you made the vow, is satisfied." Abd al-Muttalib did exactly as she said. Each time he cast lots, they fell against the boy. So after each cast, he added ten camels. Finally, at 100 camels, the lot fell against the camels. He cast three more times, and each time the lot fell against the 100 camels. Abd al-Muttalib, therefore, knew that the god had truly accepted the redemption of his son. One hundred camels were slaughtered and distributed to all the people of Mecca.

This story expresses well the ambivalence associated with chosenness. First of all, we must recall that the intended sacrificial victim of the story, Abdullah, would become the father of the prophet Muhammad. Although it was not good luck that Abdullah was chosen by the god to be sacrificed, it was deeply auspicious. His having been chosen by the deity—not by chance the most powerful deity in the Arabia pantheon of that region—demonstrated something very special about him. He was clearly unique and clearly chosen, but nobody knew what for. His distinctiveness remained a mystery for many years and might have been forgotten. But Abdullah would father the greatest and final prophet to be sent to humanity— Prophet Muhammad.

There is much more to this story than we can examine here, but some observations are in order. Abd al-Muttalib's requirement to sacrifice his son by the authority of the deity parallels that of Abraham (Gen. 22, Q. 37:109–113). The son, like Abraham's son, Isaac, of the Hebrew Bible, was not a very well developed figure in Islamic sacred history. Abdullah died even before his own son, Muhammad, was born. The key in the Arabian narrative is the product or offspring of the intended sacrifice. It was the inscrutable reversal of the divine decree that, in both the Biblical and Arabian cases, enabled the leader of the religious nation to be born. Muhammad, like his parallel in the Biblical narrative, Jacob, was the founder of a great nation, the *umma* or religious peoplehood of Islam, corresponding in Islamic tradition to the Children of Israel in the Bible.

The parallels are not accidental. We will observe below how very many themes that are basic and essential to the Hebrew Bible become at least basic, if not always essential, to subsequent scriptures among its literary/revelatory heirs.

■ WHY DID GOD HAVE TO CHOOSE?

In Scriptural discourse, chosenness or election as it is sometimes called, describes a unique relationship with God. In the discourse of the Hebrew Bible, it is the "People (or Children) of Israel"—or in Jewish parlance, simply "Israel"—that is in that special relationship.

According to the narrative of the Hebrew Bible, God did not set out to choose only one sub-community from the whole human race. On the contrary, God began creation with a primordial couple, Adam and Eve, who represented, not a particular race or people or religion, but rather, all of humanity. That couple, however, when left to their own devices in the Garden of Eden, failed to live up to the responsibility expected of them. The following generation represented by the couple's children, Cain and Abel, also failed God by committing the horrendous deed of fratricide. Their descendents in Noah's generation failed God yet again by their constant acts of overwhelming violence. And in the fourth and last example of humanity's collective failure, the generation of the Tower of Babel attempted to become like God themselves.

After such overwhelming failure in macroanthroposophy, the Hebrew Bible narrows its focus to a single nuclear family that becomes a clan, then a tribe, then a nation. The issue seems to be one of focus, and with focus, accountability. After human failure at the macro level, God no longer leaves his experiment to act according to its own devices, but narrows the focus and forbids the absolute freedom that had resulted in consistent human failure. The change is marked by the establishment of a *berit,* or covenant. God establishes the covenant and for some inscrutable reason, chooses a simple tribal sheikh named Abram.

The covenant is, in fact, a simple contract with attendant obligations. When God first discusses the covenant with Abraham in Genesis 17:1, God uses an idiomatic expression and says, *hithalekh lefanay veheye tamim,* which means literally, "Walk around before me and be innocent." Because language idioms tend to be loaded with special meaning and not literally translatable, one would be required to translate the phrase paraphrastically, that is, something like, "If you behave or comport yourself in a way that is acceptable to Me, then you will be innocent of sin and, therefore, not liable for punishment."[6] God did not tell Abraham what would happen if he *didn't* behave himself. The promises of reward and punishment would be saved for the expanded covenant with the larger multitribal nation of Israel many generations later.[7] In any case, never in the Hebrew Bible is reward and punishment articulated through a concept of afterlife. According to the Hebrew Bible, it is all realized in the life of this world.

Covenant in the Hebrew Bible is actually a technical institution that carries no particularly sacred meaning. It simply refers to a specific form of contractual relationship. There are covenants between individuals, between kings and nations, and between certain individuals or collectives and God. However, because in later years it took on a symbolic definition of the formal relationship between God and a particular people, covenant became a symbol of chosenness. The chosenness of the individuals and families of Abraham, Isaac, and Jacob, and the chosenness of the collective of Israel were formalized through the establishment of a formal relationship between God and a unique human community established as a covenant.

Being chosen in the Hebrew Bible indeed meant being singled out, being unique. It clearly conveyed preference, but this mark of distinction seems not to have been intended for privilege (although it came to be interpreted as such in some circles). The singularity seems to be tied up with steadfastness and fidelity to one God.

There is honor and status in that, to be sure, but as the Hebrew Bible demonstrates in so many different ways, the honor of chosenness was often a burden. It was not a hierarchy of race or genetics, as some have mistakenly suggested, because a "mixed multitude"[8] of tribes and peoples accompanied Israel when they were freed from Egypt and all became part of the covenant at Sinai. And there was always intermarriage between Israel and other peoples.[9] They all made their way to the mountain together—Israelites and Egyptians, individual Midianites, and other unnamed peoples—and engaged in an expanded covenantal contract with God.

There they formed a religious peoplehood for the simple reason that religion in the ancient Near East was organized ethnically.

Ethnic is neither racial nor genetic. Whereas ethnicity tends to express racial or genetic preference, ethnic identity, even including the records of genealogical relationship, is a human construct and anthropologists have confirmed long ago the tremendously porous nature of ethnic boundaries. Religious identity in the ancient Near East was virtually the same as ethnic identity. As will be discussed in more detail later, differing beliefs seem not to have defined religious communities until the emergence of monotheism, probably in combination with Hellenism. There is a clear refrain of elitism in the notion of chosenness, and because of the ethnic nature of the ancient Near Eastern religious community, that elitism was expressed in terms of peoplehood. "The Lord your God chose you from among all other peoples on earth to be His treasured people" (Deut. 14:2).

Read contextually, it becomes clear from many Biblical passages that the status of chosenness is not given unconditionally. The special relationship is coupled in virtually every case with responsibilities to engage in certain behaviors, and with prohibitions against other behaviors. Most simply, being chosen restricted freedom.

The citation from Deuteronomy 14 is coupled with the prohibition against certain activities and fashions associated with other religious communities' worship, "For you are a people consecrated to the Lord your God" (Deut. 14:1–2). That same special relationship restricted Israel from eating many kinds of foods and from engaging in the religious festivals of their neighbors. The restrictions extend beyond the ritual to the moral-ethical. Israel is required, for example, to treat even the stranger with kindness, to deal in commerce fairly.[10] All the moral-ethical and ritual expectations of behavior incumbent upon Israel are articulated in terms of the covenantal relationship.

Perhaps chosenness provided a sense of recompense or reward for a drastic reduction in personal autonomy. It certainly must have engendered a sense of elitism among some in the population, for several biblical passages express discomfort with how some Israelites understood their chosen status. This was one of the prophet Amos's complaints: "You alone have I singled out [known] of all the families of the earth. That is why I will call you to account for all your iniquities" (Amos 3:2). "To Me, O Israelites, you are just like the Ethiopians. True, I brought Israel up from the land of Egypt, but also the Philistines from Caphtor and the Arameans from Kir" (Amos 9:7).

Whether one considers chosenness in the Biblical context positively or negatively, it is essential to note that chosenness became deeply associated with monotheism. Unlike neighboring peoples, Israel is obligated to worship only the one God. As the introductory paragraph of the Ten Commandments (Exodus 20:5, Deut. 4:24) proclaims, God is a "jealous" God—*El qanna'*—who requires absolute obedience.[11]

Not surprising, however, the notion of chosenness was probably not unique to Israel. Neighboring peoples had their own tribal gods with whom they were in exclusive relationship. It appears that there existed no conceptual option for anything other than tribal religion in the ancient Near East. Gods were particular—not universal—and they were associated with individual nations or tribes. In fact, there is no evidence that changing religions was even a conceptual possibility before the Hellenistic period. One was born into a people, a tribe, a nation, and that social group had a special relationship with its own particular god. Chemosh was the tribal god of all the peoples that defined themselves as Moabite, and Dagon the god of the Philistines.[12] One could no more voluntarily change allegiance from one god to another than voluntarily change one's mother tongue or ethnic identity. "Conversion" as we know it, and, therefore, mission, were simply not conceptual options.[13]

The gods of the nations (*goyim*) surrounding Israel protected their tribes or peoples just as the God of Israel protected its own people, and there certainly must have been a sense of loyalty and elitism—even chosenness—among these peoples as well as among Israel. But they had more flexibility in their worship. Their gods were not conceived as universal gods, and they did not seem to require absolute and exclusive obedience as did the God of Israel. It would not be uncommon for a member of a tribal religion visiting a neighboring people to make an offering to the neighbor's god(s). Not so among Israel, or at least not according to the covenantal agreements.

One of the nagging issues that plagued biblical Israel was its backsliding from absolute obedience to its zealous God. Many biblical passages describe Israelites engaging in foreign devotion, the worship of other gods. This would suggest that the notion of monotheism, of a truly universal deity, was not a universal belief in ancient Israel. The Bible is a kind of devotional history of a people, and current biblical scholarship is in agreement that true and consistent monotheism does not become dominant among the Israelites until at least the time of the classical prophets. This was not until sometime around the destruction of the First Temple in the sixth century, BCE.[14]

Another thing that must be remembered is that the religious civilizations of the Moabites, the Philistines, and others did not survive, so neither did their own particular kind of religious elitism. The sense of chosenness that did survive was *Israelite* chosenness, and it is that expression that became deeply associated with monotheism in general.

Israelite religion—Israelite monotheism—somehow survived the fate of all other religious systems of the ancient world. The Israelite temples were destroyed, but Israelite monotheism somehow survived. Theologians have constructed many different meanings out of that survival, from the lesson of God's true and unfailing love for His beloved people to chastisement meant as a lesson for the inevitable emergence of a truer, more perfect expression of the divine will. From the perspective of the history of religion, however, it was the simple fact (or luck) of Israel's survivability, the very endurance of Israelite religion, that gave it such an edge as a model for all subsequent expressions of monotheism.

▪ "BEST PRACTICE" AND RELIGIOUS SUCCESS

Whatever religions' existential meaning in relation to God, creation, the universe, and the beyond, the way in which religions function in human history is influenced enormously by the actual people who make up the minions of their membership, management, and leadership. Whatever their origins or their views of themselves, religions function in real time as human institutions, and the academic study of religion observes them according to methodologies that are used to study other human institutions. Subjecting religious institutions to the same analysis as other human institutions is sometimes jarring to the religionist because it may be perceived as cheapening what is often considered, at least by the believer, to be their sublime nature. But such exercises can also offer extremely important insights. In the following, I freely use language that is often used when evaluating business. This can be quite jarring, and I am not attempting to equate religion with business in terms of authority, authenticity, or ethics. However, following others in the field I find that using this vocabulary opens up a world of understanding about the nature and behaviors of religion.

In religion, as in business, it is the best models that are emulated.[15] In modern business this is a conscious process. In religion, this seems less likely to be the case, but both successful business and successful religion need to control a certain share of the consumer market in order to maintain themselves, meaning to control enough human and material resources to "stay in business." Without the aid of a certain minimal amount of supporters' energy, commitment, personal abilities and material resources, no religion can long survive. Religious followers are consumers of religion, and their numbers represent a share of a religious market of consumers. New religious movements, like new products on the market, occasionally become available to consumers.

Sometimes new religious movements emerge out of existing religious systems. They may begin as particularly active segments of the religious body or as followers of particularly strong or charismatic leadership within a subcommunity. Usually such groups remain committed to the larger institution, but occasionally they begin to be seen (either by themselves or by the mainstream) as different enough to be considered outside the parameters of the religious institution. Sometimes they are forced out. By definition, such a new movement is defined as separate from the mainstream, and it is inevitably opposed by it. If it is not rejected entirely by the larger religious institution out of which it emerges, it is called a sect. If it moves far enough away from the core, it is called a heresy.

Sometimes, a new religious movement does not emerge from within an established religious system but from outside of it. When this occurs, it is institutionally independent, and this in our day is called a cult. Whether sect, heresy, or cult, the emerging religious movement is resisted by established religions. If it succeeds in gathering enough followers (i.e., gains a healthy enough percentage of the market of believers), it becomes increasingly difficult to marginalize and put an end to it. With the support of a large enough following (or consumer pool), the new movement can withstand the pressures of the establishment religion(s) to delegitimize it. When this occurs it begins to attain the status and influence of a religion.

In order to succeed in gaining the requisite market share, new religious movements must demonstrate to enough potential consumers that they are authentic. They must convince an adequate number of supporters that they are authoritative and represent the will of God. One way to demonstrate this legitimacy is by presenting the new religion in ways that are easily recognized by potential joiners as authentic. Such recognition can be accomplished by incorporating powerful symbols and images that are already universally acknowledged through their existence in established religions. Successful religious movements always manage to incorporate venerated aspects of established religions in their own representational systems. We must keep in mind that images, symbols, belief concepts, and rituals form the building blocks of religious traditions. They are not necessarily unique to any one of them. It is the unique version or flavor of these and their particular combinations that make for the particularity of religion.

Many aspects of Israelite customs, traditions, rituals, conventions, and symbols, for example, can be found among contemporary and more ancient neighboring religions. We have learned through archaeological digs that the altars of ancient Israel looked like Canaanite altars, the layout of the Tabernacle and architecture of the Jerusalem Temple were like those of other contemporary sacred structures in the region. The Bible itself attests to non-Israelite priests and non-Israelite prophets (Ex.3:1, Num. 22, etc.). Even religious poems with uncanny parallels to Biblical psalms have been discovered in the libraries of ancient civilizations uncovered in archaeological digs.[16] But those poems revere other gods. What made ancient Israel unique were the particular nuances of meaning associated with its religious institutions. It is less the precise item than the meanings or interpretations associated with it that provides the particularity of religion.

Keep in mind that Israelite religion was considered ancient when it was encountered by the early Greeks. It was the one great survivor from the world of the ancient Near East. The earliest Greek writers on the Jews, such as Theophrastus, Megasthenes, and Clearchus of Soli, all who lived in the fourth to third centuries BCE, gave Israel their highest compliment, for they considered Israel to be a nation of philosophers.[17] As a most ancient and hoary expression of God's communication to humanity, it was natural for Israel's religion to be emulated, whether consciously or not, by new religious movements in formation. Those that were most successful managed to integrate some of the most powerful symbols, images, and motifs from the religion of Biblical Israel. One of the most central motifs of ancient Israel was chosenness.

■ THE RELIGIOUS BACKLASH

Students of new religious movements in the West have articulated for us what we already know intuitively and from our own experience—that both the leaders and the rank-and-file of establishment religions do not care for new religions. All the names for new religious movements—sect, cult, and heresy—are designations for dubious religion at best, and usually false religion. The derogatory nomenclature and negative stance arise from the simple fact that new religious movements are threatening. They are threatening to believers who have invested so much of themselves (and often their and their family's personal salvation) to a religious tradition whose authority is challenged by the claims and even the very existence of new religions. They are also threatening to the institutional well-being of the religious establishment. Religiously affiliated parents rarely agree that their children join other religious communities, and especially those that are considered marginal. Religious leaders and functionaries preach against new religions; they polemicize against them. They often argue that the leaders of new religious movements manipulate innocent people in order to benefit themselves. They habitually maintain that leaders of new religions make metaphysical promises that cannot be fulfilled, that new religious movements are not authoritative representations of the divine will. They are not authentic, not "true religion."

One need not be a historian of religion to know that these very positions were articulated by representatives of establishment religions in reference to Christianity as it emerged in Late Antiquity. They were also articulated in reference to emerging Islam as well as new religious movements in more recent generations. However, new religious movements usually fight back, and they can be quite successful in their counterattacks by responding to the polemics of establishment religions with counterpolemics. One can observe this response quite commonly within the scriptures of Judaism, Christianity, and Islam, all of which denigrate and complain against the hypocrisy of established religion. It should be kept in mind that successful new religious movements eventually become *establishment* religions themselves, and they, in turn, denigrate and attempt to de-legitimate new religious movements that threaten *them*.

My focus of discussion here is on the scriptural response of Judaism, Christianity, and Islam to the denigration of establishment religions directed against them. scripture is both the earliest witness to the emergence of these religious traditions and the most authoritative item in their possession. As mentioned previously, one particularly successful method of combating the attempt at de-legitimization by establishment religions is, usually intuitively, to incorporate within their own institutions precisely those aspects of establishment religions that grant them their greatest credibility, and this process can be observed in all three scriptures. However, there is a danger in doing this, for if a new religious movement incorporates too much of the establishment within it, it loses its standing as an alternative to the status quo. Then again, being too far out proves its own illegitimacy. Success means maintaining a balance between likeness and uniqueness.

One of the most natural symbols of authority to be incorporated into the scriptures that emerged into human history following the Hebrew Bible was the notion of chosenness. God had chosen His beloved Abraham and his descendants (Isaiah 41:8), and the chosenness relationship with God and Israel is ubiquitous in the Hebrew Bible.[18] It was emblematic of a true relationship with God. As we have observed previously, the Hebrew Bible taught that humanity failed when it lived outside of an intimate relationship with God, and that God was only really with those with whom God was in a chosen relationship. The Greeks had characterized the religion of Israel to be ancient already in their own day, and the religions of the ancient Near East had weakened and were disappearing by the emergence of Christianity. Chosenness was thus a natural and appealing motif of ancient Israelite religion to be absorbed by new religious movements. It epitomized the unique and exclusive relationship between God and humanity, and it was emblematic of Israel's longevity and survival. Chosenness was certainly emblematic to Jews themselves, who did not hold back from referring to it in post-Biblical literature.[19]

It is not clear exactly how chosenness became so important to ancient Israel. My hunch is that chosenness was simply a feeling among all nations or peoples that had their own ethnic deity who nourished them and protected them, not only against the vicissitudes of nature, but also against the predations of neighboring peoples. Feelings of chosenness may have been the standard mode of relationship between a community and its god in the ancient Near East. There were of course many other ethnic or national communities with their particularist ethnic deities in the ancient Near East. However, whereas a Moabite or Edomite or Egyptian or Phoenician could make offerings to foreign deities on a journey to another ethnic (and, therefore, religious) region, Joshua forbids Israelites from doing so:

> Now, therefore, revere the Lord[20] and serve him with undivided loyalty; put away the gods that your forefathers served beyond the Euphrates and in Egypt, and serve the Lord. Or, if you are loath to serve the Lord, choose this day which ones you are going to serve—the gods that your forefathers served beyond the Euphrates, or those of the Amorites in whose land you are settled; but I and my household will serve the Lord. (Joshua 24:14–15)

A heightened sense of chosenness may have emerged among Israel as it made the slow transition from worshipping a tribal deity, known by its own personal name (the *tetragrammaton*), to worshipping a transcendent and unnamable power that ruled not only Israel but the entire universe. As a particular community came to believe that it and only it was in a relationship with the One Great God that would never countenance worship of other forces or powers (because such forces and powers were not separate from God itself), then feelings of chosenness would have certainly grown exponentially.

When monotheism took hold in ancient Israel, the Israelites naturally saw the essential character and quality of their relationship with their one and only universal God as different from the relationship of neighboring peoples with their limited, tribal deities. As a result of this unique *kind* of relationship, they considered their position and responsibility in the world unlike their neighbors. They were simply different, and different in a cosmic sense. Their relationship with God, whose mystery and power was so beyond human qualities that Israelites were forbidden even from pronouncing its name, was unusual enough that it engendered a feeling of being in a profound sense different than all other religious communities.

Their relationship with God thus seems to have been truly unique. As their scripture articulated it, the God of Israel singled out a small and unexceptional tribal group to stand in an absolutely exclusive relationship (Deut. 7:7–9). This zealous God required separation from the neighboring peoples with their multiple gods through cultural expectations and rules, such as special foods and eating habits, dress, and, as we observe in Deuteronomy 14, even hair styles.

Because of its status of superancient religion, its longevity, and its status in the eyes of observers as the "mother of monotheisms," the religion of Israel established the paradigmatic relationship between the one great God and humanity. This relationship is special, unique, and limited to a single community. The limitation bears all the markings of the historical context out of which the notion emerged.

Although it began as one of many expressions of personal and intimate relationship between a god and its nation or a nation and its god, the neighboring ancient Near Eastern tribal religions died out. The unique relation between one single human community (Israel) and its now universal God became the surviving expression of chosenness, and it, therefore, became the characteristic representation. So when one examines the successful monotheistic religious movements that emerged out of the crucible of ancient Western Asia, one cannot help but notice that they all incorporate that one aspect of ancient Israelite religion. A number of other common motifs are also found among them, but chosenness, often defined by covenant, is certainly a core item that was incorporated in them all.

■ MIMESIS AND INTERTEXTUALITY

We must now consider the polemical nature of emulative mimicry, or mimesis. Mimesis is imitation, and it is a natural part of human nature. We tend to imitate the qualities, traits, and styles of those whom we admire. René Girard noted how the mimetic act can cause anxiety when it appears from the perspective of the imitated that the imitator is desirous of replacing him. According to Gerard, the imitator in fact does desire (perhaps consciously but more likely unconsciously) to replace the imitated, and the resultant anxiety can grow to the point of violence.[21] It is both frightening and risky to take on the very aspects of an "other" whom one desires to replace. This is one of the reasons for the scriptural polemics associated with chosenness.

We do not have any clear ancient Near Eastern subtext for most of the Hebrew Bible, so we cannot examine its mimetic anxiety as well as we can that of the New Testament and the Qur'an. However, should you read through the Biblical chosenness texts, you will note how powerful is the image of chosenness: "*I will maintain My covenant between Me and you, and your offspring to come, as an everlasting covenant throughout the ages* (Gen.17:7), *Now then, if you will obey Me conscientiously and keep My covenant, you shall be My treasured possession among all the peoples*" (Ex.19:5).

You will see how exclusive is the language, and how harsh: "*I will bless those who bless you and curse him that curses you*" (Gen.12:3), "*[The Lord your God] instantly requites with destruction those [Israelites] who reject Him*" (Deut.7:10–11).

This language is polemical and is directed against the general and often unidentified "other" outside of the community that is loyal to the one great and zealous God. Sometimes that "other" represents those within the community itself who are unfaithful or who might become unfaithful. More often, they represent the adherents of previously established religions, and a polemical subtext can be presumed from the contentious references to them: "*...for all those abhorrent things were done by the people who were in the land before you, and the land became defiled. So let not the land vomit you out...as it vomited out the nation that came before you* (Lev. 18:27–28). We must keep in mind that the term for nation in this as in many such verses, *goy*, refers to a religious nation, because the particularism of religion and nation were identical in the ancient Near East. It is important to keep in mind also that no Biblical expressions of reward and punishment for those within or outside of the chosenness relationship with God refer to a world to come; there is no notion of reward and retribution in heaven or hell in the Hebrew Bible.

Although no scripture or scripture-like text has been discovered that predates the Hebrew Bible and may have served as a major subtext,[22] we do have the subtext of the Hebrew Bible for chosenness polemics in the New Testament, and we have the Hebrew Bible and New Testament that serve as subtexts for chosenness polemics in the Qur'an. This relationship of text and subtext is sometimes referred to as *intertextual* because of the great textual sharing in language and literary motifs, symbols, images, and narratives between them. However, although there is certainly a great deal of sharing between the scriptural texts, each scripture uses the shared items for different purpose and the result is virtually the opposite of sharing. It becomes a means of differentiating. The intertextual relationship between these scriptures thus becomes a convenient conduit for argument.

The New Testament, for example, claims a new chosenness that supersedes the chosenness of the Hebrew Bible: Jesus through David in Luke 1:30–33 (Cf. 2 Sam. 7:12–13), then Jesus through the authority of Moses and Elijah in Luke 9:28–35 (Cf. Ex.34:29, 19:9, 33:9), Jesus's atoning quality through the blood of sacrifice in Matthew 26: 26–28 (Cf. Ex. 24:6–8), coded and not-so-coded counterattacks in Acts 7:51–53 and John 10:1–15 against establishment Jews who refuse to accept the divinity of Jesus and who try to obfuscate the intertextual claims of his disciples, and then an extraordinarily effective use (or reversal) of the Hebrew Bible chosenness paradigm in Romans 9: 7–9 and Galatians 4:21–31 (Cf. Gen. 21:9–13). And, of course, there is the well-known covenantal supersessionism of Hebrews 8:6–13 (Cf. Jer. 31:31–34).[23]

We find a similar intertextual relationship in the Qur'an, classically represented by Q.3:67 ("Abraham was neither a Jew nor a Christian, but rather an early monotheist Muslim"). The Qur'an is of course a different scripture than the New Testament and born of a different time and place. Its rhetorical style and interpretive methods, its specific subtextual sensitivities, the nature of its intertextual relationship with prior scripture and the final results, therefore, differ from those of Christian scripture. The Qur'an is, however, like the New Testament, concerned with the covenantal claims of prior scripture. Rather than claiming to supersede them or declare them out of date and no longer in force, it excludes most Jews and Christians from the very covenants that are represented by their scriptures by citing their lack of commitment to them (Q. 2:124, 4:54–55, 5:12–14). There is a metamessage here, and that message is not only that Jews and Christians as collectives are no longer worthy of that special and unique status of chosenness. There is also a profound lesson for the early Muslims: those few and beleaguered followers of Muhammad whom the Qur'an is addressing and who have chosen to accept the newest and most accurate—therefore, the best—divine dispensation. The message is that they will remain in their special, privileged relationship with God only so long as they submit—that is, so long as they are absolutely loyal—to the divine will as articulated by the newly emerging religion of Islam. Although the new covenant applies to the Muslims as a collective, as individuals they, like errant Jews and Christians before them, can easily be rejected from that exclusive relationship with God.

Islam is not as preoccupied with chosenness as are Judaism and Christianity.[24] This is probably due to the fact that monotheism was not so unique in the Near East of the seventh century. Historians engaged in religious demography suggest that the majority of West Asians were already Jews or Christians (or Zoroastrians) by the emergence of Islam in the seventh century. Thus most peoples with whom the early Muslims came into contact as they spread beyond the borders of Arabia were already monotheists. As they emerged into a world of monotheisms, they could not claim truth as monotheists in a world of polytheism, as did ancient Israel, or sole possession of the ultimate relationship with the one great God in a simple bilateral competition with the Jews, as did Christianity. Muslims encountered a multimonotheist playing field in which the goal had to be, simply, to demonstrate superiority and thus claim its share of the religious market or even dominate it. The religious fellowship of Islam, the *umma* in Qur'anic parlance as articulated in Qur'an 3:110, is "the best community that has been brought forth for humanity," but only as long as its members would "command the reputable and forbid the disreputable, and believe in God."

Exactly what was meant by these requirements was not articulated unambiguously in the Qur'an. That is to say, would successfully fulfilling these three requirements be possible only within an Islamic framework? Or could Jews and Christians command the reputable and forbid the disreputable acceptably, according to Islam, within their own religious traditions? Some Qur'anic pronouncements, such as Q.2:62, repeated in Q.5:69 and suggested again in Q.22:17, say yes: "Those who believe, and who are Jews, and Christians and Sabaeans—whoever believes in God and the Last Day and who work righteousness: they have their reward with their Lord, they shall not fear nor should they grieve."

Other verses, such as Q.9:29, take a different position, which is considered by most traditional exegetes to have abrogated the more welcoming verses already mentioned.[25] According to a well-known and normative understanding, Q.9:29 requires either humility or humiliation of the Peoples of the Book (depending on how one translates a key term in the verse), thereby placing even true monotheists of the religions of the Book in a secondary position to Muslims. In the Qur'an, however, and even in exclusivist readings, chosenness is necessarily a shared item among all monotheists. In theory, at the very least, there is a place for the covenanted chosenness of Judaism and Christianity within Islam.

Before concluding we must consider one important monotheistic religion and its scripture that is usually overlooked in comparative studies. That religion is Rabbinic Judaism, and its scripture is the Talmud, also called the "Oral Torah," to be distinguished from the "Written Torah" of the Hebrew Bible. Contrary to some uninformed assumptions, the religion of Israel did not remain static after the emergence of Christianity. It continued to evolve with the destruction of the Jerusalem Temple. At about the same time that a new revelation emerged, according to Christians in the person of Jesus Christ, another revelation was emerging according to Jews who did not accept the messiahship and divinity of Jesus. Just as Christianity is not the same religion as that of Biblical Israel, so, too, is Rabbinic Judaism—the Judaism of the rabbis—not the same as the religion of Biblical Israel: different worship (no more sacrifices, different liturgy), different theologies, different behavioral obligations, and different expectations of the Endtime mark only some of the many significant distinctions; and of course, although unadvertised, an additional scripture in the oral as opposed to written Torah of Rabbinic Judaism. Such differences are the stuff that makes for a different religion.

The reason that this has not attracted more attention than it does is that the Jews representing Rabbinic Judaism, which is the basis for virtually all forms of Judaism today, did not intend to make a break with the ancient religious system as the community that accepted the saving power of Jesus as Christ-messiah eventually did. For the Christians, breaking away from the establishment religions was critical, despite the need to retain a level of continuity for reasons that we have already considered. For the Jews, it was exactly the continuity that was critical for maintaining its claim of authenticity, despite the need for radical changes in religious practice and doctrine. So the Scriptural nature of the Talmud emerged gradually and only became a doctrinal expectation for most Jews in the seventh or eighth century. However, the Talmud functions similarly to the New Testament as a hermeneutic through which the Hebrew Bible/Old Testament is read. That is to say, like the Christian New Testament, the Jewish Talmud serves as a lens through which to read and process earlier scripture. Even among the Protestant Christian denominations, which claim to go directly to scripture without interpretation through the Magisterium of the Church or its Apostolic tradition, the Old Testament cannot be read without looking at it through the lens of the New. So, too, in Jewish tradition among all but a tiny group known as Kara'ites, the Hebrew Bible is read through the eyes of the Talmud. It is certainly true that the *way* in which it is read may vary greatly among Rabbinic Jewish communities, but the broad range of Talmudic hermeneutic nevertheless concretizes the meanings of the Bible for Jews. The "revelation" of tradition that resulted in the development of the Talmud thus pushes the boundaries between revelation and interpretation even farther than the New Testament, which is also extremely exegetical in its intertextual relationship with the Old Testament. Nevertheless, its recognition in traditional Judaism as "Oral Torah" renders its status to be that of scripture.[26]

In this essay, we treat Biblical Religion as the "mother of scriptural religions," so to speak, and for the purposes of this examination, the mother of three of its offspring. There *is* no more Biblical Religion outside the text of the Hebrew Bible. Nobody practices it. The chosenness that is so central and deliberate in the Hebrew Bible is an institution or paradigm that has been absorbed in one way or another by all of its surviving monotheistic progeny.

How has Rabbinic Judaism understood chosenness? With a lot of ambivalence, clearly, and it was the experience of permanent exile that forced a high level of complexity and ambivalence within Jewish thinking about chosenness. On the one hand, Rabbinic Judaism accepts the chosenness of Israel expressed in the Hebrew Bible and applies it to the continuation of Israel's unique relationship with God among Israel's descendants, the Jews. On the other hand, the Talmud and Rabbinic Literature contain a significant amount of material that expresses unease with the notion. One repeated sentiment is that God did not choose Israel because of its inherent superiority, but rather because there were no other takers. God had tried the Torah out on many peoples, but only Israel accepted it.[27] In an alternative tradition, God eventually had to force one people to accept the difficult life of Torah commandments, and that people ended up being Israel.[28] In a third, Abraham and his progeny were chosen by the angels, but only by the casting of lots, not because Israel was inherently better than any other nation.[29] A more complex notion of an afterlife than that of Biblical Religion had also entered into Rabbinic Judaism, but it remained uncertain and, therefore, flexible. No final dogmatic solutions were reached regarding exactly who merited the world to come, and it remained possible that the righteous of any faith, whether or not from among the chosen, could enter.[30]

▪ CHOSENNESS AS A HISTORY OF MONOTHEISMS

To summarize, we have suggested that the origin of the notion of chosenness in Israelite religion derives from the nature of tribal religion in the ancient Near East in general. Whatever its origin, however, chosenness became intimately associated with monotheism and Israel by the time of the Greek colonization of Western Asia in the fourth century, BCE. Monotheism became equated with this notion of exclusive chosenness, or chosenness with monotheism. The chosen or, depending on how one reads scripture, those who chose, tended to consider themselves higher in the spiritual and religious hierarchy than those who were or did not.

In the earliest period of emerging monotheism, only one monotheistic community existed to articulate its exclusive relationship with a deity that was both its own tribal god and the God of all creation. As Martin Jaffee expressed it so succinctly, "The unique Creator of the world discloses his love and will in a unique moment of self-disclosure to a unique human community."[31] If Israel was chosen, other religious communities were not. We have posited that because chosenness came to be considered one of the central authoritative and distinguishing features of monotheism, successful new forms of monotheism naturally tended to absorb the notion and apply it to their own membership. In the earliest period of competing monotheistic truth claims, chosenness was considered something of a zero-sum phenomenon. Only one religious tradition could be the "truly chosen."

We have noted that the notion of chosenness created a certain unease as well, which is reflected in some Biblical texts. Be that as it may, as Christianity emerged successfully in competition with establishment religions such as Biblical Religion, intertestamental Judaisms and those associated with ancient Rome, it claimed that it was the exclusive heir to the unique Biblical phenomenon. Thus a "new covenant" epitomized the "new Israel" the *verus Israel* or "true Israel" of the Church. If Christians were now the chosen, then the "old Israel" could not be.

At about the same time, Rabbinic Judaism was emerging as a distinct religious tradition. It could rely on the old Biblical expressions of chosenness as a consolation after the destruction of its Temple and the forced dispersion of its people. The Temple may have been destroyed and its power and unique public status taken over by the Church, but the Jews were true to the original covenant, so they were still the "truly chosen" of God. On the other hand, Rabbinic Judaism was defeated as a political system, so it had to find other ways to understand its unique place in the world.

We have suggested that by the time of the emergence of Islam in the seventh century, when most of Western Asia was devoted to one or another variant of the two monotheistic expressions of Judaism and Christianity, it may have felt unreasonable or unrealistic for a newly emerging religion to claim a unique and exclusive chosenness. So Islam's sense of relationship with a monotheistic deity became more inclusive than either that of Judaism or Christianity, but at a price for non-Muslim monotheists. The best or "truest" expression of the divine will is reserved for Muslim believers, and only those believers have the highest social privileges and the exclusive right to rule the multireligious society that it engendered.[32]

From the perspective of the history of religion, then, one could say that the centrality of the notion of chosenness is an accident of history that became identified with the notion of religious truth as monotheism emerged with its inherently exclusive truth claims. Chosenness became a status that all monotheistic adherents felt they had to claim, and successful new forms of monotheism have made it part of their essential nature. We can observe this trend continuing into the modern era with the emergence of new religious movements such as the LDS Church. According to this perspective, it is only the vagueries of history that have made chosenness so important in the four monotheistic Scriptural systems examined here. It seems sad, even almost ridiculous from the perspective of the history of religion, that such an expectation has come to divide peoples of good faith who are intent on being upright and moral, ethical followers of their religious traditions. I conclude with some summary observations that I hope will stimulate further thinking about the problematic of chosenness and humility.

1. The early Hebrew Biblical expression of chosenness may have emerged organically out of the particularities of ancient Near Eastern religion where all religious peoples considered themselves "chosen" by their gods. It was hardly concerned about the beliefs and worship of the "other," and it had no relation with an afterlife. What occurred after this life was open to question. Israelite chosenness was about responsibility and relationship, and it provided for survival and divine protection as a small and distinct community. It also created a sense of religious elitism that became institutionalized. But the religious polity of Biblical Religion ultimately failed and was destroyed.

2. By the time of the emergence of Christianity, when Hellenistic philosophies were highly systematic and intended to be universal, chosenness became an invitation to all rather than restricted to a single group. But it was an invitation to universalism on highly particularist terms. This eventually became a chosenness of imperialism when the Roman Empire Christianized and even, in its most narrow expression, a chosenness of totalitarianism. The totalitarian tendency is articulated in the notion that only those who recognize the saving power of Christ are saved.[33] The negative of that equation is that those who would or could not must suffer unimaginable punishment, an aspect of the chosenness paradigm that does not exist in the Hebrew Bible.

3. Rabbinic Jewish chosenness is particularist and elitist, but not imperialist, probably because Rabbinic Judaism never became a religion of empire. It also continued the Biblical tradition of uncertainty about the afterlife, which

also may have affected its lack of totalitarian sentiment. Even when Rabbinic Judaism developed a more coherent view of the afterlife, it remained uncertain about it. Thus, although Israel (meaning now, the Jews) is the one community chosen by God, that does not automatically deny the entrance of the righteous among Gentiles into a positive life after death, however vague the notion of that life might be.

4. Islamic chosenness is significantly tempered because of the existence of multiple expressions of monotheism at the time of its emergence, each claiming its own chosenness. Islam nevertheless developed its own elitism. It also became imperialist through the spread of its own religious empire, but it was never totalitarian. Jews, Christians, and other Scripturalists—the "Peoples of the Book"—who are righteous and accept certain theological beliefs such as that of a final Day of Judgment, may be entitled to salvation (there is still no consensus about this among Muslim interpreters of the Qur'an and the Tradition). However, because they refused to accept the prophethood of Muhammad, thereby causing their praxis of God's religion to be flawed, they are not entitled to an equal place in the society of this world.

This historicizing of monotheisms inevitably raises some pressing questions. The first question usually asked by the "unchurched" is, "How can anyone be absolutely certain of their chosenness and their salvation?" The answer to this question is quite consistent: faith. That sense of faith can range from an automatic, knee-jerk conviction to one's superiority to a hopeful, deep, and enduring trust in an unfailing God.

Any positive response to the question of chosenness brings more questions. Is that chosenness exclusive? If yes, then what arrogance allows one to dismiss billions of intelligent human beings over the past hundreds or thousands of years who respond to different sets of faith principles? Given that different religious traditions claim a phenomelogically similar record of divine self-disclosure through scripture, by what criteria can one distinguish a single "real" truth from among the various truth claims? Can so many billions of God's human creations err, or worse, sin in their error of "wrong" belief? How is it possible to isolate only one right among the multitudes of wrong?

Rather than engage in the futility of argument over whose vision is the real truth, there is the alternative option, which consists of humbly sharing our unique perspectives and, without discarding our own particular religious systems, listening to and hearing the perspectives of our comrades on the march to the Ultimate. In my own experience, those who do so inevitably grow deeply in their own particular faith path.

In the last prophetic book of the Hebrew Bible, the prophet Malachi lamented his kinsmen straying after the temptations of alien gods with words meant to unite. His prophetic mission takes place in a depressing period of weakness among the reconstituted postexilic community of Judea, and his purpose was to look inward and prevent contact with the polytheistic religions of his day. But his words are expansive and uplifting, and can be read as uniting not his small and limited community, but rather a universal assemblage that, although made up of distinct communities, transcends the provincial nature of competitive claims for truth.

"Have we not all one Father? Did not one God create us? Why, then, do we break faith with one another, profaning the covenant of our ancestors?" (Malachi 2:10)

■ Notes

1. An earlier version of this chapter was presented as the 2005 Sterling M. McMurrin Lecture on Religion and Culture, University of Utah. The most penetrating recent articulation of the problematic discussed here is Martin S. Jaffee, "One God, One Revelation, One People: On the Symbolic Structure of Elective Monotheism." *JAAR*, 69, no. 4 (2001): 753–775). Jaffee approaches the topic from an entirely different perspective but arrives at similar conclusions. I wish to express my gratitude to Pim (Wilhelmus) Valkenberg for his astute and helpful comments on this text, but I, of course, take full responsibility for any errors or gaps in the thinking represented here.

2. The introductory paragraphs of this chapter have since been used in the introduction to my book, *Who Are the Real Chosen People?* (Woodstock, VT: Skylight Paths, 2008), although they originate here.

3. Muhammad Ibn Hisham, *Al-Sira al-Nabawiya* (Beirut: Dar al-Thiqafa al-Arabiyya, n.d.), Vol. 1, pp 142–147; English translation by Alfred Guillaume, *The Life of Muhammad* (Karachi: Oxford University Press, 1955), 62–64.

4. Firestone, *Journeys in Holy Lands* (Albany: SUNY, 1990), 63–71; Al-Tha'labi, *Ara'is al-Majalis*, trans. William Brinner (Leiden: Brill, 2002), 139–140; Cf. Genesis 21:17–19 (and Genesis 16:7).

5. Ibn Hisham, 145; Guillaume 63–64. In another version of the poem, the voice tells him that it is by the nest of the ravens, by the nest of the ants.

6. See also, Prov. 20:7, Ps. 101:2, 116:9, Zach. 10:12, Ps. 56:14. God begins his discourse with Abraham by voicing a similar command, *lekh-lekha* (Gen. 12:1), and to the Jewish mind, that "walking" (*halokh*) is intimately associated with Jewish traditional behavior norms, the *halakhah* (the simple root can also have a meaning that is akin to "behave" as in Jer. 9:3, Prov. 11:13, Ps. 86:11).

7. See Lev. 26:3–45, Deut.11:26–29, Deut. 30.

8. Ex. 12:38.

9. Deut. 23:8–9. Joseph married an Egyptian, and their two sons became the progenitors of the two Israelite tribes of Efrayim and Menashe (Gen. 41:45–52); Moses married the daughter of a Midianite priest with whom he had at least one child (Ex. 2:16–22). Later, in the Land of Canaan/Israel, Israelite intermarriage with other peoples became a problematic issue and was outlawed, though always practiced.

10. Leviticus 19:32–34.

11. Or "impassioned," often translated as "jealous," but see Brown, et al, *Hebrew and English Lexicon of the Old Testament* (Oxford: Clarendon Press, 1977, p. 888).

12. As noted earlier, the individuals who defined themselves as Moabite (or Philistine, etc.) may have derived from other ethnic or tribal units but then joined the Moabite collective through war, famine or other means and then assimilated within a few generations into the specific culture. That cultural assimilation would have included worship of the local cultural deity or deities.

13. A. D. Nock, *Conversion* (Oxford: Clarendon Press, 1933).

14. Nili Fox, "The Concepts of God in Israel and the Question of Monotheism," in eds. G. Beckman and T. Lewis, *Text, Artifact, and Image: Revealing Ancient Israelite Religion* (Brown Judaic Studies, 2006), 341–343.

15. See Rodney Stark, and Laurence R. Iannaccone, "A Supply-Side Reinterpretation of the 'Secularization' of Europe," *Journal for the Scientific Study of Religion,* 33 (1994): 230–252; Rodney Stark, "How New Religions Succeed: A Theoretical Model," in *The Future of New Religious Movements,* ed. David G. Bromley and Phillip E. Hammond (Macon, GA: Mercer University Press, 11–19); Rodney Stark and William Sims Bainbridge, *A Theory of Religion* (New York: Peter Lang, 1987; Rutgers, NJ: Rutgers University Press, 1996). This finds distinct parallels with rational choice theory. See Michael Allingham, *Choice Theory: A Very Short Introduction* (New York: Oxford, 2002); Michael Allingham, *Rational Choice Theory: Critical Concepts in the Social Sciences* (5 Vols.) (New York: Routledge, 2006).

16. H. L. Ginsberg, *Kitbe Ugarit* (Jerusalem: Mosad Bialik, 1936); T. H. Gaster, "Psalm 29," *Jewish Quarterly Review* 37 (1946–1947), 55ff; F. M. Cross, "Notes on a Canaanite Psalm in the Old Testament," BASOR 117 (1950), 19–21; Carola Kloos, *Yhwh's Combat with the Sea* (Leiden: Brill, 1986).

17. John Gager, *The Origins of Anti-Semitism* (New York: Oxford, 1985), 39, 69.

18. Gen.12:103, 17:1–14, 22:15–18; Ex. 19:1–6; Lev. 24:20–26, 26:44–45; Deut.7:6–8, 14:2; Isaiah 42:6, 43:10, 44:1, 45:4, 49:7–8; Psalm 33:12, 35:4, etc.

19. Babylonian Talmud, *Chagigah* 3a-b, *Avot deRabbi Natan* Ch.44 (Vienna Ed., p.124), Mekhilta deRabbi Yishmael *Beshalach* 3 (Horowitz-Rabin Ed., p.99), Romans 9:4.

20. The letters that are rendered in Jewish translations as "the Lord" actually spell out the name that the very early Israelites called their tribal god. It is convention among Jews not to pronounce that name, but the meaning of the sentence changes significantly if the notion of deity presented there is seen as tribal and monolatrous.

21. René Girard, *Violence and the Sacred,* trans. Patrick Gregory (Baltimore: Johns Hopkins University, 1977).

22. On the other hand, literary and phenomenological parallels between the Hebrew Bible and ancient Near Eastern texts have long been noted. See James Bennet Pritchard, *The Ancient Near East,* Vols. 1 and 2 (Princeton: Princeton University Press, 1965); Walter Beyerlin, *Near Eastern Religious Texts Relating to the Old Testament* (Philadelphia: Westminster, 1975);Frank Moore Cross, *Canaanite Myth and Hebrew Epic* (Cambridge, MA: Harvard University, 1973; H. L. Ginsberg, *Kitbe Ugarit;* T. H. Gaster, "Psalm 29."

23. Some object to the use of the term "supersessionism" and would prefer the softer "fulfillment." Although fulfillment theology is an important and commendable development that for many transforms or even abrogates the classical position of Christian supersession, the latter was dominant until recent times and it is the classic notions that are being discussed here. See Rabbi David Rosen, *Nostra Aetate,* Forty Years after Vatican II: Anniversary Conference of the Holy See's Commission for Religious Relations with Jewry (Rome, 2005 http://www.bc.edu/research/cjl/meta-elements/texts/cjrelations/resources/articles/Rosen_NA40_27Oct05.htm). Either term acknowledges the importance of mimesis and intertextuality in these scriptures.

24. Firestone, "Is there a notion of 'divine election' in the Qur'an?" in *New Perspectives on the Qur'ān. The Qur'ān in Its Historical Context 2* NY: Routledge, 2011.

25. Firestone, *Jihad: The Origin of Holy War in Islam* (New York: Oxford University Press, 1999), 48–65, esp. 64 and p.156, note 121.

26. There are many difficulties associated with the scriptural status of the Talmud. The Talmudic sage is different from the prophet, for example, and the hermeneutical nature of the Talmud is clearly interpretive in direct relation to the Hebrew Bible. It might be termed phenomenologically "quazi-scripture," but its title as "Oral Torah" (*torah shebe'al peh*) gives it authority for keeping the finite and canonized revelation of the Hebrew Bible alive in a manner that finds clear parallels with the title and role of the New Testament.

27. Babylonian Talmud (BT) *Avodah Zarah* 2b; *Mekhilta deRabbi Yishma'el, Bachodesh parashah* A (on Ex.19:2).

28. BT *Shabbat* 88a.

29. *Pirkey deRabbi Eli'ezer* chapter 24.

30. BT *Megillah* 13a, *Tosefta, Sanhedrin* 13:2.

31. Jaffee, "One God, One Revelation, One People," 760.

32. This is based on legislation derived from an interpretation of Q.9:29 plus a document called the "Pact of 'Umar" and codified in Islamic legal literature (*fiqh*). See Ibn Qayyim al-Jawzi, *Ahkam Ahl al-Dhimma* 2 vols. ed. Subhi Salih (Beirut: Dar al-'Ilm Lil-malayin, 1983).

33. This is expressed classically by the famous *extra ecclesiam nulla salus* (no salvation outside the church), first formulated by Cyprian of Carthage (d. 258) in his Letters (lxxii *Ad Jubajanun de haereticis baptizandis* as *"Quia salus extra ecclesiam non est"* and reiterated repeatedly by popes (such as Innocent III [d.1208], Boniface VIII [d.1302]) and authoritative Church statements (such as the Fourth Lateran Council [1215], the Council of Florence [1442]). There were, of course, counter positions as well, sometimes referred to as "universal reconciliation," based on the writings of Clement of Alexandria (d.211/216), Origen (d. ca 254) and others. However, this position virtually disappears from official discourse after the Christianization of the Roman Empire, and it would appear that a strict teaching of *extra ecclesiam nulla salus* was intended by most pre-modern Church leaders. This has changed since the middle of the last century, but despite the major shift in thinking on this topic expressed in Vatican II and continuing to this day, the sentiment often remains, though now largely apart from official discourse. Daniel Madigan unpacks some of the complexity of current thinking about this in his article in this collection.

7

The Belief in the Incarnation of God: Source of Religious Humility or Cause of Theological Pride?

Olivier-Thomas Venard

I was born the second of seven brothers and sisters into a strong Catholic family on my father's side, devoted to "Cross and Crown," or as we say in French, *l'alliance du sabre et du goupillon*. As a young adult with a philosophical bent specializing in literary studies, I naturally became fascinated in postmodern thought. I became aware that the best of modernity is indebted to ancient religious sources and that many of its present problems come from forgetting or denying the existence and presence of a Creator. After I entered the Dominicans, I was trained in metaphysics and Thomistic theology, which provided me with the means to better articulate this insight. The ongoing theological critique of secularism paradoxically led me to sympathize with religious (often Muslim) criticisms of the lack of doxology in our culture, while I became aware that many authorities in my field, belong to the Jewish tradition (for example, Derrida and Steiner).

My interest in interreligious dialogue grew after I arrived in Jerusalem in 2001 to research and teach at the *École Biblique et Archéologique Française de Jérusalem*. New friends there proposed that I take advantage of the diversity found in the Holy Land by engaging in interreligious discussions, either in Jewish or in Christian contexts. I became a member of the Latin Patriarchate's Commission on Relations with Judaism. How not to be fascinated by the relationship between Jews and Christians in the Holy Land? Unlike the West, Christians are a small weak minority, whereas Jews are in control.

On a day-to-day level, other religions force me to discern clearly what is essential to my own tradition. For example, I have been challenged by the question of what my religious vows of poverty and chastity (do not) mean in every-day conversations with non-Christians in Jerusalem or, the question of whether forgiveness and injustice are distinguishable, when they are identical for many Jewish and Muslim believers. I have also discovered the concrete burden of history in such discussions. Indeed, *Nostra Aetate*'s teaching on religious freedom does not erase centuries of religious conflicts. On the other hand, at interreligious meetings, I have also experienced that one's individual qualities, gifts, and insights may go across confessional borders: on such or such issue, as a Catholic, I sometimes feel closer to a Jew or a Muslim than to a fellow Christian!

In the Holy Land today, the most urgent issue in interreligious dialogue seems to be political: How to promote a separation of religion and politics to avoid the manipulations of the former by the latter? However, this question is far too simple: Is this request a neutral one, from a religious point of view, or is it not already Christian (but if it is so, why are so many present-day Western standards so at odds with the Church?) Or should we try to go beyond tolerance, and search for religious reasons, in each of our traditions, for providing at least respect if not love for people believing differently, *without yielding in relativism*? *Dialogue* is the new name for *mission*, Pope Paul VI said, a statement that may have many different meanings. If God is God, is He not the more perplexing, the more we try to approach Him? Even though we disagree on the contents of our faith, could we not share both our happiness to know God and our sadness to be so unfaithful to His requirements? Could we not share our certainty of knowing the Truth without *owning* it? Could not our learned ignorance be a common enterprise?

In the framework of the trialogue among the Abrahamic faiths, the belief in the Incarnation puts the Christians in an uncomfortable situation. They alone have to justify their form of monotheism.

Indeed, in the rabbinic Jewish tradition, the beliefs concerning Jesus are traditionally discarded as blasphemous[1] or simply not relevant.[2] In modern Jewish scholarship, the dogmatic side of Christianity is often considered a pagan idolatrous distortion[3] of the purely Jewish message of Jesus, eventually leading up to intolerance;[4] or even a credulous effeminizing[5] of the Jewish inheritance handed down by Jesus to his disciples. "If a man says to you I am God, he is a liar; if he dubs himself Son of Man, at last he shall regret it; if he says I am ascending in heaven he will not keep his promise."[6]

And in purely Qur'anic terms, the core belief of Christianity seems to be bluntly ruled out. The accusation of "associationism" (*širk*)[7] seems to rule out any concept of incarnation or of uniplurality in the Godhead[8], and thus to disqualify Christians as partners in an authentic theological trialogue: "Christians have said: the Messiah is the Son of God . . . Let God destroy them!"[9]

So much so, that a frequent tendency of Christians in interreligious dialogue has been to avoid dealing with dogmatics in general[10] and to play down what is nevertheless their core belief.[11] Indeed, their belief in the incarnation of God places Christians in a humbled and defensive condition from the outset.

Now, real dialogue can only take place between equals. So our first question will be the following: How can Christians prove that they are truly monotheist to their Jewish and Muslim friends?

■ BELIEF IN INCARNATION IN THE PRESENCE OF TRIALOGUE: HUMILITY DE FACTO

There are two strategies for Christians to postulate their monotheistic commitment history and theory.

First, historical studies open up many opportunities to renew our theological dialogues. As regards Islam, it may be argued that despite a prejudice originating in commentators, the Qur'anic tradition is not utterly deprived of means to think of the relationship between God and matter.[12] Furthermore, read closely, the Qur'an does not necessarily target the orthodox Christian faith, but a set of heresies, such as tritheism[13] or Mariolatry,[14] that can be reconstructed thanks to several ancient texts condemning them. The orthodox doctrine about Christ, it is contended, does not contradict the Qur'anic teaching on the absolute impossibility of any procession deriving *from* God.[15] So much so that according to the author of one of the best translation of the *Qur'an* in modern language, traditional Christianity escapes the reproach of associationism...[16] Of course, one may be skeptical about the real impact through historical research on the average Muslim or Christian.[17] At least, they should prevent academics from any exclusivism, which is a first achievement.

The Judaic notion of God is much richer than the standard Maïmonidean concept largely indebted to Aristotelian-Muslim metaphysics. Even in the framework of modern Judaism, the subtle approaches to God of the Kabbala or newer spiritual movements might be contrasted with the rather univocal account of the transcendence of God conveyed by many philosophers.[18] Moreover, the diversity of Ancient Judaism's understanding of God's unity is ever more researched today.[19]

Indeed, the ancient Jewish sense of God is necessary to understand the composition of the first Christological discourses and narratives in the years 30 to 50. In the Gospel narratives, Jesus is faithful to the Jewish ideal of always seeking Someone greater:[20] "nonxe is good save One."[21] Moreover, by revealing God as a loving "Father," Jesus radicalized theological assumptions formerly derived from the Jewish meditation on the cosmic and historic experience of the people. By stressing God's gratuitous behaviour as Creator and author of Providence, he stressed the fact that no necessity rules the divine act of creating.

Nevertheless, Paul's main challenge was surprisingly not to make his interlocutors believe that Jesus is God, but rather that He truly was man, born of a woman,[22] arguably over against docetic accounts of his divinity triggered by the supernatural powers he had shown forth during his ministry.[23] Indeed, straight from the literary beginning of Christology, in the very fabric of New Testament poetry and narrative, the attributes of creative Wisdom had started to be concentrated in the Person of Christ.[24]

The New Testament does not countenance reducing Jesus to the scope of a prophet or a wise man, and even less to a "man-made-God" by his followers. Embedded in practices more than expressed in discourses, the primitive "Christology" in its Jewish setting could not be but "from above."[25] It was a doctrine of the inhabitation of the Name in the flesh—understood in the sense of the full human nature. Only this, after all, could be thought and believed by pious people keeping the memory that such mysterious presence had been enacted in a column of fire or in a golden ark....[26]

If brief, What is at stake in the historical encounters of the Christian faith with Judaism or Islam is *the correct theoretical rendering of the belief in the incarnation* in its monotheistic context. In fact, it took three to four centuries, many heresies, and much philosophical speculation to Christians, first to articulate the astonishing core belief imbedded in the religious *praxis* initiated by Jesus and his disciples in Jerusalem, and then to go on confessing it rightly. It is beyond the scope of this study to tell in details the coinage of new metaphysical categories such as "subsisting relation," or the theological reshaping of those of "essence" and "person" that have been necessary to confess Christ as God[27] without reducing him to an idol, that is, without putting a human—far too human—answer in place of the divine question he asks to his disciples: "Who do you say that I am?"[28] Let a few reflections on the final phrasing of the Christological dogma defined at Chalcedon suffice.

It has been rightly described as a "riddle" pointing at "a new and surprising reality which we could not previously have thought possible," namely "the reality of Christ's *hypostasis*"[29]—a remarkable literary achievement in learned ignorance. The council reads: "the one and only Son, our Lord Jesus Christ: this selfsame one is perfect both in deity and in humanness; this selfsame one is also actually God and actually man."[30] Lest it collapse into idolatry or absurdity, this statement implies a strict logic of absolute incommensurability of God and creatures. It is crucial to the doctrinal formula[31] that the infinite difference between God and any creature[32] be carefully maintained in the case of Christ. Nevertheless, this incommensurability must not be conceived of as a mere *gap* between God and creatures, as if the difference between them were of the same kind as the "distance" between created beings. "Because of [this] incommensurability the predicates 'is human' and 'is God' do not and cannot refer to natures standing in relations of mutual exclusion."[33]

In no way is the Christological dogma an idolatrous hand snatching at the mysterious otherness and unicity of God.[34] To the contrary: in Christ, God is only "known as unknown."[35] Indeed, insofar as there is but one person in Christ— namely, the Word of God—the logic of reduplicate statements enables us to say that in Him, "what is true of the man who is God is true of the God who is man.[36] Nevertheless, "…the nature of man, as creature, is incommensurable with the nature of God, who is the creator. But it is true to say that anything predicable of the man Christ is predicable of the God Christ and *e converso*."

"…[N]otwithstanding the fact that, even in Christ, there is no possible 'common logical ground' which the divine and human natures occupy; as Chalcedon puts it, the divine and the human natures remain 'unconfused.'"[37] "Just as of one and the same shape it is contradictory nonsense to say that it is a square and a circle, so it is also 'as devoid of meaning' to say 'without explanation, that the historical Jesus of Nazareth was also God.'" "What you say of Jesus in so far as he is man cannot be said of Jesus in so far as he is God: 'Jesus is God' is true, 'Jesus was born of Mary' is true, 'Jesus died on the cross' is true; but it is not in so far as Jesus is God that Jesus was born of Mary or that Jesus died on the cross… Clearly, to say of Jesus that he is God is not to say the same thing as to say of Jesus that he is man, nor does the former entail the latter, even if both the former and the latter are true."[38]

In brief, when the theologian speaks about Christ, as when he speaks about God, he knows *that* what he utters is true, but he does not know *how* it is true. Thus, the most daring Christian theological statements are real pieces of learned ignorance.

Moreover, Christian theological discourse requires epistemological humility. Orthodox dogma challenges the rationalistic account of a mastering reason with a kenotic conception of reason. In rationalistic thought, Jesus escapes any conceptual grasp, because of his *temporal* remoteness; but within the temporal realm, reason is able to gauge the gap between facts and faith (for example, the quest for the so-called "historical Jesus" results in reconstructions trying to make sense of the traces that he has left in history without yielding in Christian faith).

In traditional, confessional thought, Jesus escapes any conceptual reduction because of the *ontological* difference between Creator and creature, which he both overcomes and enlarges. Now, reason is unable to bridge the *ontological* gap between God and man. Thus, the meditation about Christ results not in an answer silencing all questions, but in an ultimate question putting an end to all answers.

In its Christological context, reason appears nobler in *extension* and humbler in *comprehension* than in its secular context. It is not an instrument for mastering whatever it touches, but a limited light able to feel and state the presence and existence of what it nevertheless cannot conceptually grasp. The incarnation of God is thinkable, though not representable.[39]

As opposed to this epistemological humility, rationalism locks the human mind in immanence and paves the way to idolatry.[40] Indeed, worshipping images of created beings is hardly essential to idolatry. Its core is the closing of human mind, the suffocation of human desire by, and the allegiance of human existence to, only created things. Perhaps its most subtle occurrence is in the overconfidence in all-too-human conceptions, especially in religious issues, which threatens every monotheistic faith.[41] Turner's book about faith and reason is very important here, because it demonstrates that one can fall into a type of idolatry by having a notion of God that limits what he can and cannot be.

■ A COUNTERPOINT TO THE PHILOSOPHICAL AND POLITICAL HISTORIES OF THE RELIGION OF INCARNATION: INTELLECTUAL PRIDE OR MORAL HUMILITY?

Now, by working out the rational articulation of their belief, Christian theologians were led to refine considerably the sense of both the transcendence of God and the dignity of mankind. Indeed, God incarnate can no longer simply be "wholly Other," in the same sense as the otherness of creatures differing from one another. The natural sense of divinity derived from the awe aroused by the traces of the Creator in nature is overwhelmed by a new one. God is, so to say, "otherly other." The transcendence of the Creator God reflects as well His infinite closeness as the unfathomable source and cause of our being.[42] According to this other otherness, once again, the predicates "is human" and "is God" cannot refer to nature's standing in relations of mutual exclusion.

The actual, historical incarnation, remains obviously an object of faith. Once it has been discovered, its rational possibility repels the affirmation of its impossibility as potentially idolatrous. "It is perfectly reasonable to think it false to say this of any historical person. But contradictory it is not, except on some quite idolatrous account of God...God cannot be exclusive of anything at all."[43] Even though it is discovered on the occasion of the Christian preaching, the *possibility* of such a close presence of God to mankind does not need the Christian faith to be acknowledged, so long as it remains but a logical question.

Now the actualization of such a possibility in Christianity has had tremendous consequences regarding the way we conceive of mankind. For Christian thought, the dignity of human beings does not simply come from their being created by God, but also from the fact that God assumed an individual human nature in Christ at a particular historical moment, thus bestowing an incomparable nobility to the human creature. Moreover, Christ himself in the Gospel has closely linked his fate to that of the humblest people (women, children, disabled people...),[44] thereby establishing an unbreakable connection between his followers' relation to him and to the poor ones.

Human rights, as they were articulated by the end of the eighteenth century in Old Europe are very much indebted to the evangelical and Christological context, although it took nearly two centuries for the Catholic Church officially to recognize some of these rights.[45] Generally speaking, many achievements of modernity are deeply rooted in Christianity—even though dialectically. Marcel Gauchet's definition of Christianity as "the religion of the way out of religion"[46] has become a commonplace to connect modern Western secularism with the old Western Christianity from which it comes.

Thus, the existence of the will as a spiritual faculty of its own,[47] the autonomy of the individual, freedom of conscience, and even the distinction between State and religion[48] derive from the recognition of the human person as the only absolute available on earth—a conviction turned into a moral imperative by the belief in incarnation embedded in the Gospel narratives.[49] At a more theoretical level, many of our modern epistemic strategies are indebted to ancient theology, as several theologians are showing in their ongoing works, after John Milbank's *Theology and Social Theory.*[50]

At this point, the initial situation seems to be reversed. The Christian thinkers are no longer defensive about their monotheism, but perhaps can be overconfident about their language on God. The transformation of learned ignorance into intellectual humility is certainly not automatic. We are in great danger of falling into intellectual pride: "See what great achievements Christianity has brought to humanity"!

■ HISTORICAL CONSCIENCE AS A WARRANT OF INTELLECTUAL HUMILITY

Yet, that, in its turn, will soon become a cause for moral humility. Indeed, Christians have only to look back in their history to discover much personal and collective unfaithfulness and many violations of basic evangelical principles.

Too often has the defense of the interests of the Church as a human institution been substituted for the promotion of the interest of the People of God. Too often have Christians defended their power more than truth. Thus, they triggered counterreactions stressing the autonomy of the individual over against the institution at the level of religious conscience in the time of the Renaissance, and at the level of political conscience in the time of the Enlightenment. Such movements could have resulted in religious awakenings, as Henri de Lubac has shown in his studies of Pico or Cusa,[51] but unfortunately they led to new waves of hybristic self-confidence. Hence, the baby has very often been thrown out with the bath water. The reaction against the power of churchmen turned out to be a rebellion against the Creator God, as was the case during the French Revolution, which progressively rejected any reference to a Creator God.[52]

The whole "drama of atheist humanism"[53] could be evoked here. If there is no God and the only control on human behavior is human reason and logic, everything will sooner or later be permitted, for the sake of efficiency or social utility. Thus, by a dialectical subversion of the evangelical message, moral progress that could have been experienced as an opportunity to glorify the Creator came to be obscured or denied by his unfaithful creatures entrusted with the revelation and then, hijacked by irreligious people and turned into Promethean *hybris*. The climax of this drama was the ironclad system of Nazism, in which those who were killed as "useless," "detrimental" poor people were principally the Jews—namely, the People *God* has chosen.[54]

Faced with such scandals, however, the Western conscience is still tempted by diverse forms of secular humanism or by theories that often come to be but postmodern disguises of nihilism.[55] The world should be re-enchanted again: Scholars committed to their faith-traditions should strive to show the light of the Creator already present even in the chiaroscuro of the theories of their secularized colleagues! Even within the Catholic Church, I dare say, the practical consequences of the anthropologic turn, which took place in theology as a response to these dramas, were not always immune from forgetting God. The trivialization of liturgy in many Western Churches might, for example, well be one of them. In fact, recovering a genuine and shared sense of the existence and the presence of God in daily life is urgent.

Is it possible to guide the abstract transcendentalism of the moderns and the absolute indeterminacy of the postmoderns back to the concrete transcendence of God? Shall we be able to recover an authentic sense of the transcendence of God devoid of dualism, a sense of His transcendence that would help us understand that there is no rivalry between God's omnipotence and human freedom, unless His power be idolatrously construed as on the same level with any created power? We are convinced that ongoing interreligious relations are a sure path to recover this sense of God. Only the collaboration of our three traditions will enable us to recover a correct conception of the hierarchy of causes, as was already the case in the twelfth and thirteenth centuries.

■ FROM PAST POLITICAL FAILURES TO FUTURE THEOLOGICAL CHALLENGES

All of us remember the spectacular celebrations of apology and atonement presided over by John-Paul II, in the symbolical year 2000, celebrated as the 2000th after the birth of Christ. However one might gauge them, the fact is that the main motive for hope they were intended to convey could be summarized as follows: "*we* failed—God did *not*. Only He can reopen a shared future for us all."[56] We have not lived up to the moral consequences of the Incarnation and we must repent of this.

The same Pontiff, who is remembered both as a deep theologian of the Incarnation of God[57] and as a champion of interreligious meetings, is also the one who also went through both the Nazi and the Communist prometheanisms. Indeed, the need for interreligious dialogue arises first in the political field. None of the civil societies that our Christian, Muslim, or Jewish traditions have informed has been able to fulfill the great human expectations implied in the revelation with which they were endowed. In different ways, for example, we have failed in absolutely respecting freedom of conscience, restricting the use of force to the minimum required by social life, or promoting equity between men and women—yet these are moral standards possibly and diversely conveyed by our narratives, according to the apologists of every one of our traditions. Even the controversies and corrections coming from each of them have proved to be insufficient. Therefore, the political conviction animating interreligious dialogue is that what none of our traditions has really succeeded on its own, will only be achieved in partnership with the two others. Certainly, such a perspective must be favored in the political field, in order to repel the threat of any clash of civilizations.

However, permit me to point out that the deepest reason for this is not so much political or moral as theological. What is needed is not so much a simple relativizing that can result from any confrontation of different cultures, as a new appreciation of our conception of the One absolute. Indeed, the very existence of believers in both the other traditions, reminds every Abrahamic believer of the divinity of God, because, if God is God, nothing happens in his creation but with his permission. By tolerating—if not celebrating—the fact that actual other human beings bear other witnesses to the divine otherness, every one of us warrant that our God is the living and merciful God, and not an idol.

Therefore, actually meeting faithful persons of the other monotheisms is today a religious duty. It is the best guarantee to remain theocentric, by maintaining the practical conditions of a pious learned ignorance against any ideological, tribal reduction of the transcendence of God—regressions all the more dangerous as they happen in a monotheistic thought: "The more notions of the divinity tend towards idolatry, the more we will find them opposing one another like tribal gods. Yet as such 'theologies' claim to be 'monotheistic,' that opposition will be the more acrimonious in that each pretends to exclusive possession of a complete account of reality: a posture academics call 'exclusivism.' And when that complete account is reinforced by economic and political power, the opposition becomes deadly."[58]

■ THE FUTURE OF OUR TRIALOGUE: LEARNED IGNORANCE— A THEOLOGICAL WARRANT AGAINST IDOLATRY

Promoting interreligious encounters does not prevent one's being true to one's side or thinking that one's community is closer to God and his will. Ours might be *the best* without turning the other into *evil*: indeed, there are degrees in goodness. However, over against any claim to exclusive control of the truth, we religious people should continually enhance the interrelations between our traditions,[59] in order to deepen our specific faith thanks to that of the other. Our next step could be to test the ideal of mutual correction and enhancements of our three monotheisms not only in the practical, social field, but also in the properly religious field. Is it a mere dream to hope that all religious people strive to find deep grounds *in their own traditions* for being open minded and welcoming to all religious goods or truths, from wherever they may come?

Let me try and illustrate this last suggestion by a last glimpse at the Christian dogma of the incarnation. I would like to propose that Christians might be helped to go on rightly confessing Christ as true God and true man, by welcoming the light shed by the other monotheist faiths.

From its very beginning, Christological doctrine was indebted to earlier philosophical traditions for its phrasing. As Denys Turner remarks about the rules of the logic of incommensurability displayed by the theology of incarnation, "it is very hard to see how they could ever have been formulated with any degree of precision without the resources of metaphysics and logic derives from philosophical traditions far more ancient than Christianity itself."[60]

It is not less hard to imagine how this logic of incommensurability could have been elicited by medieval speculative theologians, without actual relations with Jewish and Islamic thought. Appreciation of this dialectic relationship could bring Judaism, Islam, and Christianity closer to one another. On one hand, theoretical speculation about the orthodox confession of the two natures of Christ might have deepened the biblical conception of God's transcendence to the point of bringing it to a speculative achievement never reached before. On the other hand, the discoveries of Ibn Sina, the teaching of Maïmonides, the meditation of the *Liber de Causis* taken over consecutively by the three traditions, have resulted in logical procedures and metaphysical tools articulating the unique transcendence of God and His relations to created beings. They allowed Christians to go on confessing Christ rightly without reducing Him to an idol.

As it was illustrated best a few years ago by Robert Sokolowski's illuminating account of the "Christian difference," the history of Christian metaphysics is that of a progressive disentangling from emanationist trends.[61] However, this Christian difference would probably never have been articulated without these Muslim and Jewish thinkers. Before Aquinas, they remodeled metaphysical discourse according to theological imperatives (especially the distinction between *esse* and *essentia*),[62] in order to avoid any ontotheological account of the relationship between the Creator-First Cause and His creatures.[63] Aquinas's recourse to participation, this instrument of Neoplatonic thought, to render coherent the radical introduction of a free creator into Hellenistic metaphysics "was only accomplished in conjunction with Avicenna and Moses Maimonides: an Islamic philosopher who introduced a distinction which would prove key to Aquinas' elaboration of the creator as 'cause of being,' and a Jewish thinker steeped in 'the Islamicate.' "[64] Thus, "what many regard as the classical Christian synthesis of philosophical theology, Aquinas' *Summa Theologiae*, proves in retrospect to have already been an intercultural, interfaith achievement, offering a constructive intellectual demonstration of the way that faith cannot be something which we grasp but which must grasp us; and even further, of the role those of other faiths can play in articulating one's own."[65]

If medieval theological sophistication in speaking of God turns out to be an interfaith dialectical achievement, the same must be said about theological language about Christ. Permit me to tell here a personal anecdote. During my first months in Jerusalem, I felt much annoyed by the calls for prayer shouted at our priory and church from the ever more powerful loudspeakers of the nearby small mosque. It sounded especially irritating to my ears, when it invaded the acoustic space of our basilica just as the president of our Eucharistic concelebrations was lifting up the consecrated host, to offer it to the adoration of the congregation. I experienced this imposed vocal presence as a disturbing noise, causing spiritual wounds and eliciting desire for revenge. "We should buy a huge bell," I thought, "and make even more noise than they do!" But little by little, I learned not only to cope with, but sometimes even to appreciate these calls—depending on quality of the chant, I must say. If you remove the claims to the exclusive possession of truth it includes, the call is first of all a vivid reminder of the presence of God, and it may be more fitted with the Eucharistic celebration than I thought: Yes, God is great, even greater than what human mind would have ever imagined. He is able to give Himself through such modest species.... This is maybe not the result the *muezzin* would expect from his calls, but this is surely an experience of overcoming the clash of civilization on a daily-life scale!

At a more theological level, cordial relationships with believing Jews and Muslims, together with a more serious appreciation of their requisites regarding monotheism will prevent Christian scholars from exaggerated "low" Christologies, which have sometimes resulted in rendering Christian origins rather unintelligible,[66] and Christian monotheism somewhat problematical.[67] The Church may say that she *knows* the Truth,[68] but she cannot claim to *possess* it, at least because *no person* is able to be possessed, and *a fortiori* if she believes that this person is God incarnate. Only a plain admission of the learned ignorance brought about by Jesus Christ can warrant the genuineness of the witness borne to His absolute truth. The respect of human conscience is an inescapable imperative for the followers of Christ, and the genuine dialogue with Jews, in particular, seems to be of tremendous importance do warrant it.[69]

■ CONCLUSION

For all these reasons, the ability to share in interreligious dialogue might be considered a test of faith for the Christian theologian. This is a new way indeed. Traditionally, our religions have tended to define themselves by reshaping their predecessors or caricaturing their successors. Thus, for a long time, Christians have generalized the opposition that the apostles met as they began to preach the Christ as Messiah to all the Jews. The Law was no longer a pedagogue (Paul), but became a deadly prison; and the Pharisee ceased to be the right interpreters of the Torah,[70] and became the archetype of hypocrisy. Conversely, rabbinic Judaism has mostly considered Christianity as idolatry and Christians as pagans to be avoided. In its turn, Islam did recast entirely Judaism and Christianity into its own categories. Symmetrically, Christianity has to reject the mask of heresy and logical absurdity it is being superimposed,[71] whereas Judaism wavers between admiration for the pure monotheism of Islam and rejection of the Qur'anic account of its relation to Jesus depicted as the prophet announced by Moses but rejected by his people.

New reversed forms of supersessionism have appeared since the Enlightenment. Jewish scholars have produced many learned and skilful books reclaiming Jesus from Christianity, either as a Pharisee (Abraham Geiger, 1810–1874), or as a prophet (Claude Montefiore, 1858–1938), or as a Hassidic master (Martin Buber, 1878–1965).[72] Moreover, as early as in the 1840s, taking over and subverting a medieval Christian conception,[73] Louis Geiger found the origins of Islam not among Christian heretics, but in the midst of rabbinic Judaism.[74] In recent years, a similar rhetoric has appeared among Muslim apologists reclaiming Western trust in reason as a legacy of Islam, through the Greek philosophers handed over to Christian thinkers despite their Christian dogmas.

To encapsulate and redeem this history of successive denials, anathemas, and supersessionisms, another model may be proposed: that of the lovers' quarrels. "Lovers' quarrels are not solved but in love, that is by being continued—and not by parting their ways to wait for the quarrels to disappear by themselves."[75] Clashes or silence are never a solution: we have to go on an disputing with one another sustained with the certitude that the relationship will always be more profitable to all than any rupture.

■ Notes

1. Cf. R.T. Herford, *Christianity in Talmud and Midrash* (New York: Ktav, 1975); M. Hilton and G. Marshall, *The Gospels and Rabbinic Judaism: A Study Guide* (New York: Ktav, 1988); or more recently the groundbreaking Peter Schäfer, *Jesus in the Talmud* (Princeton, NJ: Princeton University Press, 2007), pp. 66–79, 91–92, 106–107, 128–129.

2. "How does one have a dialogue when the subject in hand is of no interest to one party?," the Jewish contributor to a chapter dealing with Jesus asks in a recent trialogue (Sybil Sheridan, "Jesus from a Jewish Perspective," in eds. Norman Solomon, Richard Harries, Tim Winter, *Abraham's Children: Jews, Christians and Muslims in Conversation* [London: T&T Clark, 2005], pp. 87–98: 87).

3. Cf. G. Lindeskog, *Die Jesusfrage im neuzeitlichen Judentum. Ein Beitrag zur Geschichte det Leben-Jesu-Forschung* [Uppsala: A.B. Lundquist, 1938], German ed. (Darmstadt: Science Books Publishers, 1973), pp. 78–84; Susannah Heschel, *Abraham Geiger and the Jewish Jesus* "Chicago Studies in the History of Judaism 5. Jahrg. 10," (Chicago IL: University of Chicago Press, 1998), p. 152 quoting L. Geiger, *Das Judentum und seine Geschichte*, 3 vols. (Breslau: W. Jacobsohn, 1910); Trans. Ch. Newburgh, *Judaism and Its History* (New York, 1911) pp. 1, 134–136. Even in more recent studies such as H. Maccoby, *The Mythmaker: Paul and the Origins of Christianity* (London: Weidenfeld & Nicholson, 1986) all the blame for "dejudaizing Jesus" is still laid on Paul.

4. Susannah Heschel, *Abraham Geiger…*, p. 135, alluding to Samuel Hirsch, *Das System der religiösen Anschauungen der Juden und sein Verhältnis zum Heidentum, Christentum und zur absoluten Philosophie* (Leipzig: Heinrich Hunger, 1842).

5. Susannah Heschel, *Abraham Geiger*, 236: Christian dogma has been related to an alleged effemination of religion, as opposed to Judaism remaining a "classical religion." Effeminate Christianity lacks ethics and moral responsibility; masculine Judaism is a religion of law, commandments, and rational submission to dogmas. See on this LeoBaeck,

"Romantic Religion," in *Judaism and Christianity: Essays by Leo Baeck*, transl. and ed. Walter Kaufmann (Philadelphia: Jewish Publication Society, 1958), pp. 189–229.

6. *Talmud of Jerusalem*, tractate Ta'anit 2,1.

7. Cf. *Qur'an* 5, 72.

8. See recently Basil Mustafa, "Jesus from a Muslim Perspective," in Solomon et al., *Abraham's Children*, pp. 99–107. At 101: "The Qur'an refutes in unequivocal terms the doctrine of Jesus as the Son of God and the doctrine of Jesus as the incarnation of God *in any sense or form*" (italics mine). In fact, the quotations forwarded by Mustafa to prove this statement do not suffice. His Qur'anic quotations (19,88; 21, 25–27) are mere external denials of the propositions "The Merciful has betaken a son" or "The Merciful has chosen a son," without saying what could be referred to by these sentences.

Indeed, even speculative Muslim texts against the Christian dogma fail to understand the concept of "subsisting relation," which enables to distinguish between personal and essential attributes. (See later note 27). They have some excuse. Even Arab Christian apologetes met lexical difficulties: sometimes using the word *çifat* to refer to the Persons, rather than the word *'aqanim*, they provided a cause for confusion (the same word *çifat* usually meaning the attributes): See on this point Denise Masson, *Monothéisme coranique et monothéisme biblique : doctrines comparées*, 2ᵉ ed. (Paris: Desclée de Brouwer, 1976), p. 97.

9. *Qur'an* 9, 30.

10. See the remarks by Kallistos Ware, "Jesus from a Christian Perspective," in eds. Norman Solomon et al. *Abraham's Children...*, pp. 72–86. At p. 83, rightly stressing the fact that even for the World Council of Churches "the distinctive mark of the Christian faith" remains "the belief in Jesus as the divine and eternal Son of God."

11. Cf. C. Gore, *The Incarnation of the Son of God* Bampton Lectures (John Murray, 1891), p. 17.

12. For example, Ibn Rushd underlines the fact that the Qur'an is not decisive about whether it is possible to attribute corporeality to God, despite prohibitions such as Ghazali's. And rightly so, he thinks, because the Revelation is thus well attuned to most of the people, who cannot conceive of existence but in material fashion. If corporeality were simply excluded from the attributes of God, that could mean His inexistence (cf. Ibn Rushd, *Al-Kashf an manahij al-Adillah fi Aqaid al-Millah* [An *Exposition of the Methods of Arguments Concerning the Doctrines of the Faith*], (Cairo: Al-Matbaat al-Rahmaniyyah); Engl. transl. G. F. Hourani: *On the Harmony of Religion and Philosophy* (London: Luzac and Co.Ltd., 1961), p. 79.

13. Cf. *Qur'an* 4,171; 5,73.116. A sort of tritheism seems to have been implied in the monophysite teachings of the School of Edessa condemned by the council of Constantinople in 557 (see references in Masson, *Monothéisme*, pp. 103, n.16. See in particular Basil of Caesarea, *Homilia* 29: *adversus eos qui per calumniam dicunt dici a nobis deos tres* (PG 31, 1488C–1496C).

14. Cf. *Qur'an* 5,116. Epiphanius, *Adversus Haereses*, 19,4 (PG 41, 266) ; 78, 23 (PG 42, 735) refutes the heretical cult of Mary by the Collyridians, which appeared in Arabia in the fourth century.; Ireneus, *Adversus Haereses. De Ophitis et Sethianis*, 1, 30, 1 (PG 7,692–93) denounces those who call the Spirit the primordial Woman. According to Origen, *Commentaria in Evangelium Joannis*, 2, 6 (PG 14, 131) the Mother of Jesus was identified with the Holy Spirit in one of the *Gospel to the Hebrews* (more references in D. Masson, *Monothéisme*, p. 103, n.18).

15. Compare *Qur'an* 112, 1–4 and Fourth Council Of Lateran (1216), cap.2, "De errore abbatis Joachim": "There exists a certain supreme reality, incomprehensible and ineffable, which truly is the Father and the Son and the Holy Spirit, the three persons together and each one of them separately.... This reality neither begets nor is begotten nor proceeds; the

Father begets, the Son is begotten and the Holy Spirit proceeds. Thus there is a distinction of persons but a unity of nature." (DZ # 804-5).

16. "Although the Qur'anic texts do fight against either a vague threefold polytheism or a sort of generation incompatible with the unique and immaterial God, they do not attack the dogmas of the Trinity or the Incarnation as the Church teaches them. The tritheism in question does not match the dogma of the Trinity: God ONE as regards substance and THREE as regards Persons" (D. Masson, p. 98 and 102, our translation). Affirming this does not require denying the truth of the Qur'an. Without transgressing the borders of Muslim piety, is it not possible to construe its truth about Christianity in a contextual way, and to stress that the targeting of heresies is historically accurate, whereas generalizing it in a criticism against the Christian dogma as such may be wrong?

Christian apologists have traditionally underlined rich tensions present in the *Qur'an*, and proposed that it does encompass many positive hints of orthodox Christian beliefs. As a matter of fact, many odd passages of the *Qur'an* regarding the life of Jesus can be traced back to Syriac traditions; see the clear synthesis on this point by Neil Robinson, *Christ in Islam and Christianity: The Representation of Jesus in the Qur'an and the Classical Muslim Commentaries* (London: Macmillan, 1991), pp. 15–22; more in E. Rabbath, *L'Orient chrétien à la veille de l'Islam* (Beirut: Librairie orientale, 1980). Briefly, there is a sense in which the *Qur'an* does not deny both the divinity of Christ and his death on the Cross. See Charles J. Ledit, *Mahomet, Israël et le Christ* (Paris: La Colombe, 1956), pp. 152–156).

It must be acknowledged though, that more accurate readings often ruin the textual basis of these attempts. On the example of Jesus as Word, another specialist notes: "What in fact is Muhammad denying in this passage? Nothing more, it would appear, than that God was physically the Father of Jesus…In this passage he in fact affirms not only the Virgin birth on which the Qur'an always lays great emphasis, but also that Christ is 'only' God's messenger and His Word (*kalima*) – a spirit from Him, that is to say not carnally conceived by the divine afflatus and the divine fiat – exactly, then, what orthodox Christianity means by 'the Word made flesh'" (R.C. Zaehner, *At Sundry Times: An Essay in Comparative Religions* [London: Faber & Faber, 1958], pp. 201).

17. Cf. the rather pessimistic conclusion of Neil Robinson, *Christ in Islam and Christianity*, p. 192. Cf., more recently, B. Mustafa, n.8.

18. See the astonishing Eliott Wolfson, "Judaism and Incarnation: The Imaginal Body of God," in eds. T.S. Frymer-Kensky et al., *Christianity in Jewish Terms* (Boulder CO and Oxford: Westview Press, 2000), pp. 239–254.

19. Cf. for example Menahem Kister, "Some Early Jewish and Christian Exegetical Problems and the Dynamics of Monotheism," *Journal for the Study of Judaism in the Persian, Hellenistic and Roman Period*, 37/4 (2006):548–593, who concludes his erudite study by emphasizing the fact that Judaism, being a monotheistic religion that has as part of its inheritance the notion of divine beings, "even when [the Gnostic or Christian] theological systems are in bitter polemic with Judaism, they owe much to the inherent tension in Judaism itself as a monotheistic religion."

20. He claims to reveal the Father in the very encounter with himself (Cf. Jn. 14:8–10). Revealing God as a person, he makes Him escape any reifying grasp. The God of Jesus, it is often contended, is very close to mankind, so close that he may be called *Abba* (Mk. 14:36). Thus, Jesus continues and deepens the teaching of *Sefer Devarim*. Dt. 4:7–8, 32–34 (cf. Jer. 29: 13–14; Ps. 145: 18; 147: 19–20; 148: 14).

However, Jesus often enhances God's transcendence by speaking in paradoxical, aporetic, or apophatic ways. The dispute about the title "son of God" in John (Jn. 10:33–36) might be construed as an anti-idolatry polemic: the opponents of Jesus are shocked by his use of this phrase, though it can be justified by Scripture; is it not because they tend to understand "God" in a pagan manner, according to Greco-Roman standards (the Emperor was "son of God"; and it was very probably the only meaning the Roman officer at the foot of the Cross was able to intend, cf. Mk. 15: 39)?

21. Jesus's apophatism clearly appears in Mt 19:16–18; Mk 10:17–22; Lk. 18: 18–23. When called "good teacher," Jesus reminds the person of God's sole goodness and of the observance of the law: "here ran one to him, and kneeled to him, and asked him, Good Teacher, what shall I do that I may inherit eternal life? And Jesus said unto him, Why callest thou me good? None is good save one, [even] God. Thou knowest the commandments…" (Mk. 10: 17–19).

22. Cf. Eph. 4: 21, Rm. 1: 3; Gal. 4: 4–5. Paul uses already *Lord* to refer both to the tetragrammaton and to the risen Christ, as has been shown by David Capes, *Old Testament Yahweh Texts in Paul's Christology*, WUNT 2:47 (Tübingen: Mohr, 1992).

23. Cf. Flavius Josephus hands over a memory of Jesus as a wonder maker (Cf. S. Bardet, *Le Testimonium flavianum: Examen historique, considérations historiographiques* (Paris: Cerf, 2002). Despite their polemic shaping and their controversial interpretations, Talmudic passages sometimes referring to Jesus, like *Sanhedrin* 43a (?) *Sanhedrin* 106a (?) could confirm these views (see more in Peter Schäfer, *Jesus in the Talmud*).

24. See for example not only the prologue in John, but also the typological features of Jesus as Wisdom in Mt. as well. Important features projected on Christ in the New Testament are later attributed by rabbis to the Torah. For example, by describing Christ as the way, the truth and the life (Jn. 14:5), the evangelist bestows on him features later related to the study of the Torah (cf. G. A. Anderson, "Adam and Eve in Judaism and Christianity," last chapter of *The Genesis of Perfection: Adam and Eve in Jewish and Christian Imagination* [Louisville: Westminster John Knox Press, 2001]).

25. How was it possible to hinge the universal doctrine related to creation upon such an individual and brief life as that of Jesus, and in such a peculiar culture as his—Palestinian Judaism of the first century? Neither the old rationalist, nor the present-day deconstructivist approaches to Christian origins answer these questions in a plausible way. Both tend to reduce it to *a posteriori* theological constructions. Christian origins are thus rendered undecipherable, insofar as Paul, both a learned Jew and the first Christian author, was already given by the (Jewish) first communities a creed (1Cor. 15: 3) and several hymns (Eph. 1:3ff; Phil. 2: 6–11) articulating a few years after the events a very high Christology. As early as in the mid-50s, Paul claims to be remembering what he had been handed over.

The so called "ascendant Christologies," sometimes also dubbed "Christologies from below," are historically implausible. No Jew would have identified such an idolatrous Christ as Emmanuel (Mt. 1: 23) or the image of the invisible God (Col. 1: 15). Rather would they have dismissed him as an idol "unable to save" (Dt. 32: 37–38; Jer. 2: 28). Compare K. Rahner, "The Two Basic Approaches of Christology," in transl. D. Bourke *Theological Investigations, XIII*, (London: Darton, Longmann & Todd, 1975), pp. 213–223, with J.–M. Garrigues, "Jésus: le salut comme chute et relèvement d'Israël," in idem, dir., *L'unique Israël de Dieu : Approches chrétiennes du Mystère d'Israël* (Limoges: Criterion, 1987), pp. 41–58, esp. 53. Genuinely Christian Christology must be simultaneously *katagogic* and *anagogic*. It must deal with both Jesus in history and his being One of the Trinity, in the manner the New Testament speaks about Jesus (cf.Wolfhart Pannenberg, *Jesus: God and Man* [London: SCM Press, 1968]; John Arthur Thomas Robinson, *The Human Face of God* [London: SCM Press, 1973]).

26. When searching for the Jewish preparation for the belief in the incarnation, Nicolas Wright quite convincingly turns his attention to the Temple. "The Temple was of course in this period the heart and centre of Judaism, the vital symbol around which everything else

circled. It was supposed to be where YHWH himself dwelt, or at least had dwelt and would do so again." (Nicolas Wright, The *Challenge of Jesus: Rediscovering Who Jesus Was and Is* [Downers Grove, Ill.: Intervarsity Press, 1999], pp. 62–63). Indeed, the metaphor central to John's teaching about the incarnation of the Word in his Prologue (John 1: 1–18) is that of ŠKN (*eskenosen*). Word, Wisdom, Spirit, Temple and Torah are the main symbols of God's presence and saving action in favor of Israel in the world: all are conflated in the Prologue, "and I suggest that they are also major themes in the Synoptics" (N. Wright, "Jesus' Self-Understanding," in Stephen T. Davis, Daniel Kendall, Gerald O'Collins, *The Incarnation: An Interdisciplinary Symposium on the Incarnation of the Son of God* [Oxford: Oxford University Press, 2002], pp. 47–61, 57). Arguing about the Temple was common in all parties.

The ongoing research for a "purely Jewish" construal of the faith in Jesus Christ in "Messianic Jewish" milieus, might supply us with a sort of life experience of the birth of Christian dogmas: cf. the survey of the main attempts by Richard Harvey, "Jesus the Messiah in Messianic Jewish Thought: Emerging Christologies," *Mishkan: A Forum on the Gospel and the Jewish People*, 39 (2003), pp. 4–19.

27. For a brief summary involving all these notions, see Thomas Aquinas, *De rationibus fidei contra Saracenos, Graecos et Armenos, ad Cantorem Antiochenum*, chap. 4, (ed. Marietti: Roma, 1954, 969–971). On the use of "essence" about God, see *idem, Summa Theologiae*, Ia pars, qu. 2, a. 2, c. About the reshaping of "person" in the language about God, cf. *Ibid.* Ia pars, qu.29, a. 3 and qu. 13 a. 2. For the concept of subsisting relations: Ibid., Ia pars, qu. 28, a. 2, c.: "whatever has an accidental existence in creatures, when considered as transferred to God, has a substantial existence; for there is no accident in God; since all in Him is His essence. So, in so far as relation has an accidental existence in creatures, relation really existing in God has the existence of the divine essence in no way distinct therefrom. But in so far as relation implies respect to something else, no respect to the essence is signified, but rather to its opposite term. Thus it is manifest that relation really existing in God is really the same as His essence and only differs in its mode of intelligibility; as in relation is meant that regard to its opposite which is not expressed in the name of essence. Thus it is clear that in God relation and essence do not differ from each other, but are one and the same."

28. Matt. 16: 15. Kallistos Ware in "Jesus from a Christian Perspective" (p. 85) notes: "For all Christians, not just for the 'Nicenes' but for the others as well, there is something profoundly puzzling about Jesus. He is, to adapt Paul's phrase, 'unknown, yet well known' (2 Cor. 7: 9) ... We speak of the mystery of Jesus ... something that is indeed revealed to our understanding, yet never totally revealed because it reaches into the depths of God."

29. Sarah Coakley, "What Does Chalcedon Solve and What Does It Not? Some Reflections on the Status and Meaning of the Chalcedonian 'Definition,'" in eds. Stephen S. Davis et al., *The Incarnation*, pp. 153–163 at 155. The same A. rightly speaks about Chalcedon as "linguistic regulation" (p. 145), and proposes the following list of questions deliberately left unanswered by that Council: "Thus: (1) Chalcedon does not tell us in what the divine and human 'natures' consist; (2) it does not tell us what hypostasis means when applied to Christ; (3) it does not tell us how *hypostasis* and *physeis* relate to one another (the problem of *communicatio idiomatum*); (4) it does not tell us how many wills Christ has (5) it does not tell us that the *hypostasis* is identical with the pre-existent Logos; (6) it does not tell us what happens to the *physeis* at Christ's death and in his resurrection; (7) it does not tell us whether the meaning of *hypostasis* in this christological context is different, or the same, from the meaning in the trinitarian context; (8) it does not tell us whether the risen Christ is male" (Ibid., pp. 163–164).

30. A deft summary of the sinuous way to Chalcedon can be found in Thomas Weinandy, *Does God Change? The Word's Becoming in the Incarnation*, in Studies in Historical Theology 4, (Still River, MA.: St. Bede's Publications, 1985).

31. Council of Chalcedon, 30: "[…] One and the same Christ, Son, Lord, only-begotten, acknowledged in two natures which undergo no confusion, no change, no division, no separation; at no point was the difference between the natures taken away through the union, but rather the property of both natures is preserved and comes together into a single person and a single subsistent being; he is not parted or divided into two persons, but is one and the same only-begotten Son, God, Word, Lord Jesus Christ, just as the prophets taught from the beginning about him, and as the Lord Jesus Christ himself instructed us, and as the creed of the fathers handed it down to us."

32. "In Thomas Chalcedonian Christology, as in general in his philosophical theology, the pseudo-Denys's formula applies: 'the Cause of all is beyond similarity and difference'; as does Meister Eckhart's formula: 'God is distinct by virtue of indistinction' " (D. Turner, *Faith, Reason and the Existence of God*, (Cambridge: Cambridge University Press, 2004), p. 219). Cf. also Robert Sokolowski, *God of Faith and Reason* (Washington DC: Catholic University of America Press, 1990).

33. D. Turner, *Faith, Reason*, p. 217. Turner here replies to John Hick, in John Hick ed., *The Myth of God Incarnate* (London: SCM Press, 1977), p. 178.

34. As regards the immutability of God preserved in the incarnation, cf. a long discussion in Thomas Aquinas, *De rationibus fidei contra Saracenos, Graecos et Armenos, ad Cantorem Antiochenum*, chap. 4, (ed. Marietti: Roma, 1954, 979–981. The core of the argument is encapsulated in *Summa theologiae*, IIIa pars, qu. 1, a. 1, *ad* 1: "The mystery of Incarnation was not completed through God being changed in any way from the state in which He had been from eternity, but through His having united Himself to the creature in a new way, or rather through having united it to Himself. "

35. Thomas Aquinas, *Super Boethium de Trinitate*, qu. 1, a. 2 *ad* 1.

36. This is what is traditionally known as the *communicatio idiomatum* (the "communication of properties" between man and God in the language about Christ).

37. D. Turner, *Faith, Reason…*, p. 221.

38. Ibid., p. 218. Cf. Thomas Aquinas, *Summa Theologiae*, IIIa pars, qu. 16, a. 5, c. and a. 11, c. But "if it false to say that '*qua* God, Jesus died on the cross', still, because Jesus is God, it *does follow*, if Jesus died on the cross, that 'God died on the cross' is true. And if it is false to say that '*qua man* Jesus is the Son of God', still, because the second person of the Trinity became man, it *does follow* that 'the man, Jesus, is the Son of God'. If it is false to say that '*qua* God, Jesus was born of Mary', still, because the baby born is God, it is true and it follows that, as Nicaea says Mary is *theotokos*, the 'mother of God.'" (D. Turner, *Faith, Reason…*, pp. 219–220).

39. "Reason, as we might put it, is governed by an incarnational logic: it has that 'kenotic shape' because, rooted though it is in our animality, reason opens up, in its own kind, into the mystery which lies unutterably beyond it, for it can, out of fidelity to its own native impulse, ask the question which it knows it could not answer, the asking being in its powers, the answering being in principle beyond them." (Ibid, p. 261. Turner beautifully adds: " 'reason' is a point of entry into the 'darkness of God' in its way, just as, in its own distinct way, the human nature of Christ is, as Bonaventure tells us, a *transitus* into the *Deus absconditus* of Christian faith," also p. 261).

40. To be fair to the philosophers of the Enlightenment, one should add here that Kant's pietism, for example, attempted to rescue his thought from idolatry with the concept of "rational faith."

41. Besides the cancer of fundamentalism, present in any religion with a sacred text, a list of the side effects of such self-confidence could include: for *Judaism*: the ritual, or the community (in the Holy Land sometimes wrongly identified with the political state) when they tend to be viewed as ends *in se*; for *Christianity*: overappreciation of the sacramental

structures (from the Church's institutions to the sacraments themselves) making absolutes of them, despite their being means turned toward eschatological fulfilment; for *Islam*: too abstract a confession of the Uniqueness and Greatness of God may turn into an "ideological shelter" for whatever will of power.

42. So much so, that it might be represented at best as a musical interval in which what is remote and what is near are inseparably connected (David Bentley Hart, *The Beauty of the Infinite : The Aesthetics of Christian Truth*, [Grand Rapids MI: W.B. Eerdmans], 2003), pp. 188–89.

43. D. Turner, *Faith, Reason…*, *op. cit.*, p. 218.

44. Cf. Matt. 25: 35–40.

45. It takes more than one thousand pages for Fr. Basile, *La Liberté religieuse et la tradition catholique. Un cas de développement doctrinal homogène dans le magistère authentique* (Le Barroux: Abbaye Sainte-Madeleine, 1998) to harmonize the *Syllabus of Errors* condemned by Pope Pius IX in 1864, with the *Declaration on Religious Freedom "Dignitatis Humanae" on the Right of the Person and of Communities to Social and Civil Freedom in Matters Religious* promulgated by Pope Paul VI in 1965.

46. Marcel Gauchet, *Le désenchantement du monde: Une histoire politique de la religion* (Paris: Gallimard, 1985).

47. Cf. the key role of the Monothelite controversy of the 7th century in the elaboration of a theory of will. To explain the evangelical narrative of Jesus in agony in an orthodox manner, it allowed the invention of the distinction between *energeia* (faculty of action) and *praxeis* (multiple actions produced by the faculty). Cf. Philippe Fontaine, *La morale : Le devoir, la volonté, la personne* ("Philo-Notions ," Paris: Ellipses Marketing, 1998); *La volonté* ("Philo-Notions," Paris: Ellipses Marketing, 2001).

48. Cf. Matt. 22: 15–21.

49. From François-René De Chateaubriand, *Le génie du christianisme, ou Beautés de la religion chrétienne* (Paris: Mercure de France, 1803) down to René RÉMOND, *Les grandes inventions du christianisme* ("Domaine Biblique," Paris : Bayard éditions, 1999); *Le christianisme en accusation. Entretiens avec Marc Leboucher* (Paris: Desclée de Brouwer, 2000), apologetic works demonstrating the Christian inheritance of modernity have never ceased to be released.

50. Cf.John Milbank, *Theology and Social Theory, Beyond Secular Reason* (Oxford: Blackwell Publishers, 1990). Milbank here shows how the founders of "sociology" had to alter the real man, to suppress a large part of the concrete life experience of the person's life in society, in order to "scientifically" develop a "natural human being," a "social reality" or "secular society" outside Divine Revelation.

51. In his *Pic de la Mirandole* (Paris: Aubier-Montaigne, 1974), Henri "de Lubac points out […] that this shift of microcosmic reference from cosmic immanence to supernatural transcendence is an explicitly *Christian* shift, linked to acknowledgment of the supreme glory of God" (J. Milbank, *The Suspended Middle: Henri de Lubac and the Debate Concerning the Supernatural* [Grand Rapids MI / Cambridge UK: Eerdmans, 2005], p. 54); "For Pico,… the human spiritual creature, precisely *as* drawn beyond itself by grace, is self-constructing, just as, for Cusa and Bérulle, we 'give ourselves to ourselves' just *because* we are through and through divine gift. Our 'autonomy' and openness is in fact the counterpart of a radical receptivity which renders even our own action at a higher level utterly passive. Thus we are, for Pico, cultural creatures beyond nature because we are also engraced creatures beyond nature" (ibid., p. 53).

52. To qualify this statement, though, cf. Dale K. Van Kley, *The Religious Origins of the French Revolution: From Calvin to the Civil Constitution,* 1560–1791 (New Haven, CT: Yale University Press, 2000).

53. Henri de Lubac, *The Drama of Atheist Humanism* [*Le Drame de l'humanisme athée*, Paris: Spes, 1945], trans. E.M. Riley, A.E. Nash & M. Sebanc (San Francisco: Ignatius, 1995).

54. Remembering survivors of the Nazi deportation arriving in Paris, François Mauriac is reported to have said as early as 1958 "the dream of Progress, Enlightenment, and Science has ended up vanishing in front of these trains." In the same vein, A. Kaspi : "The history of the Shoah sounds as a counterpoint to modernity, to the belief that progress leads us or the philosophy of Enlightenment guides our steps." (André Kaspi, "Qu'est-ce que la Shoah? Conférences et séminaires sur l'histoire de la Shoah, Université de Paris I, 1993–1994," *Les cahiers de la Shoah* 1 [Paris: Les Éditions Liana Levi, 1994], read online: http://www.anti-rev.org/textes/Kaspi94a/index.html; our translations). This was a key theme of the teaching of Cardinal J.-M. Lustiger.

55. With the authors of *Radical Orthodoxy* (cf. eds. John Milbank, Catherine PIckstock & Graham Ward, *Radical Orthodoxy: A New Theology* [London-New York: Routledge, 1999]), we might interpret the history of western thought since the eleventh century as an increasing neglect of the participation of *all* being in the divine Being, accelerated especially by the establishment of "onto-theology," beginning with Duns Scotus. Having disconnected the appearances of things from the depths of their natures, we are no longer capable of fathoming the diversity of the ways in which beings are manifested, beginning with their coming-to-be. In order to grasp the real, then, we have sought to contain its ceaseless flux in a sort of network of stable laws—i.e., the *mathesis* to which knowledge has gradually been reduced. But the desire to conceive of finite being in strict categories without questioning its relation to Being—the separation of epistemology from ontology—comes to a dead end in the tormenting question of whether there is ontological depth behind appearances, and the conviction that certain knowledge has no necessary link to the really existent. Following Jacobi, Milbank speaks in this sense of an ultraradical Kantian "nihilism": Kant ends up discussing reality in itself as though it were *nothing*. Thus, the paradox of modernity is that it dissolves the real in the very gesture with which it claims to recognize the substance of reality. This resonates with John Paul II's own diagnosis of present-day western culture. Cf. John Paul II, Encyclical letter *Fides et Ratio*, September 14, 1998 (Libreria Editrice Vaticana), par. 46, where the pope underlines the connection between rationalism and nihilism.

56. The head of the oldest Christian institution was begging his fellow human beings to forgive many crimes or sins committed by its members over the centuries. Insofar as God alone can forgive past sins (neither reparable by their actual perpetrators, nor forgivable by their actual victims) such an action was indeed reckoning the ongoing presence of God in those human beings who had been victims and their descendants. See for example Pontifical Commission for ReligiousRelations with the Jews, *We Remember: A Reflection on the Shoah* (Vatican, 1998) John Paul II, Apostolic Letter *Tertio Millennio Adveniente*, November 10, 1994, n. 33: AAS 87 (1995): 25.

57. See his first Encyclical letter, *Redemptor hominis* (Rome: Libreria Editrice Vaticana, 1979), with the par. 17 dedicated to human rights.

58. D. Burrell, "Anthropomorphism in Catholic Context," Claremont Conference on Philosophy of Religion 11–12 February 2005, quoted from a draft kindly communicated by the author, p. 2.

59. This move begins as soon as in the Torah, where Moses is described as learned in all the wisdom of Egyptians (Exodus 2: 5, 10)—a feature polemically remembered by Stephen in his preaching (Acts, 7: 22)—and does not hesitate to apply the judicious advise of Jethro his Madianite father-in-law (Exodus 18: 1, 19–23).

60. D. Turner, *Faith, Reason…*, p. 221. The author adds "in themselves, however, these constraints are imposed upon the theologian as necessities of thought imposed by the articulation of Christianity's own central doctrines, and especially of Christological faith."

61. Cf. R. Sokolowski, *The God of Faith and Reason: Foundations of Christian Theology* (Notre Dame, IN: University of Notre Dame Press, 1982; Washington, D.C: The Catholic University of America Press, 1997).

62. "The conceptual material came to the west in the form of Ibn-Sina's observation that existence (*wujud*) is not included in what we understand of things—their essence (or quiddity, *mahiyya*)—but can only be said to 'happen to' them. In Aquinas's hands, this distinction will become the key to conceiving created beings in relation to their creator, as well as articulating what distinguishes the source of all that is for everything else" (D. Burrell, *Knowing the Unknowable God: Ibn-Sina, Maimonides, Aquinas*, [Notre-Dame IN: University of Notre-Dame Press, 1986], pp. 17–18, alluding to Avicenne, trans. G. C. Anawati *La Métaphysique du Shifa*, (Paris: Vrin, 1986), par. 108).

63. "Indeed, customary western attempts to separate creatures from the creator falsify the relation as effectively as some 'eastern' attempts to collapse the two. Fear of pantheism has moved western thinkers to parse the *distinction* as a *separation*, yet I shall argue that this strategy has diluted the specific assertions of Jewish-Christian-Muslim faith in a creator, so demoting the creator to 'the biggest things around' and promoting a secular ethos" (David B. Burrell, "Creation in the Three Monotheisms, Lecture at the E.B.A.F., Jerusalem, December 12, 2006," quoted on typ.: 6; David B. Burrell, "Creation, Metaphysics, and Ethics," *Faith and Philosophy* 18 (2001): pp. 204–221.

64. D. Burrell, *Anthropomorphisms...*, p. 2 The author refers to R. teVelde, *Substantiality and Participation in Aquinas* (Leiden: Brill, 1996) and for the crucial role of an Islamic text in this process, to his own "Aquinas' Appropriation of *Liber de causis* to Articulate the Creator as Cause-of-Being," in ed. F. Kerr, *Contemplating Aquinas* (London: SCM Press, 2003), pp. 55–74, and *Knowing the Unknowable God* (Notre Dame IN: University of Notre Dame Press, 1986). "Islamicate" was coined by M. Hodgson, *Venture of Islam* (Chicago: University of Chicago Press, 1974).

65. D. Burrell, ibid.

66. Etienne Nodet has remarkably related the birth of the "two-source theory" (considering *Mark* as the first Gospel written down, and as the source, with "Q," of the two other synoptic Gospels) to the agenda implied by the sociocultural conditioning of its inventors. They lived in the context of *Kulturkampf*: Prussia was struggling for its independence and any "foreign" dominion was proscribed: anti-Catholicism (against Rome) joined the traditional anti-Semitism. Theologians involved in that move tried to find a direct contact with Jesus, beyond institutional mediations. The simple pattern of *Mark* contrasting a brilliant ministry in a semi-pagan Galilee with a catastrophe in the narrow-minded Jewish Jerusalem, fitted at best with their wish to get rid of traditional dogmas and institutions. Cf. E. Nodet, *Histoire de Jésus ? Nécessité et limites d'une enquête*, "Lire la Bible" (Paris: Cerf, 2003), pp. 89–90.

Indeed, in *Das Jahrhundert des Heils* (Stuttgart: E. Schweizerbart, 1838), p. 132, August Friedrich Gförer, a former student of Baur, condemned the Pharisees by comparing them to Catholics: "The Pharisees closed the gate of the tradition much more eagerly than did the papacy; they plugged the fountains from which any kind of renewal in their church circle might flow." The Sadducees would have been the Reformers of "catholic" Pharisees.

67. Jewish and Muslim theologians may rightly wonder at the discourses about "God's suffering" or "God's death," sometimes awkwardly proposed by Christian thinkers legitimately concerned with the existence of evil, but forgetting too quickly the logics of incommensurability without which the discourse about God collapses into absurdity. On a more practical level, interreligious dialogue may have a corrective effect even in popular devotion: "The overflowing of popular devotions in the Roman Church seems to weaken among Catholics the sense of mystery and divine transcendence. The Incarnation, the doctrine of God-with-us, God close to us, turns out to be a temptation of laziness, of familiarity. The

mild elderly man with a white beard, the 'sweet Jesus,' Mary the 'good mother'..." (D. Masson, *Monothéisme*, n. 4 , p. 206).

68. Grounded in John 14: 6.

69. Indeed, Jesus tends to destabilize the self-definitions of both Judaism and Christianity. "Read in post-modern categories, as cross-dressed, Jesus is at once both a signifier and that which signifies the undecidability of signification, pointing towards himself, but also towards the place where he is not. In this way, Jesus destabilizes the self definitions of both Judaism and Christianity, pointing out that the former could not retain its hegemony over monotheism and the Bible, while the latter eternally reinvented...its own origins" (S. Heschel, Abraham *Geiger and the Jewish Jesus*, p. 239). The story of the invention of a Jewish "historical Jesus" shows how each religion has tried to inscribe the other through the mediation of Jesus.

70. Matt. 23: 3.

71. Cf. ed. and trans. T. Khalidi, *The Muslim Jesus: Sayings and Stories in Islamic Literature*, (Cambridge, MA and London: Harvard University Press, 2001).

72. In our times, Geza Vermes, *The Religion of Jesus the Jew* (Minneapolis: Fortress Press, 1993), pp. 214–215, calls "unjustifiable" to continue to represent Jesus as the founder of the Christian Church.

73. Peter the Venerable, *Summa totius haeresis Saracenorunm* (1143), presented Islam as an offshoot of a Jewish-Christian heretical sect, against the former prejudice assimilating Islam to a form of paganism.

74. Later he would say the same about Christianity, depicted as derived from Pharisaic Judaism. See S. Heschel, *Abraham Geiger*. p. 51: "This was a counter-history of Western civilization that placed Judaism, not Christianity, as its center. It is from Judaism that both Christianity and Islam derived their major ideas, and even modernity itself, with its openness to critical thinking, is a Jewish phenomenon, according to Geiger."

75. Jean-Louis Chrétien, "La parole blessée," in eds. J.-L. Chrétien, M. Henry, and J.-L. Marion, *Phénoménologie et théologie* , "Critérion-idées," (Paris : Critérion, 1992), p. 55.

8 Supernatural Israel: Obstacles to Theological Humility in Jewish Tradition

Shira L. Lander

My intrigue with people of other faiths began in my childhood. I was raised in a predominately Christian town where most of my closest friends were religious. My father was the campus rabbi, and we were the only observant Jews on our street, the only house with a *mezuzah*. Our neighbors welcomed us to join them for their holidays, and we reciprocated on ours. School was more of a challenge. Many of the adults had difficulty pronouncing my name and questioned my absences at holiday time. However, my difference was generally celebrated and embraced. My classmates expressed genuine interest in my religion. Every Jewish holiday I would bring in ritual objects and/or food and give a spiel about the holiday's significance.

I encountered my first interfaith theological quandary around fourth grade. I had begun singing in the school choir, and we were preparing for the Christmas/Holiday concert. Most of the Christmas carols were really winter songs, but then there was "Silent Night." What a beautiful melody. I was captivated by its lullaby gentleness, but the words in the second verse, "Christ the Savior is born" stuck in my throat. Should I or shouldn't I sing them? Would I be seen as proclaiming this as my own belief, or was I singing it so someone else could affirm their faith? I brought the question to my wise father, who, in typical rabbinic fashion, answered my question with a question, "What do *you* think?" After serious thought, I decided I would drop out during the words "Christ the Savior," and then come back in on the rest of the line. That got me through the next eight years of school and community choir singing. Music was really my most significant entrée to Christian worship. As either a vocalist or musician for many Masses, Passions, Requiems, and, of course, Handel's Messiah, the music conveyed a connection to God that transcended the particularity of the text. How could Leonard Bernstein have written a Mass if this weren't the case?

In addition to the Christian piety that surrounded me, I was exposed to the interfaith circles that my father traveled in. As a campus rabbi, he worked in one of a series of clergy offices with a minister, priest, and nun, focused on common concerns. Our home continually welcomed various clergy who seemed as comfortable in our living room as any of our other visitors. As a campus rabbi later myself, part of the "God squad on the quad," I would realize the theological significance of working together as a religious team— each of us bringing different skills and goals to produce a vibrant and vital tapestry of campus religious life. It was this healthy model of interreligious cooperation and understanding to which I determined to devote my life.

In college this fascination turned academic and subsequently in rabbinical school my area of focus was early Christianity and interfaith relations, which sent me to my first job—at the Institute for Christian and Jewish Studies in Baltimore. As an interfaith professional, I learned so much Torah from my Christian study partners, and I learned how to challenge my tradition and some of the assumptions of my faith. When I returned to graduate school for a degree in religious studies, I studied Islam in addition to my focus on Christians and their Others in Antiquity.

My academic training, coupled with my experience in interfaith dialogue, has taught me that dialogue is absolutely necessary for healthy religion. Religion is social, and just as human beings cannot thrive without healthy human interaction, so too with religions. Honest and respectful dialogue nurtures humility and offers a corrective to the excesses of our own traditions. Dialogue can create trust and imbue a sense of security to help overcome the suspicion and fear our traditions have often instilled about the other. By forging bonds of support and solidarity across religious boundaries, people of religious good will can help overcome ethnic and national xenophobia. I believe that this is the challenge confronting people of faith today.

Jewish tradition is replete with appeals to personal and theological humility. Over the centuries, and to this day, many arks containing the sacred Torah scrolls are emblazoned with the rabbinic admonition "Know before whom you stand" (adapted from the Mishnah, *Avot* 3.1), referring to God, the supreme, awesome and Holy One of Blessing. Being in the presence of God, who is revealed and manifest through the text of Torah, elicits modesty and a sense of the worshipper's own insignificance, as recited in the daily morning prayer:

> What are we? What is the value of our lives?... What can we say before you, Lord our God and God of our ancestors? Before You the mighty are as nothing, the famous as if they have never been; the wise are without wisdom, the clever without reason. For most of their deeds are worthless, and their days are like a breath. Measured against Your perfection, our preeminence over the beast is negligible, for we are all so trivial.[1]

Of course there is no *guarantee* that humility before God will engender concomitant humility toward one's fellow human beings. Thus the concluding meditation following the central daily prayer, the Amidah, reminds the worshipper to approach not only God but fellow human beings with humility and self-restraint: "My God, guard my tongue from evil and my lips from speaking guile. To those who curse me, let my soul be silent, and let it be like dust to everyone."

When dealing more specifically with the non-Jewish "other," Jewish tradition has navigated between two poles. On the one hand, the Roman period rabbinic work, the Mishnah, declares: "all among Israel merit a portion in the world to come" (*Sanhedrin* 10:1), with no apparent provision for gentile salvation. On the other hand, the contemporaneous Tosefta preserves the view of Rabbi Joshua that "the righteous among the nations merit a portion in the world to come" (*Sanhedrin* 13:1).[2] The latter view was widely accepted by Palestinian rabbinic authorities, as preserved in the affirmative opinion of Rabbi Judah the Prince when asked by the mid-second-century Roman Emperor Antoninus Pius (used here as a type for the quintessential non-Jew, as he was the most powerful and prominent of all Roman pagans at the time) whether the Emperor would merit the world to come. The twelfth-century theologian and philosopher Moses ben Maimon (Maimonides), who fled the North African invasion of his native Spain to eventually become court physician to Caliph Salah al-Din (Saladin) in Cairo[3], expressed this same positive evaluation when he stated that "all the righteous of the nations merit a portion in the world to come."[4] This medieval theologian would go even further, writing:

> The missions of Jesus and Muhammad have helped pave the way for the coming of the messiah by improving the nature of mankind through the universal worship of God that has brought them near to His service....[5]

This remarkably progressive attitude toward non-Jews was not shared by all Jewish commentators. Jews living in European Christian countries or less tolerant of Muslim empires, who experienced economic instability, social isolation, political subordination, and sporadic persecution and expulsions, tended toward a more exclusivist view of divine favor and salvation. Jews construed the actions of non-Jews as signs of their moral and spiritual character, as articulated by the thirteenth-century Rabbi, physician, and philosopher Moses ben Nachman (Nahmanides) in his account of the Barcelona Disputation with convert and Dominican monk Pablo Christiani:

> {T}he Christians spill more blood than the rest of the nations, and they also lead immoral lives.... {Despite your claim that the messiah has already come}, you [still] consider it advantageous to have [weapons and] mail-covered steeds.[6]

A strain of polemical writing emerged from such religious debates, which were publicly staged with the aim of encouraging Jewish conversion. Theological trends in both the *halakhic* (behavioral) and *aggadic* (ideational) literature promoted a more parochial stance particularly constitutive of the people Israel in relation to non-Jews, whom Jews regarded as situated outside the covenantal circle. These traditions disrupted the predominant heritage of collective theological humility and reinforced a reaction formation to negative experiences throughout Jewish history that could be characterized as self-importance or superiority, or perhaps even arrogance. Although I hesitate to use this latter term because it carries the historical baggage of anti-Jewish accusations by those who sought either to supersede or to eliminate the Jewish people through conversion, I think that the sources investigated in this paper warrant such usage. I am not, however, in a position to assess the statistical extent of this attitude; yet the fact that it appears in mystical, exegetical, philosophical and legal literature throughout all periods of history suggests that it is not aberrant.

Jewish theological arrogance is rooted in the central concept of peoplehood, or *am yisrael*. There is little evidence for individualistic theological hubris. One of the greatest Jewish theologians, Moses Maimonides, would ultimately and unequivocally affirm a *theologia negativa* or even *negationis*, despite his many theological expositions (*Guide* 51).[7] This reticence on the part of Jewish scholars to define God is representative of the entire tradition of Jewish thought. Nevertheless, Judaism's preference for predicate theology is reflected best in the Jewish liturgical tradition. This sentiment was expressed well by the fifth century Church scholar, Prosper of Aquitaine, as *Lex orandi, lex credendi* (the law of prayer is the law of belief). It is in prayer that we find numerous attributes and actions attributed to God. When these qualities are also attributed to the people Israel, collective theological humility recedes and arrogance rises in its place.

Although there is fluidity between the biblical terms *bnei yisrael* (children of Israel) and less frequent *am yisrael* (nation of Israel), the post-Biblical concept of *yisrael* develops an ethnocentric, xenophobic trend that parts ways with its biblical antecedents.[8] I will trace this development primarily through classical rabbinic and medieval *aggadic* sources, concluding with the contemporary work of philosophers Michael Wyschogrod and David Novak.[9] Even though the notion of election has been identified by numerous critics of the biblical concept as the primary source of Jewish hubris, I suggest that election is insufficient for producing the type of hubris displayed in the later traditions. Rather, this development is rooted in the tendency of Jewish theologians and scholars to make definitive claims about the characteristics of the people Israel that bordered on or even participated in the supernatural, a realm generally reserved for God.[10]

Three supernatural attributes are assigned to *am yisrael*: (1) eternality; (2) moral (and perhaps intellectual) superiority and authority; and (3) oneness, including indivisibility. The association of these attributes with Israel lies at the heart of Jewish self-understanding, since corporate identity is fundamental to Judaism's theological structure. This corporate identity can be seen in Judaism's post-Temple mechanism for repentance (confession of sins—*vidui*—in the first person plural), its liturgical requirement for a quorum, one of its primary names for God (*Eloheinu* = "our God," inflected in the first person plural possessive), and its concept of redemption (Ex. 13.14, as repeated in the Passover Haggadah, e.g.).

First I will investigate the sources of these aggrandizing attributions. Second, I will explore whether the attribution of these qualities to *am yisrael* is necessary in order for Judaism to remain coherent. Finally, I will excavate resources within the tradition for a more humble understanding of *am yisrael*.

■ SOURCES OF ARROGANCE: ETERNALITY

Am yisrael chai (the people Israel lives!) is the most blatant formulation of the eternality of Israel. Made popular by the musical setting of Shlomo Carlbach during the Soviet Jewry movement, it likely has its origins in German Zionism.[11] Yet its sentiment has much earlier roots, which are most evident in medieval cosmology and eschatology. Israel's holiness guarantees her eternality, as the Talmud observes, "Just as whatever is holy exists forever (*kayyam leolam*), so shall they exist forever (*leolam kayyamin*)."[12] Although the original passage refers to the righteous of Israel, the sixteenth-century Italian commentator, physician, and philosopher Sforno reinterprets it to suggest that *all* of Israel is eternal: "A nation that shall never perish but shall exist forever among men, as it shall be in future time..."

(Sforno, commentary on Ex. 19.6). Israel is one of the pre-existing primordial *logoi* that was destined for a particular historical event, as advanced in classical rabbinic literature:

> Six things were created before the creation of the world. Some were created, and others were intended to be created (*alu bemachshava*): the Torah and the Throne of Glory were created;...the ancestors, Israel, the Temple, and the name of the messiah were intended to be created (*Gen. Rabba* 1.4).[13]

The twelfth-century Spanish scholar Yehudah HaLevi quotes this Rabbinic source in the *Kuzari* when discussing seemingly false rabbinic passages that upon closer examination reveal deeper truths.[14] The primordial status of Israel is elevated further in the Zohar, the central text of the Kabbalah, which understands Israel to be part of the Godhead, as Novak points out: "Everything real is in truth a manifestation of the Godhead.... Accordingly, Israel and humanity are in essence synonymous. There is no humanity outside Israel."[15] Kabbalah expresses divine agency in terms of principles, or *sefirot*, often depicted as an interconnected chain of spheres extending from heaven to earth.[16] Israel partakes of the *sefirot* Wisdom (*Hokhmah*) and Understanding (*Binah*), emanations of the divine self:

> Israel has two portions: One from the side of Kingship (*mesitra demalka*), in which Israel has an uppermost portion, as it is written, "while you, who held fast to the Lord your God [are all alive today]" (Deut. 4:4) as well as "For the Lord's portion is His people" (Deut. 32:9), and one from the uppermost side of Holiness (*mesitra alah dekadesh*), in which Israel has an uppermost portion, as it is written, "You shall be people of holiness to Me" (Ex. 22:30) as well as "Israel is holiness to the Lord" (Jer. 2:3).[17]

Having been created out of the very same substance as the Divine, Israel's holiness is ontological. Returning to the rabbinic notion of Israel as primordial, the idea that Israel is part of the Godhead explains how Israel can be considered to have existed prior to creation and before time.

The Zohar then traces Israel's descent from the primordial eternal realm into history. Following the act of creation, Israel began to emerge in time through the patriarchs, Abraham, Isaac, and Jacob, and reached its fruition at Sinai with the reception of Torah. It is the gift of Torah, through the observance of *mitzvoth* (divine commandments), that enables Israel to achieve the supernatural ability to survive all historical vicissitudes. By following the commandments, Israel is protected from harm. This is taken quite literally as referring to the apotropaic value of the two particular *mitzvoth*: circumcision and Passover. The blood of the lamb on the doorposts of the Israelite houses in Egypt protected them from the angel of death who slew the Egyptian first-born, which is re-enacted in the yearly Passover observance. The blood of circumcision likewise protects Israel from harm.[18] The fulfillment of other commandments also ensures Israel's survival, as expressed by HaLevi:

> ....God has a secret for keeping you alive. God used the Sabbath and festivals as one of the most important ways to preserve your identity and splendor.... Whatever efforts you make for these days benefit you both in this world and the World to Come, as your expenditures for these days are for the sake of Heaven (*Kuzari* 3.10.1, 3).[19]

Thus, Israel is the beneficiary of God's "specific providence (*hashgacha p'ratit*)," which includes subversion of the natural law: "All the world will be guided by the laws of nature (*haminhag hativ`i*), except for you.... Through all this you will see that you are not governed by normal laws of nature, but rather by Divine will" (1.109.2–3).[20] The fifteenth-century Spanish sage Isaac Abravanel affirms the notion of God's special providence for Israel:

> Scripture means that when God bequeathed the land to the nations, "and set the divisions of man" (Deut. 32.8) and when they built the tower [of Babel] and he divided them and confounded their languages.... he cherished them [the children of Israel] in the desert when he was revealed at Sinai with speaking (*bedibrot*), and in clouds of Glory, and gave them understanding which was the Torah, and with this he distinguished them from all the other nations, and this is what Scripture says, "The Lord alone did guide him [no alien god at his side]" (Deut. 32.12). From that time on, they remained designated for his divine providence in particular....[21]

This protection is achieved in various ways, including, Abravanel claims, through the exile. In a rather unusual interpretation of dispersion, he writes: "When Israel is concentrated in one spot, the enemy can easily destroy her... Dispersion was, thus, a great kindness ensuring our survival and deliverance."[22]

A Talmudic excursus on astrology suggests that Israel's fate is determined differently from that of other nations:

> R. Johanan maintained: Israel is immune from planetary influence. Now, R. Johanan is consistent with his view, for R. Johanan said: How do we know that Israel is immune from planetary influence? Because it is said, "Thus says the Lord: Learn not the way of the nations, and be not dismayed at the signs of heaven, for the nations are dismayed at them."... From R. Akiba too [we learn that] Israel is free from planetary influence. For R. Akiba had a daughter. Now, astrologers told him: On the day she enters the bridal chamber a snake will bite her and she will die. He was very worried about this. On that day [of her wedding] she took a brooch [and] stuck it into the wall and by chance it penetrated into the eye of a serpent. The following morning, when she took it out, the snake came trailing after it. "What did you do?" her father asked her. "A poor man came to our door in the evening," she replied, "and everybody was busy at the banquet, and there was none to attend to him. So I took the portion which was given to me and gave it to him." "You have done a good deed," said he to her. Thereupon R. Akiba went out and lectured: "But *tzedakah* delivers from death" (Prov. 10:2): and not [merely] from an unnatural death, but from death itself (*Shabbat* 156a-b).

Not only is Israel "immune from" the natural order of the cosmos, but the covenant, through its requirement of *mitzvoth*, creates an almost parallel universe in which Israel is protected by her covenantal obligations. Akiba's daughter's performance of the *mitzvah* of *tzedakah* results, *quid pro quo*, in the saving of her own life. The twelfth- to thirteenth-century French exegete David Kimhi explained that "... these nations [Edom and Moab] are not known today, except Israel, since they were separated from the idolatrous nations by means of their Torah..."[23]

Israel's charmed existence is explained not only by the performance of *mitzvoth*, but by the protection of the "Divine Presence" (*Shechinah*), as an early rabbinic commentary on Numbers states: "Whenever Israel was exiled, the *Shechinah* went with them…"[24] This is true even when Israel was unclean.[25] Interpreting Isaiah 63:9 "and the angel of His presence saved them," the Zohar comments:

> Whenever Israel is in exile, *Shechinah* accompanies them, as they have established, for it is written… *YHVH your God will return, [with] your captivity and have compassion on you*… (Deut 30.3). Alternatively, *And the angel of His presence saved them—Shekhinah*, who accompanies them in exile. But how can you say that he *saved them*? Yet certainly so! These are the pledges of the blessed Holy one in exile, and since *Shechinah* is with them, the blessed Holy One remembers to help them and bring them forth from exile, as it is written, *I have remembered My covenant* (Ex. 6:5), first, and then, *Here, the cry of the Children of Israel has come to me* (Ex. 3:9).[26]

Like a force field, the *Shechinah* protects Israel from being overwhelmed by the violence of the nations in the Diaspora. HaLevi puts it metaphorically:

> [T]he Divine Presence was in the midst of the Jewish people like a soul resting in a person's body. It provided them with a Divine life force and a radiance and splendor in their bodies, their clothes, and their abodes (*Kuzari* 2.62).

This protection is an act of grace rather than merit, according to Kimhi. Indeed, Israel may have "occasionally, from time to time, deserved annihilation, but God protected [her] from generation to generation… until she became a covenant people."[27] In fact, God's protection of Israel is for God's own purposes, rather than Israel's: "[A]nd this is for the future Messianic days, so there will be a need for her to be a covenant people."[28]

God's gracious and special providence is affirmed by the modern Orthodox philosopher Michael Wyschogrod: "Hashem ["The Name," i.e., God] lives among and in the Jewish people, both individually and collectively.… It is the national or collective existence of the Jewish people that is the dwelling place of Hashem."[29] Wyschogrod cautions, though, against construing this idolatrously:

> This does not mean, God forbid, that Israel is Hashem… To say that Hashem dwells in the Jewish people does not deify the Jewish people any more than to say that Hashem dwells in the Temple in Jerusalem is to deify the stones of the Temple.[30]

Although Israel's existence is the direct result of God's presence, the distinction between the two entities, for Wyschograd, is never effaced: One is finite, the other infinite.[31]

The eternality of Israel is realized in the end of days, when redemption will be made available to all the nations of the world through this tiny people. This notion is well articulated in the ninth century *Pesikta Rabbati*:

> In the hour when King Messiah is revealed… God will brighten the light of King Messiah and Israel, so that all the nations who are in darkness and in gloom, will walk in the light of the Messiah and of Israel, as Scriptures says, 'And the nations shall come to your light' (Isa. 60:3).[32]

Abravanel envisioned Israel's fulfillment in the end time as an ideal: "Thus in the Days of the Messiah, Israel will represent the materialized ideal of a People of God, of a Holy Nation."[33] Wyschogrod interprets this future redemption as physical as well as spiritual:

> The prophetic picture of the end of days envisages a reconciliation among the peoples of the world, so that the redemption of Israel is also the redemption of humanity. The election of Israel [is]...the means chosen by Hashem for the redemption of humanity.... The circumcised body of Israel is the dark, carnal presence through which the redemption makes its way in history. Salvation is of the Jews because the flesh of Israel is the abode of the divine presence in the world.[34]

This "apocalyptic view" of the messianic era, as David Novak calls it, expresses the expectation that the nations will derive benefit from Israel's salvation.[35] In the end time, the generic "nations" lose both their specificity and their identity as non-Jews, as they adopt the righteous ways and divine devotion of Israel, whose identity is not only preserved, but completed.[36]

Israel's existence, therefore, before creation, throughout history, and in the messianic age attests to its eternality. Is Israel thus co-extant with God? To the extent that Israel is perceived as the "incarnation of Torah," one is forced to answer in the affirmative.[37] Because supernatural Israel was the predestined recipient of Torah, where Torah, being God's *logos*, is considered co-eternal with God, supernatural Israel would consequently be co-eternal with God as well. That Torah existed prior to the creation of the world is suggested by the statement of R. Akiba: "Beloved are Israel, since God gave them a precious vessel...through which the world was created."[38] The classical rabbinic view is affirmed by Maimonides, who asserts that the Torah "is forever and all eternity."[39] The Zohar, by seeing Israel as part of the Godhead, infers the eternality of Israel from that of Torah. Novak takes a similar position when he writes:

> The Jewish people is at least as much for the sake of the Torah as the Torah is for the sake of the Jewish people. Here there must be something about the Torah, for which they live as much as it lives for them, that is part of the prehistorical, created order.[40]

Wyschogrod, however, rejects this position, positing that Torah, and, therefore, Israel, is historically contingent. Torah emerges specifically out of God's command to his people Israel; it "is addressed only to Israel."[41] For Wyschogrod the Torah, philosophically speaking, is an accident of her election:

> The Torah grows out of Israel's election and Hashem's saving acts performed for his people.... The Torah is not a demand that exists apart from the being of Israel. Once the Jewish people is, the Torah has also come into being and once the Torah is, the Jewish people, to whom it applies, is made necessary.[42]

What follows from this symbiosis is the understanding that "Israel thus remained in history...in theory."[43] Although Israel's exile removed Israel from the historical stage, thus qualifying this people's historicity, Israel still remained bound by historical contingencies.[44] For Wyschogrod, then, historical Israel cannot acquire the characteristic of eternality, because Israel is constrained by the finitude of history. He separates the body of Israel from its soul; thus, even if the spirit or essence of Israel may be eternal, corporeal Israel is certainly not.

Novak attempts to reconcile the eschatological and historical dimensions of Israel by suggesting that Israel's election, while having "primordial status," is only granted that status *post facto*.[45] This rabbinic idea of retrojection, or *bereira*, allows Novak to preserve Israel's cosmic role without attributing undesirable qualities.[46] The examples Novak gives, however, demonstrate that the rabbis employ this concept for *halakhic* cases such as Shabbat boundaries [*eruv*], and marriage, and not for issues like election. The distinction that the *midrash rabbah* makes (mentioned earlier) between items that existed before creation and those "intended to be created" suggests that the rabbis were aware of this philosophical dilemma. The cases of divine knowledge and intention seem to be of a different order than these *halakhic* examples. The idea that the divine forethought of Israel's election is only confirmed retroactively after the fact of Sinaitic revelation raises other problems regarding divine omniscience and what is meant by divine foreknowledge. Novak's attempt to resolve this dilemma by using the technique of retrojection subordinates Israel's election to divine revelation. In full recognition of this limitation, he attempts to salvage both the doctrine of Israel's election together with the doctrine of revelation without subsuming one under the other, as we shall discuss later.

■ SOURCES OF ARROGANCE: MORAL SUPERIORITY AND AUTHORITY

Regardless of how Jewish scholars treat the relationship of Torah's eternality to that of the people Israel, they tend to agree that the two are in some way irrevocably linked. Israel's observance of the commandments not only has ensured the nation's survival without the usual requisites of land and sovereignty, as we saw earlier, but it also has enabled this people to achieve a higher, more ethical and spiritual, level than other people. This achievement may not be rewarded in this world, but earns Israel final authority in *olam habah* (the world to come).

The Jewish condition of moral superiority was apparently more obvious to classical rabbinic and medieval theologians than to modern interpreters. Despite this chronological disparity, these traditional formulations deserve examination, because residual attitudes persist in contemporary colloquial piety. This exploration requires a brief digression into *halakhic*, or legal, matters.

The classical rabbinic assertion of Israel's moral supremacy declares that Israel is held to a higher *halakhic* (legal) standard. Thus, "One who robs from a gentile is liable to return. Robbing from a gentile is viewed more strictly than robbing from an Israelite."[47] Abravanel raises this issue in his discussion of 2 Kings 17.34–5: Why is Israel punished for her idolatry once she enters the land, but the idolatrous nations who were there previously were not punished?[48] He reasons that

> Scripture makes clear that they [the nations] weren't obligated by it [the Torah] and weren't liable [for punishment].... Behold after the children of Israel came to the land and received the Torah and the commandments and heeded the words of the prophets and providence cleaved to her (but Israel's cleaving to the gods of the land was greater than in earlier times)...they were not denied His divinity, His portion, and His providence.[49]

Israel is liable for punishment because the covenant holds her to Torah standards. However, punishment for Torah infractions does *not* entail the abrogation of God's covenantal promises. That this eternal status of election extends to individuals is suggested by the Talmudic phrase "even a sinner in Israel is in Israel (*af al pi shecha-tah yisrael hu*)."[50]

A double standard with regard to purity also suggests that Israel has a higher degree of holiness: "R. Simeon b. Yohai said: The graves of gentiles do not defile, for it is written, 'For you my flock, flock that I tend, you are human (*adam*; Ezek 34.31)'; only you are designated 'human'. "[51] This disparity in holiness is caused by gentile contact with idols, the quintessence of impurity. A parallel version of this *halakhah* takes an even sharper tone: "You are called *human* [*adam*], Gentiles are not called *human*."[52] This binary antithesis reaches its height in the Zohar, according to which not only is Israel alone created as a reflection of God's image, but the spirit that dwells in nations of the world is part of the *sitra achra*, the cosmic demonic.[53]

For Halevi, the disparity between Israel's holiness and that of the nations is evinced by Israel's ability to prophesy:

> God rested His Divinity upon them, so much so that all of them heard God's words. This Divinity passed over to the Jewish women as well, who also became prophets... [T]hey were elite descendants, as is evidenced by their ancestry, their innate qualities, and their ability to sire elite descendants.[54]

Thus, HaLevi concludes, "only Jews from birth can achieve prophecy."[55] Converts to Judaism can therefore be "wise and saintly," but they cannot be prophets.[56] Because of their "distinguished Divinity," the Jews are a "different level or species (*min*) of creation, that species being angelic in nature."[57] Therefore, Jews are called "the 'choicest' (*hasegulah*) of all mankind."[58]

As a result of Israel's higher moral level, she will either rule over the other nations in the Messianic era or the nations will be converted to Israel's ways.[59] The Talmud derives the former notion from the eschatological visions of Isaiah:

> It is written, 'He will destroy death for ever, My Lord God will wipe the tears away from all faces [and will put an end to the reproach of his people over all the earth]' (Isa. 25:8), while it is written elsewhere, 'No more shall there be an infant or gray-beard who does not live out his days. He who dies at a hundred years shall be reckoned a youth [and he who fails to reach a hundred shall be reckoned accursed]!' (Isa. 65:20). There is no con-tradiction: the former refers to Jews, the latter to gentiles. But what business do gentiles have there [in the Messianic era]? [They are] those about whom it is written, 'Strangers shall stand and pasture your flocks, aliens shall be your plowmen and your vine-trim-mers' (Isa. 61:5).... And according to Samuel, who maintained: 'This world differs from the Messianic era only with respect to their serving foreign powers.'[60]

In the Messianic age, gentiles will be Israel's servants. Kimhi states it more baldly:

> All the idolaters will be under Israel's rule (*tachat yedei yisrael*)... Now, in the Babylonian exile, they [the strangers] rule over them [Israel], but after they are brought out of exile and He chooses Israel again in the Days of the Messiah, the stranger will escort them...[61]

Maimonides expresses the expectation thus: "Israel will exercise dominion over the world...rule over the heathens...be exalted by the nations...[and] eat, drink, and rejoice."[62] The perspective is repeated by the eighteenth-century Galician rabbi David Altschuler, "The house of Israel shall inherit them [the nations] being on their earth as slaves for them."[63] The nineteenth-century Russian rabbi Meir Lob ben Yehiel Michael, Malbim, combined the notion of conversion and hegemony by envisioning the eschatological role of the gentiles in two stages:

> At the beginning [of the Messianic era] they [Israel] will receive converts who will be converted before the final tranquility (*shalvah*), but afterwards the idolatrous nations will take be taken and brought to their places and no more converts will be accepted. Rather, Israel shall inherit them (after they will already be "on the soil of God") as male and female slaves.[64]

Israel not only survives into the end of days but is proportionately recompensed for her suffering in this world through an inversion of the sociopolitical order.

The seventeenth-century Dutch philosopher Baruch Spinoza, whose Jewish status is debated, offers a most trenchant critique of this elevated status, since it incurs the wrath of the nations: "[Israel] vaunted themselves above all men—indeed despising all men."[65] One can indeed interpret the phenomenon psychologically, as Spinoza did, claiming that this moral arrogance is a defensive reaction to the Jewish experience in exile. This understanding of morality also helped Jews understand why they were often targets of violence. This is clearly the context of the twelfth-century Provençal scholar Joseph Kimhi's statement about the comparative morality of Jews and Christians:

> [T]here are no murderers or adulterers among them [Jews]. Oppression and theft are not as widespread among Jews as among Christians who rob people on the highways and hang them and sometimes gouge out their eyes. You cannot establish any of these things with respect to the Jews.... Are you {Kimhi's fictional Christian antagonist} not then ashamed and embarrassed to say that you are a good people since you regularly and publicly encourage these sins. [You are] not from a people that will prevent this sort of thing. On the contrary, [your children] become accustomed to sin.... No one can deny that all these good traits which I mentioned are found among the Jews and [that] their opposites [are found] among Christians.[66]

Kimhi argued that Jews, by following Torah, had attained a higher level of morality than their lawless Christian neighbors.[67]

■ SOURCES OF ARROGANCE: ONENESS

The biblical assertion of God's oneness that became virtually doctrinal in postclassical rabbinic Judaism is the *Shema*, recited daily: "Hear O Israel, the Lord is our God, the Lord is one" (Deut. 6:4). The oneness of Israel mirrors God's unity, as illustrated by 2 Samuel 7:23 and Exodus 15:11: "Who is like your people Israel, a unique nation on earth!" and "Who is like you, Lord, among the gods!"[68] The parallelism of the two qualities of oneness is used in the following Talmudic *aggadah* (narrative):

> R. Nahman bar Isaac said to R. Hiyya bar Avin: These *tefillin* [phylacteries] of the Master-of-the-world, what are written inside of them? He said to him: "Who is like your people Israel, a unique nation (*goy echad*) on earth!" ... God said to Israel: You have made me uniquely beloved in the world and I have made you uniquely beloved in the world. You have made me uniquely beloved in the world as Scripture states, "Hear O Israel, the Lord is our God, the unique Lord (*echad*)." I have made you uniquely beloved in the world as Scripture states, "Who is like your people Israel, a unique nation on earth!"[69]

Novak uses this *aggadah* to illustrate the singularity of God's relationship with Israel and, consequently, Israel's relationship to the world and God's relationship to the world, which is how the passage has been read throughout Jewish tradition.[70] On the other hand, this anthropomorphic projection reveals a more disturbing aspect of rabbinic piety that emerges in the Kabbalistic tradition, namely, that Israel and God are homologous:

> Come and behold: regarding the nations of the world, the Holy One, blessed be He, did not want any of them except Israel exclusively. He made them a unique nation in the world. He called them "one nation," like His name. ... The Holy One, blessed be He, who is One, involves Himself with one. For the King involves Himself only with what befits Him. This Scripture states: "But He is one (*echad*), and who can turn Him?" (Job 23:13) since the Holy One, blessed be He, dwells and is found only in one ... and not in any other place.[71]

Israel's attribute of oneness emerges out of the supernal oneness of God. They are part of a supreme whole: "'One' [in Deut. 6.4] is the congregation of Israel (*knesset yisrael*); all [of the *sefirot*] are one wholeness and are interconnected one with the other. There is no division among them; they are all one."[72] It is actually Israel's utterance of the word *one* in the course of reciting the daily *Shema* that causes this oneness to come into being.[73] In essence, God's oneness relies on Israel's oneness.

Altschuler does not equate Israel's oneness with inherent supernaturalness:

> 'Who is like your people Israel, a unique nation on earth!' meaning insofar as none other. Whether this one or that one from among the nations is upright and praiseworthy as are your people Israel, they are a special (*meyuchad*) nation on earth.[74]

Evidently the uniqueness of Israel is an act of God's own doing, as is apparent from the rest of the 2 Samuel verse: "whom God went out to redeem as a people for himself, and to make a name for himself...." This trajectory of thought belongs to the strain of eschatology that sees the purpose of Israel's election as bringing in the other nations to recognition of the one true God, as "a light to the nations." Indeed, Altschuler interprets Isaiah 42:6 "And you shall be a light to the nations" as "to enlighten the eyes of the nations. All will know that Adonai is God." Israel's oneness, then, is by God's design: it is for the ultimate purpose of revealing God's oneness.

Like Altschuler, Wyschogrod asserts the transcendental oneness of Israel while eschewing the Kabbalistic tendency to conflate the divine and the human: "[There] exists the metaphysical, mystical unity of the Jewish people. It always has and it always will [be]."[75] Despite the factionalism that threatens to divide contemporary

Israel, or world Jewry, Wyschogrod argues, maintaining unity is philosophically necessary because "Jewish thought must serve two masters: God and Israel."[76] Although these masters are not equal, "God appears in history as the God of Israel and there can therefore be no thought about God that is not also thought about Israel."[77] This is a radical statement about the theological enterprise. It is certainly the case that the two monotheistic religions that followed Judaism, namely, Christianity and Islam, referred to God's historical relationship with their predecessor Israel (whether positively or not). Yet as a normative, prescriptive statement, Wyschogrod's assertion is philosophically troubling, despite its biblical grounding, because it seems to limit God's ability to act freely in history and makes God appear to be historically contingent.[78]

Not all commentators, however, claim that Israel is ontologically one. Some assert that Israel's oneness will not be achieved until the eschaton, once Israel returns to the land of Israel. Only then will the two factions led by the two Messiahs, ben David and ben Yosef, be united under the one Messiah ben David.[79] This alternative suggests that while Israel may function in history as a people divided by conflicting ideologies and practices, her metaphysical unity (as seen from God's perspective, which is the eschatological view) is mysteriously retained. In other words, Israel's oneness is a factor of God's action and perception rather than of humanity's.

Hermann Cohen, the late nineteenth- early-twentieth-century German-Jewish philosopher, distinguished God's oneness, or *Einzigheit*, from Israel's, which he called *Einheit*. Because God is eternal and humanity is finite, the oneness of God is a radical and absolute singularity, whereas Israel's oneness is "one among many."[80] Although this distinction is philosophically appealing, Novak's critique of its functionalism, namely, that Israel's oneness serves the eschatological purpose of bringing the nations to the worship of the one, true God, is convincing. Novak argues that Israel's election, and hence oneness, is "not provisional," because it "is always central to the relationship of God and man."[81]

■ SOURCES FOR CORRECTIVE THEOLOGY

The problem of Israel's eternality is philosophically resolved by Wyschogrod's insistence on the historical contingency of this particular people and by Novak's recognition that truth is not confined to Torah as understood by human beings in their historical contexts. On the other hand, moral arrogance is difficult to address, because it subsequently evolved into a secular cultural *Weltanschauung*, as reflected in the expressions *yiddishe kopf* vs. *goyishe kopf* (Jewish vs. Gentile sense). Acknowledgment of the non-Jewish influences on Jewish tradition and thought (as external sources of truth) would go a long way to correcting this theological trend.

Regarding the oneness of both God and Israel, Novak's emphasis on "relational" rather than "substantial" distinctiveness relieves some of the burden of arrogance, because it allows room for additional distinctive relationships between God and other peoples. An alternative is to view the oneness of Israel as a quality that can only be recognized and understood by God. It is neither within Israel's power nor her job description to comprehend or maintain her own unity. "Who is like your people Israel, a unique nation on earth!"(2 Sam. 7:23) is an affirmation of God's love for (one of) His people, and, although it may be a side effect of Israel's performance of her covenantal obligations, it does not, in and of itself, constitute a commandment. Israel is commanded to be a "kingdom of priests and a holy nation" (Ex. 19:6), and to "be holy" (Ex. 22:31; Lev. 19:1), but never to be "one."[82] It may be humanly desirable for Jews to work toward maintaining some kind of sociological or even theological unity, but whether oneness is achieved or not cannot influence the future of the world and its salvation, because salvation is up to God. Can the same be said for Israel's continued existence?

Israel surely needs God, whether acknowledged or not, but is the reverse true: Does God *need* Israel in order to achieve His purpose for the world? HaLevi would answer in the affirmative: "Were it not for the children of Israel, the Torah would not have existed."[83] To the extent that God's purpose for Israel and the world is revealed in Scripture, those Jews who understand that revelation to be mediated through the limitations of human experience might assess biblical prophecies such as Isaiah 42.6, Ezekiel 11.27–20, 28.25–6, and Zechariah 2.15 and 8.20–23 as ethnocentric projections. The biblical view that God intends for His name to be universally recognized is so pervasive that it cannot be adjusted for human mediation. The role of Israel in that plan, however, is less clear, and is, therefore, more open to theological speculation. Novak writes that "the ultimate consequence of the election of Israel is the final redemption itself (*ge'ulah*). However, it is not the automatic result of what transpires now in the present."[84] Theology cannot assert, therefore, a logical formula, such as "if Israel keeps the covenant, the world will be redeemed." In other words, Israel can be understood as a necessary but not sufficient condition for redemption, or as Novak asserts: "God's redemption of Israel will be central to this cosmic redemption."[85] Jews are just as unredeemed—in the Jewish understanding of that word—as everyone else. Torah is thus a blueprint for Israel's private covenantal obligation and limited understanding of the universe; it is not a manual for salvation.[86]

I agree with Novak that the Jewish understanding of God's purpose in the world must emerge out of the covenantal experience. For a *halakhic* Jew, this covenant is fully delineated in Torah, both written and oral. As opposed to the view of Wyschogrod, Novak's understanding of universal justice, that it is not "reducible to the singularity of election," skillfully avoids the narcissistic arrogance detected in HaLevi and the Zohar, however excusable this stance might be given their historical contexts.[87] For Novak, the *mishpatim*—those laws that roughly correspond to civil and criminal legislation—apply to relationships among all human beings, albeit from Israel's point of reference. Because these cannot be subsumed by the covenant, they allow for God to relate to the entire world, a world that extends beyond Israel.[88] This understanding of the *mishpatim* mitigates the type of arrogance that sees Israel as the sole repository of holiness and truth, as above all the nations morally. *Huqqim*, on the other hand—those arbitrary particularistic commandments that defy rational explanation—delineate the "limits of Israel's election."[89] These laws act as a bulwark against Israel's arrogance, because they are to be observed merely out of divine obedience, in order to recognize the limits of human understanding before God's.[90] Israel must function *within* the covenant, whereas God transcends it. Interestingly *tefillin* fits into this latter category. This approach renders the notion of "God's *tefillin*" discussed earlier as merely poetic; the *aggadah* cannot withstand theological scrutiny.

For a non-*halakhic* Jew, however, this framework is not useful. The *huqqim* are precisely those laws that Reform Judaism sought to discard. From Novak's view, this probably appears to have been an act of supreme arrogance, a defiant act of hubris to overthrow God's inscrutable sovereignty. Despite the resurgence of ritual observance in American Reform congregations, it is unlikely that *huqqim* will experience a full-scale revival. What is more possible is to recover the philosophical purpose that these rituals serve: to orient the non-*halakhic* Jew to God's incomprehensible dominion over humanity and the entire universe. This is attainable, perhaps, through the recitation of blessings and through prayer. Blessings acknowledge the source of all being, focusing worshippers' attention at profound and banal events on the One who made all things possible. Recited with this *kavanah* (intention) out of a sense of deep gratitude and obligation, and not reflexively, blessings offer an antidote to arrogance. The fact that blessings all begin with praise of God by name and of God's sovereignty invites such theological reflection. Prayers also inspire humility. Although few daily or weekly prayers directly declare Israel's smallness, most do address God's majesty. The concomitant reflection should be on Israel's sinfulness, both corporate (as a whole people) and individual (as single human persons).[91] Prayers are often accompanied by liturgical choreography that physically expresses this humility. If these actions are performed with the awareness that bending the knee, stepping back, bowing at the waist, covering one's head, are not generic acts of *kavod* (respect), but bodily recognitions of human smallness and divine grandeur, humility can be embodied. This interpretation must be explained to worshippers in order to inculcate the appropriate *kavanah*, rather than performed merely as rote imitation, pseudo-piety, or uninformed attempts at spirituality. Of course, there is no *guarantee* that humility before one's fellow human beings will accompany humility before God. But if all of God's creation, including the diversity of human form, beliefs, and practices, is truly appreciated, the chances of inspiring humility toward fellow human beings are increased.

■ CONCLUSION

I conclude with a hermeneutical reflection. Those Scriptural passages that appear to suggest Israel's eternality, moral superiority, or even supernatural unity, and that have invited Jewish commentators throughout the ages to imagine a Jewish messianic triumphalism should not be read proleptically. Neither should they be read proscriptively or descriptively. These verses are not to be construed as ontological assertions to any degree. To avoid the type of theological arrogance such readings produce requires a thoroughly different approach. I borrow here from both the late Rev. Paul van Buren and again from David Novak.[92] Such passages are private expressions of an intimate relationship between Israel and God that, in human terms, is best approximated by analogy to marriage.[93] Novak writes:

> In a marriage deeply lived by its participants, the husband and wife believe themselves both chosen and choosing in unique ways, ways having a significance beyond the mere experience of *a* man and *a* woman. To and for each other, he is *the* man and she *the* woman. Moreover, in this profound situation, the husband and wife make very special demands on each other, demands that would be totally unreasonable if extended outside their own communion. But in their relations with the outside world, he is just a man and she is just a woman [emph. original].[94]

Because Novak refers here to a covenantal type of marriage, the metaphor can be understood only by those who have either experienced this themselves or who conceptualize marriage in the terms he describes. Unlike many contemporary Jewish marriages, however, the relationship between God and Israel is hierarchical. Framing that relationship in covenantal terms leaves open the possibility for the nature of the covenant to adapt to the changing of both parties over time. Those changes will be governed internally by the relationship and externally by the way each partner encounters the world. However, the *commitment* to the covenantal relationship does not change. It is this eternality of relationship that Israel has sometimes confused for its own eternality. Israel has occasionally confused God's particular expressions of love and devotion for general declarations of universal truth, perhaps as consolation when God seems distant and inattentive. However, the limitations of such speech need always be kept in mind to avoid encroaching on God's freedom and infinitude.

Despite the illumination such a powerful metaphor of marriage conveys, it founders on the issue of polygyny, the ways God relates to the many peoples of the earth.[95] Here we would do well to recall that the Bible, as humanly understood, is not the full expression of God's wisdom. Whether God's wisdom extends specifically to the oral Torah, as Novak argues, or beyond—to other human endeavors guided by divine norms—we have not yet heard God's final word.[96] That God's teaching can come from sources *outside* Israel is apparent from the prophet Balaam.[97] Jews are reminded of this fact every morning in the opening of worship, where Balaam's prophecy is quoted. Jews begin the orientation to God, therefore, with the recognition that *all* are related to God. The liturgy then moves from the general to the particular, which culminates with the core prayer, the Amidah (which substitutes for the Jerusalem Temple sacrifices that can no longer be performed) and three times a week with the Torah reading, which is like the *ketubah* (marriage contract) between God and Israel.[98] The concluding prayer, known as *Aleinu*, pans out to the larger worldview with which the service began, but this time the view is from the future rather than the past. Israel's destiny will somehow be tied to that of all peoples, regardless of how Jews have traditionally (or wrongly) interpreted that connection in triumphalist terms. All that can be hoped for is that "On that day God will be one, and his name will be one." Neither the worshipping community nor any Jew should be so arrogant as to claim to know what that oneness will look like.[99] The people of Israel can merely be content knowing that by committing itself faithfully to that God now, it can catch a glimpse of what will some day, God willing, unfold.

Notes

1. Sidney Greenberg and Jonathan D. Levine, eds. *Siddur Hadash: A New Prayer Book for Sabbath & Festival Mornings*, (Hartford, CT: Hartmore House, 1992).

2. Gilbert S. Rosenthal explores this positive trajectory, particularly as it appears in Italian rabbinic authorities from the Middle Ages through the modern period ("Jewish Attitudes towards Other Faiths: The Italian Model," *Journal of Ecumenical Studies* 44.2 (Sp 2009): pp. 203–225). A salient exception to the more negative French-German tradition is the eighteenth-century German Talmudist, Rabbi Jacob Emden, who wrote that "the Nazarene [Jesus] brought a double blessing to the world. On the one hand, he strengthened the Torah of Moses majestically.... and on the other hand, he did much good for the gentiles...by doing away with idolatry and removing the images from their midst.... In the name of heaven, we are your brothers! One God has created us all" (*Seder Olam Rabbah Vezuta*, as quoted in Rosenthal, *Modern Jew*, p. 207).

3. Joel L. Kraemer, *Maimonides: The Life and World of One of Civilization's Greatest Minds* (New York: Doubleday, 2008), p. 215. Not all historians consider this claim of Ibn Abi Usaybi'a to be accurate.

4. Maimonides, *Mishneh Torah* (Hilkhot Teshuvah 3:5).

5. Maimonides, *Mishneh Torah* (Melakhim 11:4), uncensored, as quoted by Gilbert S. Rosenthal, *What Can A Modern Jew Believe?* (Eugene, Oregon: Wipf & Stock Publishers, 2007), p. 204.

6. Nachmanides, *The Disputation at Barcelona*, trans. Charles B. Chavel (New York: Shilo Publishing, 1983), p. 21. Square brackets are Chavel's; curly brackets are mine.

7. Maimonides, *The Guide for the Perplexed*, trans. Friedlander (New York: Dover, 1956).

8. See Ex. 1.9, 2 Sam. 18.7, 19.41, and 1 Chron. 17.21, for example, for *am yisrael*.

9. The *halakhic* material is well-documented in the controversial book by Israel Shahak, *Jewish History, Jewish Religion: The Weight of Three Thousand Years* (Boulder, CO: Pluto Press, 1994) and the inflammatory article by Gush Emunim rabbi David Bar-Chayim, "Yisrael Nikraim Adam [Jews Are Called 'Man']," *Tzfiyah*, v. 3 (1989): pp. 45–73.

10. Many scholars use the term *supernatural* to identify the type of thinking I will explore. See, for example, Jacob Neusner, *Recovering Judaism: The Universal Dimension of Judaism* (Minneapolis, MN: Augsburg, 2000), p. 13ff. Alon Goshen-Gottstein, following the Zohar ('*ila-ah*), uses the term "supernal Israel," in eds. Arthur A. Cohen and Paul Mendes-Flohr "People of Israel," *Contemporary Jewish Religious Thought. Original Essays on Critical Concepts, Movements, and Beliefs*, (New York: Macmillan, 1987), p. 703. I use the former term, *supernatural*, to connote an extra-historical phenomenon, while reserving the latter, *supernal Israel*, for a purely cosmological sense.

11. Jacob Birnbaum, "Re: Four Questions on Am Yisroel Chai," May 13, 2003, *Jewish Music*, 4/5/07 <http://www.mail-archive.com/jewish-music@shamash.org/msg02297.html>. The twentieth-century philosopher and Holocaust survivor Emile Fackenheim wrote a reflection on the *Shoah* by this title in *The Christian Century* series "How My Mind Has Changed," 87 (May 6, 1970): 563–568).

12. Talmud *Sanhedrin* 92a.

13. Israel is not included in the lists given in the Talmudic parallels (*Pesachim* 54a, *Nedarim* 39b).

14. Yehuda HaLevi, *The Kuzari. In Defense of the Despised Faith*, trans. N. Daniel Korobkin (Mahwah, NJ: Jason Aronson, 1998), 3.73 (9).

15. David Novak, *The Election of Israel. The Idea of the Chosen People* (Cambridge University Press, 1995), p. 17. See also p. 218.

16. For the sake of simplicity I employ the term "Kabbalah," though I realize that this grossly reduces the variety of Kabbalistic traditions to an artificial singularity.

17. Michael Berg, ed., *The Zohar*, vol 16, ch. 22 (*Emor*), §106, pp. 166–167 (New York: Yeshivat Kol Yehuda, 1999).

18. Rashi on Ezek. 16.6, A. Berliner, *Rashi 'al ha-Torah* (Frankfurt, a.M., J. Kauffmann: 2nd ed., 1905). See also M. Berg, *Zohar* 16.15 and 3.36 (excurses on circumcision).

19. HaLevi, *Kuzari*, pp. 135–136.

20. Ibid., p. 48. The observation about God's providence is also Korobkin's.

21. Abravanel on Deut. 32.6 (Avishai Shotland, *Perush ha-Torah le-Rabenu Yitsḥak Abravanel* [Jerusalem: Horev, 1997]).

22. Abravanel on Deut. 32.26 (*Perush ha-Torah*). This view is suggested as early as *Gen. R.* 76.3 on Gen. 32.9.

23. David Kimhi (Redak) on Isa. 11. 14 (*Mikraot Gedolot haKeter. Isaiah. A Revised and Augmented Scientific Edition*, ed. Menahem Cohen [Ramat Gan: Bar-Ilan University Press, 1996]).

24. *Sif. Num.* Beha'alotecha 84, f 22b, trans. H. Loewe, in ed. C.G. Montefiore & H. Loewe, *A Rabbinic Anthology*, (New York: Schocken, 1974), p. 64.

25. *Sif. Num.* Naso 1, 1b.

26. *Zohar* 1.120b, in trans., Daniel Matt, *The Zohar. Pritzger Edition* vol. 2, pp. 200–201 (Stanford, CA: Stanford University Press/Zohar Education Project, 2000); Hebrew from Berg, *Zohar,* vol. 3, Ch. 38 (*vayerah*), §511.

27. Redak on Isa. 49.8 (*Mikraot Gedolot haKeter*).

28. Redak on Isa. 49.8 (*Mikraot Gedolot haKeter*).

29. Michael Wyschogrod, *The Body of Faith. Judaism as Corporeal Election* (New York: Seabury Press, 1983), p. 103. Wyschograd explains his use of the circumlocution "Hashem," for God as best expressing the Jewish understanding of the supreme divine being in relation to the Jewish people.

30. Ibid., p. 212.

31. So Hermann Cohen, *Ethik des reinen Willens,*4th ed. (Berlin: B. Cassirer, 1923), 466, cited by Novak, *The Election of Israel,* p. 60.

32. *Pes. R* 162a-b, trans. H Loewe, *A Rabbinic Anthology*, p. 607.

33. Benzion Netanyahu, *Don Isaac Abravanel. Statesman and Philosopher* (Philadelphia: Jewish Publication Society, 1968), 241.

34. Wyschogrod, *The Body of Faith*, pp. 103–104 and 256.

35. Novak, *The Election of Israel*, p. 159. Novak contrasts this view with the "extensive view of eschatology" advocated by Maimonides, Franz Rosenzweig, and Hermann Cohen, wherein Israel has a vocation as "a light to the nations" (158), which he critiques for its implicit proselytism. This view of Israel's messianic role is found as early as the Roman period (Tannaitic) *Gen. R.* 44.23.

36. Alternatively see Ibn Ezra and Kimhi on Isa. 60.12, who write that the nations will be physically annihilated. The eighteenth-century Galician rabbi David Altschuler interprets "shall perish" as referring to the nations' governments. Commentaries can be found in *Mikraot Gedolot haKeter.*

37. Wyschogrod, *The Body of Faith*, p. 211. As Novak points out, since Wyschogrod does not hold the eternality of Torah, his understanding of Israel as Torah's incarnation does not produce this result (Novak 242). The classical rabbinic formulation, however, does imply Israel's eternality as well.

38. *Avot* 3.18 (*Sayings of the Fathers*, ed. J.H. Hertz [New York: Behrman House, 1945]).

39. *Mishneh Torah* 14.11.3 on Kings, in trans. Isadore Twersky, *A Maimonides Reader*, Library of Jewish Studies (New York: Behrman House, 1972), p. 223.

40. Novak, *The Election of Israel,* p. 246.

41. Wyschogrod, *The Body of Faith,* p. 211.

42. Ibid.

43. Wyschogrod, *The Body of Faith,* p. 179.

44. *Contra* Franz Rosenzweig, who interprets Israel's exile as a superhistorical existence (Barbara Galli, trans., *Star of Redemption* [Ann Arbor: University of Wisconsin Press, 2005], p. 367): "Thus the bridge of eternity arches for us—from the starry sky of the promise that arches over the mountain of Revelation from where the river of our eternal life sprang, up to the countless sands of the promise upon which the sea washes up into where that river empties, the sea out of which one day the Star of Redemption will rise, when like waves the earth will foam over with knowledge of the Lord." Elsewhere Rosenzweig writes "He who is begotten as Jew bears witness to his faith by continuing to beget the eternal people" (363). Thus the paradigmatic relationship in Christianity is the sibling one, which is synchronic, while in Judaism the diachronic, cross-generational link between grandparent and grand-child embodies "the eternal people" (367).

45. Novak, *The Election of Israel,* pp. 206–207.

46. Ibid., p. 205.

47. Tosefta *Nezikin* 53, in ed. Lieberman, trans. S. Fraade, "Navigating the Anomalous: Non-Jews at the Intersection of Early Rabbinic Law and Narrative," *The Other in Jewish Thought and History. Constructions of Jewish Culture and Identity,* eds. Laurence J. Silberstein and Robert L. Cohen (New York: NYU Press, 1994), p. 150.

48. This state of grace did not extend to idolaters who lived in the land after Israel had entered it; as articulated in Lev. 18.14–18, they were clearly punished.

49. Abravanel on 2 Kings 17.34–5.

50. Talmud *Sanhedrin* 44a. I am indebted to Reuven Firestone for this reference.

51. Talmud *Baba Metziah* 114b.

52. Talmud *Yevamot* 61a, trans. Daniel Matt, *Zohar,* vol. 1, p. 156, note 380.

53. *Zohar* 1:20b (122).

54. HaLevi, *Kuzari* 1.95.1, 8.

55. Ibid. 1.115.3.

56. Ibid.

57. Ibid., 1.103.1.

58. Ibid.,1.27.1.

59. Only in the former case does the identity of the nations remain intact. The latter case is what Novak calls the "extensive eschatology," a view he rejects.

60. Talmud *Sanhedrin* 91b. A similar notion is expressed, albeit more briefly, in *Gen. R.* 44.23, tied to the fulfillment of Deut. 7:1.

61. Redak on Isaiah 11.14 and 14.1 (*Mikraot Gedolot haKeter*).

62. Maimonides, *Mishneh Torah* 14.12.4 on Kings, trans. Twersky, *Maimonides Reader,* p. 225. I have taken this quotation out of its original context, where Maimonides makes the point that Israel longs not for these worldly pleasures of the Messianic era but for the opportunity to study Torah in the world to come. Bear in mind that for Maimonides, following classical rabbinic eschatology, the Messianic era is merely a transition period from this world to the next. Though note that elsewhere Maimonides seems to take an opposing view: "The sages and the prophets did not desire the days of the Messiah in order to rule over the whole world nor to exercise authority over the gentiles nor that the nations might lift them up over them..." (*Mishneh Torah* on Kings, 12.1.4.)

63. *Metzudat David* on Isa. 14.2 (*Mikraot Gedolot haKeter*).

64. Malbim on Isa. 14.2 (*Mikraot Gedolot haKeter*).

65. Spinoza, *Tractatus Theologico-Politicus* ch. 1, p. 70, as quoted in Novak, *The Election of Israel*, p. 44. As Novak indicates, xenophobia is an age-old pagan accusation against the Jews, going back to writers like 3rd century BCE Egyptian Manetho and 1st century CE Alexandrian Apion.

66. Kimhi, *Book of the Covenant*, trans. Talmage (Toronto: Pontifical Institute of Mediaeval Studies, 1972), pp. 32–35, as excerpted in Frank Talmage, *Disputation and Dialogue. Readings in the Jewish-Christian Encounter* (Jersey City, NJ: Ktav, 1975), pp. 11–12.

67. This theme also appears in the thirteenth-century disputation record of Nahmanides: "But since the days of Jesus up to the present the whole world has been full of violence and rapine, the Christians more than other peoples being shedders of blood and revealers likewise of indecencies" (Talmage, *Disputation*, p. 87).

68. Redak points out the parallelism in his commentary on 2 Sam., paraphrasing the 2 Sam. 7:23 verse to make it structurally parallel to the Ex. 15:11 verse: "Who is like you, Israel, among the nations!" (*Mikraot Gedolot haKeter. Samuel I-II. A Revised and Augmented Scientific Edition*, ed. Menachem Cohen [Ramat Gan: Bar-Ilan University Press, 1993]).

69. Talmud *Berakhot* 6a, trans. Novak, *The Election of Israel*, p. 13 (slightly expanded and modified).

70. Novak, *The Election of Israel*, pp. 13–14.

71. *Zohar*, ed. Berg, vol. 16, ch.3, §20–22 (*kedoshim*) on Lev. 19:1 "You shall be holy."

72. *Zohar*, ed. Berg, vol. 22, ch. 8, §59 (*vaetchanan*) on Deut. 6:4.

73. *Zohar*, ed. Berg, vol. 22, ch. 9, §61–64 (*vaetchanan*).

74. *Metzudat David* to 2 Sam. 7:23 (*Mikraot Gedolot haKeter*).

75. Wyschogrod, *The Body of Faith*, p. 240.

76. Ibid., p. 175.

77. Ibid.

78. See, for example, Ezek. 34.30. Ultimately Wyschogrod may be asserting a paradoxical mystery of the antidocetic variety: Once God creates the world, God is both inextricably tied to Israel (that is historically contingent) and supernatural (noncontingent).

79. Malbim on Ezek. 37:20–22 (*Mikraot Gedolot haKeter. Ezekiel. A Revised and Augmented Scientific Edition*, ed. Menachem Cohen [Ramat Gan: Bar-Ilan University Press, 2000]).

80. Cohen, "Einheit oder Einzigkeit Gottes" (1917), *Jüdische Schriften*, ed. B. Strauss (Berlin, 1924), vol 3, pp. 87ff, as discussed in Novak, *The Election of Israel*, p. 66.

81. Novak, *The Election of Israel*, p. 77.

82. Jews are commanded, of course, to *love* one another (Novak, *The Election of Israel*, p. 234; see Lev. 19.18). Whether love leads to unity, though, is uncertain.

83. HaLevi, *Kuzari* 2.56.2, translation slightly modified.

84. Novak, *The Election of Israel*, p. 252. Compare this with HaLevi, echoing Talmud *Pesachim* 87b, who sees Israel's exile as the seed of redemption. Once planted, its effect on its surroundings and its ability to ultimately produce fruit is virtually inevitable (HaLevi, *Kuzari* 4.23.2).

85. Novak, *The Election of Israel*, p. 253.

86. I am referring to the notion that human beings' understanding of Torah is historically contingent, not that Torah itself is.

87. Novak, *The Election of Israel*, pp. 248–249.

88. Ibid., p. 251.

89. Ibid. Novak also discusses *edot*, those commandments that symbolically reference covenantal events, which I have omitted because these are not relevant to the discussion here.

90. Awareness of the ways these laws function seems to be a prerequisite for their ability to function in the way Novak describes. HaLevi expresses a similar philosophy when he writes, "If most of us [Jews] would have accepted our lowliness (*dalut*) with subservience (*kniyah*) to God and His Torah, then Divinity would never have left us for so long" (HaLevi, *Kuzari* 1.115.1).

91. The two penitential prayers, *Vidui* and *Tahanun*, provide liturgical opportunities for daily confession of corporate and private sins, yet this practice is waning among Orthodox congregations, is even less observed in Conservative congregations, and is absent from the Reform daily liturgy. Relegating confession to once a year (Yom Kippur) fails to achieve the desired outcome and often has the unintended consequence of making people feel bad rather than humble. Jewish guilt may be the secularized, psychological expression of this theological humility; it maintains a dimension of communal identity despite its individualized context.

92. I recall van Buren's interpretation of Matthew 5:13 from a Scripture study at the Episcopal Church of the Redeemer in Baltimore in the early1990s.

93. The parent-child metaphor falls apart, as Wyschogrod's (disturbing) reflection reveals: "As a father, God loves his children and knows each one as who he is with his strengths and weaknesses his virtues and vices. Because a father is not an impartial judge but a loving parent and because a human father is a human being with his own personality, it is inevitable that he will find himself more compatible with some of his children than others and, to speak very plainly, that he love some more than others" (pp. 64–65). It seems to me that Wyschogrod has confused genuine, particular love with a more egocentric emotion, like desire, affection, or companionship. A "favorite child" turns out to be one who is easier for the parents to raise, or the best reflection of the parents, or one who fulfills the parents' expectations, none of which has anything to do with love.

94. Novak, *The Election of Israel,* p. 222.

95. See Amos 9.7.

96. Novak, *The Election of Israel,* p. 172.

97. See Num. 23–24. How Israel is able to recognize the divine origin of these words is unclear, particularly since immediately following these prophecies Israel sins by mixing with the Moabites and adopting their worship (Num. 25). Perhaps the juxtaposition is meant to remind Israel that although Jews should learn from the wisdom offered by those outside Israel, it does not follow that they should abandon their own specific calling and assimilate. This is how I interpret the Aleinu verse, "who has not made us like the nations of the lands, and has not put us as families of the earth. He has not assigned our portion like theirs nor our lot like all their multitudes."

98. *Ex. R. (Ki Tissa)* 46:1 (Vilna, 1887).

99. Even the prophetic visions preserved in the Hebrew Bible do not agree. See Ps. 22:27, 86:9, Zech. 14:16 vs. Zeph. 2:11.

9

Walking on Divine Edge: Reading Notions of Arrogance and Humility in the Qur'an

Afra Jalabi

Once upon a time, and beyond time, God announced a new project. "Behold, the Lord said to the angles: I shall create a vicegerent on earth." The angels objected to the creation of a new species. They had concern and doubt, and questioned God. They laid down their assumptions and expectations. "They said, 'Will You place therein one who will make mischief and shed blood, while we celebrate Your praises and glorify You"(Qur'an 2: 30).[1]

God's answer to the angels, found in the same verse, captures the Qur'anic perception of humanity. "He said [to the angels] *I know what you know not.*"

In a small sentence, transcending the angelic *prediction*, and in less than a statement, God justified his creation with His *knowing*. This dialogue appears early in the first pages of the Qur'an, in a passage that holds in tension humanity's future between the angels' prediction and divine knowledge, the angels voicing doubt and accusations and God's transcending knowing of his own creation. We are forced to realize that the angels made an accurate prediction when considering historical facts, and yet, looking at our future, we need to be reminded of God's knowing. The prediction was concrete and specific and has come to pass. God's knowing is open and is up to us to actualize.

The picture presented here of humanity transcends religion, nationality and culture. We are brought to a scene that symbolizes the existential primordial status of humanity in the universe. Implicit in God's answer to the angels is divine faith in this project, humankind, which throughout the Qur'an is shown to be a single organic unity, where the totally of our kind is seen as a single self (6:98). God's answer to the angels stands pregnant with potential and radiates with possibility. We get a sense of a divine trajectory of humankind but without limiting it to any form. It is a statement that transcends angelic predictions but one that does not decide or dictate a specific outcome for humanity, and hence the subtle reference to the free choosing nature of this species. It is for this reason that the late Muhammad Iqbal said, it was not without a great risk to permit the emergence of a free choosing ego because the freedom to choose good involves also the freedom to choose the opposite of good. "That God has taken this risk shows His immense faith in man," writes Iqbal, "it is for man now to justify this faith."[2]

Divine faith is shown in the Qur'an when God gives humanity the choice to carry the Trust, the *response-ability* that humanity accepted to undertake, when all of creation, with its heavens, earth, and mighty mountains all declined it (33:72). So whether we transcend the angelic prediction or step up to the possibilities of

170

God's knowing remain as options within ourselves, neither of which is predetermined or imposed. In surah Fatir, we are told it is ultimately our choice whether we step up to our *khilaphah* (viceregency) or deny it. "He is who has made you *khaliphas* (viceregents) upon the earth, and if any do deny (or reject it), against themselves is their denial." (35: 39). In the same surah, we read how our redemption as a species is not inevitable although we are invited and supported to awaken to our divine potential and creative status. "If He so pleased, He could blot you out and bring in a New Creation. Nor is that difficult for God." (35: 16–17). However, in the same surah, we are also shown the noncoercive nature of the divine, in accordance with many Qur'anic references to God's patience with human erring and His waiting. God suspends immediate consequences to our straying and hence gives us the chance to always fine tune our alignment to Truth, repent, and reverse our confusion. "If God were to take human beings to task according to what they have earned [by their thoughts and actions], He would not leave on the surface of the earth a single living creature, but he gives them respite to a stated term [or end], and when their term expires, God has in his sight all His servants." (35: 45).

In the three Abrahamic religious traditions, the image of God blowing his breath into humanity is central. It captures the source of our agency in how God forms and directs our destiny, and yet also demonstrates our tendency for elating ourselves and exceeding our limits. We were made in the image of the Lord. It is our blessing, but also our curse. It is the edge we are here to learn to walk, to step up to our viceregency, on whose two sides lie the imbalances of either tyranny or victimhood.

We have a tendency to perceive ourselves as gods, placing ourselves above others through an exaggerated sense of self. We presume to bestow life and love or take it away. Creating or destroying; healing and yet devastating. We have been endowed with choice—this is our inescapable existential reality—we have the divine in us, yet it is a double-edged status. The laws of the divine cannot be made manifest without human agency, making us recognize the "narratives" of this intertwined enterprise present and dominant in these three Semitic traditions. We realize that we are blessed with this "creative" status while also burdened with this very responsibility. We are the co-creators of our destiny, and hence the plotters of history, while also making "choice" the biggest human challenge—simply due to the fact that we cannot escape from making choices. Therefore, even inaction, is a form of action as Jean Paul Sartre expressed in his writings in the last century.

■ LOOKING BACKWARD

A strong common visual image that captures our status in the three traditions is the romantic image of blending earth and water and then God blowing His divine breath into this mixture of different elements. Our nonresistant, pure, and transparent living nature reflects water and our ability for humility and surrender reflects our earthly origin. Transcending the duality is the divine breath bringing this mixture of opposites into a whole conscious being. It is through our nonresistant, earthly nature, that all these three traditions, including the Eastern traditions, reconcile these two marvelous and yet competing innate tendencies—the propensity to dominate and the ability to surrender.

In this chapter, by examining the practical ways in which humility is presented in these traditions, particularly from a Qur'anic perspective, we see the creative ways we are encouraged to pursue in order to reshape and evolve and reach out toward our divine potential, beyond the assumptions of angels who are keeping their watch on us in this dark night of the human self.

The Qur'an eloquently and elegantly condenses the malaises of humanity into two major tendencies: wrong perceptions and desire, or, as stated earlier, attachment to opinion and tendency to control and dominate. However, the real emphasis in the Qur'an is on the problematic nature of mental perceptions and the way humans misperceive reality. The verse that discusses wrong perceptions and desire is preceded by a discussion on the misleading nature of language itself. The Qur'an shows the intimate connection between idols and language. The former being made by the hands and the latter being spun in the mind. In surah Al-Najm, we are told about the ways we name the world and create idols, "These are nothing but names which you have devised—you and your fathers—for which God has sent down no authority whatsoever. They follow nothing but perceptions (or opinion) and the desires of their own selves." (53:23). I am translating "dhan" as perception or opinions, which sometimes is translated as "guesswork," because the word is also used in Arabic to refer to a thinking that is not based on facts or clear evidence.[3]

In Arabic, even to this day, the verb "dhan" is used to express the vernacular, "I think," when in reference to issues that are not based on facts. So it is interesting to see how the Qur'an constantly brings up this particular word to discuss the nature of human thinking, which is mostly perceptions, opinions, speculations, and guesswork, all spun in the mind irrespective of reality or facts. This explains why the Qur'anic focus on arrogance is not cast in mystical and spiritual terms but, rather, in socioeconomic and political ones. It always asks us to "observe" reality, and to examine the large scale consequences of confusion or tyranny in history. Humanity's propensity for arrogance is presented as humanity's main challenge in the very first revelation. It is as if the genetic code of the Qur'an was planted into this initial small passage. (96:6)

There are several major terms used in the Qur'an to refer to arrogance: *istikbar* (to perceive oneself as bigger) and *uluw* (to perceive oneself as higher) or *tagha*, (to transgress bounds). These words capture attitudes in which the mind has become delusional in regard to size or altitude or boundaries. They are terms describing different illusions: an overblown perception of oneself, or a context gone awry, or limits ignored. In one instance in the Qur'an, we see how Pharaoh is caught up in both: "Then we sent Moses and his brother Aaron, with our signs and a manifest authority. To Pharaoh and his chiefs; but they acted arrogantly (*istakbaru*) –perceived themselves as bigger—as they were people who elated themselves ('*aleen*')—those who placed themselves higher." (23: 45-46).

In the New Testament, we find the same practical references instead of theological or philosophical notions about humility. Elegant frugality is a central message for Jesus, a much needed concept in the age of excesses of global inequities, consumerism, and environmental destruction: "Do not store up for yourselves treasures on earth, where moth and rust destroy, and where thieves break in and steal. But store up for yourselves treasures in heaven... For where your treasure is, there your heart will be also."[4] We also read in Isaiah:

> Spend yourselves on behalf of the hungry and satisfy the needs of the oppressed, then your light will rise in the darkness. And your night will become like noonday. The Lord will give you always; he will satisfy your needs in a sun-scorched land and will strengthen your fame. You will be like a well-watered garden, like a springs whose waters never fail. Your people will rebuild the ancient ruins and will raise up the age-old foundations; you will be called Repairer of Broken Walls, Restorer of Streets with Dwellings.[5]

It is the way this passage ends that gives us an insight into why we want to look backward. After all, it is legitimate to question our attachment to these sacred texts given all the horrific deeds caused and still being caused by religious people and their religious traditions. I would like to suggest that the practical and direct propositions in the Scriptures, or as well put in Isaiah, "the age-old foundations," have not yet been allowed to manifest their actual potential. Rather, they have become ancient ruins. This is reminiscent of Jesus who talks about the "stone," which is rejected by the builders and yet which has become the cornerstone. Just because the religious traditions have been established within large communities, with certain canonized "dogmas," does not necessarily mean that these were true expressions of the original teachings. Social norms, which we see in many historical contexts, have lasting impact and strongly resist new teachings.

I would like to argue that sometimes it is not the search for truth or justice that attracts people back to their religious traditions, but rather nostalgia, either out of an innocent naivety for a lost golden age or out of political agendas bent on usurping power. It is misfortunate that many religious movements, although on the surface invoke ritual, symbolism, slogans, and spiritual wording, go awry and subvert the core principles of their tradition, reminding us of why Jesus so aptly warns: "Watch out for false prophets. They come to you in sheep's clothing, but inwardly they are ferocious wolves." But Jesus's alarm is not raised to cause fear or chasm, but rather to create discernment. He even provides a methodic tool for verification—something that we can appreciate better in the age of science with its emphasis on observation and consequence—when he says to his disciples: "By their fruit you will recognize them. Do people pick grapes from thornbushes, or figs from thistles? Likewise every good tree bears good fruit, but a bad tree bears bad fruit... Every tree that does not bear is cut down and thrown into the fire. Thus, by their fruit you will recognize them."[6] This is practical advice that borders on being a social science, and a much needed approach in an age with many religious slogans. This is also consistent and similar to the Qur'anic emphasis on consequence, as we will see later in connection to tyranny and injustice.

The sheer survival of these major religious traditions and their indisputable grip on the imagination of billions of people speak to a great potential and the light of Truth within these ancient teachings, which have yet to bear fruit:

The dictum that truth always triumphs over persecution, is one of those pleasant false-hoods which men repeat after one another....History teems with instances of truth put down by persecution. If not suppressed for ever, it may be thrown back for centuries.... The real advantage which truth has, consists in this, that when an opinion is true, it may be extinguished once, twice, or many times, but in the course of ages there will generally be found persons to rediscover it, until some one of its reappearances falls on a time when from a favorable circumstances it escapes persecution until it has made such head as to withstand all subsequent attempts to suppress it.[7]

The values of equality, nonviolence, gentleness, and intellectual and spiritual humility, although part of the core teachings of the major world traditions, have been co-opted by previous major paradigms of domination. Many of these patterns of behavior and exploitation still survive. In fact, much of what we consider modern and still embrace in our contemporary world has been opposed by prophets and sages long ago. Many practical guidelines for humility and compassion still seem alien and marginal in our world, if not outright mad. Our current reality reflects many of the opposite values. We live arrogantly, violently, and with elaborate structures of global superiority and domination. We reconcile ourselves with the veto right, a Roman legacy, in the Security Council of the United Nation, a modern institution that stands for the assembly of our planet's nations.

■ HUMILITY AND ARROGANCE IN THE QUR'AN

Although the theme of humility has been discussed over the centuries in the various Islamic traditions and even formed schools of thought, especially in the mystical tradition, I would like to focus here directly on the Qur'anic conceptions of arrogance and humility. The Qur'an describes arrogance as humanity's malaise because it represents its major misconception of itself. It does so in both the very first verse revealed to the Prophet Muhammad, as well as in the story of creation, and also throughout its subsequent various themes. The first verses revealed to Mohammad deal with arrogance and connects it directly to social and political tyranny:

> Read in the name of your Lord, Who created humanity out of a clot. Read And your Lord is Most Generous (Bountiful). He Who taught with the use of the pen. Taught humanity that which they knew not. Nay but humanity transgresses. In that it looks upon itself as self-sufficient. Verily, to your Lord is the return of all...(96: 1–8).

And naturally the Qur'an also connects Pharaoh, the archetypical tyrant, to *tagha*: "And with Pharaoh, lord of Stakes. Those who transgressed (*taghaw*) in the lands, and heaped therein corruption." (89: 10–12). Toshihiko Izutsu, the Japanese academic, who is one of the stellar modern scholars of Islam, discusses the different terms used in the Qur'an to refer to arrogance or haughtiness. He argues that *Taghut*, which is a central term in the Qur'an, is connected to *Istikbar*:

> This verb is another synonym of "*istakbara*" [to conceive oneself bigger than others] which plays an important role Qur'an. Starting from the image of the water rising so high as to exceed the bounds and overflow the banks....The Arab philologist, al-Baydawi, in his commentary on Surah XXIII, 77 says that *tughyan* (nominal form)

implies 'an excess in *kufr*, man's being too puffed up with pride (*istikbar*) to accept the Truth, and an open hostility against the Apostle and the believers.' *Tughan* is often used in combination with *kufr*, showing that the two words are almost synonymous.[8]

However, I would like to suggest that in most instances we come to see that *istikbar* (to perceive oneself bigger) is a term that captures cultural discourses of superiority and self aggrandizement, that is, ethnocentrism, whereas *taghut* is generally used in the Qur'an in contexts in which *istikbar* has become the social and political reality, and where it has been put to practice and hence leading to *taghut*, that is, tyranny.

A significant theme, therefore, emerges here in relation to the identity of the *Kafir* (infidel). Rather, certain traits and patterns of behavior bring someone within the bounds of being *Kafir* and further away from being with God. Izutsu goes further and states that arrogance is the central trait of a *Kafir*:

[An] important element in the semantic structure of the concept of *kufr* is 'haughtiness' or 'arrogance'. We should remark that in the Quranic conception the inborn arrogance of the mind is not simply one of the various features of *kufr*. The Qur'an never tires of laying special emphasis on this element in the structure of *kufr*, so much so that in many cases it is made to represent the most typical characteristic of a *Kafir*. A *Kafir* is an arrogant, haughty man in a religious sense. Even a cursory examination of the Scripture will convince anyone that it looks at the phenomenon of *kufr* mainly from this angle. In the Qur'an the insolent boaster walks around as the central figure in the province of negative properties.[9]

Moreover, the term *kufr* in Arabic is derived from the root three-letter verb K F R, which is, although used in the context of rejecting faith, is a verb for denial. Hence, a *Kafir* (infidel) is someone who is in denial of truth and equal bounds with others. Another way to understand the subtlety of the term *kufr*, is to note what the Qur'an contrasts it with. In many instances, *Kufr* is contrasted and the opposite of, not faith, but rather gratitude. Gratitude is the ultimate and highest level of faith, that is, the joyful appreciation and acknowledgment of God's blessings and the measured balance and justice in existence. Hence, *Kufr* is the denial of all that.[10]

The Qur'an provides an optimistic vision of humanity. Arrogance is not integral to humans, but only a human propensity. Therefore, humans can escape its beguiling grip. The Qur'an, in the first story of creation, as we see also in the Old Testament, establishes the first scene of humanity's journey. Our first encounter with arrogance in the Qur'an is not committed by Adam or Eve; rather, it is committed by Satan who is arrogant toward God and his new creation: "It is We who created you and gave you shape; then We bade the angels, Bow down to Adam, and they bowed down except *Iblis* [Satan]; he was not among those who bowed down. He said [God]: What prevented you from bowing down when I have commanded you? He said [Satan]: I am better than he; you created me from fire and him from clay." (7: 11–12). We encounter here the first act of arrogance—defiance toward God on the basis of origins. Then God drives Satan out of paradise because he has committed arrogance—the Qur'an uses a word similar to *istikbar*: "He said [God]: "Get down from this place: it is not for you to be arrogant here for you are now among the smallest of creatures." (7:13) It is noteworthy that Satan's state is described in the active form of being small, *saaghir*.[11]

Satan belittled himself when he pretended to be better and bigger than Adam and Eve. Just as arrogance is an act of literally making oneself bigger than one is, *saaghir* is the noun form, in Arabic, for the one who makes oneself smaller than one is. Thus, Satan humiliated himself by the very act of arrogance; he made himself smaller by the act of attempting to make himself bigger. Poetic justice is done when he exceeds his limits. By exploding with arrogance, he imploded with humiliation. Nevertheless, Satan stays the course of defiance toward God and his arrogance, instead, increases. He asks God to give him time (in 7: 14): "[G]ive me respite until they [human beings] are raised."[12]

God grants him his wish. However, Satan's arrogance increases yet one more time even when given freedom of expression. He then accuses God and threatens: "Now that you have thwarted [or tempted] me, I shall most certainly lie in ambush for them all along your straight path, and shall most certainly fall upon them openly as well as in a manner beyond their ken, and from their right and from their left; and most of them you will find ungrateful." (7:16–17) Only then God says, "Go forth from here, disgraced and disowned." (7:18)

Satan here is a figure whose traits draw one away from being in a state of peace with God, away from being in a true state of surrender. We see that he is arrogant on two levels. He is racist and he is also someone who places blame outside himself for his moral failings. In the first instance, he uses his origin—fire—to raise himself above Adam and Eve who were created from mere clay. In the second instance, his arrogance is intellectual and ideological. He accuses God of thwarting him and making him fall in error and thereby redeems and absolves himself of any wrong. Then his commitment to his arrogance turns ideological when he challenges God and promises to spread his ideas till the end of time. He shows no sign of self-reflection; rather, he is utterly convinced beyond any doubt of his own path, which he promises to adhere to until the Day of Judgment. Moreover his determination to propagate his ideas gives us a rather humorous insight into evil's desperate need for propaganda and "hard work ethic." So we come to see that his steadfast stance and the complete lack of self-reflection turn his ideology into an inflexible dogma. Satan is arrogant, and he is fundamentalist.

On the other side of this story are Adam and Eve. Soon enough, Satan goes to work and starts his campaign and persuades them to eat from the forbidden tree. "Your Lord only forbade you this tree lest you should become angels, or among the immortals." (7: 20) And then we read in the Qur'an how he swears to both Adam and Eve about his sincerity. Then he succeeds in making them eat from the tree. But then "their Lord called unto them: Did I not forbid you that tree, and tell you that Satan was an avowed enemy unto you?" (7:22) The response of Adam and Eve in the Qur'an sets them completely apart from Satan's ideology. Here, even though God is acknowledging Satan's agency and involvement in their violation of the rule, they themselves, however, take a moral stance, based on personal accountably, where they do not even attempt to blame Satan— although he clearly misled them as we are told—nor do they insist on their wrong doing. On the contrary, they say: "Our Lord! We have been unjust to ourselves. If you forgive us not and bestow not upon us your mercy, we shall certainly be among the lost." (7:23)

In contrast to Satan's arrogance, Adam and Eve provide the alternative model. They take moral responsibility for their mistake, act with accountability and immediately admit their wrongdoing using a phrase that is unique to the Qur'an—"being unjust to oneself"—and which is one of the repetitive Qur'anic phrases. What makes this a unique concept is the way the Qur'an contextualizes injustice as an aberration from the balance and equality of existence. It describes, therefore, a phenomenon not caused by only external forces and outside enemies, but also as the result of one's own doing. Again, this has to do with the theme of "transgression"—going beyond the proper bounds and stepping out of the equilibrium intended by God. Consequently, in the Qur'an, injustice is not simply a one-sided affliction for which we blame others; it is rather a state of imbalance in which both victim and victimizers are responsible for its occurrence. Hence, one sees in the Qur'an the unity of "injustice," because it is presented as a moral failing by both those who inflict the injustice and those who receive it. Both sides are agents in the imbalance and transgression. The wronged side is not merely a helpless victim. The Qur'an stresses the agency of both in the equation of the power game. In one verse, we see blame being thrown back and forth between the two sides as they argue in a scene that foreshadows the hereafter. The Qur'an uses the term the "unjust" to refer to both sides of the power equation.

Could you but see when the unjust will be made to stand before their Lord, throwing back the Word [blame] on one another? Those who have been oppressed [rendered weak] will say to the arrogant ones: "Had it not been for you, we should certainly have been believers!" The arrogant ones will say to those who have been oppressed: "Was it we who kept you back from Guidance after it reached you? Nay, rather it was you who transgressed." (34: 31–32)

In this exchange of blame, we see the earlier themes of blame and loss and the close connections between injustice and transgression. What emerges in their dialogue—or actually, bickering—is the inability of both aggressors and the oppressed to take moral accountability. As we have seen in the story of creation, it is this refusal of self-reflection and the obstinate unwillingness to repent and make a U-turn that keeps one on the path of injustice, be it tyrant or victim. Consequences, *awaqib* in the Qur'an, therefore, are the ways to measure such levels of misalignment to truth and the degrees of arrogance and transgression. Again, we are brought back to practical grounds, because the Qur'an focuses on tracing history to see the *awaqib* of arrogance playing out in the landscape, both in individual instances and in the collective narrative of nations. The Qur'an specifically and repeatedly asks believers to travel the earth and examine the consequence of bygone nations. "Do they not travel through the earth, and see what was the consequence of those before them." (40:21) It also specifically calls to see the consequence of injustice, and in 28: 40 we read "look at the consequence of the unjust ones."[13] It urges us to look especially at how arrogance and inequity destroyed them: "We were not to destroy a town unless its people were unjust," (28:59) and why had they been destroyed? In 16: 118 we read "We were not unjust to them; they were unjust to themselves."[14]

Calling for humility, self-reflection, and a commitment to align back to the right path is the "warning" messengers bring to arrogant people to spare them the consequences of decline and destruction.

■ THE WORD OF EQUALITY

This call to aligning to God's immutable laws, creates a whole different paradigm between arrogance and victimhood. The human condition swings between polar states of being: arrogance and self-pity, superiority and inferiority, oppression and victimhood. The challenge, therefore, is not to avoid just arrogance but also victimization. By acknowledging one's agency and role in the equation of power, humanity, standing at either end of the pole is called to avoid going to excess in either direction of the power game. The idea is a practical command to return to a "Word of Equality," which is a call to return from both extremes: to the powerful, to exercise responsibility and avoid injustice; to the victims, to disobey and not worship power. The Qur'an, when addressing the "Other," places "equality" at the center: "O, people of the Book! Come to a Word of Equality between us and you: that we worship none other but God, that we associate no partners with him, that we take not each other as gods above each other." (3:64)

Upon tracing the concepts and terms relating to arrogance, it becomes clear that the Qur'anic antidotes to arrogance are practical ones: repentance, which implies self-criticism; equality as the alternative model to arrogance and dominance; and humility through practical applications that would ensure the treatment of others neither as superior nor inferior. Of course, there are other central commands, again with an emphasis on the practical, about sharing wealth and knowledge.

In particular, the concept of being unjust to oneself is, therefore, connected to being both the aggressor and the receiver of aggression—because injustice is presented in the Qur'an as a state of disequilibrium, a loss of the "Word of Equality." The Qur'an does not always present this disequilibrium, as we discussed earlier, as exclusively the result of external forces; rather, injustice is a state of imbalance from within and without. Therefore, injustice is the manifestation of ideas and conceptions coming from within. By being on a path of self-destructive behavior and hanging on to self-limiting notions, a human being is falling into "self-injustice," which is why arrogance is not just a form of "self-elation" above the others, but equally a "self-injustice." It does this because arrogance leads individuals to stagnate and stumble on their path of knowledge and growth, and it leads arrogant societies to decline and destruction. This sad state of affairs is somewhat reminiscent of Platonic conceptions of justice and the just life where beautiful parallels can be found between rational Greek conceptions of justice and the Semitic spiritual notions of equality in relation to monotheism.

When the Qur'an connects this human ability to recognize "self-injustice" with self-awareness, it highlights our capacity to change course. therefore, it stresses human agency in social change. We see the beauty of our empowered and dignified status, which we have as a result of having divine breath within our being. However, in order to maintain our connection to the divine and our connection to the creative force of the universe, we need to come to a state of humility and actually learn to be in this state of self-reflection or repentance. Thus, this openness to the sense of possibility and potential is connected to a process rather than a trait. Therefore, "learned ignorance" is an appropriate term for such spiritual evolution. "Learned ignorance" can not occur without responsibility, accountability, self-reflection, and self criticism. Repentance is what leads to consciousness and is the practical response to moral failures because it gives us the ability to adapt to changing times and circumstances. This state of perpetual self-reflection captures the centrality of repentance in the spiritual traditions the world over. The process of repentance creates humility and, therefore, balances the divine and clay forces within ourselves. Humility becomes the path to our own very survival and growth. In contrast, arrogance becomes our boulevard to destruction because it puts individuals and entire societies in a static stance and in the grip of ideology. Arrogance stems from a perception of self as perfect, which creates an atmosphere of finality and, therefore, a sense of closure. Most importantly, it robs us of the ability to adapt and evolve, on both the micro and macro levels.

By examining examples of both arrogance and humility, it becomes obvious that the Qur'anic emphasis is not due to metaphysical or purely spiritual dimensions. Rather, we see that intellectual and spiritual forms of arrogance are condemned precisely because they have earthly, political and material consequences which affect people's actual conditions on earth. All forms of arrogance and hubris are presented as dangerous traits. We are warned against arrogance because it turns, as we saw in the story of Satan, into an ideology of dogma and stagnation, and in the story of Pharaoh, as the legitimization of collective and horrific political crimes. We are asked to travel through the earth and examine the practical histories of annihilation and enslavement of the "other," which in turn is followed by a destruction of "self." The connection between injustice toward others and self-destruction, in the Qur'an, is presented as a universal law and a pattern governing history.[15]

■ FACE OFF: PHARAOH AND MOSES

The story of creation sets the tone and parameters of arrogance in the models of superiority and humility, and in repentance and self-reflection. Subsequently, all the stories in the Qur'an have elements of this original blueprint. When following the Prophetic narratives, one comes to see how the Qur'an repeatedly describes these dimensions as the major challenge that faced the Prophets: oppressive, arrogant societies. The Qur'an relentlessly reminds us that in the past nations were destroyed because they were unjust to themselves. Because these nations were arrogant and elated themselves in the land and above others, they also destroyed themselves. "We were never to destroy towns unless its people were unjust."(28:59) In the Qur'an, Pharaoh is the archetype of arrogance and oppression, and Moses is the archetype of the intellectual who opposes him. So Moses is portrayed as a prophet, as an intellectual in the face of power. He is presented as the one who tells truth to power. "Go to Pharaoh," God instructs Moses, "for he has transgressed [or acted in tyranny [*tagha*]." (20:24) And Pharaoh is presented as the archetype of tyranny and as representative of a culture whose arrogance unfolds in multitudes, "Pharaoh gathered people and called out. He said, 'I am your Lord, Most High'" (79: 24). But the Qur'an also traces the consequences of his arrogance on sociopolitical levels: "Pharaoh elated ['ala] himself in the land and broke up its people into sects, oppressing a group of them; their sons he slew, their women he enslaved for he was indeed among the corrupt ones" (28:4).

And gradually the Qur'an establishes the path of arrogance as distinct from the path of Prophets whose main command in the Qur'an is to, "worship God and eschew tyranny" (16:36). Those inflicted with arrogance are those who have been won to the path of Satan, yet the door is always open for repentance and realignment with the truth. The prophetic message is presented as a humble call to bring back people to the path of equality and compassion, away from arrogance and dominance. The Qur'an gives the command to Muhammad (18:110):

Say: "I am but a human being
Like yourselves,
But the revelation has come to me
That your God is
One God
Whoever expects to meet his Lord
Let him work righteous,
And in the worship of his Lord,
Admit no other gods.

The Qur'an generalizes the message of the prophets as constantly confirming their humanity and equality with their other fellow humans:

Their messengers said to them: 'We are only human like yourselves, but blessed those whom He wills among his servants. It is not for us to bring you an authority except as God permits. And in God shall believers put their trust. No reason have we why we should not put our trust in God after He had guided us to our paths. We shall certainly bear with patience all the harm you cause us. For those who put their trust should put their trust in God.'(14:11–12)

After such a message of unilateral equality and nonviolence, how do their societies respond to prophets? In stark contrast to the prophets' humility and proactive efforts at establishing peace, they respond with arrogance and threats of exile and intolerance. "And the unbelievers said to their messengers: 'Be sure we shall drive you out of your land, or you shall return to our religion.' Then God revealed to them, We shall cause the unjust ones to perish" (14:13) And here we see that arrogance and humility are present on both sides. The law will not spare the arrogant ones and promises their end. However, it is not the prophets who are commanded to destroy such unjust societies. On the contrary, they are the messengers who are to spare people destruction. They are carriers of warnings and are asking their people to re-align themselves and spare themselves annihilation. This is a repeated plea by all the prophets who are always commanded to use only nonviolent means and the Word to warn their people of the consequences of arrogance.

▨ EQUALITY, HUMILITY, AND UNIVERSALISM

Equality and justice take paramount place in the Qur'anic paradigm. Justice is one of the central repeated commands "If you judge, judge in justice between them. For God loves the just ones" (5:42). All believers are strongly and poetically called to stand firmly for justice: "O, you believers, stand out firmly for justice, as witnesses to God, even against yourselves, or your parents or your kin, and whether it be rich or poor. For God can best protect both. Follow not your whims, lest ye swerve, and if you distort [justice], verily God is well-acquainted with all that you do" (4:135). All prophets are presented as carriers of this teaching to humanity. Immediately following this strong injunction for justice, the Qur'an lays down another injunction: to believe in all the prophets and their scriptures: "O, you believers! Believe in God, and his Messenger, and the scripture which He has sent to His Messenger. And the scripture which He sent to those before. Any who denies God, His angels, His books, His Messengers, and the Day of Judgment, has gone far, far astray"(4:136). Of course, this is not surprising since the Qur'an constantly informs us that all the prophets and messengers were all sent to call for justice:

> We sent aforetime our messengers with clear signs and sent down with them the Book and the Balance, so that humanity may stand forth in justice. And we sent down Iron, in which is severe might as well as many benefits for humanity, that God may test who it is that will help him, Unseen, Him and His messengers. For God is full of Strength, Exalted in Might. (57:25)

We notice how justice and balance, in the Qur'an, which refer to refined and measured equality, are juxtaposed with the element of Iron to invoke might and in turn is connected to God's might and strength. This poetic alignment of all these spheres casts justice, not just as a value or merely a moral trait, but also as a law of nature, akin to its mightiest substance and also as the law of the mighty creator.

Due to this tone of universalism and the unity of prophets, the Qur'an does not place the path of Muhammad as superior or inferior to other religious traditions and messengers. The Qur'an, rather, affirms the spirit of equality it calls for by also presenting Islam as part of a larger universal human journey. Just as the prophets, in the Qur'anic narratives, place themselves in equality with their fellow humans, the Qur'an also places itself in equality with the rest of human heritage, as being part of a larger chain of human knowledge and wisdom. "We make no distinction between one and another of his messengers. And they say, 'We hear, and we obey. We seek Your forgiveness, Our Lord, and to You is the end of all journeys'"(2:285) Moreover, the Qur'an opens the door of the message of God to all in an inclusive embrace of humanity when it expands the frontiers beyond the ones included in the Qur'an, and hence opening up the Semitic tradition to a larger global view. "And messengers from before We have related to you; and some whom We have not"(4:164). The Qur'an even commands Muhammad not to claim any distinction in regard to other religions when he addresses his people. The Qur'an also stresses his humanity, vulnerability, and lack of knowledge about what the future may hold: "Say, 'I am not an anomaly among his messengers. I do not know what will be done with me or with you; for I only follow that which was revealed to me and

I am nothing, but a plain Warner" (4:69). The verse continues to refer to the reason behind the peoples' rejection of Muhammad's prophets and says to them, "Say: 'You see if this teaching be from God, and you reject it, and a witness from among the children of Israel testifies to its similarity [with earlier scripture], and has believed while you are arrogant. Verily God does not guide unjust people' " (46:10). Here we see that the arrogance condemned in the people of Mecca extends beyond their rejection of Muhammad to their arrogance toward other scriptures and traditions, to which the Qur'an connects Muhammad. The passage in Surat Al Ahqaf goes even further to make the Qur'an a scripture that confirms and continues the message of Moses. "And before this, there was the Book of Moses, a guide [imam] and mercy; and this Book is confirming the truth [of the Torah] in the Arabic tongue, to warn those who commit injustice and a glad tiding to those who are compassionate" (46:12). The Qur'an places itself within the Semitic heritage by creating a continuity of the leadership and mercy of Moses and his heritage as "imam." The parameters of this passage are yet again extended further into a full-blown and all-inclusive universal message, by emphasizing ethics beyond simply religion and messengers: "Those who say, 'Our Lord is God, and become straight; on them there shall be no fear nor sorrow. Such shall be the dwellers of Paradise in recompense for their deeds"(46:14).

■ LOOKING FORWARD

These Qur'anic verses carry great potential in creating a modern universalistic ethos in Muslim societies. It is important to stress these themes of universalism and equality in the Qur'an, especially given the increasing religious sensibilities and political frustrations of Muslim societies. By bringing forward the centrality of universalism and equality in the Qur'an, which have been overlooked by traditional and medieval interpreters due to the sociopolitical realities of their eras, modern values and theses could ring true and authentic in Muslim societies. Given the revival of strong Islamic waves in the Muslim World today, these empowering verses that advance intellectual and spiritual humility along a universal vision of humanity can serve in creating paradigm shifts to the dominant postcolonial feelings of alienation and anger. These values can empower Muslims to reclaim a history and tradition much richer and more layered with nuance than the reductionist discourse of those with immediate political agendas.

Unfortunately, the Qur'an and Islamic heritage, which for centuries have been tolerant toward minorities and other religious groups, have recently been co-opted to produce a deformed, horrific, and fanatical fragmented postmodern pastiche—a sort of political Frankenstein, stitched together hastily in an atmosphere of angst and frustration in societies barely waking up to modernity. The fragmented and decontextualized understating of Islam by some Muslims especially contributes to the current levels of oblivion to its rich heritage in ethics, philosophy, and multitudes of spiritual paths and movements. These tendencies also occurred in an era in which Muslim found themselves as the objects of global spiritual and intellectual rejection, and reacted then with their own rejection. They rejected not just others but also themselves, further confirming why the Qur'an always connects injustices and hostilities toward the Other as an ethos also directed toward Self. Western colonialism created deep levels of alienation in the Muslim world. This alienation resulted not just in an anti-Western ethos but also created an epistemological disconnection for Muslims from the larger Islamic heritage and history. Muslim rejection of the West today encapsulates a profound rejection of Self, and, hence, a severe and profound discontinuity with the Islamic tradition itself. In his *Culture and Imperialism*, Edward Said argues poignantly that the ethnocentric European "one-way gaze" into other corners of the world created equally reactionary "one-way gazes" back onto the Western world. According to Said, an ethnocentric Europe fueled, in turn, ethnocentric and nationalist liberation movements in which the Other had no place in Western discourses of superiority and empire except as curious objects; in response, those corners of the world, as they attempted to regain their agency, rendered the West obsolete.[16] Of course, when rejecting others, one is also rejecting the humanity they have in common, which naturally results in a rejection of their own self. All this leads to revisionist puritanical and arrogant renditions of one's own imagined history. Because intolerance has been brewing for millennia on all sides, examining the propositions and themes of the religious traditions around the world could play a healing and proactive role in creating a far more universally based spirituality and inclusive political and cultural discourses.

We now live in times in which intellectual humility is no longer a matter of enlightened luxury, an exercise in spiritual gymnastics or mysticism. We are in dire need of intellectual humility as a new paradigm for the world. Real lives, blood, and bread are at stake. World resources and global safety are at stake.

The scriptures and religious traditions, and the heritage of sages, philosophers, and poets over the past centuries provide people of all traditions in the world with ample sources for constructing new paradigms, ones that remain authentic to the indigenous peoples—paradigms that affirm their history and identity while encouraging them to become members of a larger world community. When human beings feel affirmed, respected, and admired, they become more self-critical while also becoming less afraid to open themselves to the outside world. This is why, during any political strife or crises, we see over and over the closing down of cultural bridges between people, the imploding of Self, and the rise in nihilistic tendencies. As a result, increasing anger and despair take severe forms of aggression by both the powerful and weak and create either monsters who level the landscape, or fanatic rebels with misguided causes. We need to revisit the practical propositions of these traditions to combat, in concrete ways, the rise in the "spirituality of arrogance" all over the world.

For Muslims, just as for believers in other religious traditions, humility is a model for practice. Humility was defined by Muhammad in the *Hadith* tradition, just as discussed earlier in relation to the Qur'an, as having practical implications. It is not to be confused with dignity and beauty. The Prophet Muhammad once told his companions that "a person does not enter paradise as long as in his heart there remains a drop of arrogance." A man sitting in his company said, "but a man likes to dress in beautiful garment and to wear beautiful shoes." Muhammad then replied, "God is beautiful and loves beauty. But arrogance is to reject truth and oppress people."[17] Once again, arrogance is presented here in connection to truth and oppression, and it is distinguished from human's search for beauty and excellence, which is even commended. Once again we are confronted with this double-edged challenge: striving toward excellence or falling into arrogance, but it is *attitude* that misaligns a person to the truth and leads him or her to act in unjust ways. This is what defined arrogance for Muhammad.

Humility, therefore, is not merely a spiritual generosity with which we oblige the "other." Rather, in the Islamic tradition, it is the law of the universe that we see in other previous traditions. Analogies with the physical universe are constantly drawn in all the three traditions to give further explanation to the laws governing the moral realm. These analogies take us beyond justice. Both in the Gospels and the Qur'an we are asked to love our enemies and repel animosity with compassion. We are asked to enter a higher realm, one that can seem harder. But love in the Gospels and Qur'an is presented again in practical and even empirical ways. Jesus tells the crowd:

> You have heard that it was said, 'Love your neighbor and hate your enemy.' But I tell you: Love your enemies and pray for those who persecute you, that you may be sons of your father in heaven. He causes his sun to rise on the evil and the good, and sends rain on the righteous and the unrighteous. If you love those who love you, what reward will you get?[18]

In the Qur'an, resisting animosity with active compassion is similarly presented as a statement of fact: "Goodness and wrong are not equal. Repel back with compassion; then will he between whom and you was animosity become as it were you friend and intimate"(41:34).

We see here how love and compassion are not presented as charities or commands to struggle with, which can be arrived at only through strenuous spiritual work, but rather as laws of the universe that affect the self and society. These commands are given within statements about the nature of good and compassion. Hence, they come across as an emotional paradigm shift.

So, just as humans had to change their perceptions of the movement of the Sun and Earth, these notions of love and humility are presented as new ways of perceiving what is good. Love is presented as integration between intellect and emotion, where both are aligned with the universe. Resistance is really futile. It is only self-destructive, just as it is when a human being defies physical laws and decides to jump off a high tower. Jesus opposes the Devil who tempts him to jump from the top of the Temple, but refuses to "tempt the Lord." He then comes back from the desert and re-aligns our emotional landscape with that of planetary physics, where love and the way the Sun shines are correlated. Similarly, in the Qur'an, we find that "of the bounties of your Lord, We bestow on all, these people and those people; for the giving of your Lord is not limited [or exclusive to either side]" (17:20). Just as we are not in control of the movement of the planets or planetary physics, so are we bound to the laws of love and compassion, not as metaphysical values but rather as earthly laws with specific consequences.

The Syrian scholar, Jawdat Said, compels us to observe our all-too-common dysfunctional ideas that lead to inequality and war:

When Louis Pasteur was looking in vinegar bottles to understand the way organic corruption occurs in biological entities, people were dying around him of different contagious diseases. But for Pasteur, mourning the dead was a less effective way of understanding the mechanisms of disease. Similarly, those who look into our cultural bottles will be able to discover the small mental entities spread in our intellectual food and sanctified cultures, enabling us to practice intellectual hygiene.[19]

Just as we discovered how to disinfect and pasteurize our food, Said says, humanity will also be able to disinfect our cultural materials from intellectual germs—from wrong perceptions as the Qur'an constantly states. Given the real consequences of our wrong perceptions, he proposes that we should also find methods of mental anesthesia, so that our operations will be less painful when removing harmful tissue, that is, nullify harmful ideas and notions. Said writes that "We are still at that level culturally. People have always been preached to, during Sunday sermons, to love their enemies; yet, they did not feel the contradiction when they sanctioned the burning of those who disagreed with them in opinion."[20]

He urges to find ways to placing such intellectual germs under the microscope. Is it yet possible to analyze and understand the cultural environment in which such a germ flourishes? This question, he writes, should become a priority, because for him, we devote certain amounts of funds to researching AIDS and cancer to gain control over them. Most people are concerned and follow the results of such efforts closely. But the question for Said is whether we can arrive at a level of consciousness and popular interest in intellectual health?[21]

Said makes it clear that humility is not a theoretical indulgence; rather, it is an ethic of practice where one always combats the potent germs that create hallucinations of perceiving oneself better, bigger, or higher than others. It is also why the opposite of arrogance is, in the Qur'anic paradigm, dangerous, that is, when people perceive themselves as smaller, lower, less or simply victimized. It is in establishing the equilibrium of equity with other beings that constitutes in the Qur'an the challenge for human beings. We are asked constantly to check this balance to see whether we are in positions of power or victimhood. We are asked, therefore, when in power, to practice compassion and tolerance and a just form of governance. When oppressed, we are asked to oppose injustice and reclaim our agency. Hence the image that emerges is magnificent. We are spiritually given the injunction to always hold each other as equals, repelling the tendency to oppress others and checking for the vulnerability of victims. The humility and spirituality found in the original teachings gives us a raw and direct image of all of us relating to each other in constant flux while maintaining the law of equality, the equilibrium of life. The very act of worshipping God is an act similar to the way the planets are held in orbit by the equality of the forces of gravity and repulsion. The beauty in the human endeavor as presented in these traditions is our capacity for choice and, therefore, our ability to create our planetary physics at will—whether we would hold each other as equal planets in each others' orbits, or collide and destroy ourselves, or float apart and become alien.

Karen Armstrong discusses the importance of study, *darash* in Rabbinic Judaism, as a perpetual pursuit of new insights. In a rather poignant tale, she tells a Talmudic story about Rabbi Eliezer ben Hyrcanus, who was engaged in an intractable argument with colleagues about a point of Jewish law. Armstrong writes that he could not convert them to his point of view, so he wanted God to back him up by performing some miracles. God obliged by making a tree move four hundred cubits of its own accord, water in a conduit flowed backward, and the walls of the house of studies started shaking so dramatically that the building seemed about to come down. But Rabbi Eliezer's companions were not impressed. Finally, in desperation, he asked for a "voice from heaven" (bat qol) to come to his aid. Obligingly the divine voice declared: "What is your quarrel with Rabbi Eliezer? The legal decision is always according to his view." But Rabbi Joshua rose to his feet and quoted the book of Deuteronomy: "It [the Law] is not in heaven," he said. "So we pay no attention to a *bat qol*."[22] The teaching of God was no longer confined to the divine sphere. It had been promulgated on Mount Sinai, and was, therefore, the inalienable possession of every single Jew. It did not belong to God anymore.[23]

This story rather beautifully captures the agency the faithful have toward change and the trust God placed in them. "Scripture was not a closed book," argues Karen Armstrong. The revelation, she argues, was not a historical event that had happened in a distant time, closed to renewal. Rather, every time a Jew confronts the text, he opens himself to it, and applies it to his own situation. For Armstrong, this dynamic vision could set the world afire.[24]

This same sentiment is what propelled Indian philosopher and poet Muhammad Iqbal to explain the liberating implications behind the Qur'an's claim to be the last revealed Scripture.[25]

This claim was not meant to seal knowledge, nor to place Islam above other traditions, argues Iqbal, but to give closure to a certain phase in human history and to usher in a new dawn where, precisely as those Rabbis argued, Scripture was no longer confined to the divine sphere, but would become a possession of humanity so that we can claim our agency through reason. Humanity was no longer in need of "divine revelation," argued Iqbal, because it was gradually endowed with tools to liberate it into larger fields of knowledge. Iqbal explained that a human being is in a place to shape and direct the powers around him. For him, a human being has the capacity to build a much vaster world in the depths of his or her own inner being, wherein he or she discovers sources of infinite joy and inspiration. "Hard his lot and frail his being, like a rose-leaf, yet no form of reality is so powerful, so inspiring, and so beautiful as the spirit of man! Thus in his inmost being, man, as conceived by the Qur'an, is a creative activity, an ascending spirit who, in his onward march, rises from state of being to another: 'It needs not that I swear by the sunset redness and by the night and its gatherings and by the moon when at her full, that from state to state shall ye be surely carried onward'" (84: 16–19).[26]

Although the Qur'an was revealed long before the age of science, its emphasis on the immutable laws of God in history, nature, and self was, for Iqbal, a celebration of humanity's ability to reason for itself and to engage with the world around:

> It is the lot of man to share in the deeper aspirations of the universe around him and to shape his own destiny as well as that of the universe, now by adjusting himself to its

forces, now by putting the whole of his energy to mould its forces to his own ends and purposes. And in this process of progressive change God becomes a co-worker with, provided man takes the initiative.[27]

Iqbal then quotes a verse in the Qur'an that connects both divine law and human agency: "Verily God will not change the condition of a people unless they change what is in themselves" (13:11). This is precisely the opposite of the fundamentalist religious view, where history has ended or, at best, has been locked into some golden bygone era. Fundamentalism is the height of intellectual arrogance. This sense of finality renders the religious quest into a tool for opposing the forces of history and nature. It is an arrogant attempt to stop the will of God from unfolding. There is no stopping the will of God, the Scriptures assure us. So does the "earth reveal its stories" as the Qur'an urges humanity to travel upon the landscape and trace the consequences of this dynamic nature of history. (99:4) It is only arrogant people who stop their destiny from unfolding. There is neither an end to knowledge, nor an end to God's Words. The Qur'an forcefully challenges such a static imaginary with a powerful poetic image (31:27):

> And if all the trees
> On earth were pens
> And the ocean were ink
> With seven oceans behind it
> To add to its supply
> Yet would not the Words of God be exhausted....[28]

■ Notes

1. For Quranic references, I did my own translation while consulting the translations of Abdullah Yusuf Ali, *The Holy Quran: Text, Translation and Commentary* (Brentwood: Amana Corporation, 1989), and the translation of Muhammad Asad, *The Message of The QUR'AN* (Gibraltar: Dar Al-Andalus, 1980). I made my changes and edits to bring the translation closer to its original Arabic as I saw fit.

2. Muhammad Iqbal, *The Reconstruction of Religious Thought in Islam* (Pakistan: Shaikh Muhammad Ashraf, 1960), p. 85.

3. Karen Armstrong notes in her recent book, *The Great Transformation*, how the Qur'an is skeptical and critical of theological speculation, dismissing it as "self-indulgent guesswork." She stresses that the Qur'an commands "practical compassion": "It was wrong to build a private fortune selfishly, at the expense of others, and good to share your wealth fairly and create a just and decent society where poor and vulnerable people were treated with respect." Karen Armstrong, *The Great Transformation: The Beginning of Our Religious Traditions* (New York: Alfred A. Knopf, 2006), p. 386.

4. John, 6: 19–21.

5. Isaiah, 58: 10–12.

6. Matthew (7: 15–20).

7. John Stuart Mill, *On Liberty*, (Oxford/New York: Oxford University Press 1991) p. 34.

8. Toshihiko Izutsu, *Ethico-Religious Concepts in the Qur'an* (Montreal & Kingston: McGill-Queen's University Press, 2002), p. 149.

9. Ibid., p. 142.

10. See how the Qur'an places notions of "infidels" and "those in gratitude," or the act of rejecting faith and the act of gratitude, as the polar opposites in these examples: Surat Anaml (27: 40), Surat Lukman (31: 12), Surat Al Inssan (76: 3) and Surat Al Baqarah (2: 152). See also Izutsu's discussions of these terms.

11. The term *saaghir* is distinct from *sagheer*, although both are derived from the root SGHR. *Sagheer* is the word for *small* without connotations of lowliness, whereas *Saaghir* is used to refer to those who are belittled and lowly.

12. See the chapter, "Satan and Evil" in Fazlur Rahman's *Major Themes of the Quran* (Minneapolis: Bibliotheca Islamica, Inc. 1989), pp. 121–131.

13. Also see Surat Yunus (10: 39). "They charged with falsehood that whose knowledge they cannot compass, even before the elucidation thereof has reached them. Thus also did those before them, make charges of falsehood. But see what was the end of those who did wrong." And given the rejection of absolute generalizations in the Qur'an, we see an exception made here, as we see elsewhere throughout the Quran when stating historical tendencies, "Of them there are some who believe therein, and some who do not. And your Lord knows best who are corruptive." (10:40)

14. See also Surat Hud (11: 101), Surat Al Zukhruf (43: 76), and Surat Ali Emran (3: 117).

15. See the work of Jawdat Said, *Hatta Yughayiru Ma Bi Anfassihim (Until They Change Themselves)*, (Damascus: Dar Al Fikr Al Mu'asser, 1996). He examines the ways the Qur'an presents laws of history and social change through the Qur'anic term, "Sunnah," meaning law or immutable and fixed patterns, and the notions of consequence and its connections to the social imaginary of a given people.

16. Edward Said, *Culture and Imperialism* (New York: Vintage Book, 1993).

17. Mustafa Al Bugha, ed., *Mukhtassar Sahih Musslim* (Damascus: Dar Al- Ulum Al- Insaniyah) pp.27–28.

18. Matthew (5: 43–46).

19. Jawdat Said, "Prophetic Method of Social Change," *Journal of Law & Religion* (Hamline University), XV (2001): 148.

20. Ibid.

21. Ibid.

22. Armstrong, *The Great Transformation*, p. 382.

23. Ibid.

24. Ibid.

25. Iqbal, *Reconstruction*.

26. Ibid., p. 12.

27. Ibid.

28. Also, in Surat Kahf, we read a similar verse: "If the ocean were Ink to the Words of my Lord, sooner would the ocean be exhausted than would the Words of my Lord, even if we added another ocean like it for its aid"(18: 109); see also the Gospel of John, 21:25.

PART III

Violence, Apologies, and Conflict

10 After Augustine: Humility and the Search for God in Historical Memory

Elizabeth Groppe

I grew up in rural Indiana in the flat lands of corn and soybean farming in a town of 5,200 people, one Catholic church, one small Episcopal church, and thirty Protestant congregations. There were no synagogues, mosques, or meditation halls. My first interreligious experience resulted from an invitation from South Bend's Temple Beth-El to graduate students in the theology department at Notre Dame to attend their annual weekend workshop on Judaism for Christian clergy and religious educators. On a Shabbat evening, I listened to the beautiful voice of the cantor and the prayers of the congregation and sat stunned. This service alive with spirit was not at all what I had anticipated. Raised in a post-Vatican II Catholic Church that had begun a dramatic transformation of its relationship to Judaism, I realized that I had internalized nonetheless an image of Judaism as a lifeless and legalistic religion.

Eager to learn more about the living Judaism I had experienced, I audited a course with Michael Signer at Notre Dame and began reading Jewish authors such as Abraham Joshua Heschel, in whom I found a profound expression of faith and spirituality that renewed my approach to the mystery of God. I have been moved by the Jewish reverence for the ineffable divine name and the Jewish emphasis on the inadequacy of all our attempts to speak of God. And I have come to feel a deeper connection with the person and faith of Jesus of Nazareth. Standing before the open Torah with a Jewish congregation, I have a new appreciation for what it meant for Jesus to stand to read the Isaiah scroll in the synagogue (Luke 4:16).

Interreligious dialogue has also been a painful but necessary encounter with the dark side of my own tradition. As a participant in a Notre Dame trip to Auschwitz, I saw the consequences of what Jules Isaac termed the Christian "teaching of contempt" for Jews and Judaism. I am haunted by the knowledge that although this alone does not account for the *Shoah*, Christianity, as the U.S. National Conference of Catholic Bishops acknowledges, "did lay the groundwork for racial, genocidal anti-Semitism by stigmatizing not only Judaism but Jews themselves for opprobrium and contempt."[1] I have learned that we must be ever vigilant to protect our religions from complicity in prejudice and violence and to keep our paths steady in the way of peace that is ultimately at the heart of our traditions.

This is one reason interreligious dialogue is so imperative. Another is that dialogue can transform our own egoisms. Augustine recognized that there is a part of us that wants to deify ourselves, to make our own selves the center of the universe. Our predilection for autobiography, Charles Mathewes comments, can be symptomatic of this spiritual pathology. There is also a certain presumptuousness to the autobiographical genre, an assertion of fixed identity that can blind me to the fact that I am still in *media res* and that I must continue to be open to the transforming presence of God's grace. Augustine, Mathewes notes, subverts these temptations by addressing his *Confessions* to God and beginning not with his own words but with the language of the psalms. His "anti-autobiographical autobiography" is the work of one who "has been redeemed from the ceaselessly futile task of trying to tell one's own story."[2] Religious communities, too, can fall prey to the spiritual pathologies of self-deification and blinding fixed identities. By living and telling our communal stories in dialogue with one another, we can counter these temptations and help one another to continue to be open to the transforming grace of the Spirit of God, the ultimate author of a story that is still ongoing.

The *Confessions* of Saint Augustine, composed between 397 and 401, are a classic account of the Christian quest to know and love God. They recount a search that founders on the tumultuous waves of human pride (*superbia*) and finds remedy in the humble wood of the cross, a raft that carried Augustine safely across the sea of pride to the homeland he glimpsed on the horizon.[3] "Let your faith board the wood of the cross," he exhorted his congregation, "You won't be drowned, but borne up by the wood instead."[4] Clement of Alexandria, Origen, Gregory of Nyssa, Basil, Hilary of Poitiers, and Ambrose preceded Augustine in their emphasis on humility as the paramount Christian virtue, but no one, writes Deborah Wallace Ruddy, "was more insistent about its primacy in the Christian life than St. Augustine," whose theology has had a deep and lasting influence on Western Christianity.[5] In this chapter I will introduce Augustine's theology of pride and humility, using his autobiographical *Confessions* as my primary source. I will then attempt to follow Augustine in a search for God that journeys through historical memory as I walk the labyrinthine streets of Jerusalem with my Jewish and Muslim trialogue companions.

▨ SUPERBIA AND HUMILITY IN AUGUSTINE'S CONFESSIONS

"You are great, Lord, and highly to be praised" (Ps 47:2).[6] This line from the psalms opens the *Confessions*, which are simultaneously a public acknowledgment of sin and a statement of the praise and glorification of God. Augustine's masterpiece spans the years of his infancy in Thagaste (354 CE) through his consecration as bishop of Hippo (397 CE) and offers reflection on many issues germane to our consideration of intellectual humility and learned ignorance: the temporal distention that distinguishes our mode of consciousness from that of God; Scripture as a revelatory text that mediates but does not reify God's timeless truth; and the transcendent character of truth that we will know in full only in the eschaton.[7] I will focus here on just one dimension of Augustine's contribution to our trialogue theme: his confession of pride as the primal obstacle to knowledge of God and the humility of Christ as the remedy.[8]

Augustine's *Confessions* analyze the pervasive reach of pride through examination of his own life, beginning with the jealousies of infancy and proceeding with reflection on his youth and schooling in Thagaste. In the intellectual culture of his day, he recalled, "It was set before me as my moral duty in life to obey those who admonished me with the purpose that I should succeed in this world, and should excel in the arts of using my tongue to gain access to human honours and to acquire deceitful riches."[9] When he neglected lessons in grammar and arithmetic in preference for ball games, he was chastised by the canes of schoolmasters, who were themselves engrossed in adult contests of wealth and glory.[10] Latin poetry was one subject that he did study eagerly, delighting in tales of wooden horses full of armed soldiers and weeping as Dido was dying for love of Aeneas—yet he shed no tears at his own alienation from God.[11] The skill with words that he honed as he polished his recitations of Virgil in the hope of accolades was good, he later confessed, but "my sin consisted in this, that I sought pleasure, sublimity, and truth not in God but in his creatures, in myself and other created beings."[12] This misorientation of soul he terms *superbia*, the pride of placing oneself or a creaturely good in a position that belongs to God alone.

For Augustine, *superbia* is the primal sin, the cause of the fall of the rebellious angel, and the cause of Adam and Eve's disgrace. "If you eat," the serpent tempted them, "you shall be like gods" (Gen. 3. 5).[13] This sin of attempted self-deification is replicated each time the self with its lusts and desires for pleasures becomes the ultimate arbiter and criterion of the Good. *Superbia* operates, not simply in the heart of the individual school boy enamored of Virgil and eager for praise, but in the subtle complexities of a social world warped by the fundamental misdirection of human desire. Behind the curtains of the classroom doorway, the models held up for Augustine's imitation were men who were embarrassed by a lapse in grammar but received praise and self-congratulation when they "described their lusts in a rich vocabulary of well constructed prose with a copious and ornate style."[14] Augustine depicts a society in which the love of God that should be the cornerstone of the social order is eclipsed by a corrupted form of self-love, and, as a consequence, the entire culture founders. Language, for example, unmoored from divine justice and goodness, becomes a mere human convention rather than an expression of truth. Accolades are given not to one who strengthens the moral conscience of humanity but to the orator who pronounces the word *homo* with the initial aspirate.[15] "These were the qualities for which I was praised by people whose approval was at that time my criterion of a good life."[16]

Superbia also cast its shadow on Augustine's young adulthood. As he pursued his studies of law in Carthage, he was beset again with a desire for social recognition. At the top of his class in the rhetor's school, he reflected, "I wanted to distinguish myself as an orator for a damnable and conceited purpose, namely delight in human vanity."[17] At the impressionable age of nineteen, Cicero's *Hortensius* redirected his vision. The text was presented as an exemplar of eloquence, but Augustine was moved by Cicero's call to the love of wisdom, and he renounced his plans for a legal career. "The book changed my feelings. It altered my prayers, Lord, to be towards you yourself. It gave me different values and priorities." At the same time, it kindled an ardor that it could not satisfy, for its pages were void of the name of Christ that "my infant heart had piously drunk in with my mother's milk, and at a deep level I retained the memory."[18]

Seeking the name that had been so deeply rooted in his memory by the love of his mother Monica, Augustine turned to the pages of Scripture, available to him in an unrefined Old Latin translation. Its prose lacked the dignity of the masters of rhetoric in whom Augustine had been schooled, and its content was beset with difficulties, such as anthropomorphic images of God and discrepancies in the genealogies of Jesus. "Puffed up with pride..." Augustine reflected, "I was not in any state to be able to enter into that, or to bow my head to climb its steps."[19] He turned instead to the conventicles of the Manichees, a group founded in the third century that had spread throughout the Christian Roman world and into the Far East. Christ was for the Manichees the principle of wisdom, and their Scriptures consisted of an edited version of the letters of Paul supplemented by oracles of Mani recorded in beautiful parchment volumes that told of a battle between the kingdom of light and the kingdom of darkness. The human person lives amidst this cosmic conflict, and the elect among the Manichee performed elaborate rituals and prayers to liberate shards of the deity of light from the darkness in which they were entrapped. Augustine was for nine years a second-tier aspirant who served the first-tier Manichee elect. Unable to conceive of a purely spiritual reality, he mistook the sun and shards of light for the reality of God. He also accepted the Manichaean doctrine that a good human soul is part of the very substance of this deity of light. "What could be worse arrogance," he later confessed to God, "than the amazing madness with which I asserted myself to be by nature what you are?"[20] This anthropology enabled Augustine to identify himself only with the substance he shared with the deity of light and to deny his own complicity in sin: "I still thought that it is not we who sin, but some alien nature which sins in us. It flattered my pride to be free of blame and, when I had done something wrong, not to make myself confess to you that you might heal my soul; for it was sinning against you" (Ps. 40: 5).[21] While a Manichee aspirant, Augustine taught the liberal arts in Carthage and Thagaste, seeking "the empty glory of popularity, ambitious for the applause of the audience at the theatre" and its garland of grass.[22]

Augustine's allegiance to the Manichees waned when their famed teacher, Faustus, was unable to resolve the discrepancies between Mani's cosmology and astrological science; meanwhile, his appreciation for the Latin Bible was bolstered by bishop Ambrose of Milan, who introduced him to spiritual exegesis. However, it was the *Platonici* that enabled Augustine's complete divorce from the Manichees at the age of twenty-nine. In the Roman Empire at this time, a renaissance in philosophy was underway, inspired by the works of Plotinus (204/5–270 CE) and his disciple Porphyry (234?–305? CE). Augustine encountered this school through friends in Milan, and the Latin translations of Plotinus and other Greek writers produced by Marius Victorinus, and this "most genuine philosophy" was soon engrafted into his own thought.[23] Book Seven of the *Confessions* is rich in allusions to Plotinus as Augustine searches restlessly for God amidst the things of this world. At the outset, he is weighed down by physical images, conceiving even God as an infinitely large being permeating the entire mass of the world. "I was fixing my attention on things contained in space, and there I found no place to rest in, nor did those external things receive me so that I could say 'It is enough and it is well.' "[24] Admonished by the Platonic books to return to himself, he began a journey through the intellect, which mediates between the multiple, mutable things of this world and the changeless One from which all originates. With the eye of the soul, Augustine perceived an immutable brightness that was not the noonday sun but an utterly different and transcendent light, the light of eternal truth and love and Being: "And you cried from far away: 'Now, I am who I am' [Exodus 3: 14]. I heard in the way one hears within the heart, and all doubt left me."[25] From this summit, he realized that God is not an all-pervasive physical substance but infinite in a sense that cannot be perceived by the flesh. His Manichaean dualism was over-turned in the realization that everything that has being is in some sense good, and that wickedness is "a perversity of will twisted away from the highest substance, you O God, towards inferior things, rejecting its own inner life…and swelling with external matter."[26] For those engaged in interreligious dialogue, it is note-worthy that Augustine wrote as Bishop of Hippo of the disciplined methods of pagan philosophers as a path to true knowledge of God.

However, Augustine's contemplation was fleeting. In the climax of contempla-tion "I was astonished to find that already I loved you, not a phantom surrogate for you. But I was not stable in the enjoyment of my God. I was caught up to you by your beauty and quickly torn away from you by my weight. With a groan I crashed into inferior things. This weight was my sexual habit."[27] Again, he attempted the Platonic *itinerarium intus*. Step by step, he moved his attention from the percep-tible bodies of the created world to the soul that perceives through the body, and then to the inward force of the soul that registers external sensation. From here he progressed to the power of reasoning that has the ability to judge the sensations received by the senses, a power that his intelligence recognized to be mutable. Simultaneous with this recognition was the certainty that the unchangeable is superior to the changeable—an insight that implies actual knowledge of the unchangeable. "So in the flash of a trembling glance it attained to that which is. At that moment I saw your 'invisible nature understood through the things which are made'" (Rom. 1: 20). But once again, he confessed, "I did not possess the strength to keep my vision fixed. My weakness reasserted itself, and I returned to my cus-tomary condition."[28] Neo-Platonism gave Augustine the intellectual tools he needed to ascend to true knowledge of God, but not the affective power of conversion of will that could sustain this knowledge in a soul warped by *superbia*. Indeed, Platonic *noesis* actually fostered *superbia* insofar as it tempted one to believe that knowledge of God had been attained by one's own powers.[29]

And so, Augustine turned elsewhere. In the books of the Platonists he had read of a divine word through whom all things were made, but he did not read that "the Word was made flesh and dwelt among us" (John 1:14), or that "he took on himself the form of a servant and emptied himself, was made in the likeness of humanity and found to behave as a human, and humbled himself being made obedient to death, even the death of the cross" (Phil 2:6–11).[30] In the garden of a lodging in Milan, Augustine agonized over the passive bondage of his will and then opened Paul's letter to the Romans and read: "Put on the Lord Jesus Christ and make no provision for the flesh in its lusts" (13:13–14).[31] This text that spoke so directly to

Augustine's struggle is part of the broader New Testament narrative of the Word made flesh (John 1:14) who emptied himself for us on the cross (Phil 2:6–11). It was this vision of divine compassion and humility that inspired the tears that flowed freely as Augustine continued with preparations for baptism.

Augustine's desires were so entrenched in habituated disorder that even certain knowledge of God was inadequate to sustain contemplative *noesis*. He had schooled himself in a culture of pride, loved created beings with a kind of love due only to the Creator, and flattered himself with the divinizing Manichaean anthropology. He needed not simply a path for the ascent of the mind to God, but a medicine to heal his disordered will, a knowledge that was not only intellectual but also cura-tive and salvific. What alone had the power to heal him was the compassion manifest in the Word that assumed flesh and willingly suffered a humiliating form of death for the sake of human beings—humans who had become foul and unworthy of love. "You pierced my heart," Augustine testified, "with the arrow of your love."[32] His conversion was an affective experience in which the love of God mediated by the humility of the crucified Christ became the new integrating force of his personality.

Jesus Christ, like a good physician, offered a cure appropriate to our disease of *superbia*. "The Son of God came down and was made human" in order to heal pride with humility.[33] The remedy prescribed by the doctor of humility (*medicus humilis*) was sometimes painful. It required of Augustine that he recognize in himself things that he would rather not see and admit need of a mediator who had descended from God that we might be healed of pride. "The healing of humility," explains Wallace Ruddy, "involves an initial period of exposure and a 'remedial pain.'"[34] But the remedy, if accepted, removes the underlying cause of our disease, and the good physician encourages us to take the medicine by drinking of it himself. "So he is the doctor," Augustine preached to his congrega-tion, "who in no way needs any such medicine; and yet to encourage the sick person he drinks what he had no need of himself. . . . 'The cup,' he says, 'which I am to drink'" (Matthew 20: 22).[35]

■ SEARCHING FOR GOD IN HISTORICAL MEMORY ON THE STREETS OF JERUSALEM

The God of humility that Augustine found after years of restless searching was a God that at some level he had always known. Although he rejected Plato's position that our souls pre-exist our bodies such that acts of learning are simply a recollec-tion (*anamnesis*) of knowledge from this prior state, he did maintain that knowing is a form of recognition. This is true in a unique and particular way of theological knowledge, for God, Augustine testified, was more intimate to him than he was to himself (*interior intimo meo*), the primary agent who was seeking Augustine even before Augustine began the search for God.[36] Augustine's "discovery of God," Denys Turner explains, "is the *re*discovery of God, the return to a truth already somehow known, to a knowledge already somehow present within the searching itself."[37]

Augustine's quest employed the Neo-platonic *itinerarium intus*, a journey through memory that ultimately led beyond the inner self to the eternal and boundless Truth of God.[38] However, as John Cavadini emphasizes, Augustine's transformative encounter with the Word humbly made flesh gives Neoplatonic *noesis* a profoundly new character: "Our contemplative regard is pushed outward, from the consideration of a static metaphysical self essentially disconnected from the uncomfortable realm of the bodily and historically contingent—that realm which defines our ontological distance from God—to that very realm itself and to the blood [of Christ], irreducibly contingent and irreducibly historical, which for Augustine became its central node."[39]

There is no better reminder of the irreducibly historical character of Christian faith than the stone streets within the gates of the Old City of Jerusalem, which we walked together as a trialogue group during our meeting at Tantur. In the Christian quarter of this city, which is a holy place for the three religions of Abraham and Sarah, our sandals trod the same narrow labyrinthine paths that Jesus walked 2000 years ago. We witnessed pilgrims walking the *Via Dolorosa*, retracing the steps of Jesus through streets hemmed with shops and vendors, singing and praying in Korean, English, and Spanish. Intermittent signs along the limestone walls marked the Stations of the Cross. We turned from the crowded street into the courtyard of the Church of the Holy Sepulcher and sought refuge from the fierce sun in the shade beside a stone wall. It was the Emperor Constantine's mother Helena, Fr. Michael McGarry explained, who identified the site on which the church now stands as the place of Christ's crucifixion, burial, and resurrection. We filed slowly through the tall wooden doors whose keys, we learned, are in the custody of a local Muslim family because the various Christian groups who maintain the building cannot agree amongst themselves as to whom should hold them. In the hushed, cavernous church we ascended a winding stone stair case that led us to the Chapel of the Nailing of the Cross, marked by a twelfth century mosaic of the crucifixion, and a Greek Orthodox Chapel enshrining the Rock of Calvary. Whether Queen Helena was precisely right in her attempt at historical reconstruction, it was surely somewhere in this vicinity that Jesus Christ was crucified. Here, in this place or somewhere nearby, in time and history and flesh and blood, Christ suffered and cried out in lamentation. Augustine wrote in a reflection on the passion:

> The only thing to cleanse the wicked and the proud is the blood of the just man and the humility of God; to contemplate God, which by nature we are not, we would have to be cleansed by him who became what by nature we are and what by sin we are not. By nature we are not God; by nature we are humans; by sin we are not just. So God became a just human being to intercede with God for sinful humans.... It was surely right that the death of the sinner issuing from the stern necessity of condemnation should be undone by the death of the just man issuing from the voluntary freedom of mercy....[40]

Approached through Augustine's eyes, the Church of the Holy Sepulcher is a cathedral of humility and compassion.

But the stones of the streets of Jerusalem echo not only the footsteps of the *Via Dolorosa* of Jesus Christ. The realm of the bodily and the irreducibly historical holds memories beyond those enacted by the Christian pilgrims who come here to mark the way of the cross. In the eleventh century, as my Muslim companions well know, the Church of the Holy Sepulcher became the focal point of the First

Crusade. Stirred by accounts that the Turks had conquered territories of the Byzantine Empire and committed atrocities against its Christian peoples, Pope Urban II delivered a sermon in a public square in Clermont, France exhorting those gathered to bring aid to the Christians of the East and "to destroy that vile race from the lands of our friends."[41] The Crusaders were to rescue lands recently occupied and then proceed to Jerusalem, which had been under the control of Muslims since 638 CE. "Set out on the road to the Holy Sepulcher," Pope Urban reportedly declared, "take the land from that wicked people, and make it your own.... This royal city is now held captive by her enemies, and made pagan by those who know not God."[42] According to Robert the Monk, the assembled people cried out with one accord "It is the will of God, is the will of God!" (*Deus hoc vult!*) Urban enjoined the Crusaders to vow to complete the journey to Christ's Sepulcher wearing a cross on their brows or breasts and offering themselves as a holy and living sacrifice.[43] In return, they were promised remission of sin. The Pope embarked on a preaching tour and enlisted bishops throughout western Europe to echo the call, and, by the spring of 1096, five armies of an estimated 60,000 soldiers set off toward the East, a walk of several thousand kilometers. The following autumn, 100,000 followed.

They had undertaken a harsh and perilous journey and many perished en route. Others began an unauthorized battle before reaching their destination. In May of 1096, Count Emich of Flonheim and his band canvassed the Rhineland, attacking the Jews at Speyer on the Sabbath. Several weeks later, they massacred Jews at Worms and desecrated Torah scrolls. By the end of the month they reached Mainz, a major center of Jewish culture; apprised of their approach, Archbishop Ruthard first sheltered the Jews in his palace but then fled, and hundreds of Jews were murdered while others choose suicide or even took the lives of their own children. On May 29, Emich's Crusaders burned the synagogue of Cologne, and attacks followed in neighboring Neuss and Wevelinghoven. In the words of a Jewish witness, their rationale was as follows:

> Look now, we are going a long way to seek out the profane shrine and to avenge ourselves on the Ishmaelites, when here, in our very midst, are the Jews-they whose forefathers murdered and crucified him [Jesus Christ]for no reason. Let us first avenge ourselves on them and exterminate them from among the nations so that the name of Israel will no longer be remembered, or let them adopt our faith and acknowledge the offspring of promiscuity. [44]

Emich moved on, but attacks continued for weeks, perpetrated by other bands of *crucesignati* or local opportunists. In June and July there were attacks on Jews in Trier, Metz, Xanten, Mehr, Ellen, Geldern, Dortmund, and Mörs.[45]

It took three years for the various bands of crusading armies to reach Jerusalem. On July 15, 1099, troops posted around the walls of the city eventually broke through with the help of a tower constructed from the masts and cords of a Genoese ship. For the next three days in the promised land of milk and honey, the streets ran with blood. "Piles of heads, hands and feet were to be seen...," recounted Crusader Raymond d'Aguilers. "It was necessary to pick one's way over the bodies of men and horses ... [I]n the Temple and the porch of Solomon, men rode in blood up to their knees and bridle reins. Indeed, it was a just and splendid judgment of God that this place should be filled with the blood of unbelievers, since it had suffered so long from their blasphemies."[46] Historian Christopher Tyerman writes:

> The massacre in Jerusalem spared few. Jews were burnt inside their synagogue. Muslims were indiscriminately cut to pieces, decapitated or slowly tortured by fire (this on Christian evidence)....The city was comprehensively ransacked: gold, silver, horses, food, the domestic contents of houses, were seized by the conquerors in a pillage as thorough as any in the middle ages. Profit vied with destruction; some Jewish holy books were later ransomed to the surviving community in exile. Violence overcame business on 16 July when Tancred's prisoners in the al-Aqsa mosque were butchered in cold blood, possibly by Provençals who had missed the previous day's action. The city's narrow streets were clogged with corpses and dismembered body parts, including some crusaders crushed in their zeal for the pursuit and massacre of the defenders. The heaps of the dead presented an immediate problem for the conquerors; on 18 July many of the surviving Muslim population were forced to clear the streets and carry the bodies outside the walls to be burnt in great pyres, whereat they themselves were massacred, a chilling pre-echo of later genocidal practices.[47]

The Church of the Holy Sepulcher, meanwhile, filled with pilgrims. "How they rejoiced and exulted," wrote Raymond d'Aguilers, "and sang a new song to the Lord!"[48]

The Second Crusade, called by Pope Eugenius III in 1145 in response to instability in the Holy Land, again precipitated attacks against Jews in Speyer, Worms, Neuss, Mainz, Cologne, Trier, Rameru, Stahleck, Bonn, Wolkenburg, Aschaffenburg, Würzburg, and Bacharach. And the chambers of the streets of Jerusalem harbor memories beyond those of the Crusades. Inscribed in the pages of Jewish history books, and in the dirges of Jewish liturgies, and in the memorials at Yad Vashem are many others accounts of violence perpetrated by Christians against European Jews. False accusations of host desecration led to attacks and massacres of Jews in Westphalia (1292), Laa-an-der-Thaya in northeast Austria (1294), and throughout the entire region of Franconia—Röttingen, mid- and upper-Tauber, Rothenburg and its environs, Würzburg and the lower Tauber valley, the Jagst and mid-Necker valleys, and Nuremberg (1298).[49] The Armleder massacres (1336–1338) began when King Armleder sought vengeance for the death of his brother and then continued on spurred by accusations of host desecration throughout the regions of Alsace, Austria, Styria, and Swabia.[50] The Chmielnicki Massacres (1648–1649) began with Bogdan Chmielnicki's revolt against the Kingdom of Poland, but the spreading violence that took the lives of thousands of Jews in Poland and the Ukraine was fanned in part by religious animosity.[51] In Russia in 1881, as the country reeled from a terrorist attack that took the life of Alexander II, the *Novorossiiski: Telegraf* published rumors that the approaching Easter holidays would bring attacks upon Jews, and a *pogrom* (Russian for "massacre" or "devastation") took place in Elizavetgrad on April 1, and violence spread to 253 other towns and villages.[52] In Kishinev on Easter Sunday, 1903, another pogrom was inspired in part by rumors that Jews in the nearby town of Dubossary had killed a Christian boy and taken his blood for use in the preparation of Passover matzah.[53] A call to settle scores with the Jews accused of crucifing Christ and taking Christian blood for Passover was also a factor in the murder of many hundreds of Jews in the village of Radziłów in German-occupied Poland (1941), a massacre preceded by that of Wąsosz and followed by that of Jedwabne.[54] In Germany itself, Robert Ericksen and Susannah Heschel write, the Christian churches played a much more important role in the success of Hitler's genocide than is often supposed.[55] This is patently clear in the case of the German Christian Movement (*Glaubensbewegung "Deutsche Christen"*) founded in 1932 as a *Volkskirche* defined by Aryan blood. But many Protestants and Catholics met the Nazi's anti-Jewish agenda with silence, and some actively contributed. At the end of Hitler's reign of terror, for example, survivors of the once vibrant and now decimated Jewish communities of Poland were attacked and murdered by Catholics in Kraków and Kielce (1946).[56] "I was fixing my attention on things contained in space," Augustine recounted, "and there I found no place to rest in, nor did those external things receive me so that I could say 'It is enough and it is well.'"[57] Augustine wrote poignantly of the inability of the finite and mutable to satisfy our longing for God. But the external also fails to satisfy when the space of a history graced with the Incarnation of the Word becomes a nightmare of bloodshed.

■ MEDICAMENTUM HUMILITATIS?

"Alas," exclaimed Augustine, "for the sins of humanity!" (Isa 1:4)[58] The Bishop of Hippo would surely be appalled by the history of Christian persecution of Muslims and Jews. It is contrary to God's precepts, he wrote, to hate another human being.[59] Moreover, in the era of John Chrysostom's virulent diatribes against the Jews of Antioch, Augustine maintained that the Jews were to be protected. Although he described them as "the House of Israel which [God] has cast off" and urged them to convert from their stubborn blindness to Christian truth, he believed that, in their dispersal throughout the world, the Jews bore witness through their Scriptures to the prophecies of Christ.[60] This ambivalent theology helped protect the Jews of Europe for centuries, even as it legitimated their exile and *diaspora*.

What, then, would the Bishop of Hippo say of a history in which *crucesignati* murder Jews in an archbishop's palace and kill Muslim women and children seeking sanctuary in a mosque? Why did these atrocities happen? There are limits to our knowledge of the varied motives of the Crusaders and those Christians who perpetuated other acts of violence against Jews.[61] Yet, if Augustine is correct in his position that *superbia* is the root of all sin, we should expect to find evidence that it lurks behind the piles of corpses that filled the streets of Jerusalem in 1099 and bloodied villages and cities throughout Europe. Indeed, Augustine's probing analysis of the dynamics of *superbia* can help diagnose the spiritual ailments of Christian history in several ways. First, Augustine was no stranger to the spurious pleasure that can be derived from watching or participating in the suffering of another. He confessed his own fascination with the fly-catching tactics of lizards and spiders, and he wrote of a wish to be feared by people for the apparent joy that is derived from such power—a joy that is in fact wretchedness.[62] One cause of violence, Charles Taylor elucidates, is our proclivity to see destruction as divine and then to identify ourselves with this destructive power. This gives a metaphysical meaning to violence that may mitigate the terrible fear that violence arouses, and it also distinguishes us from that which is being destroyed. Violence is raised "to the level of the sacred, making it a way of participating in the power of God" and "we purify ourselves of what seems evil … in our aggression."[63] "*Deus hoc vult!*" was the rallying cry of the Crusaders. This is a form of *superbia* insofar as we divinize our own acts of destruction.

Second, there is a form of *superbia* implicit in the cry for vengeance that characterized many of the incidents of Christian violence that historians have chronicled. The First Crusade was conceived as a penitential war rooted in love of God and Byzantine neighbor—and a war of vengeance upon the Muslims who had occupied Christian holy places. All three Hebrew Chronicles agree that vengeance for the crucifixion was a rallying cry in Count Emich's attacks against the Jewish communities encountered en route to Jerusalem, and revenge for the death of Christ was also a striking theme of the Crusader song "*La Chanson d'Antioche.*"[64] In many of the subsequent Christian attacks on European Jews, vengeance for alleged host desecration or ritual murder was the stated justification. Actions in the name of vengeance give one a strong sense of self-righteousness. I, the victim, am justly righting a wrong that has been done to me. I am also, Augustine enables me to see, blinding myself to my own capacity for evil. It had flattered the pride of Augustine the Manichee to think that it is not we who sin but some alien dark nature within. I, likewise, flatter my pride when I think it is not I who do evil but some alien person—a Jew, a Muslim—upon whom I righteously exact revenge. In so doing, I blind myself to the fact that in acts of vengeance I am committing against another something I deemed evil when it was perpetuated against my own community. The self-deception intensifies when the supposed wrong for which I seek retribution is falsified or fabricated. There was absolutely no factual basis to the deeply ingrained belief that Jews used Christian blood to prepare matzah for Passover, and historian Jan Gross suspects that Catholics who justified attacks on Jews with charges of the ritual murder of Christian children knew this at some level.[65] As to the longstanding Christian practice of blaming the entire Jewish people for the death of Jesus Christ, this, according to Eugen Drewermann, is a projection of guilt about our own sin onto another.[66] This displacement of our own capacity for evil is another manifestation of a soul jaded by *superbia*.

Finally, a common feature of the Crusades and subsequent massacres and pogroms is the expropriation of property. Crusaders went to great expense and often incurred tremendous debt to equip themselves for the long journey and anticipated battles. In this sense, they practiced a relinquishment of possessions. At the same time, it was assumed that a spiritual triumph would also be a worldly victory.[67] "Stand fast all together," was the battle cry at Dorylaeum in 1097, "trusting in God and the Holy Cross. Today, please God, you will all gain much booty."[68] In varying degrees, economic tensions or a desire for Jewish property also contributed to the massacres and pogroms of European history.[69] To murder another human being in order to take their goods is, in Augustine's analysis, a form of *superbia*, for one supplants the divinely intended order of being with a self-serving hierarchy of utility that attributes value to created beings on the basis of their service to our own needs, avarice, or lust.[70] We value gold coins more than human persons made in God's image.

And so, I return to the humble Christ, the *medicus humilis* who was doctor and healer of Augustine's soul. *Superbia* contributed to the dynamics of the Crusades and subsequent massacres and pogroms, and in the wake of this history we have need of the medicine of Christ the physician of humility. Yet as I stand together with Jews and Muslims in the conflicted city of Jerusalem amidst the irreducible realities of memory and history, the balm of Augustine's medicine of humility (*medicamentum humilitatis*) is not immediately within reach. The Church of the Holy Sepulcher in which I kneel in the company of my trialogue companions has an ambiguity that it would not have had for Augustine. The cross, wrote the Bishop of Hippo, has a unique significance because Jesus Christ knowingly and willingly accepted this lowest and most humiliating form of death: "not even in his mortal flesh did he suffer anything out of necessity, but everything of his own free will. And so it may rightly be assumed that by every single deed that was carried out and recorded about his passion he also wished to signify something to us."[71] If it is Christ's freedom that gives his death on the cross the significance of humility and compassion, so, too, does the freedom of the *crucesignati* who willingly traveled to the city of the Holy Sepulcher give the cross another layer of meaning. For the Jews of Mainz in 1096, the cross visible on the garments and hats of Crusaders who "threatened to annihilate us all, even infants and sucklings" was "an evil symbol."[72] This history casts shadows yet today over the terrible conflicts in this holy land, and the sign of the cross cannot speak to me without ambiguity, even as I make careful distinctions between the humble person of the Word made flesh and the actions of persons baptized in Christ's name. The balm of the *medicamentum humilitatis* is itself, then, in some ways, a medicine in need of purification.

Augustine opened his *Confessions* with a similar problem. He desired to praise God—*Magnus es, domine, et laudabilis valde* (Ps 47:2)—and yet the language available for his psalmody was the Latin of the rhetorical schools imbued with the *superbia* of his culture. Augustine's choice of the genre of confession is in part a response to this problem; he portrays language itself as a casualty of a culture of pride in need of conversion and cleansing before it can be properly used in praise of God. Today, the very cross that was such a powerful symbol of humility for Augustine is for many a symbol embedded in memories of Christian violence. In the aftermath of this history, we can follow Augustine in practicing theology in the mode of confession. The church, he exhorted his own congregation, is "confession and comeliness. Confession first, then comely beauty."[73]

We can also scrutinize our theologies, catechesis, and liturgy to determine if they contain elements that may legitimize or even sacralize humiliation and violence. Augustine's theology is not immune from critique in this regard. The *Confessions* convey an overwhelming sense of the gentleness and mercy of God: "The heart is aroused in the love of your mercy and the sweetness of your grace."[74] At the same time, Augustine affirmed that God can use pain and suffering as instruction for the wayward. It is preferable, he wrote, that free curiosity motivate the learning of a schoolboy, but, failing this, the schoolmaster's cane can be an effective discipline.[75] Augustine himself authorized the use of coercion in an attempt to restore Catholic unity in the conflict with the Donatists, a schismatic group in North Africa, "for many have found advantage (as we have proved, and are daily proving by actual experiment), in being first compelled by fear or pain, so that they might afterwards be influenced by his [God's] teaching."[76] Tyerman, Asbridge, Allen, and Amt identify Augustine's Christianization of the Greco-Roman just war tradition as one of the origins of Crusader holy-war theology.[77] Beyond Augustine, whose theology of compulsive discipline was rooted in his views of divine providence and his awareness of the instability of human impulses, there is a danger that a religious tradition that venerates an instrument of crucifixion may cast a sacred aura on acts of humiliation and violence.[78] During the Crusades, writes Tyerman, "the preaching of the cross emphasized meritorious Christian violence, the legitimacy of revenge and religious vendetta and the suffering of Christ Crucified."[79] Today there are some that speak of a "return of the Warrior Jesus."[80] At the same time, efforts are underway to develop a Christian theology and practice of active nonviolence, and these vital initiatives are a balm for our ills.[81]

Finally, in the wake of our history, there is need to consider another ailment of our soul that may be just as primal as the *superbia* that Augustine identified. German theologian Eugen Drewermann concludes from a psychoanalytic reading of Genesis that our fall into pride comes only after a prior descent into fear.[82] In Genesis 3, the serpent in the garden casts doubt on the trustworthiness of God's instruction to abstain from eating of the tree in the middle of Eden, assuring Eve that anyone who partakes of its fruit will not die, as God had said, but rather will become like God, knowing good and evil. These words undermine the primal trust that Eve and Adam had placed in God, and fear becomes humanity's *existenzialer Entwurf*.[83] An abyss of mistrust now separates us from a heteronomous God, Drewermann believes, even if this does not come to conscious awareness. We fear in our psychic depths that our existence is not ultimately justified, and we attempt to compensate for this ontological insecurity by absolutizing something finite, attempting to be like God, making our own group the center of the world, or competing with Cain against our siblings for God's acceptance.[84] Augustine identified this self-deification and absolutization of the finite as the sin of *superbia*. But Drewermann's analysis of fear adds another dimension to Augustine's probing of the human psyche, and his theology finds corroboration in the history of the Crusades and the Holocaust. According to Asbridge, the lay aristocracy among the Crusaders was motivated by spiritual concerns, particularly "an acute awareness of the danger of sin and an associated terror at the prospect of damnation."[85] The success of recruitment for a Crusade that promised remission of sin, Tyerman corroborates, stemmed not only from wealth, social order, and mobility, but also from "skilful manipulation of cultural habits of violence and spiritual fears of damnation."[86] In the ensuing centuries, according to Gavin Languir, among the mixed motives for the violence perpetrated by Christians against European Jews was "the anger or fear aroused when believers who recognize that disbelief exists on the frontiers of their faith are seriously upset by the recognition that their faith is not unchallenged."[87] In the troubled Germany of the 1930s, according to Drewermann, Hitler rose to power because he capitalized on a pervasive sense of insecurity, while the church failed to still people's fears.[88] Fear, in the judgment of Jan Gross, was the underlying cause of the multiple murderous attacks on the surviving Jews of beleaguered post-Hitler Poland. Violence such as that which took place in Kielce in 1946 cannot be explained by the charge that Jews had kidnapped a Christian child, which was patently untrue, but rather by the unease provoked by the presence of persons who were unwitting reminders of ordinary Poles' widespread collusion with the Nazis "and a threat that they might need to account for themselves."[89] Moreover, the fact that Jews had been reduced to a subhuman status was a sign that this could also happen to Catholic Poles. The Jewish survivors "induced fear in people by reminding them of the fragility of *their own* existence, of the propensity for violence residing in *their own* communities, and of *their own* helplessness vis-à-vis the agents of pseudospeciation."[90]

We need, then, not simply Christ the physician who heals our pride through the medicine of humility, but also Christ the healer of our deeply rooted ontological insecurities and fear. Christ, writes Drewermann, overcame fear through trust in God, and the church, in turn, should be a place that calms our primal fears and heals the sickness of the human spirit.[91] The Eucharist is a sacrament in which we can know in grace that our existence is, in fact, justified, that we are unconditionally loved and embraced by a primordially maternal God.[92]

Although Drewermann's work is focused on the Christian church, it is clear that there is a necessary interreligious dimension to the healing that he advocates. Primal fear and ontological insecurity shaped our history of interreligious bloodshed and contribute to the tensions of our conflicted world today. In Bethlehem, just beyond Tantur, someone has written in large letters on the Palestinian side of the concrete and steel wall that divides Israel and the occupied territories: "Fear builds walls, hope builds bridges." There is truth to these words, but it is also true that hope can only bloom when fears are allayed. Given the history of the Jewish people, it is to be expected that fear is deeply engraved in the Israeli psyche, and Christians bear tremendous responsibility in this regard.[93] This fear is only exacerbated by the 889 terrorist attacks that occurred within the Israeli Green Line from September 2000 to mid-February 2005, or by the words of an Arab leader who called for Israel to be "wiped off the map."[94] Meanwhile, fear spreads among the Palestinians because of their dislocation, economic insecurity, and subjection to occupation. "We are all afraid," a Palestinian social worker testifies, "I, the Israelis, and the children whom the mothers bring to me for help."[95] Our trialogue also discussed with concern the growing global phenomenon of Islamophobia, while innocent Muslims, in turn, live in fear of being stereotyped as terrorists or even of losing their lives and loved ones. Healing the fears that estrange us will require interreligious encounter and relationship building. There is an urgent need to cultivate opportunities in which the sons and daughters of Sarah and Abraham might come to know one another as accepted and embraced by one another and by the one God whom we all worship.

■ CONCLUSION

Augustine contributes to our reflections on intellectual humility a profound analysis of the psychological, social, and spiritual dynamics of *superbia*. The pride that ails intellectual culture and obstructs our knowledge of God is just one manifestation of the primal sin at the root of all other sin—the *superbia* of placing ourselves or other created beings in a position that belongs to God alone. I can recognize all too readily my own culture, my own soul, and the history of my church in the pages of Augustine's analysis. We are truly in need of the *medicus humilis*, the balm of the incarnate Word who humbly shares in human suffering and death despite our unworthiness of this love. Yet much has transpired since that day when the compassion of Christ moved Augustine to conversion and tears. "You pierced my heart," he confessed to God, "with the arrow of your love."[96] "And you," the dead of Jerusalem testify to those baptized in Christ's name, "pierced our bodies." Our bloodstained history has altered the meaning of the cross of Christ, but the true meaning of the symbol may be restored by the lives of Christian communities authentically living out the compassion and active nonviolence of Christ the good physician. We must also seek an antidote to fear. We need not only the *medicamentum humilitatem* but also the balm of the resurrected Christ who greeted Mary Magdalene, an unidentified Mary, and the disciples with the words "Do not be afraid" (Matt 28:10). As Christians, we receive these words in dialogue with Jews and Muslims, listening openly to their own fears and to their testimony of the experience of a covenantal God of divine *pathos*,[97] a God revealed to Muhammad by the name of the Compassionate and the Merciful.[98]

■ Notes

1. Secretariat for Ecumenical and Interreligious Affairs, National Conference of Catholic Bishops, *Catholic Teaching on the* Shoah: *Implementing the Holy See's* We Remember (Washington, DC: United States Catholic Conference, 2001), p. 10.

2. Charles T. Mathewes, "The Presumptuousness of Autobiography and the Paradoxes of Beginning," in *A Reader's Companion to Augustine's Confessions*, eds. Kim Paffenroth and Robert P. Kennedy (Louisville, KY: Westminster John Knox Press, 2003), pp. 7–24.

3. The image of the cross as a raft occurs throughout Augustine's writings. See, for example, *De Trinitate*, 4.4.20.

4. Sermon 131.2, trans. Edmund Hill, in *The Works of Saint Augustine*, ed. John E. Rotelle (New York: New City Press, 1990), III/4.317.

5. Deborah Wallace Ruddy, "The Humble God: Healer, Mediator, and Sacrifice," *Logos: A Journal of Catholic Thought and Culture*, 7.3 (Summer 2004), p. 87.

6. Augustine, *Confessions*, trans. Henry Chadwick (Oxford, England: Oxford University Press, 1991), 1.1.1.

7. See Paula Fredericksen, "Patristic Pramā and Pramāna: Augustine and the Quest for Truth," in *Religious Truth*, ed. Robert Cummings Neville (Albany, NY: SUNY, 2001), pp. 116–24.

8. For a comprehensive account of Augustine's theology of *superbia* and additional bibliography, see John C. Cavadini, "Pride," in *Augustine through the Ages: An Encyclopedia*, ed. Allan D. Fitzgerald (Grand Rapids, MI: Eerdmans, 1999), pp. 679–84.

9. *Conf.* 1.9.14.

10. *Conf.* 1.10.16.

11. *Conf.* 1.13.20–21.

12. *Conf.* 1.20.31.

13. For commentary, see *De Genesi contra Manichaeos*, 11.5; *Tractatus in Johannis Evangelium*, 25.16.

14. *Conf.* 1.18.28.

15. *Conf.* 1.18.29.

16. *Conf.* 1.19.30.

17. *Conf.* 3.4.7.

18. *Conf.* 3.4.8.

19. *Conf.* 3.4.9.

20. *Conf.* 4.15.26.

21. *Conf.* 5.10.18.

22. *Conf.* 4.1.1.

23. *Contra Academicos*, trans. Mary Patricia Garvey (Milwaukee, WI: Marquette University Press, 1942), 3.19.42.

24. *Conf.* 7.7.11.

25. *Conf.* 7.10.16.

26. *Conf.* 7.16.22.

27. *Conf.* 7.17.23.

28. *Conf.* 7.17.23.

29. *De Trin.* 4.15.20. On the *superbia* or *tolma* of the Platonists, see also John M. Rist, *Augustine: Ancient Thought Baptized* (Cambridge: University Press, 1994), p. 104.

30. *Conf.* 7.9.13–14.

31. On this text in relation to *superbia*, see D. J. Macqueen, "Augustine on *Superbia*: The Historical Background and Sources of His Doctrine," *Melanges de science religieuse* 34 (1977), pp. 207–11.

32. *Conf.* 9.2.3.

33. *Jo. ev. tr.* 25.26. The theme of the humility of Christ pervades Augustine's writings. See, for example, *Serm.* 341A; *Jo. ev. tr.* 3.1–15.

34. Wallace Ruddy, "The Humble God," p. 92.

35. *Serm.* 142.6.

36. *Conf.* 3.6.11.

37. Denys Turner, *The Darkness of God: Negativity in Christian Mysticism* (Cambridge: University Press, 1995), pp. 58–59; cf. Fredriksen, "Patristic Pramā," p. 117.

38. Turner, *Darkness of God*, pp. 68–69.

39. John C. Cavadini, "The Structure and Intention of Augustine's *De trinitate*," *Augustinian Studies* 23 (1992), p. 109.

40. *De Trin.* 4.1.4.

41. The text of Urban's actual speech has not survived. There are several accounts of eye-witnesses, but they were written after the successful capture of Jerusalem. This quotation is from *A Source Book for Medieaval History: Selected Documents Illustrating the History of Europe in the Middle Ages*, eds. Oliver Thatcher and Edgar McNeal (New York: Charles Scribner's Sons, 1905), p. 517.

42. *Ibid.* pp. 519–20.

43. *Ibid.* p. 521.

44. *The Chronicle of Solomon bar Simson*, trans. Shlomo Eidelberg, *The Jews and the Crusaders: The Hebrew Chronicles of the First and Second Crusades* (Madison, WI: University of Wisconsin Press, 1977), p. 22. Cf. p. 26. Clearly, as Eidelberg explains, the Jewish narrator adds his own perspective to this account by referring to the Holy Sepulchre as a "profane shrine" and Jesus Christ as an "offering of promiscuity."

45. On Emich, see Christopher Tyerman, *God's War: A New History of the Crusades* (Cambridge, MA: Harvard University Press, 2006), pp. 100–106; Jonathan Riley-Smith, "The First Crusade and the Persecution of the Jews," in *Persecution and Toleration*, ed. W. J. Sheils (Padstow: Basil Blackwell, 1984), pp. 51–64.

46. Crusade account of Raymond d'Aguilers, Canon of Puy, in August C. Krey, *The First Crusade: The Accounts of Eye-Witnesses and Participants* (Princeton: University Press, 1921), p. 261. According to Tyerman, this is an allusion to Rev 14:20. *God's War*, p. 31.

47. Tyerman, *God's War*, pp. 157–58.

48. Crusade account of Raymond d'Aguilers, in Krey, *First Crusade*, pp. 261.

49. Miri Rubin, *Gentile Tales: The Narrative Assault on Late Medieval Jews* (New Haven, CT: Yale University Press, 1999), pp. 48–54.

50. *Ibid.* pp. 55–57.

51. Translator's Introduction to Nathan Hanover, *Abyss of Despair: The Famous 17th Century Chronicle Depicting Jewish Life in Russia and Poland during the Chmielnicki Massacres of* 1648–1649, trans. Abraham J. Mesch (New Brunswick: Transaction Books, 1983), p. 2.

52. I. Michael Aronson, *Troubled Waters: The Origins of the 1881 Anti-Jewish Pogroms in Russia* (Pittsburgh, PA: University of Pittsburgh Press, 1990).

53. Edward H. Judge, *Easter in Kishinev: Anatomy of a Pogrom* (New York: New York University Press, 1992), pp. 40–44.

54. Jan T. Gross, *Neighbors: The Destruction of the Jewish Community in Jedwabne, Poland* (Princeton, NJ: Princeton University Press, 2001), p. 65 ff.

55. Robert Eriksen and Susannah Heschel, eds. *Betrayal: German Churches and the Holocaust* (Minneapolis, MN: Fortress, 1999). On the German Christian Movement, see also Doris Bergen, *Twisted Cross: The German Christian Movement in the Third Reich* (Chapel Hill, University of North Carolina Press, 1996).

56. Jan T. Gross, *Fear: Anti-Semitism in Poland After Auschwitz: An Essay in Historical Interpretation* (New York: Random House, 2006).

57. *Conf.* 7.7.11.

58. *Conf.* 1.7.11.

59. *Conf.* 1.18.29.

60. *City of God*, trans. Henry Bettenson (London: Penguin, 1972), 18.46. On Augustine and the Jews, see Franklin T. Harkins, "Nuancing Augustine's Hermeneutical Jew: Allegory and Actual Jews in the Bishop's Sermons," *Journal for the Study of Judaism* 36 (2005), pp. 41–64.

61. On the limits of our knowledge of the First Crusade and the psychology of the Crusaders, see Tyerman, *God's War*, pp. 60–61 and 111.

62. *Conf.* 10.36.59.

63. Charles Taylor, "Notes on the Sources of Violence: Perennial and Modern," in *Beyond Violence: Religious Sources of Social Transformation in Judaism, Christianity, and Islam*, ed. James Heft, S.M. (New York: Fordham University Press, 2004), pp. 17–19.

64. Eidelberg, *Jews and the Crusaders*, pp. 22, 80, 99 and 103; Riley-Smith, "The First Crusade and the Persecution of the Jews," pp. 67–71. For pertinent excerpts from "La Chanson d'Antioche," see *The First Crusade: The Chronicle of Fulcher of Chartres and Other Source Materials*, ed. Edward Peters (Philadelphia: University of Pennsylvania Press, 1998), pp. 302–306.

65. Gross, *Fear*, p. 245–46; on ritual murder, see also *Neighbors*, p. 123.

66. Eugen Drewermann, *Das Matthäusevangelium* (Olten: Walter, 1992), pp. 102–39; cf. Matthias Beier, *A Violent God–Image: An Introduction to the Work of Eugen Drewermann* (New York: Continuum, 2004), pp. 239–32. Notably, *Nostra Aetate*, the Second Vatican Council's "Declaration on the Relation of the Church to Non-Christian Religions" definitively reputiated the deicide charge: "Even though the Jewish authorities and those who followed their lead pressed for the death of Chirst (see Jn 19:6), neither all Jews indiscriminately at that time, nor Jews today, can be charged with the crimes committed during his passion" (no. 4).

67. Tyerman, *God's War*, pp. 84 and 111; Thomas Asbridge, *The First Crusade: A New History* (New York: Oxford University Press, 2004), p. 68. Plunder, notes Riley-Smith, was also simply a matter of sheer survival for the Crusaders. "The First Crusade and the Persecution of the Jews," pp. 57–58.

68. Cited in Tyerman, *God's War*, p. 73.

69. See, for example, Gross, *Neighbors*, pp. 65 and 110.

70. *City of God*, 11.16. Cf. Cavadini, "Pride," p. 680.

71. *Serm.* 218.1.

72. *Mainz Anonymous*, in *The Jews and the Crusaders*, p. 99.

73. *Enarrationes in Psalmos*, trans. Maria Boulding, *Expositions of the Psalms* (Hyde Park, NY: New City Press, 2003), 103.1.6. Pope John Paul II led the Catholic Church in this direction on the first Sunday of Lent in the Jubilee year 2000. The Lenten prayer of contrition included a confession of "sins against the people of Israel" and a call for repentance for "enmity toward members of other religions." "Service Requesting Pardon," *Origins* 29 (2000), p. 647.

74. *Conf.* 10.3.4.

75. *Conf.* 1.14.23.

76. *The Correction of the Donatists*, trans. J. R. King, in *St. Augustine's Writings Against the Manichaeans and against the Donatists*, ed. Philip Schaft, *NPNF* vol. 4 (Grand Rapids, MI: Eerdmans, 1974), 6.21. For a critique of Augustine's endorsement of coercion, see Gerald W. Schlabach, "Augustine's Hermeneutic of Humility: An Alternative to Moral Imperialism and Moral Relativism," *Journal of Religious Ethics* 22 (1994), pp. 299–330.

77. Tyerman, *God's War*, p. 34; Asbridge, *First Crusade*, 33, 36; S. J. Allen and Emilie Amt, eds. *The Crusades: A Reader* (Ontario: Broadview Press, 2003), pp. 7–9.

78. The passage from Philippians 2:8–9 that so influenced Augustine came from a stratified society in which Christ's death on the cross was interpreted as a profound humiliation. (See Joseph H. Hellerman, "The Humiliation of Christ in the Social World of Roman Philippi," *Bibliotheca Sacra* 160 [2003], pp. 321–36 and 421–33). Christians, in turn, have perpetuated humiliation against others. Crusader Raymond d'Aguilers, for example, rejoiced in "the justification of all Christianity, the humiliation of paganism" (In Krey, *First Crusade*, p. 261). Today humiliation remains such a grave dimension of conflict that Evelin Linder, Neil Walsh, and Judy Kuriansky believe that the field of Human Dignity and Humiliation Studies offer an interpretation of global relations that is an alternative to Samuel Huntington's *The Clash of Civilizations* (New York: Touchstone, 1997). (See Linder, Walsh, and Kuriansky, "Humiliation or Dignity in the Israeli-Palestinian Conflict," in Kuriansky, ed. *Terror in the Holy Land: Inside the Anguish of the Israeli-Palestinian Conflict* [Westport, CT: Praeger, 2006], p. 99. See also Linder, *Making Enemies: Humiliation and International Conflict* [Westport, CT: Praeger, 2006].)

79. Tyerman, *God's War*, p. 104.

80. David D. Kirkpatrick, "Wrath and Mercy: Return of the Warrior Jesus," *New York Times* (4 April 2004), p.WK1.

81. *By Little and By Little: The Selected Writings of Dorothy Day*, ed. Robert Ellsberg (New York: Knopf, 1983); Philip Hallie, *Lest Innocent Blood Be Shed* (New York: HarperPerennial, 1994); J. Denny Weaver, *The Nonviolent Atonement* (Grand Rapids, MI: Eerdmans, 2001); *Peacebuilding: A Caritas Training Manual* (Caritas International, 2002); Walter Wink, *Jesus and Nonviolence: A Third Way* (Philadelphia, PA: Fortress, 2003); Jack Nelson-Pallmeyer, *Worship in the Spirit of Jesus: Theology, Liturgy, and Songs without Violence* (Cleveland, OH: Pilgrim Press, 2005); *Cross Examinations: Readings on the Meaning of the Cross Today*, ed. Marit Trelstad (Minneapolis, MN: Fortress, 2006); John Howard Yoder, *The War of the Lamb: The Ethics of Nonviolence and Peacemaking*, eds. Glen Stassen, Mark

Nation, and Matt Hamsher (Grand Rapids, MI: Brazos, 2009); *Peacebuilding: Catholic Theology, Ethics, and Practice*, eds. Robert Schreiter, R. Scott Appleby, and Gerard F. Powers (Maryknoll, NY: Orbis, 2010).

82. Drewermann, *Strukturen des Bösen*, 3 vols. (Paderborn: Schöningh, 1985–86); cf. Beier, *A Violent God-Image*, pp. 27–34.

83. Beier, *A Violent God-Image*, p. 28.

84. Ibid., pp. 119, 45, 105, 113, 128–29, 133, 143, 239, and 260.

85. Asbridge, *The First Crusade*, p. 71. Cf. 39.

86. Tyerman, *God's War*, 78.

87. Gavin I. Langmuir, "At the Frontiers of Faith," in *Religious Violence Between Christians and Jews: Medieval Roots, Modern Perspectives*, ed. Anna Sapir Abulafia (Hampshire: Palgrave, 2002), p. 139. The attacks against Jews that accompanied the Crusades were, in his judgement, "indisputably religious violence." From 1250 on, however, the violence was instead psychopathological: "I mean violence that was motivated and explicitly justified by the irrational fantasies of paranoid people whose internal frontiers of faith were threatened by doubts they did not admit." *Ibid.* p. 53. This position is corroborated by Robert Chazan, who finds that the new anxieties and doubts of the 13th century were fertile ground for "irrational suggestions about Jewish malevolence" and bred "wholly unrealistic fears." Chazan, *Daggers of Faith: Thirteenth-Century Christian Missionizing and Jewish Response* (Berkeley, CA: University of California Press, 1989), p. 30.

88. Beier, *A Violent God-Image*, p. 26.

89. Gross, *Fear*, pp. 247–48. One should not conclude, he notes, that Poland is hostile to Jews. Because Poland had once been such a haven for Jews, there were more Jews in Poland before the war than anywhere else in Europe. Opportunistic complicity with Nazism occurred throughout Europe—in Paris, Amsterdam, Vienna, etc.—but because of the large Jewish population in Poland and Hitler's use of the country as a location for so many death camps, there were simply more opportunities for collaboration. On Jews and Poland, see also Stanisław Krajewski, *Poland and the Jews: Reflections of a Polish Polish Jew* (Kraków: Wydawnictwo Austeria, 2005).

90. Gross, *Fear*, p. 256.

91. Beier, *A Violent God-Image*, p. 255.

92. *Ibid.* pp. 105, 100, 112, 203, and 253.

93. On our objective common responsibility for past wrongs, see the International Theological Commission's "Memory and Reconciliation: The Church and Faults of the Past," *Origins* 29 (March 16, 2000), p. 637.

94. The statistic on bombings is from Ruth Pat-Horenczyk, "Terror in Jerusalem: Israelis Coping with 'Emergency Routine' in Daily Life," in Kuriansky, *Terror in the Holy Land*, p. 68. The Arab leader is cited in Julia DiGangi, "Homeland, Helplessness, Hate, and Heroes: Psychosocial Dynamics in the Israeli-Palestinian Conflict," in Kuriansky, *op cit.*, p. 8.

95. Nahida AlArja, "Cries for Help: A Palestinian Worker's Story," in Kuriansky, *Terror in the Holy Land*, p. 57. Essays in this volume cite numerous studies documenting high levels of trauma, anxiety, and fear throughout both the Israeli and Palestinian populations.

96. *Conf.* 9.2.3.

97. On the divine *pathos* see Jewish theologian Abraham Joshua Heschel's *The Prophets* (New York: HarperCollins, 1962, 2001), pp. 285–98.

98. Qur'an 1:1.

11 Apology, Regret, and Intellectual Humility: An Interreligious Consideration

Michael B. McGarry

Although my study of interreligious *relations* has lasted well over thirty years, my experience of interreligious *dialogue* began a few years later: my early years were confined to study *about* the Jews. Only later did I actually start talking *with* the Jews. At the University of Texas where I first served and taught, I contacted the local Hillel director and local Catholic leaders to help me become involved in the Jewish-Christian dialogue.

From this and many years' experience of dialogue, I have learned at least these two lessons: First is the *irreplaceable* talking-with-the-other—in this case, the Jews—in order to *learn about them*. In the process, I have learned that Jews do not define themselves (as some popular, naïve Christian notions supposed) in terms of "denying Christ" but rather in terms of peoplehood and, for religious Jews, in terms of Torah and, even more so, of Talmud and Midrash. I have come to appreciate the wealth of their practice of ongoing interpretation of their sources. And my appreciation has not been merely an archeological or historical one. Rather, I have discovered a *living* tradition and a *living* people.

Second, I have learned that dialogue helps me to *learn about myself and the God we as Christians believe in*. I am convinced, through my own experience of dialogue, that the God we commonly believe in is faithful to His promises. God has not abandoned the Jewish people. Learning about the bloodstained history of my Christian tradition and especially about the *Shoah* has made me (I hope) humbler in my expression of Christian belief. The paradox, then, is that in coming to understand the Jews in all their diversity, I have also come to understand more deeply why I am a Christian.

So what have I learned from dialogue with Jews and Judaism? I have learned about them and their faith, and about me and my faith. We learn from listening to one another address some of the same, and some different, questions. Sometimes we learn that Jewish questions yield interesting Christian reflections, and sometimes we learn that we have different answers to the same questions.

Finally, although there are many significant issues in the dialogue, I mention but two: first in importance is religion's relation to peacemaking; second, having lived in the Middle East for nine years, I have become increasingly persuaded that *cultural* differences need to be explored and appreciated more thoroughly. As a local Palestinian priest cautioned me, "Dialogue is a Western import; it does not apply in the Middle East." The mindset and practices emanating from

Western society often do not find easy correspondence here in Israel/Palestine. For communities who have not gone through the Western intellectual movement known as the "Enlightenment," approaching "the other" as partner with whom one may share and from whom one may learn can be quite daunting. The massive shadow of Israeli-Palestinian *political* relations regularly impinge on anything so "pure" as *religious dialogue*. Indeed, in this part of the world, religion and politics are not so easily separated. Peacemaking and cultural differences—these are always peering over us as we talk with one another.

■ INTRODUCTION

Among the many striking dimensions of his twenty-six-year pontificate, the late Pope John Paul II's eager and warm outreach to the Jewish people, as well as to the peoples of Islam and other world religions, stands out as exceptionally significant. In his relationships to "the other," one event is most remarkable: on March 12, 2000, Pope John Paul, on behalf of the Roman Catholic Church, confessed many sins and asked for forgiveness for its harmful behavior toward some within and many outside the Church. The press marked, measured, and graded "how far" the Holy Father went in "apologizing" to others: to other Christians for the Church's persecuting and condemning them, to the Jews for the suffering the Church inflicted upon them, to peoples of other cultures and religions for distorted missionary efforts that violated their rights and showed contempt for their culture and religious traditions. However, as a matter of fact, in the "asking of forgiveness," the Pope did not once use the word "apology," and this for a variety of reasons outlined a few months before.[1] To prepare for the dramatic liturgy on the First Sunday of Lent 2000, at the instigation of Joseph Cardinal Ratzinger, the Catholic Church's International Theological Commission explored the meaning of and relation among confession, forgiveness, responsibility, and repentance in its document "*Memory and Reconciliation: The Church and the Faults of the Past*" (*MR*).[2] It defined the requirements and distinctions necessary for a self-critical Church coming to terms with its faults through history. Thus, the document provided an *historical, theoretical*, and *theological* framework for the March 2000 papal litany of repentance, officially entitled the "Universal Prayer: Confession of Sins and Asking for Forgiveness." Among its many agenda, *MR* distinguished apology (appropriate only between perpetrator and victim) from regret (appropriate for descendants of the perpetrators to descendants of the victims).[3]

Drawing upon this recent Church experience, I wish to explore, from a Catholic Christian perspective, the place of apology in interreligious relations and its relation to our "learned ignorance" of the other. Around this fundamental question, we will consider a constellation of other questions, including: Is requiring an apology from the other a way of humiliating, or at least "taming," the other? Is "going only so far" (e.g., saying that some *members* of the church, but not the church itself, are guilty), a way of "having one's intellectual integrity-cake and eating it too"—that is, the institution gets credit for humility and honesty, but its integrity and truth claims remain insulated from any damage?[4] When the Church is keenly (but perhaps privately) conscious of its own shortcomings, can it afford to be publicly vulnerable in an interreligious situation where some others may be waiting to see who will acknowledge their lack of integrity? Furthermore, is apology possible or desirable where, because of cultural differences, it is seen as a weakness rather than a strength? Even though Pope John Paul II had long before promised that such a "purification of memory" would be forthcoming (see later), forces within the Church were alternately skeptical and critical. They feared that such public confession would compromise the Church's teaching role.

A particularly illuminating case with regard to interreligious relations and apology was the exchange between some Muslims and the Vatican in response to Pope Benedict XVI's lecture to the faculty at the University of Regensburg in late summer 2006.[5] I wish to reflect on the place and meaning of apology, intellectual humility, and interreligious relations by examining both the general "nonapologies" of Pope John Paul II and the specific "nonapologies" of Pope Benedict XVI. Reflecting on and analyzing these cases, I will conclude with a suggestion about the place of apology in an intellectually humble interreligious encounter.

■ TWO POPES: REGRETS OR APOLOGIES?

In 1994, Pope John Paul II, reflecting on the Biblical meaning of the Jubilee Year and preparing for the year 2000, wrote in his Apostolic Exhortation *Tertio Millennio Adveniente* about the church's need to "purify her memory":

> It is appropriate that as the second millennium of Christianity draws to a close the church should become more fully conscious of the sinfulness of her children, recalling all those times in history when they departed from the spirit of Christ and his Gospel and, instead of offering to the world the witness of life inspired by the values of faith, indulged in ways of thinking and acting which were truly forms of counter-witness and scandal...[the Church] cannot cross the threshold of the new millennium without encouraging her children to purify themselves, through repentance, of past errors and instances of infidelity, inconsistency and slowness to act. Acknowledging the weaknesses of the past is an act of honesty and courage which helps us to strengthen our faith, which alerts us to face today's temptations and challenges, and prepares us to meet them.[6]

The promise of 1994 took shape in a twofold movement. First, in late 1999, the already-mentioned Congregation for the Doctrine of the Faith's *MR* both explained the Papal intentions and sought to neutralize curial fears that such admissions would harm the Church's proclamation of the Christian faith. The second movement came on Sunday, March 12, 2000, with the "Universal Prayer of Confession of Sins and Asking for Forgiveness" during which Pope John Paul II expressed regrets for some Church members' sins toward a variety of communities. The world's eyes watched closely for the Litany of Sins: Who would be mentioned? Which sins would make the list? Were such sins adequately described? One example, especially germane in our context, was the confession of the Church's sins against the Jewish people.

For many, Pope John Paul II's expressions of regret with regard to the Jewish people on March 12, 2000 did not go far enough. Indeed, for them, it was quite disappointing.[7] A week later, during the Papal visit to Israel, they listened carefully to the Holy Father's words at Yad Vashem to see if he would go further than the previous week's Litany by actually apologizing for the Church's role during the *Shoah*. He did not. In the end, the words of the March 12 Litany became the words inscribed on the prayer card that he inserted during his prayer at the Western Wall.[8] Pope John Paul II did not and would not apologize.

Moving from these general Papal expressions of regret to a specific incident, we turn to Pope Benedict XVI's lecture at Regensburg. One has to say that public attention to his lecture, which sought to explore the relation between faith and reason, quickly focused on a few sentences in his third paragraph. What did he actually say?

> Without descending to details, such as the difference in treatment accorded to those who have the 'book' and the 'infidels,' he [Byzantine emperor Manuel II Paleologus] addresses his interlocutor with a startling brusqueness on the central question about the relationship between religion and violence in general, saying 'Show me just what Mohammed brought that was new, and there you will find things only evil and inhuman, such as his command to spread by the sword the faith he preached.' The emperor, after having expressed himself so forcefully, goes on to explain in detail the reasons why spreading the faith through violence is something unreasonable. Violence is incompatible with the nature of God and the nature of the soul.[9]

It did not take long for many Muslims to react to their perception that the Pope had insulted the Prophet. To the outraged voices, the Vatican's secretary of state responded on behalf of Pope Benedict. He said that the Pontiff

> did not mean, nor does he mean, to make that opinion [of the Byzantine emperor] his own in any way. He simply used it as a means to undertake...certain reflections on the theme of the relationship between religion and violence in general, and to conclude with a clear and radical rejection of the religious motivation for violence, from whatever side it may come.[10]

At the same time, what is notable for our discussion is the absence of apology in this Vatican response. In effect, speaking for the Pope, Bertone said, "You didn't understand me, this is what I meant, and since this is what I meant, there is no need for an apology." With varying degrees of insistence, calls for a papal apology from many sectors of the Muslim world continued. Within a week, as the fury spread, the Vatican responded three times, the second of which is the more considered from the secretary of state already quoted.[11] These were not enough for some. For example, the Kuwaiti leader of the Islamic National Party, Hake al-Mutairi contended the Pope must declare that "he is sorry for the wrong done to the prophet and to Islam, which preaches peace, tolerance, justice and equality."[12]

For the third reply, on September 17, in his regular Sunday address, Pope Benedict said:

> I wish also to add that I am deeply sorry for the reactions in some countries to a few passages of my address at the University of Regensburg, which were considered offensive to the sensibility of Muslims. These in fact were a quotation from a Medieval text, which do not in any way express my personal thought.[13]

In other words, "I am sorry you feel bad about passages I quoted, which some think were offensive." For some Muslim leaders this was enough; others continued to demand a full apology. Still others observed that more, and more honest, dialogue was still needed.[14] After these, one might conclude that none of the three responses from the Vatican—first from the Pope's spokesman, then from the Vatican Secretary of State, and finally from Pope Benedict himself—amounted to a real apology. Unlike what was actually said, a genuine apology would sound like, "I am wrong, I shouldn't have said that. I personally do not agree with what I quoted, and I am sorry that I said it." The official replies sounded more like, "I am sorry you were offended by what I said. You didn't correctly interpret what I said, and what I quoted is not my personal opinion anyway." It is, as Lazare puts it, the use of an apology, or, more accurately, the use of the words "I'm sorry," to assure the offended party that "I am a compassionate person who would not intentionally hurt your feelings." What was happening in the back-and-forth between the Vatican and some Muslim leaders?

Living in the Middle East (Jerusalem) for the past eight years has impressed upon me the profound importance of cultural difference. Although attentive to Edward Said's warnings to Western scholars about the dangers of essentialism,[15] I nonetheless began to wonder if the main problem between the Vatican and some in the Arab Muslim world was, at root, an expression of a cultural chasm between the protagonists (one could hardly call them interlocutors, as they spoke about the other to the media and did not address one another directly). Indeed, an editorial cartoon "Dry Bones: Pushing the Pope" from *The Jerusalem Post* caught the drift of my intuition: In the first panel, the Pope says, "They want me 'to apologize again'?!!" Anonymously from the side, a reply comes, "We're doing an exact translation from the Arabic, Holy Father, and a more precise rendering would be 'to grovel even lower.'"[16]

Were those who were demanding an apology really asking for *only* an apology? Or was there something else going on that kept the Pope from issuing a "real apology"?

I propose that, among other things, a cultural miscommunication was occurring here that (1) prevented the Pope from apologizing and, (2) precluded Arab Muslims from understanding and/or accepting the Papal talk and the papal explanation.

Anthropologists alert us to different cultural expressions and values in the world. In one part of the world, a raised middle finger brings shivers to a shocked opponent; in another part of the world, exposing the underside of one's shoe to the face of the other can provoke hostile reactions. On a level deeper than signals and signs, one can identify values that are core to one society and those that are core to another.

One may observe—oversimplistically—that the Western post-Enlightenment world is an economic, results-oriented, individualistic culture. One takes responsibility for one's conduct, and accepting blame or praise reflects only on the individual. Economic metaphors and measures riddle Western language and give it immediate meaning: The question, "What's the bottom line?" can as easily describe one's bank account as one's core personal values. Life is lived for the future, and life is a problem to which there is always a solution. A future orientation always pushes to solving the problem, because the future is where we are moving and where our imagination dwells. So, no matter what happened in the past—whether last week or last century—the answer is the same: "Let's get on with living." "Let go of it!" we chide. "We don't study history, we make history," as one wag put it.

In the Middle East, other values shape the consciousness and frame daily life. Anthropologists claim that the Middle East (and many other parts of the world) partake in an honor-shame culture.[17] Bruce Malina observes, "Mediterranean society and culture was dominated by honor and shame."[18] What does honor mean here? Honor is the claim to social worth and the public acknowledgment of that claim. Shame is the opposite of honor: a claim to worth that is publicly denied and repudiated. In such a culture, how one is viewed (reputation) is more important that how one views oneself (self-esteem). A leader must be a person of honor. One's actions reflect, most importantly, on one's family, one's tribe, one's community and seldom are attributed simply to the individual. Conversely, to insult one person is to insult the that person's family, tribe, or people, and, supremely, to insult the Prophet is the greatest insult to the people.[19]

Furthermore, culturally endorsed and reinforced values require a vocabulary. A culture—determined by and determining a stable of words that express its values—possesses an array of concepts to express its values. The words available to speak—and to hear—a message are necessarily limited in number. Sometimes vocabularies between cultures do not overlap. As the great Protestant theologian and missiologist Leslie Newbigin, in speaking about transcultural communication of the Christian gospel, noted:

> Any attempt to preach the gospel involves using the language spoken by the hearers. That language has been shaped by and has shaped their experience of life. It is the form in which they seek to grasp and make sense of the whole range of human experience. It embodies their beliefs about life and death, about sin and virtue, about guilt and forgiveness, about salvation and damnation, about soul and body, about time and eternity, about God and man. None of the language is 'neutral'; it embodies beliefs to which its users are committed.[20]

I suggest that this observation about language availability, and the meaning of that language, provides an insight into the cross-cultural communication gap between some Arab Muslims and the Pope. Perhaps pressing the Pope for an apology was not really trying to get him to "grovel," but coming from an honor-shame society, it was not simply asking him to do the "gentlemanly thing."

Merely a novice in colloquial Palestinian Arabic, I went to my dictionary to explore the words for *apology*. I was unsuccessful. In correspondence with a long-time resident of the Middle East and expert in Arabic and Middle Eastern culture, Dr. Kenneth Bailey, I asked about the words for *apology*. He noted that, in Arabic, there really is no exact equivalent for the Western word *apology* as a public acknowledgment and expression of sorrow for doing something wrong with a resolve not to do it again.

In an honor-shame culture, as I have known it, to "apologize" in the English language sense is considered shameful. Three words are relevant to the subject. (1) *Asif,* "This means, 'No, I can't do it.' This is the word used when you bump into someone in the hall and say, 'Sorry.' You are not admitting that you have made any serious mistake. This also applies when you turn down a request. 'I can't come to the meeting—*asif.*' (2) *A'tazar.* 'This word is used when you have promised to go to a meeting and send 'your regrets.' It is used for something you would like to do but don't have time to do. Arabic speakers of English translate this with 'He apologized.' A more precise translation would be 'He sent his regrets.' (3) *A'tarif.* This is used theologically for confession in a liturgical setting. It is acceptable to confess your sins to God even though you never do so to humans. This word is used to define relations between people and usually appears in the context of telling secrets previously withheld. In colloquial English this would be equivalent to, 'Previously I have not told you but I must confess so-and-so is untrustworthy.' Put back into Arabic this sentence would use the above word.[21]

Presuming Dr. Bailey's correct defining of related, but not exact, words for apology, I sought recourse in a Middle Eastern text: the Bible, both Old and New Testaments. A word-search of the *New Revised Standard Version* (*NRSV*) and *New International Version* translations of the Bible turns up hardly an instance of "apology" or "apologize." One does find, in the *NRSV,* about a dozen references to an expression of sorrow, but not to "apology" in an everyday Western sense.[22] And where the word "sorry" is used, these act rather as synonyms for "regret" than as expressions of claiming responsibility for one's actions and intending not to do them again.[23] Although a Western perception associates "apology" with fundamentally (but certainly not uniquely) Christian behavior, it is quite surprising to find little biblical or early patristic evidence for its importance as a Christian virtue.[24]

If apology's root location is the relation between two people, one of whom has harmed the other, then one explanation why one does not find "apology" in the Bible is because "[t]here is very little in the Hebrew Bible about interpersonal repentance and forgiveness."[25] In the Bible, the place of repentance or forgiveness is between the sinner and the Holy One. Confession of sin, when it happens, is directed to God (cf., *a'tarif* as explained earlier). Post-Biblical development, in both Judaism and Christianity, evolved into the interpersonal, individual relationship, reaching its apex after the Enlightenment. In the case of English, the Oxford English Dictionary (OED) notes that the definition of *apology,* in the sense of an admission of fault between two people, emerged only in the sixteenth and seventeenth century, again roughly the Enlightenment period. So from two Middle Eastern resources (the Bible and the Arabic language), we find a paucity of material on apology either as a religious or cultural value.[26]

And so we return to Benedict and his Muslim interlocutors: (1) Why did the Pope not oblige their repeated requests for an apology? Did he—or his advisers—recognize that apologizing carried far more serious consequences than simply a "political" mistake that could easily be disposed by saying "I made a mistake, I'm sorry"? (2) What were Arab Muslims asking from the Pope if they themselves do not have valued, available concepts for apology in their own stable of words?

With regard to the first question, if we proceed from the OED definition that to apologize is to "acknowledge and express regret for a fault without defense, by way of reparation to the feelings of the person affected,"[27] then it is clear that Pope Benedict did not apologize to the Muslims. Perhaps he was cautioned by the passage from *MR* "that the recognition of [the Church's] faults is, for the most part, one-sided and is exploited by the Church's detractors, who are satisfied to see the Church confirm the prejudices they had of her."[28] So, the pope couldn't apologize, with a Western intention, if he understood that such an apology would be heard as an admission that Christianity was wrong.[29]

Although it is true that he used "apology-sounding" words, Pope Benedict's explanation quickly transformed these apologetic words (*I'm sorry*) into an expression of regret. As Tavuchis and Lazare point out, words of apology that move into explanations often shift the responsibility for the hurt or offense on to the person offended (i.e., "you didn't understand my words," "these are the sentiments of someone else; I, as a compassionate person, would not hold that view myself," etc.). As Nicholas Tavuchis notes, a proper apology elicits forgiveness; an expression of regret elicits understanding.[30] Benedict was seeking understanding.

However, an expression of regret *may* elicit forgiveness if such persons, although not personally responsible, continue to benefit from the sin of their ancestors (e.g., slavery, stealing of land). Although both apology and regret are performative utterances that invite a response from the addressed party, Pope John Paul II's words in 2000 were properly speaking, expressions of *regret* rather than apology. As already noted (see note 3), only a perpetrator—someone in personal responsibility and in the wrong—can apologize.[31] Benedict was the perpetrator—he *could* have apologized. Why didn't he? Here I continue to be tutored by Dr. Bailey in his correspondence with me in September 2006:

> I have often heard Middle Easterners discuss the question of publicly admitting mistakes. Their response is: "if the Prime Minster admits he has made a mistake he is not fit to be a Prime Minister" (the point being admitting mistakes is shameful and if the PM shames himself in public he is not fit to hold office). Anyone who "apologizes" in our sense of the word is someone who is humiliating himself in public and such activity is to be avoided at all cost. The closest a Middle Easterner can come, generally speaking, is to vocalize some form of "let bygones be bygones." The point being: "I cannot admit that I made a mistake but I do want a relationship with you so let's forget the past."

In other words, whereas some apologies in the West may communicate strength, honesty, sincerity, and integrity, they may be perceived in the East as weakness, shame, and inadequacy. Furthermore, in an honor/shame culture, a collective, more than an individualistic, self-understanding prevails. So in the West, a sincere apology may cast only a solitary shadow; in the East, it will probably cast a collective shadow.[32] Simply speaking, from a Western individualistic culture, when one person acts, he acts on his own; in an honor/shame culture, he transmits shame onto the whole community. So, when the Pope spoke, he spoke for all Christians, not just for himself as a scholar or even as one Christian. For him to apologize, to admit a wrong, a mistake, then, would not have been seen as the voice of an individual, but as the voice of the collective. The various Vatican spokesmen speaking to the Muslim community, while never apologizing for the offending remark, perhaps disclose how the Vatican saw the problem, at least as it should be interpreted to the Muslims: not so much, "let bygones be bygones," but rather "I will not admit that I made a mistake, but what I said was misunderstood. Now let us dialogue, let us speak good words to one another." This was essentially Pope Benedict's message when he met with representatives of the Muslim Community:

> I have already had occasion to dwell upon them [the events around the Regensburg talk] in the course of the past week. In this particular context, I should like to reiterate today all the esteem and profound respect that I have for Muslim believers...In a world marked by relativism and too often excluding transcendence and universality of reason, we are in great need of an authentic dialogue between religions and between cultures, capable of assisting us, in a spirit of fruitful co-operation, to overcome all the tensions together.[33]

Some would say that these words were not the closure for the "Regensburg Affair." That moment, in such an interpretation, came in November of 2006 when Benedict prayed in the Istanbul Mosque. The final word, then, was a gesture, whose image said more about respect for the Muslim community than the cautious, well-crafted words of the Vatican State Department and papal spokesmen.

With regard to the second question—what were Arab Muslims asking of the pope if culturally apology did not hold the same meaning for them as for the West?—it should be noted that most observers thought that Benedict, however he tried to distance himself from the quotation, nonetheless had insulted the Prophet. For some, it was a deserved insult,[34] but for most, that the Pope would quote such a crude emperor's words shocked them. Those words, whatever the explanation, were hurtful and the Prophet and his people felt insulted. I believe that some of the Muslims who called for an apology were conversant with Western grammar, literally and figuratively, and sought an apology as a way both of regaining the honor from an insult and of showing the inadequacy of Christianity on the public stage. Benedict sought to achieve the former without risking the latter.

■ CONCLUSION

Many years ago, I heard a Japanese Jesuit, son of Buddhist and Roman Catholic parents, claim that *dialogue* was the gift of the Holy Spirit to the Church of the twentieth century.[35] The Holy Spirit's gift necessarily implies two things: that we have something to say (we have always believed that) and that we have something to learn (we have not always believed that). We Catholics had nothing to learn from the other because the outsider was the heretic (other Christians), the infidel (members of other world religions) or "perfidious" (Jews). An ethos of "error has no rights" pervaded many parts of the church until the Vatican Council II (1962–1965). Since then, the Catholic Church has committed itself to a posture of dialogue vis-à-vis other Christians and persons of other world religions—for now, we understand, we have something to learn. But what is the place of apology—a particular kind of discourse—between dialogical partners?

Our topic of "learned ignorance" about the other, I think, is amply illustrated in the case study mentioned earlier about a dialogical situation in which an apology—from the perspective of many persons—was required and which, in the end, did not happen. Reflecting on this event (which, admittedly, was not a dialogue as such) suggests the following conclusions:

First, our "learned ignorance" of the other, in this case our Middle Eastern Muslim brothers and sisters, includes at least two things: first, we come from different cultures that value different things (indeed, in one culture, an apology is a virtue, in another it is a shameful act). Second, anything that approaches an insult to the Prophet, even if merely quoting a Medieval emperor in an academic setting, touches a very sensitive nerve, because, in the world forum, there is no neutral setting.

Second, part of our "learned ignorance" of the other devolves from a lack of listening to the others: to their dreams, their values, their memory, their narrative, and their religious convictions. Had Pope Benedict submitted his lecture to an expert in Islam, especially someone who had lived in the Middle East, would he have left his Regensburg speech's third paragraph intact? I think not.

Third, to reverse our "learned ignorance" of the other does not mean a simple choice of "dialogue," as it is not a cure-all. Indeed, in this chapter, we have not clearly defined what constitutes dialogue in general or interreligious dialogue in particular—or how dialogue can be used to maintain a *status quo* rather than to liberate both parties.[36] How many of us have endured interreligious dialogues that were little more that parallel soundtracks? Furthermore, a simplistic understanding of dialogue privileges the verbal, and the verbally adept, the clever, the debater. It devalues the slow, the fumbling, the poet, the artist, the mystic, the dreamer, the dancer. It values declaration and orthodoxy; it neglects beauty and the intuitional. In three very provocative chapters in his book *Holy War, Holy Peace*, Marc Gopin suggests nonverbal gestures, symbols, and exchanges that might be helpful in religious contributions to peacemaking.[37] Pope Benedict, in a profound way, finally resorted to the gesture when he prayed in the Istanbul mosque in November 2006.[38]

Fourth, our "learned ignorance" about the other begins inevitably with the small worlds we grow up in. Conversely, how much wider is our perspective when our world has included—as perhaps a friend—someone from the other community?[39] It may be a cliché to say "some of my best friends are Jewish"…but what if *none* of my friends are Jewish? One can only speculate on how Pope Benedict might have spoken differently if he had Muslim friends. What might happen to him if he develops some? Our "learned ignorance" of the other is guaranteed by not having friends among the "other."

Fifth, our understandable, but *curable* ignorance about other cultures will inevitably cause us to bump into the values of others. Nonetheless, the place of apology in interreligious relations will emerge only after some kind of positive relations have begun. Our learned ignorance of the other, coming from our (not blameworthy) parochial backgrounds may develop to places where apologies are needed…but only when the meaning of apologies are mutually acknowledged and commonly valued. Although I believe that Pope Benedict made a major mistake in his Regensburg lecture, damaging the Catholic Church's newly forming relations with the Muslim peoples, he was correct in not apologizing—at least not in a Western sense—for the reasons already suggested. The relationship between Catholics and Muslims should be one of equality and mutual exchange of stories, insights, narratives, pains, and challenges. These need to build on the strengths of each community and not on humiliation or taming of the other.

Sixth and finally, between the two communities is a sea of memories and mutual recriminations. As Nigerian Cardinal Francis Arinze, a veteran of Catholic-Muslim dialogue, observed:

> One of the problems that arise in interreligious relations is the impact of the historical memories of conflicts and misunderstandings. It is difficult for many people to move beyond the past, to forgive wrongs that were committed by one group against another. As a result they find themselves not relating as well intentioned persons living in the present, but rather as representatives of traditions which have long histories of mutual recrimination and wrongdoing. We need to heal our memory.[40]

Indeed memories need to be healed and individually remembered histories need to be addressed. This was Pope John Paul II's 1994 commitment to an ecclesial "purification of memory." In many ways, the Catholic Church has sought to do this with the Jewish community and, I submit, needs still to do so with the Muslim community. However, a "purification of memory" is a delicate process, as we know the church's experience with the Jewish community has not always been smooth. Rabbi Leon Klenicki has often expressed his frustration with some of his fellow Jews' need to exercise a "triumphalism of pain" in repeatedly listing the many ways and times that the Christian Church has badly treated the Jewish people. Rightly, the Church must listen to and come to terms with this litany, but it must not be paralyzed by it. Similarly, in our relations with the peoples of Islam, for many of whom a legacy of suffering at Christian hands is as fresh as yesterday's newspaper, regret and a purification of memory may still be necessary, but only when, on a level floor, both can look at each other and offer gifts, memory, narrative, and silence in a mutual gift exchange.

■ Notes

1. Members of the press were not the only ones to mislabel the pope's action as "apologies." See the otherwise fine articles by Christopher M Bellitto, "Teaching the Church's Mistakes: Historical Hermeneutics in *Memory and Reconciliation: The Church and the Faults of the Past*," *Horizons* 32, no. 1 (2005): 125–135. Bradford E Hinze, "Ecclesial Repentance and the Demands of Dialogue," *Theological Studies* 61 (2000): 207–238.

2. All references to this text (hereafter *MR*) come from the English translation found on the Vatican website <www.vatican.va> under the links associated with the documents of the Congregation for the Doctrine of the Faith. *MR*'s full text was published in *Origins* 29 (16 March 2000): 625–644. I will use the Section Outline Numbers for reference, because page numbers do not line up among the various places where this document may be retrieved.

3. *MR* 1.3: "[T]he imputability of a fault cannot properly be extended beyond the group of persons who had consented to it voluntarily, by means of acts or omissions, or through negligence." Or later (5.1), "asking for forgiveness [apologizing] presupposes a contemporaneity between those who are hurt by an action and those who committed it [and are subjectively responsible for it]."

4. Indeed, traditional Catholic teaching contrasts the "indefectibility of the Church" and the sinfulness of her members, or, using another metaphor, between "the Bride of Christ 'with neither blemish nor wrinkle ... holy and immaculate' (cf. Eph 5:247), and her children, pardoned sinners'" (*MR* 1.2. citing *Lumen Gentium* 8). In another place (3.2), *MR* contrasts "holiness *of* the Church" and "holiness *in* the Church."

5. "*Faith, Reason and the University: Memories and Reflections*," [hereafter FRU], September 12, 2006. See text at the Vatican web site <www.vatican.va>.

6. Pope John Paul II, "*Tertio Millennio Adveniente*," *Origins* 24, no. 24 (24 November, 1994), par. 33. In addition to Papal calls for ecclesial examinations of conscience, in recent years one sees a veritable explosion of public apologies in civic and political life. These in turn have spawned a growing academic study on the subject. See, e.g., Robert Browning and Roy Reed, *Forgiveness, Reconciliation, and Moral Courage: Motives and Designs for Ministry in a Troubled World* (Grand Rapids, MI: Eerdmans, 2004); Aaron Lazare, *On Apology* (New York: Oxford University Press, 2004); Nicholas Tavuchis, *Mea Culpa: A Sociology of Apology and Reconciliation* (Stanford CA: Stanford University Press, 2004); Michael R. Marrus, "Official Apologies and the Quest for Historical Justice," *Controversies in Global Politics & Societies*, 3 (2006), http://www.utoronto.ca/mcts.

7. See Randolph L Braham, ed., *The Vatican and the Holocaust: The Catholic Church and the Jews During the Nazi Era* (New York: Columbia University Press, 2000). But see the statements by the Central Conference of American Rabbis (Reform; see http://www.bc.edu/research/cjl/meta-elements/texts/cjrelations/resources/documents/jewish/ccar.html) and the Rabbinical Assembly (Conservative) and The Rabbinic Committee for Interreligious Dialogue (http://www.bc.edu/research/cjl/meta-elements/texts/cjrelations/resources/documents/jewish/response_JPII.html). All these references are available on the web site of Boston College's Center for Christian Jewish Learning (http://www.bc.edu/research/cjl).

8. "God of our fathers, you chose Abraham and his descendants to bring your Name to the Nations: we are deeply saddened by the behaviour of those who in the course of history have caused these children of yours to suffer, and asking your forgiveness we wish to commit ourselves to genuine brotherhood with the people of the Covenant." Even before *MR*, historians were noting Pope John Paul's frequent appeal to language of "regret"; see Luigi Accattoli, *When a Pope Asks Forgiveness: The Mea Culpa's of John Paul II*, trans. Jordan Aumann, O.P. (New York: Alba House, 1998). One notes, too, that not once in these many "*mea culpas*" did Pope John Paul use the world "apology."

9. *FRU*, third paragraph. For a trenchant critique of the Papal talk, see David Burrell, "Benedict's Misreading," *Christian Century* 124, no. 10 (15 May 2007): 28ff.

10. Statement of His Eminence Cardinal Tarciscio Bertone, Vatican Secretary of State, explaining the Papal intention, September 16, 2006, in *Origins* 36 (2006), pp. 246–247.

11. More to the point of an apology is ibid.,: "The Holy Father thus sincerely regrets that certain passages of his address could have sounded offensive to the sensitivities of the Muslim faithful, and should have been interpreted in a manner that in no way corresponds to his intentions." In other words, not an apology per se, but rather "I am sorry you misinterpreted his words." The first Vatican reactions came from the Pope's chief spokesman, Fr. Federico Lombardi, who said "It was certainly not the intention of the Holy Father to do

an in-depth study of *jihad* and Muslim thinking in this field and still less so to hurt the feelings of Muslim believers." (quoted in *New York Times,* by Ian Fisher, "Muslim Leaders Assail Pope's Speech on Islam" <http://www.nytimes.com/2006/09/14/world/Europe/15papalcnd. http>) In other words, "he did not mean to hurt your feelings."

12. Ian Fisher, ibid.

13. From the Official Vatican translation of Pope Benedict XVI's remarks, as accessed from <http://www.washingtonpost.com/wp-dyn/content/article/2006/09/17>.

14. See the Muslim Scholars and Academics, "Open Letter to His Holiness Pope Benedict XVI," *Islamica,* no. 18 (2006): 26–32.

15. Edward W Said, *Orientalism* (New York: Vintage Books, 1979).

16. Dry Bones, *Jerusalem Post,* September 25, 2006, p. 14. Since the Pope actually did not apologize once, he could not have apologized "again." *Dry Bones* perhaps had a different target.

17. See, *inter alia,* Carolyn Fluehr-Lobban, *Islamic Society in Practice* (Gainesville, FL: University Press of Florida, 1994). "The entwined relationship of honor and shame has been long recognized in both and [sic] Arab and Muslim societies as well as in the generalized Mediterranean social complex." See also the suggestive George E. Irani and Nathan C. Funk, "Rituals of Reconciliation: Arab-Islamic Perspectives," in *Kroc Institute Occasional Paper 19:OP:2* (Notre Dame: Joan B. Kroc Institute for International Peace Studies, 2000).

18. Bruce J. Malina, *The New Testament World: Insights from Cultural Anthropology* (Louisville: John Knox Press, 1981), pp. 25ff; see also John J. Pilch and Bruce J. Malina, eds., *Biblical Social Values and Their Meaning: A Handbook* (Peabody, MA: Hendrickson, 1993), Jerome H Neyrey, *Honor and Shame in the Gospel of Matthew* (Atlanta: Westminster John Knox Press, 1998).

19. The Papal effort to buffer his own responsibility from the meanness of his quotation about the Prophet was successful with only a few Muslims. Indeed, we may get a small "feel" of this if we attended a lecture in which the speaker quotes a friend who says, "Your sister is very ugly." We would be offended and perhaps not completely placated by an explanation that said, "That your sister is ugly is not my opinion but that of the person I quoted – surely it is not my opinion." One still wonders why he quoted that person and to what degree that quotation was essential to advancing his argument . . . but this takes us too far afield.

20. Lesslie Newbigin, *The Open Secret: An Introduction to the Theology of Mission* (Grand Rapids, MI: Eerdmans, 1978), p. 64.

21. Private correspondence from Dr. Kenneth E. Bailey, Author and Lecturer in Middle Eastern New Testament Studies, Canon Theologian of the Episcopal Diocese of Pittsburgh, USA., September 20, 2006.

22. Although see Sirach 13:3, "A rich person does wrong, and even adds insults; a poor person suffers wrong, and must add apologies," and Acts 16:39, "so they came and apologized to them. And they took them out and asked them to leave the city."

23. For expressions of God saying He was sorry for doing something, see Genesis 6:6 ff; 1 Samuel 15:35; Jeremiah 42:10.

24. Indeed, in its Biblical section, *MR* 2.1–4, the Theological Commission finds no biblical precedent for confessing sins of previous generations' sins against others.

25. Solomon Schimmel, "Interpersonal Forgiveness and Repentance in Judaism," in eds. Fraser Watts and Liz Guilford, *Forgiveness in Context: Theology and Psychology in Creative Dialogue* (London: T&T Clark, 2004), pp.11–28, at 14. One does find the word *sorry,* but meaning "regret" rather than "apologize." See, e.g., Genesis 6:6: "And the LORD was sorry that he had made humankind on the earth, and it grieved him to his heart." See

also Genesis 6:7; 1 Samuel 15:35, 22:8; Psalm 38:18; Jeremiah 42:10; Tobias 2:10; 2 Corinthians 7:8.

26. Of course, in the Middle East, one cannot neatly divide "social," "religious," or "cultural" values.

27. Tavuchis, *Mea Culpa*. p 16. Other languages are also problematic: "A profound difference exists between the word 'apologize' in English and the words used for apology in other languages. Because the English word 'apology' has no root that acknowledges guilt or blame... 'apology'... has lost much of its precise meaning by being confused with the compassionate 'sorry'" from *Lazare, On Apology*, p. 31.

28. *MR* 1.4. In his article "When Civilizations Meet: How Joseph Ratzinger Sees Islam," Samir Khalil Samir, S.J., tellingly writes that "some Muslims have asked that the Pope ask forgiveness for the Crusades, colonialism, missionaries, cartoons, etc. He is not falling in this trap, because he knows that his words could be used not for building dialogue, but for destroying it. This is the experience that we have of the Muslim world: all such gestures, which are very generous and profoundly spiritual, to ask for forgiveness [apologize?] for historical events of the past, are exploited and are presented by Muslims as a settling of accounts: here, they say, you recognize it even yourself: you're guilty. Such gestures never spark any kind of reciprocity." See *www.chiesa* (2006), http://www.chiesa.espressonline.it/dettaglio.jsp?id-53826&eng=.

29. It was certainly not the case, as one commentator said, claiming to be a "Vatican expert," that Pope Benedict could not apologize because that would have jeopardized his infallibility.

30. Tavuchis, *Mea Culpa*, pp. 19–21.

31. Ibid., p. 33; see also Lazare, *On Apology*, pp. 41ff.

32. As one unrelated example illustrates, for many Westerners, it was both puzzling and touching when many Koreans expressed their sorrow for what Cho, the Korean-American shooter in the 2007 Virginia Polytechnic University massacre, did to his fellow Americans. In an honor/shame culture, the act of one person casts a shadow of shame on all who are from that—in this case Korean—community.

33. From the Papal meeting with representatives of the Muslim community, led by Cardinal Paul Poupard, President of the Pontifical Council for Interreligious Dialogue, at Castel Gandolfo on September 25, 2006; accessed from <vatican.va>.

34. One local Jerusalem Christian said to me, "Finally the Pope had the courage to say what others should have said long ago." This was not a typical response among my coreligionists in the Holy City.

35. See the fascinating article by John Borelli about the history of the word "dialogue" in the Catholic Church: "The word *dialogue*, missing in the acts of the previous 20 general councils of the church in the West from the fourth to the 19th centuries, explicitly appears in no fewer than six documents, and the other 10 documents of Vatican II imply the concept... In this [interpersonal] form of dialogue all parties learn from one another and progress to a greater understanding of truth." John Borelli, "University Students and the Mandate of Interreligious Dialogue," *Origins* 36, no. 14 (September 14, 2006), p. 222.

36. Someone once said that monologue is when one person talks to himself, dialogue is when two persons talk to themselves.

37. Marc Gopin, *Holy War, Holy Peace: How Religion Can Bring Peace to the Middle East* (New York: Oxford University Press, 2002), especially chapters 6, 7, 8.

38. For the three "iconic moments" of Pope John Paul II's journey to the Holy Land – which spoke more eloquently than all his words – see my essay in Lawrence Boadt, CSP and Kevin di Camillo, eds., *John Paul II in the Holy Land: In His Own Words with Christian and*

Jewish Perspectives by Yehezkel Landau and Michael McGarry, C.S.P., A Stimulus Book (Mahwah, NJ: Paulist Press, 2005).

39. More than a few have credited Pope John Paul II's openness to the Jewish community to his lifelong friendship with Jews. And who can deny Richard Cardinal Cushing's invaluable support to the Second Vatican Council's *Nostra Aetate,* which perhaps had its roots in his weekly Sunday dinners with his Jewish brother-in-law?.

40. Cardinal Francis Arinze, "Interreligious Relations in a Pluralistic World," *Origins* 25, no. 14 (September 21, 1995): 221.

12 Islamic Theological Perspectives on Intellectual Humility and the Conditioning of Interfaith Dialogue

Mustafa Abu Sway

Although there were many events in my life that I can consider as the beginning of my involvement in interfaith dialogue, I think that it has a lot to do with my upbringing and the sociopolitical context in which I live; the "other," especially the Palestinian Christian, was always part of my life.

I began my elementary studies at the Anglican St. George School in Jerusalem before the year 1967. I studied for all my three university degrees at Catholic Universities (Bethlehem University and Boston College).

The centuries old *convivencia* between Judaism, Christianity, and Islam in the Holy Land, meant an ongoing, lived trialogue, even during times of conflict. The introduction of formal dialogue is a recent phenomenon, and it takes place in the shadow of the Israeli occupation!

If I have to choose a specific date for my formal involvement in interreligious dialogue, I would say that it began almost twenty-five years ago. I was invited by one of my Christian professors at Bethlehem University. It is still customary for Muslims to be invited to such interfaith dialogue. It was only within the last few years that I took the initiative and began creating opportunities for trialogues, especially in Jerusalem, including local and international Jewish and Christian participants.

Despite the general reluctance of Muslims to participate in interfaith dialogue, I consider it a religious duty (i.e., *wajib*) for Muslim scholars to engage in dialogue. The interfaith dialogue is an excellent educational forum, where participants can discover common ground and develop a common agenda, especially where there are conflicts, internal within the same society, or external involving other countries.

Interfaith dialogue could be used as a healthy venue to clarify differences and to present one's worldview. Of course, interfaith dialogue presents us with the wonderful opportunity to listen directly to the voice of the "other," unmediated. It presents us with the opportunity to engage the participants and to share our concerns vis-à-vis general issue such as xenophobia, or certain specific issues such as vandalism or attacks at places of worship. Ambassadors of goodwill could emerge out of these gatherings.

Therefore, it is hoped that interfaith forums help in breaking stereotyped images so that societies could accept the "other" in their midst, without conflicts. It is equally important that interfaith forums challenge the false ideological premises of every occupation that exists in the world today.

Interfaith gatherings provide an opportunity for partnerships that promote *convivencia* and cooperation between the various civilizations.

Although I argue for a theology of "soft-otherness," based on Islamic textual sources, the dialogue itself could be a source for softening the "other"! This soft-otherness falls somewhere between two extremes, eliminating differences and eliminating commonalities.

Interfaith dialogue provides an opportunity for participants to express empathy without patronizing the "other." This is based on mutually respecting each other's right to be religiously different, in a multicultural global village.

I have been involved in formal interfaith dialogue for about a quarter of a century, but being part of *convivencia* social settings as the "dialogue of life" is the story of every Palestinian, including mine. Palestinian Muslims have always lived along with their brethren from among the "People of the Book." Palestine witnessed the presence of many peoples and cultures, including Jews; but when Muslims arrived historically during the time of the second caliph Umar Ibn Al-Khattab, it was the Christians who were sovereign. The "Pact of Umar" was concluded with Bishop Sophronious; it protected the life, property, and religious rights of the Christians, including protection of their churches and crosses.

This, I believe, was the first interfaith document in the history of Palestine. Jerusalem was conquered tens of times in its history, often ending in bloodbaths, as in the chilling account of what happened to Muslims in Jerusalem at the hands of the Franks (i.e., Crusaders). There is a need to deconstruct the in-built ideology that allowed such atrocities to take place. As for the Muslim conquerors, they preserved the sanctity of life in Jerusalem. This pact should be seen, however, in its own historical context and not as a document that should be upheld *verbatim* indefinitely. Its spirit, nevertheless, continues to shape Muslim-Christian relations in the Holy Land and beyond, until today. Many Muslim intellectuals and scholars today write about citizenship, regardless of religious background, as the criterion for enjoying rights.

Furthermore, Umar Ibn Al-Khattab put his knowledge into practice. When Bishop Sophronious invited him to pray at the Church of the Holy Sepulcher, Umar declined. In his wisdom, he knew that had he accepted the generous offer, future Muslim generations might claim it as a right. He stepped outside and, where he prayed, Muslims erected a mosque and named it after him. Only a wall separates the mosque and the church. In fact, in many Palestinian towns, the mosque and the church rub shoulders, because these towns have mixed populations, reflecting a unique situation. Respecting the religious space of the "other" is the core of Umar's position. Such respect should be the teleological aim of the discussion on Jerusalem's holy sites, and any other place of contention.

Umar's practical wisdom is yet confirmed by another independent source. It should be noted that there were no Jews in Jerusalem when Muslims arrived in 638 CE. The Cairo Jewish Geniza manuscripts state that Umar Ibn Al-Khattab allowed

Jews to return, establish houses of worship, and rebuild their community, rights not accorded to them by their former rulers.

The Geniza manuscripts should be part of the criteria used to deconstruct the addenda that were woven into future versions of the "Pact of `Umar." One of these versions states that Jews were not allowed to live in Jerusalem. To accept Christian presence and deny Jewish presence in the city of Jerusalem is a condition that cannot be supported by the Islamic Shari`ah. Umar Ibn Al-Khattab would have never accepted such a condition. In addition, some of the later versions use colloquial and awkward Arabic. They are full of grammatical and spelling mistakes, some of which reflect linguistic constructs that could not have emerged before the Ottoman period.

An important earlier covenant was concluded between the Prophet himself and the Jews of Medina to form the political foundations of the newly established community. This covenant became known in later times as the Constitution of Medina. It stated that "the Jews of the Bani `Awf tribe constitute one *Ummah*[1] with the Muslims: for the Jews their religion, and for the Muslims their religion."[2] The covenant then continued to mention all the Jewish tribes, one after the other. Unfortunately, this opportunity was lost, and the text of the covenant is rarely mentioned or celebrated. I do believe, despite the fact that the world scene is dotted with military conflicts, with the occupation in Palestine being the focal point, that intellectual humility paves the way for highlighting and reviving the ethos of such a remarkable covenant, which recognized a multicultural society.

The Christians of Najran, an area in the south-western region of the Arabian Peninsula, sent a delegation comprising fourteen people to meet with the Prophet; he hosted them for many days at the mosque of Medina. Ibn Sa`d mentioned in *Al-Tabaqat Al-Kubra* that they performed their prayers inside the mosque.[3] This presence is extremely important in formulating a legal ruling on the permissibility of hosting the "People of the Book" inside mosques. Today, especially in the west, many Jews and Christians are welcomed into mosques. The covenant that they concluded with the Prophet granted them his protection (i.e., *Dhimmah*) "to them, their religion, land, property, those [Christians] who were present and those who were absent, their churches. . . ." This *Dhimmi* pact concluded with direct mention of the protection of the vows of priests and monks. Christians would spend the next fourteen centuries living under such protection. A breach of this pact happened at the hands of the Isma`ili Shi`ite Fatimid dynasty, who ruled from Egypt between 910–1171 CE. During this period, Christian churches in Jerusalem suffered, but these were bad times for everyone, including Sunni Muslims.

I used the word *dhimmi* here on purpose. Islamophobes wrote frivolous attacks on this Islamic legal term. They interpreted it in terms of second-class citizenship and, at times, as slavery. The previously mentioned covenants reflect an essential Islamic position; theological differences do not prevent *convivencia* from taking place. The Islamic worldview inculcates a strong sense of being continuous with the previous revelations. It is quite remarkable that the dominant story in the Qur'an is that of Moses and the Children of Israel. Chapter 19 of the Qur'an is named after Mary, mother of Jesus Christ, the only woman to be mentioned by name.

■ POINTS OF COMMONALITY

That Jews and Christians are "People of the Book" softens their otherness, and legally allocates them a status that permits different healthy relationships, such as marriage, which essentially means a social fabric with Muslim children having maternal families that are Jews and Christians. The Qur'an renders the food of the "People of the Book" lawful for Muslims, and Muslim food lawful for them[4]; this permits social interaction between both sides.

Probably the most important aspect in this relationship is that "there is no compulsion in religion."[5] Continuous Jewish and Christian presence in the Muslim world is a reflection of this verse, and answers the claims that Islam was spread by the sword. One could only add that Muslims were required to communicate with the "People of the Book" with excellent manners:

> And argue not with the People of the Scripture unless it be in (a way) that is better, save with such of them as do wrong; and say: We believe in that which hath been revealed unto us and revealed unto you; our Allah and your Allah is One, and unto Him we surrender.[6]

The civilizational interaction between Muslims and the "People of the Book," who lived together manifested itself in different situations. The translation movement could not have taken place without the help of the Christian and Jewish translators. After digesting Greek knowledge and building on it, the Muslims transferred this knowledge to Europe through different points of contact, especially Andalusia. The latter civilizational force was brought to an end in 1492. Thereafter, Europe moved from one success to another in the sciences, and the role of Muslims shifted from providers to recipients of Western science and know-how, especially through more than two centuries of direct colonialism.

■ POINTS OF DIFFERENCE

Modern western colonialism in different parts of the world, including the Muslim world, sends a clear message of the need for a different world order that neither permits nor condones colonialization. There are no good excuses for belligerent foreign policies. Changing the rational for invading Iraq, as an example, cannot fool even the foolish. Colonialization not only perpetuates human suffering; it is also the largest obstacle in the face of interfaith dialogue and civilizational *convivencia*. In the age of nuclear proliferation, it is of the utmost importance to save the future of humanity, and to rethink the conditions that are prerequisites to peace and prosperity.

It is not clear to me whether theories that make conflicts normative begin or rather end in think tanks. I am inclined to say that some of these think tanks are nothing but unofficial arms of departments of states or foreign offices, depending on which side of the Atlantic they are, entrusted with providing an intellectual framework for whatever the current foreign policy is. This is why Samuel Huntington's *The Clash of Civilizations and the Remaking of World Order* is best interpreted through the second part of the title; it is a "remaking of the world order" through the invention of a cultural clash between the existing civilizations. This theory ignores all the real economic issues that could ignite conflicts such as oil and water. It wants people to believe that conflicts are inevitable because we are culturally different. Rather, the truth is that we are moral agents, and to create a conflict is a decision made by people who have lost their moral compass. It has nothing to do with cultural differences that could go unnoticed. Unfortunately, some misguided Muslims, who never thought of this theory before on their own, adopted the same thesis and reproduced it using Islamic garb.

Humility necessitates reconsidering international relations from the Islamic point of view. It is a well established principle in the Shari`ah that Muslims ought to fulfill treaties to which they are signatories. This is a religious obligation. What is better than conflict resolution is not to have a conflict in the first place. A just world order is needed, and it should aim at eliminating power structures that prevent the administration of justice, such as the permanent seats in the UN Security Council and the veto "rights." The Security Council is undemocratic and reflects the will of the powerful. This structure ensures continued double standards, preventing the implementation of UN resolutions, which perpetuated, for example, the plight of the Palestinian people.

In other words, to spend forty years under Israeli occupation, since 1967, you grow from a child of ten to the adult who marries and has children of his own, to the children becoming adults, where the prospect of having grandchildren, still under occupation—all this haunts you. You live under occupation long enough to see your people's suffering continuously unfolding in homes being demolished, land confiscated, colonies erected, olive trees uprooted, an unholy wall that cuts through your dreams before it brutally dissects the tiny body of the Holy Land, and loss of life, all in violation of international law! You start questioning what is wrong with the world community. Still, you try to rise above your wounds and reach out to the other in the hope that dialogue would rescue victim and victimizer. This path of dialogue does not resonate well with many Muslims.

■ THE NEED FOR DIALOGUE

There are Muslims who are suspicious about interfaith gatherings; they are afraid that the Muslim participants will either compromise their religion or give up their political rights. Interfaith gatherings do aim at a specific *telos*, and sometimes more. I can argue theologically that it is imperative for Muslim scholars to participate in such *fora*. Although one cannot and should not ignore the political implications of interfaith dialogue, one should try to understand the dialogue with the other *qua* religious. A religious person does not necessarily identify with his or her government's policies, foreign or domestic. It is my conviction that the non-Muslims who participate in these gatherings are people who care about humanity and are outspoken against the injustices around the world, even when they are perpetuated by their own governments. The same applies to us Muslims; we do not necessarily identify with those in office, especially those who are well-known dictators. We condemn acts of terror, such as the ones that visited New York, London, and Madrid. It should be noted that state, group, and individual terrorisms have the same traits, the same genetic code, for they breed each other. Only the magnitude differs.

It remains that interfaith dialogue is about engaging those who have different faiths and worldviews. These *fora* do provide a chance to explain one's position and search for the common good. These differences, however, do not preclude the possibility of learning from the other and growing in one's own faith as a result. In addition, these dialogues could lead the participant to explore areas in one's own worldview that were not part of her consciousness.

■ THE ONENESS OF GOD

The Islamic worldview revolves around the notion of *Tawhid*, or oneness of God, and, as such, this paper will explore the way the knowledge enterprise is related to *Tawhid*. It should be clear that the notion of ignorance here is not synonymous with the state of ignorance (*jahiliyyah*) that predated Islam, nor is it simply the state of lacking knowledge. In this paper, "learned ignorance" could be defined in terms of a learning process that leads the human being to be self-conscious of her epistemological limitations and, therefore, lead to intellectual humility.

Islam advocates strict monotheism, which necessitates the negation of that which is not. The first part of the declaration of faith, "there is no god except Allah, and Muhammad is His messenger," confirms God's oneness and uniqueness, and rejects other deities or whatever does not befit *Tawhid*. His "Beautiful Names" (i.e., *Al-Asma' Al-Husna*) can be understood by the human intellect, and that is precisely why they are revealed. However, the knowledge of His "essence" is beyond human comprehension. In addition, our natural language, because it is modified by our human experience of the world, is not fit to deal with this transcendental realm. Therefore, the Qur'an explains divine essence by negating that which it is not:

> [He is] the Creator of the heavens and the earth. He hath made for you pairs of yourselves, and of the cattle also pairs, whereby He multiplies you. *Nothing is as His likeness*; and He is the Hearer, the Seer.[7]

Alas! One cannot know this aspect of God, because it is not that the knowledge of divine attributes leads automatically to peaceful alignment with God's Will. Accepting one's ignorance in this case means that one concentrates on that which could be known.

The Beautiful Names of God include, for example, the name *Al-'Alīm*, the Knower. The names and attributes of God always reflect the absolute; the article *the* (Arabic: *Al*) means that only God is Omniscient. In the case where human beings are permitted to use some of these attributes as adjectives to describe a human being (e.g., *'Âlim*) (notice the difference in the use of long and short vowels) it only reflects partaking in the attribute in a less than perfect sense. In fact, the Arabic grammatical form of a noun, when it does not have the prefix "A" is called "*nakirah*" (i.e., an indeterminate noun). The etymology of its root, "*n-k-r*," connotes a certain element of ignorance, an area that one is not acquainted with, or the unknowability of the object of learning in a complete and wholesome way. In a way, the "*nakirah*" is a projection of one's inability to know. Hence, the human being could have been called *homo ignarus* rather than *homo sapien!*

Our knowledge is limited. Therefore, The Qur'an reminds us of the limited nature of one's knowledge, especially compared to God's:

> We raise to degrees (of wisdom) whom We please: but over all endued with knowledge is one, the All-Knowing (*Al-'Alîm*).[8]

Moreover, the existence of "degrees" of wisdom is a clear indicator that this is also true in relation to other human beings. One could potentially be more or less knowledgeable than others, but it is recognizing and accepting others to be potentially higher than oneself that could foster humility. This ethos is embodied in the well-known statement of Imam Al-Shafi'i (d. 820 CE), the founder of the Shafi'i School of Jurisprudence, who said: "[When I think that] my opinion is right, it could be wrong, and [when I think that] the opinion of the other is wrong, it could be right."

Muslim scholars, despite being themselves called "'*Ulama*', sing '*Âlim*," have been careful not to use the word "'*Arif*" (i.e., knower) in any grammatical form to describe God. It is reserved for human beings, for it reflects knowledge after being in a state of ignorance. "'*Arif*" is also used to describe the state of the Sufi (Muslim mystic) who attains such a title for "knowing" God.

Every human being begins life in a state of natural disposition (*fitrah*). The *hadith* that addresses the notion of *fitrah*, compiled by Al-Bukhari and Muslim, alludes to a priori knowledge of God, of His existence, and His oneness. This a priori knowledge is universal. *A posteriori* theological knowledge might or might not be reconciled with the *fitrah*. There is, potentially, a very serious problem with inherited postrevelational constructed theological notions that could contradict to *Tawhid*. In the text of the same *hadith*, it is non-*Tawhidic* parents who are responsible for steering their children away from the state of natural disposition. Of course, teachers of all sorts could also be sources of distorted knowledge. One cannot ignore the possibility of children assuming that older people have epistemic authority. Imitation (*taqlid*) becomes a problem when it leads people to follow previous generations blindly. To avoid imitating means adopting the principle of verification and a healthy dose of doubt, so that one could trek on the epistemological path to more reliable certitude.

Imam Al-Ghazzali (d.1111CE) went through this. He wrote about his intellectual and spiritual crises in *The Deliverance from Error*; the crisis was the turning point in his life. He cited the *hadith* of *fitrah* at the beginning of his book, the rest of which narrates the different stations of a journey that led him to be a mystic. He reached the level where he was no longer sure of the truthfulness of the knowledge that he had acquired in his life. He doubted the senses and the intellect as reliable sources of knowledge. At the time, he was the scholar par excellence of the Muslim world. When he regained his trust in his senses and intellect through "a light that God has cast into his chest," he went into a deep spiritual crisis. He realized that he wasn't sincere in his work. His actions weren't for the sake of God since he had egoistical motivation. He realized that his fame, academic position, social status, and wealth were hindrances to sincerity. He abandoned them all. For about eleven years he chose to live as an unknown person, literally trekking the deserts and going to cities away from Baghdad, where people would recognize him. He ended up being a Sufi. There are many remarkable moments in Al-Ghazzali's life. In one of them, he admits that, despite being a great scholar, his knowledge of the science of *hadith* is modest, a common problem amongst Sufis.

Seeking knowledge, therefore, is a religious commandment. Prophet Muhammad (Peace be upon him) said: "Seeking Knowledge is obligatory on all Muslims [male and female]." This is reflected in the grammatically imperative language used by the Qur'an, beginning with the very first revealed word:

> *Read* in the name of your Lord Who created
> He created man from a clot
> Read and your Lord is Most Honorable
> Who taught (to write) with the pen
> *Taught man what he knew not*
> Nay, but man does transgress all bounds.[9]

The potential to learn and the conditions conducive to learning are created in us and for us. A question that could be raised here is whether human beings use the knowledge they acquire to transgress and become epistemologically arrogant? A proper *reading*, even of these few verses, reflects a humanity indebted to God. It is He who provided humanity with guidance. That guidance can be innate, as in the notion of *fitrah*, which is the result of the primordial covenant between God and humanity; or it can be external, as in the continued guidance throughout the history of revelation and through being equipped intellectually to decipher the endless signs that dot the universe.

Humanity has a better cumulative *reading* of the universe on all levels. A proper *reading* on the individual level should reveal quickly one's role in the history of knowledge, which knowledge may be compared to a drop in the ocean. For no matter how knowledgeable persons can become, there is always an area that they would never know. This should be a humbling experience. The Qur'an refers to such a state of limited knowledge that is open for the human being:

> Allah! There is no other god save Him, the Alive, the Eternal. Neither slumber nor sleep overtakes Him. To Him belongs all that are in the heavens and on the earth. Who is he that intercedes with Him except by His leave? He knows that which is in front of them and that which is behind them, *while they attain nothing of His knowledge except what He wills*. His throne encompasses the heavens and the earth, and He is never weary of preserving them. He is the Sublime, the Great.[10]

The Qur'an invites us to think about the creation of the universe, understand that it was not in vain, and finally conclude by remembering the name of God. There is a direct connection between pondering and contemplating natural phenomena and spirituality. The Qur'an establishes a link between the state of being humble and being spiritual and, therefore encourages people to construct that link:

> Has not the Time arrived for the Believers that their hearts in all humility should engage in the remembrance of Allah and of the Truth which has been revealed [to them], and

that they should not become like those to whom was given Revelation aforetime, but long ages passed over them and their hearts grew hard? For many among them are rebellious transgressors.[11]

But one does not stay passive vis-à-vis his or her "share" of knowledge. The Qur'an encourages people to ask God to facilitate more knowledge for them. The following verse originally addressed the Prophet:

> Supremely exalted is therefore Allah, the King, the Truth, and do not make haste with the Quran before its revelation is made complete to you and say: O my Lord! Increase me in knowledge.[12]

■ THE UNEDUCATED EDUCATOR

This shows that lack of knowledge is neither a preferred state, nor is it a precondition for humility. The very nature of "learned ignorance" presupposes a learning process that culminates in an insight that transforms the soul. It is a very humbling experience, indeed, when the educator par excellence is an illiterate person:

> Those who follow the messenger, the unlettered (*Ummi*) Prophet, whom they will find written in the Torah and the Gospel that are with them, enjoining on them that which is right and prohibiting them from that which is wrong. He will make lawful for them all good things and prohibit for them only the impure things; and he will relieve them of their burden and the [legal] shackles that were on them. Then those who believe in him, and honor him, and rally around him, and follow the light which is sent down with him: they are the successful. Say: 'O people! I am sent to all of you, as the Messenger of Allah, to Whom belongs the dominion of the heavens and the earth: there is no god but He; He creates life and causes death. So believe in Allah and His Messenger, the Unlettered Prophet, who believes in Allah and His Words: follow him so that you may be guided'.[13]

As a rule, the uneducated educator poses a challenge to the well-educated. The other Qur'anic meaning of "*Ummi*" is goy, a member of the nations. This is also challenging to those who are not Muslims, and who expect a Messiah from among the children of Isaac, rather than a prophet from the children of Ishmael who biblically became an outcast and was expelled into the desert, after the birth of his brother Isaac. Are the Palestinian Arabs being treated like Ishmael? Are they being turned systematically into outcasts because they are the children of Hagar, the bond-woman, and, therefore, cannot inherit with the legitimate children of Abraham? How are we to explain that Abraham behaved like a good citizen and paid 400 shekels of silver for the Cave of Macphelah to bury his wife Sarah (Genesis 23:16), if the Holy Land were given to him and his progeny exclusively?

In addition, the fact that Prophet Muhammad was poor and many of his followers were poor posed a challenge to many affluent people whose arrogance prevented them from joining the ranks of the wretched. The Qur'an narrates the story of those who rejected Prophet Noah's call; they cited his followers' background among their reasons for rejection:

> The leaders of his folk, who disbelieved, said: We see that you are nothing but a human being like us, and we see not that any follow you save the most wretched among us, without reflection. And we see in you no merit above us—rather, we think you are liars.[14]

The limitation of human understanding is not reflected, usually, in academic titles; being a scholar, a professor, or, indeed, an `Arif, in the Sufi sense, does not reflect a humble state of affairs. The problem is that if we coin a title to reflect such a humble state and bestow the title on someone, the person honored might be tempted to take pride in the newly bestowed title! Imam Al-Ghazzali critiqued titles per se and said that they are "from the devil!"

Perhaps it is to encourage humility that Muslim scholars call themselves "Students of Learning" (i.e., Talabat `Ilm) rather than calling themselves scholars (`Ulama'). It could be argued still, that it is ultimately the affairs of the heart that matter most, in which case sincerity is what renders an action acceptable to God. There is no immunity to arrogance when one is described as a "student of learning."

True scholars are, therefore, cautious about presuming absolute understanding about everything in the Qur'an. Although the Qur'an refers to itself as being accessible to its readers, it nevertheless has the following description of the status of scholars and the way they relate, hermeneutically speaking, to the Qur'an:

> He it is Who has revealed unto you [Muhammad] the Book wherein are verses with exact meaning—they are the foundation of the Book—and others which are allegorical. But those in whose hearts there is perversity, they resort to [the verses that permit] allegorical interpretation seeking to cause dissension by twisting their meaning. But none knows its [absolute] interpretation save Allah. And those who are deeply rooted in knowledge say: We believe therein; the whole is from our Lord; but only people of sound intellect could apprehend this.[15]

It is rather clear that it is not possible for any human being to encompass all available knowledge, let alone potential knowledge about the universe in which we live. It should be a humbling experience to realize our inability to know everything and that we could only attain that much. To be humble here means that one should not inflate her image as someone who knows more than she does. One of the popular Arabic proverbs reflects this need for humility:

> May Allah be merciful to anyone who knows the right estimate of oneself.

Although one should be especially humble in the prime of life, when one is at the peak of his or her intellectual powers, one is still reminded by the Qur'an of the potentially deteriorating intellect of the aged:

> And Allah creates you, then causes you to die, and among you is he who is brought back to the most abject stage of life, so that he knows nothing after [having had] knowledge. Lo! Allah is Knower, Powerful.[16]

So, the human being potentially moves from the state of fitrah to acquiring knowledge, only to lose it at very old age. God is the primary cause of knowledge; He requires that, in exchange for knowledge, one should remain aware of Him. The reward for humility is to be elevated in the sight of God to high degrees. Abu Hurayrah reported part of a *hadith* that the Prophet said: "No one humbles himself for the sake of Allah, except that Allah will raise him [to higher degree]."[17]

■ THE DANGERS OF PRIDE

There is an impressive list that describes the "servants of Allah" in the Qur'an; the first of these mentions humility:

> And the servants of (Allah) Most Gracious are those who walk on the earth in humility, and when the ignorant address them, they say, 'Peace!'[18]

Such a verse highlights humility as an attribute of those who are accepted by God; it helps pave the way back to paradise. The opposite is true: arrogance distances us from God. In the story of Satan and his refusal to respect Adam, Satan's pride was the reason for his expulsion from paradise: [Allah] said: "Get thee down from this: it is not for thee to be arrogant here: get out, for thou art of the meanest [of creatures]" (Qur'an, 7:13). An earlier verse explained Satan's source of his false sense of pride; he thought he was created from better substance than man, a very early form of social-Darwinism:

> [God] said: What hindered thee that thou didst not fall prostrate when I bade thee? [Iblis] said: I am better than him. Thou createdst me of fire while him Thou didst create of mud.[19]

Humanity wasn't left without guidance. God sent prophets with revelation to educate people and guide them back to God. Humility appears to be a primary attribute of the prophets of God. This can be detected in the story of Noah; his humility motivated him to go on for a very long time, with only a handful of the meek people believing in him, while his own people ridiculed him for building the ark. This is why the Qur'an asks Prophet Muhammad to "lower [his] wing" (Qur'an, 15:88) as a sign of humility. The Qur'an mentions other necessary attributes that fall under the umbrella of humility:

> For Thus it is due to mercy from Allah that you deal with them gently, and had you been rough, hard-hearted, they would certainly have dispersed from around you; pardon them therefore and ask forgiveness for them, and take counsel with them in the affair; so when you have decided, then place your trust in Allah; surely Allah loves those who trust.[20]

In addition to the public sphere, the Prophet's humility manifested itself in the privacy of his home where he did house chores, mending his own clothes and fixing his shoes, milking the she-goat, and putting things in order. His acts made these chores genderless.

The Islamic worldview warns against arrogance and promotes humbleness. Muslim narrated in the *hadith* that the Prophet said: "Allah, Most High, revealed to me that you should humble yourselves, so that no one shall pride himself over another, and no one shall be unjust to another."[21] The order of the *hadith* indicates that pride could lead to inflicting harm on others, but humility prevents that.

No degree of arrogance is tolerated. In another tradition, Muslim narrated that the Prophet said: "He, who has arrogance the weight of one atom, does not enter paradise."

This is why the Qur'an includes pride among the list of bad manners that should be avoided. Remember Luqman's advice to his son:

> And swell not thy cheek (for pride) at men, nor walk in insolence through the earth; for Allah loveth not any arrogant boaster.[22]

Arrogance is met with Divine rejection. The arrogant will face the consequences of being deprived of seeing the manifest signs: "Those who behave arrogantly on the earth in defiance of right—them will I turn away from My signs…"[23] The arrogant faces a grim end in the hereafter: "Is there not in hell an abode for the proud?" asks the Qur'an rhetorically.[24]

■ CONCLUSION

Humility, ultimately, is the total submission to divine will, a peaceful alignment with what is right, humbling oneself in prostration before God, lowering one's wing before humanity for His sake, engaging the other compassionately in search for the common word and common ground, working for one humanity under God, but also acknowledging that differences do exist:

> And if thy Lord had willed, He verily would have made mankind one nation, yet they cease not differing.[25]

By recognizing the differences, we also recognize that which is common. When we argue theologically for the accommodation to the other, along with her differences, we hope that we are accorded the same treatment and allowed room to grow on our own terms. Dialogue, I trust, does help.

■ Notes

1. "*Ummah*" is usually used to describe all Muslims of the world. It goes beyond "nation" or "community."

2. Ibn Hisham, *Al-Sirah Al-Nabawiyyah* (Al-Mansurah: Maktabat Al-Iman, 1995) vol. 2, p. 98.

3. Ibn Sa'd, *Al-Tabaqat Al-Kubra* (Beirut: Dar Al-Kutub Al-'Ilmiyyah, 1998) vol.1, p. 358.

4. Qur'an, 5:5.
5. Qur'an, 2:256.
6. Qur'an, 29:46.
7. Qur'an, 42:11.
8. Qur'an, 12:76.
9. Qur'an, 96:1–6.
10. Qur'an, 2:256.
11. Qur'an, 57:16.
12. Qur'an, 20:114.
13. Qur'an, 7:157–58.
14. Qur'an, 11:27.

15. Qur'an, 3:7.

16. Qur'an, 16:70.

17. Narrated in *Sahih Mulsim, Book* 32, # 6264. Notes (17 and 21) are references to well-known compendia of Prophetic traditions available in English translation. See: http://www.usc.edu/schools/college/crcc/engagement/resources/texts/muslim/hadith/

18. Qur'an, 25:63.

19. Qur'an, 7:13.

20. Qur'an, 3: 159.

21. Narrated in *Sunan* Abu Dawud, Book 41, # 4877. See: http://www.usc.edu/schools/college/crcc/engagement/resources/texts/muslim/hadith/abudawud/041.sat.html

22. Qur'an, 31:18.

23. Qur'an, 7:146.

24. Qur'an, 39:60.

25. Qur'an, 11:118.

PART IV

Religious Pluralism

13 A Meditation on Intellectual Humility, or on a Fusion of Epistemic Ignorance and Covenantal Certainty

Stanislaw Krajewski

"There is no truth without humility, no certainty without contrition."

—Abraham Joshua Heschel[1]

I was born in Warsaw in 1950, studied there, received a PhD in mathematics, and later another degree (so-called Habilitation) in philosophy. I am currently a professor at the Institute of Philosophy at the University of Warsaw. I have been doing research in the area of logic and the philosophy of mathematics. For example, I wrote a book (in Polish) entitled *Gödel's Theorem and Its Philosophical Interpretations: from Mechanism to Postmodernism*. More recently, I have been studying and teaching the philosophy of religion and inter-religious dialogue. How I got into these most recent areas of study is rather unusual.

I was raised in post-World War II Poland with no religious affiliation. My father, a philosophy professor and member of the Communist party until 1968, was a declared atheist. When as a young adult I began to learn about Judaism. I understood that, similar to my ancestors, *I* was personally responsible for its survival, that "Shema Israel" was directed to *me*. I became more and more observant and involved in traditional Jewish life, but I never lost touch with my Christian and other friends. If anything, I got closer to them, because I could appreciate their religious involvement better. In a relatively short time, I began publicly to represent Jews and the Jewish perspective, especially in interreligious settings. For example, I was the only Jewish person of my generation who took part in all (three) of the Polish meetings of Pope John Paul II with Jews.

I was involved in the anti-Communist human rights movement, and a member of the initial, but then underground, "Solidarity" movement. It was only after 1989, in free Poland, that I became involved in institutional Jewish life, sitting from 1997 to 2005 on the board of the Union of Jewish Communities in Poland. In addition, from 1989 to 2006, I was a member of the advisory International Auschwitz Council. From 1992 to 2009 I was Poland's consultant to the American Jewish Committee. I have also been working as a member of the team preparing a major Museum of the History of Polish Jews in Warsaw. My publications on Judaism, Polish Jewish issues, and Christian-Jewish themes include the following books: *Jews, Judaism,*

Poland (in Polish); 54 *Commentaries to the Torah for Even the Least Religious Among Us* (in Polish); *Poland and the Jews: Reflections of a Polish Polish Jew*, (in English; published by Austeria, Cracow 2005); *The Mystery of Israel and the Mystery of the Church* (in Polish); *Our Jewishness* (in Polish).

I feel that interreligious dialogues in general, and the Christian-Jewish one in particular, are essential for the world. Not less important, they are central for me personally. I have been the co-chair of the Polish Council of Christians and Jews since its formation in 1989, right after the collapse of Communism. Our Council is a member of the International Council of Christians and Jews; I served on its board from 1992 to 1998. In 2000, immediately after the Jewish declaration on Christianity *Dabru Emet* had been issued, I translated it and had it published in the largest selling Polish daily paper.

I think that the interreligious dialogue is primarily a matter of attitude. Knowledge is important, but it is second. Therefore, the problem is how to form dialogue-oriented attitudes. On a more theoretical level, I think that one of the most important goals before us is to develop within religious traditions adequate theologies of other religions. They must be true to one's own tradition and, at the same time, not misrepresent those of others. Although this objective may be impossible to achieve fully, the need of an appropriate vision, or rather individual visions, poses a challenge to all of us who are part of the interfaith scene. A related task is how to accept such an external description of my own religion—a difficult step even when that description is made with good will.

Perhaps intellectual humility means something very simple: We cannot be sure we can know things as they really are. This is as much an everyday observation as a philosophical one. Kant has taught us that we are unable to know things in themselves, a realization that has been called "Kantian humility."[2] Whether we are learned or not, we should accept our fundamental ignorance. We all know, however, that there are things of which we can be sure. What is emphasized, be it ignorance or certainty, seems to depend on one's personal disposition and, probably even more, on experience.

Humility is a human virtue. Can it mean more than a behavioral and psychological attitude? Certainly, humble behavior and one's feeling of not being *that* important in dealing with others are necessary aspects of humility. But can humility point to a higher dimension, one that has a religious significance? And would such humility possibly have an interreligious implication?

It seems that humility and respect imply each other: Humility leads to the respect of others and their points of view, and one who really respect others is necessarily humble. Respect of other persons and of other religions is commonly seen as a principal premise of interfaith dialogue. Therefore, so should humility be such a premise.

■ HUMILITY

The Biblical lesson about humility is given principally in the story of Moses. From the standpoint of the Jewish tradition, Moses has been the greatest religious personality. It is, therefore, highly significant that Moses was called *anav*, humble (Numbers 12:3). Incidentally, this verse is in the Torah portion, *parshah*, of the very week that the Trialogue group that has produced the present volume was meeting for the first time in Boston in June of 2006. In fact, Moses is called *very* humble, or meek, "above all the men which where upon the face of the earth."[3] He thus becomes a paradigm of humility. But even more than that can be said. Joseph Telushkin observes[4] that humility is the *only* virtue that Torah attributes to Moses. He is not called courageous or wise, even though so many of his deeds justify the use of such adjectives. This characteristic of humility may be accidental; however, the tradition suggests that no circumstance detected in the Torah should be seen as inconsequential. The importance of humility is, by itself, a significant statement that is granted a prominent place in the Jewish tradition, and, of course, in other traditions as well. Does it point to something more? The mention of Moses's humbleness appears when he refrains from reproaching Miriam and Aaron for their attack against their brother's monopoly in contacts with God. He paid no heed to the injustice, and God himself intervened, stating that his message reached Moses directly, "from mouth to mouth," not like in the case of other prophets. Can we, ordinary mortals, so far from anything that Moses or the prophets represented, learn anything from that story?

Apparently, the most unusual and unsurpassable quality Moses possessed, namely, the ability of a direct communication with the Creator, did not make him think that he knew, saw, or that he was shown so much more than others that he could reject the accusations of those who pretended to be as advanced as he. He seems to accept the possibility that others could do as well as he did. We all remember that, during the burning bush revelation and at Sinai, Moses obtained a clear message but no insight into the nature of the *Hakadosh baruch hu* (The Holy one, may He be blessed). In fact, in the verse stating his humbleness, he is described as the one who saw *temunat Hashem*, (a similitude of God) but not his essence. At least, this is the way the prevailing Jewish tradition sees it. More specifically, what he was receiving, we are told, was not so much truth as commandments—not what the world or God is like, but what is to be done. This constitutes a lesson that is relevant to our topic, because it stresses the fallibility of the wise and the particularity of obligations.

Thus, first, Moses could remain humble because he knew not so much higher truths about another world but rather obligations relating to life in this world—obligations applied to him as much as to the rest. This distinction has two consequences. First, the person who knows that the obligations are shared knows that a deeper knowledge of the obligations means a more difficult challenge for him. More knowledge means more to be done or avoided, and this means that failure will be easier. Such an awareness does not support arrogance, nor does the observation that higher abilities mean bigger responsibility necessarily lead to arrogance. This is best illustrated by a well-known story told in the Mussar movement, developed in Polish lands in the nineteenth century. The founder of Mussar, Israel Salanter, has been reported to say, "I know that I have a mental capacity of a thousand men." This sounds like the utmost of arrogance. Yet he said that as an introduction to the next statement, "Because of that my obligation is also that of a thousand men."

The second consequence of the perception of revelation as commandments rather than truth is more theoretical and even more closely related to the interfaith relations. Whereas truth necessarily involves an appeal to universality, commandments can be directed to a particular group. This idea deserves a closer look.

■ TRUTH

Even the most erudite scientists will occasionally admit that they know little. Here we are dealing with intellectual humility of an epistemic variety. The more we learn about nature, the more new questions arise, and the more some fundamental things appear unexplained. Fundamental principles of physics, like the conservation of energy or various mathematical symmetries, are taken as basic premises that are justified by their fruitfulness. The case is similar with the natural sciences. It should be clear that our ignorance of matters divine can be stated even more strongly. Various theories of the ultimate and of the inaccessible realm are possible. Incidentally, a most striking expression of that ignorance is to be found in the midrash, which explains why the Torah begins with the letter *beth*; its shape, ב, is open in only one direction, which is interpreted as suggesting that all attempts to search about the matters that are above, below, or that had happened before should be eliminated. We cannot know much, if anything at all, about God; however, some of the theses involving the Almighty are traditionally stated so strongly that they seem to be beyond doubt. And some of them remain certain to a majority of contemporary Jews. They include, I believe, the concept of Jews as being chosen.

Thus, although our knowledge of matters divine is at best highly inadequate, we know something essential: the call. The challenge resulting from revelation is not something we can take lightly. Indeed, as is well known, the revelation appears to us in the form of law. Even though in the tradition the commandments are perceived as certain, they have been questioned and modified in recent generations. The specific requirements (commandments) may be debatable, but surely not the fact of being called. We know with certainty that we are called—at least I do, as well as every Jew—as long as I place myself inside the tradition. I do not believe there is any other sensible way of being Jewish than placing oneself within the tradition, even if the tradition is to be questioned (do things look really different in other religions?). Questioning the tradition, however, seems to suggest that such activity is outside the realm of intellectual humility. Can we harmonize the doubt and the certainty? The method is, again, to distinguish knowledge from obligations and, more specifically, truth claims from responsibility.

What is needed for deep interreligious dialogue is an appropriate attitude. The source of this attitude is not clear. No single pattern of experiences is responsible for that. Just compare Abraham Joshua Heschel and Franz Rosenzweig—both deeply committed Jews sharing reverence for Christianity, but, most probably, they hardly shared any specific experiences in their relations with the Church. Whatever the role of psychological factors, child memories, upbringing, attitudes of parents and teachers, personal experiences, the fact remains that a positive attitude to interfaith dialogue in which the partner is fully approved can be achieved. Moreover, the presence of contradictory truth claims that have been so important for traditional religious exchanges is not perceived by the dialogue practitioners as a disaster. The necessary proper attitude leads to carrying out one's (religious) obligations, more than just repeating religious truths.

One obvious problem with this approach is that it can lead to reducing truth to subjective truth, and if so, we are faced with relativism. What remains are private opinions or preferences, and no common standard is possible. This is unacceptable to many. David Novak, himself deeply involved in the dialogue, warns against this as "especially dangerous to the dialogue because it denies that some things are true all the time everywhere for everyone."[5] He gives examples: claims like "God elects Israel" or "God is incarnate in Jesus." The proof that truths are not subjective is provided by the requirement of martyrdom, "the ultimate expression of belief...the personal affirmation of public, universal, and perpetual truth." Relativists, says Novak, think that "the martyr is the biggest fool."

Though Novak makes a powerful argument, it does not prove to me that the martyr is ready to die for a statement, a thesis that is true all the time everywhere for everyone. Truth does involve universality but obligations do not. At least, in the Jewish tradition, the requirement of *kiddush hashem* (martyrdom literally means the sanctification of the Name) applies when one is forced to engage in idolatry, murder, incest, or inadmissible *behavior*. Truth claims as such do not entail the need of martyrdom. Even the statement "God exists" does not require martyrdom. One who says in his heart that there is no God may be a fool but the order of the world is not shaken. In my understanding, martyrdom is required when a Jew is being forced to commit idolatry. Idolatry involves some action, not just assertions.

Let us try to imagine a situation in which we would be ready for martyrdom. When I do that, and I am able to imagine such a situation, and can only humbly hope I wouldn't be faced with such a test, or if I were, I would be able to pass it. Such a test is always some behavior, not just a mere assertion of a sentence. Of course, saying some religious declaration publicly, in the presence of appropriate religious authorities, constitutes more than an assertion; it is an oath of loyalty. In logical terminology, to use Austin's terms, it is a performative utterance. Clearly, such behavior, which is unacceptable to me, may be something that, when performed by others, as is the case for example with Christian rituals, I accept, and, moreover, fully respect.

I am not suggesting that it is easy to overcome the problem of truth claims. Whereas the idea that truths are part of larger networks, frameworks, forms of life, language games, and so on is a common topic in contemporary philosophy, I am not suggesting that the question about objective truth can be eliminated. We can relativize some truths but not all truths. Much can be explained as myth, in the noble sense of the term, but not everything. The articles of faith that relate to history seem to require belief in the historical reality of something to which they refer. Something, not everything.

Let me be more specific. In the Jewish calendar, the ninth of Av is singled out to commemorate the two cases of *hurban*, the destruction of the Jerusalem Temples. Well, I am not convinced that *literally* both destructions took place on the same day of the Jewish year. Nor am I convinced that, in addition, some major disasters in later times, namely, the capture of Bethar (in 135 CE) and the ploughing up of Jerusalem, occurred on that day, as is stated in the Talmud (Taanit 4:6). I rather suspect that the rabbis cut down history "to manageable size."[6] Still, *some* historical truth remains to be believed; we cannot explain away everything. Thus, for example, I believe the statement that Jerusalem temples *existed*. The line between literally true and, on the other hand, not literally true but significant, or true in another sense, is put differently by different people. It depends on what other sources of authority you adopt, in addition to your religious tradition. For example, I accept the findings of natural and historical sciences, with no reservation other than the general proviso that they are hypothetical, and though confirmed better than any other views, are still subject to revision.

Some Christians would probably be ready to say similar things on some of the statements about the story of Jesus, just as some Muslims would about statements about Mohammed. But they assume as a literal truth, for example, that Jesus existed as did Mohammed. We may ask whether they should make this assumption necessarily. I will not go into an analysis of Christian beliefs, but let me say something about Moses. His time was much earlier, and we have no historical proof of his existence. It is conceivable, and some historians have made the claim, that there was no historical person Moses. I am not scandalized by that. I do not, however, deny the existence of Moses. I do think he initiated in some way the traditions we find in Judaism or rather that these traditions were initiated by someone whom we call Moshe Rabbenu. It should not be surprising that we have no independent proof. After all, even the evidence about Jesus is found only in Christian sources. I must say that, even if it were true that Moses did not exist, and if it were possible to prove that—an extremely improbable event—I would still feel comfortable within the Jewish tradition. I believe that the tradition started with events that were absolutely unusual, unique, and that they were expressed and transmitted in the way accessible to humans of that time. The Torah in the broad sense is its result. It contains truths that are not expressible otherwise. Moses is a central character in that tradition, and he will remain such, whatever the historians will find or miss.

■ ATHEISM

Mathematicians reflecting on the philosophy of mathematics feel very uncertain. They know so much about hard mathematics and at the same time they cannot decide if they believe in the existence of mathematical objects or not, or if they want to retain the naïve conviction that mathematical worlds are real, or if they are ready to reduce their ontology to mathematical texts and the belief in their significance. A well known joke is that working mathematicians are Platonic realists during the week and formalists on week-ends (when asked philosophical questions). A leading mathematician of the past century, John von Neumann, admitted how humiliating it was for him to repeatedly change his views on the nature of mathematics. This has consequences, I believe, for our views of religion. If mathematicians are so uncertain, how much more we all should be with regard to religious matters!

One thing, however, is certain: Religion or rather religions constitute an important part of our life. Religious activities are no less real than mathematical ones. The problem is how to understand them. What is their basis? To understand the sense of religion must be even more difficult than to understand the sense and foundations of mathematics. We can deny the existence of numbers without affecting mathematical activity. We can deny the existence of God, but does such a denial affect religion?

Atheism is not such a great threat from the Jewish perspective. Levinas stresses its importance and constructive role as a purifying force, helping believers to attain mature religiosity, to eliminate childish religiousness, magical religious beliefs, religion as *mysterium tremendum*, and so on.[7] On this view, holiness is not an internal property of things but rather a quality of our approach to things, and this quality is truly present in the ethical realm, in our relations with other persons. God is a trace, not presence similar to other beings; he is "otherwise than being." I am definitely not saying that most Jews are mature in the sense of Levinas, but his insight is very deep. And it agrees with my own experience, and that of (many?) others. Atheism can be counterbalanced by the conviction that the Jewish tradition is valuable anyway. Of course, not all Jews agree with that. Even if the tradition is not literally true, some Jews would say, it is life giving. The Jewish tradition of stressing law rather than belief is inclusive of nonbelieving Jews. This may look like an abandonment of faith, but it isn't. Can the story of Moses appeal to nonbelievers? As explained earlier, Moses, or rather *Moshe Rabbenu*, remains the central figure of tradition, regardless of whether he was a historical figure.

As is well known, in Judaism Orthopraxy is required more emphatically than Orthodoxy. This means that even when a Jew undergoes a crisis of faith, he can remain acceptable provided he fulfills his obligations. And it is possible to be faithful without having faith, a statement that is much less paradoxical in Judaism than in some other traditions. The loss of faith can be temporary; it can result from the understandable inability to understand hidden things. It can also be a consequence of intellectual humility. As long as one fulfills one's obligations—ethical, social, and ritual—one is accepted with no reservations. And this stress on Orthopraxy is extremely helpful in interreligious relations. It is not surprising to me that some authors advocating pluralism of religions tend to stress the aspect of orthopraxy more than their own tradition normally maintains. Thus Paul Knitter, a Catholic theologian, remarks that "one lives one's faith rather than one has one's faith"[8] According to him, early Christians excluded others because of orthopraxy rather than orthodoxy. In those times it meant rejection of relativism and syncretism. The acceptance of pluralism of that era would have offended against "the kind of God and the kind of society that were integral to Jesus's vision of God's reign."[9] Not any more, says Knitter. Quite similarly, I believe that there is no need for Jews to continue the old fight against idolatry in a world where the sin of idolatry is understood to a very large extent along Jewish lines. True, there are idols around us, and we should beware. The rites of our neighbors, however, are understood along monotheistic lines. Even atheists know that idols are bad.

The case for the inclusion of an atheistic tendency in Judaism should not be overstated. After all, the standard interpretation of the first commandment of the

Decalogue (in the Jewish counting) is that it states the presence of God. Traditional Judaism assumes the existence of God. But it does not discuss the statement. I believe that this can be compared to the assumption that the world exists. We all assume it, even if philosophers like to question it. It deserves no serious discussion among normal people in normal circumstances. The same is happening with God in the Jewish tradition. Our obligations are to be discussed, but not God as such. To be sure, the obligations are seen as relating us to God, but the nature of God is inaccessible.

Having said that, I must admit that the picture is more complicated. Tanakh and the traditional literature do say a lot about some aspects of God's "life." This is used, however, to draw lessons concerning persons and our obligations. Abraham Joshua Heschel has called our attention to the fact of the *pathos* of God, the Most Moved Mover,[10] who passionately cares about us and our behavior. This description is used to justify an unparalleled character of prophetic statements and the need of a modern regaining of the sense of prophecy. Levinas expressed a similar insight about God. He quoted Rabbinic sources implying that the power of God is often accompanied by God's humility, that is, his lowering himself to suffering humans. This is presumably a non-Christian motif of kenosis.[11] Thus, even God is humble in some way. This is a reassuring and at the same time a humbling teaching, which should have an impact on our behavior.

■ CERTAINTY

Heschel emphasized that truth requires humility. This humility is expressed in the Jewish tradition by preserving diverging opinions that occur in the Talmudic disputes, even when earlier decisions favor one view. The school of Hillel is praised and given the upper hand precisely for its meticulousness in quoting and considering the opinions of the opposing school of Shammai. This is intellectual humility at its best. At the same time, there is a certainty shared by all sides of the Talmudic debate, and, by extension, by all Jews who place themselves in the tradition. This is the awareness of being chosen, that is, of special obligations that matter to the world and to its Creator. We can call it a *covenantal certainty*.

This covenantal certainty of being called *can* be combined with hesitation and intellectual humility. It must be admitted that the concept of election, the certainty of being chosen is never very far from arrogance. Being chosen means more obligations but it also means possessing so much more significance for the world. Perhaps the fusion of this certainty with humility is a good definition of Judaism. The humility is epistemic.

Now, is there something that we could call an ontological humility? What would it be? My modest proposal is to consider the feeling of *not deserving* the call. We all remember the statements to the effect that Israel did not represent anything that made her deserve the covenant. This, too, begins with the story of Moses who initially did not want to engage in his mission. A good example is provided by the small letter aleph in the word *vayikra* appearing in the standard text of the Torah at the beginning of the book *Vayikra*, Leviticus. We face here an interesting tension between the textual criticism and the Rabbinic unconditional affirmation of the significance of each detail of the Torah as we know it. Thus, according to scholars of ancient texts, two consecutive alephs, one ending a word and another beginning the next word, could be reduced to just one aleph. That is why there could be one aleph in the phrase *vayikra el*, and "(God) called to Moses." Presumably when the aleph was reinstated it was made small to indicate its lack in earlier versions. The Rabbis say something entirely different. Moses, perceived as the author of the Torah, did not want to have a longer, more respectable word than had Balaam who, in Numbers 23:16, is described by *vayikar*, meaning "and God met Balaam," or rather "happened upon"[12] him. According to Baal ha-Turim, while God instructed Moses to put the aleph in, he was so humble that he made it smaller. Apparently Moses did not feel he was any more deserving to be called than was Balaam.

The call has been made. Not to deserve the call does not mean not to respond to it. We cannot abstain from the obligation. Can we respond in a way that will respect both the covenantal certainty and the humble feeling of not deserving the covenant? Perhaps a Rabbinic comment can be of help. In a Talmudic passage (Berakhot 6b)[13] we can read a surprising opinion: "Whoever sets a particular place for himself to pray [in the synagogue—this follows from the context], the God of Abraham comes to his aid, and when he dies, people say of him, 'What a humble [*anav*] and pious [*hasid*] person he was, of the students of Avraham Avinu.'" What is so praiseworthy about a particular, regular place for worship? And what has it to do with Abraham and "the God of Abraham"? On the face of it, it is just a reference to the supposed initiation of morning prayer in a regular place by Abraham, and the suggestion that if someone imitates Abraham in this respect, he would follow his footsteps as similarly humble and pious. Later, the custom of having a regular place in the synagogue is recommended in the Shulchan Arukh. Still, the praise for following this custom seems to be unjustified unless a deeper reason is found than its similarity to the supposed ways of Abraham. A modern student of Mussar, Alan Morinis, gives one: namely, "fixing yourself to one spot you free up all the other space for others to use."[14] This is indeed a striking explanation, and one relevant to the scene of religious pluralism and interreligious encounters. If each of our religions has a set place in the world "synagogue" of religions then the rest of the space is left for others. This provides a design for both humility and certainty. Of course, to stretch the metaphor a little, one could ask what is the rite used in the "synagogue of religions." Probably the best answer is none—or, at least, this is a Jewish answer.

The vision also helps to solve our problem of how to combine certainty with humility. We have a place, but it is only one among many. Our tradition prevails in our place, but in other places there are other religious traditions. We do not try to impose our way in the "synagogue of religions," neither on our partners nor on the space as such.

■ HUMILITY IN THE FACE OF PLURALISM

A humiliated mathematician can be our guide in the theology of pluralism. We must do all we can to acknowledge another religion on its own terms. And yet even with the best of intentions, a perception on my own terms seems unavoidable.

Let me explain this by considering the methodological problem of the conceptual space in which we place religions.

The fact of religious pluralism and interreligious dialogue can be acknowledged in two different ways:

Approach I (supra- or metareligious; objectivism): There is a neutral space with respect to religions: no religion is distinguished, no tradition is normative. An objective perspective exists from which we perceive religions.

Approach II (from within a specific religion; subjectivism): No neutral space exists since there can be only a particular religion or tradition-specific visions of the whole scene, the panorama of religions.

Approach I is natural for every scientific study of religion. One assumes a sociological, psychological, comparative, or just common-sense perspective. Rationalist and philosophical approaches also belong here. On the other hand, Approach I, when applied to various theoretical visions, is seen by modern humanities as illusory, and the uncovering of particular assumptions and prejudgments, necessarily rooted in a tradition, makes inevitable something like Approach II. Although postmodern attitude is often too extreme, denying any objectivity, it certainly does apply to religious traditions, visions, and truths. Thus, "there simply does not exist any universal (or metareligious) standpoint from which one can stand outside the different religions in order to look down on and evaluate them all."[15] This is not to say, however, that we are doomed to dwell in separate cells of a cultural-linguistic prison. With effort, a degree of understanding is possible; and with more effort and good will, even more understanding is possible.

To understand religions one must be religious somehow. Now, one cannot be just religious, that is, religious "in general." One must be religious according to a specific tradition. Even if one is far from Orthodoxy, nobody invents religion for oneself. One adopts a tradition, or perhaps adapts a tradition, and possibly more than one tradition. It is important, therefore, to know how a given religion views other religions. Although traditional approaches are usually far from being adequate and often present caricatures of other religions, one can try to represent another religion using the concepts of one's own religion, without violating a modern dialogical attitude. Indeed, using familiar concepts of our tradition is usually the only available approach. Some exceptional individuals can know two traditions, but each of us knows in depth only one's own tradition! If done with care and an awareness of its limitations, we can, in our terms, understand others through a reinterpretation. This approach after all is an approach that helps us create a proper Christian theology of Judaism or Jewish theology of Christianity. Thus, the step from Approach I to Approach II can be fruitful. For sure, this movement can illuminate things invisible from the outside, as is seen in the aforementioned Rabbinic explanation of the shape of *vayikra*, which ignored the objectivistic textual criticism.

To begin an understanding of an unknown subject one should try to study it making as few assumptions as possible. Thus, those who adopt the objectivist approach make an important first step and abandon their particular standpoint in order to explore the meaning of religions. Although this is necessary, I do not believe it is enough. A second step is necessary, namely, adopting some particularistic view in accordance with Approach II. The following examples explain my point well.

John Hick is perhaps the best know advocate of religious pluralism. In one of his latest books, *The Fifth Dimension*,[16] he operates wholly within Approach I. He basically adopts scientific rationalism, along with an acceptance of the spiritual realm or "signals of transcendence." He is sympathetic to great religions, but he inevitably flirts with a reductionist, suprareligious position. He assumes that the essence of all religions is the same, and it is precisely he who is expressing it. He assumes that he sees the elephant, and each religion sees only a part of it. However, this is an arrogant view, a suprareligious one, and his mystical understanding of transcendence is hardly neutral. It is one possible view that has been, in fact, influenced by Far Eastern traditions.

What authors step from Approach I to Approach II? One such author is Jacques Dupuis, who, in his book *Christianity and the Religions: From Confrontation to Dialogue*,[17] provides an interpretation of Christology that makes possible acceptance of other religions as ways to redemption. His thinking remains Christocentric but pushes the inclusivist approach to its limits. From a Jewish perspective, Irving Greenberg has also taken this second step (he is not without predecessors). In his essays, collected in *For the Sake of Heaven and Earth*,[18] he takes the concept of covenant with God and presents an expanded vision of plurality of covenants, which enables one to affirm Christianity and possibly other religions. Both Dupuis and Greenberg are among the most passionate theologians of pluralism, but rather than seeking a common denominator, they try to develop their own theologies in the way that can support pluralism and dialogue.

Another example of a fruitful step to Approach II is specifically Jewish. Kabbalah provides schemes for understanding various phenomena. Marc-Alain Ouaknin[19] quotes Rabbi Eli Munk and uses the concept of columns made of *sephirot* to describe major world religions. The three columns are: *chesed* (composed of *chokhmah, chesed, netzach*), or love, on the right; *din* (composed of *binah, gevurah, hod*), or justice, on the left; and *tiferet* (composed of *keter, tiferet, yesod, malkhut*), or harmony, in the middle. Christianity emphasized *chesed*, Islam *din*, and Buddhism *tiferet*, the middle way. It is an interesting picture that provides an insight into religions. What is more, it is not necessarily an expression of superiority. Although Judaism is perceived as trying to harmonize all three columns, Ouaknin says that each of the religions enables its adherents first to reach divinity, and that, Judaism is also in danger of losing the balance, that is, the proper appreciation of all columns.

To me, the most interesting example of a particular religious approach attempting to understand another religion's mystery is a Jewish perception of Jesus. I once realized that many of the Christian statements about Jesus that seemed to me ungraspable, strange, meaningless become perfectly understandable and even natural when I make a certain translation of them into Judaism. Briefly, Jesus is Torah. Jesus can be understood from the Jewish perspective as possessing the qualities Torah has in the Jewish tradition. Think of the text from the Gospel of John where Jesus is described as "the way, the truth, and the life"

(14:6). Of course, this is exactly how we describe the Torah! Now, I have not become a Christian believer: I would not say that Jesus is Torah to me. I just say that he functions in a similar way in another framework. I am not saying that I have uncovered a historical truth about Jesus. I do not claim I understand the mystery of Christianity as Christians do. Still, I find the parallel strikingly useful and positive. With whomever I share it, and I have seen others expressing the same insight, the reaction is always one of interest and a feeling of understanding. Extensions of this comparison may be possible. During our meeting in Jerusalem, in June 2007, Jim Heft said how he understood dogmatic statements: dogmas are not primarily explanations but protections of the truth of faith. This reminds me of the role that "fence around Torah" plays in traditional Judaism. Dogmas about incarnation would then be like the fence around the mystery of Christ.

The preceding examples show that the step from Approach I to II seems necessary. But it is not the final step. Sooner or later we must use some objective approach again. We agreed that we are not locked in isolated cells. We naturally try to find a common ground, or make a step to Approach I. After all, this is not unexpected because there is a common natural space (we as animals), and a common secular space (we as human individuals). Dangers of the just-mentioned approaches are obvious: naturalism (we are essentially only animals) and extreme liberalism (we are only individuals). This realization again pushes us to Approach II. However, as already mentioned, we cannot remain in the framework of Approach I indefinitely. So we go back and forth.

I can propose a way out of the dilemma of Approach I versus Approach II. I propose a solution as modest as it is unstable. Indeed, a certain instability itself is taken as inevitable, as a fact of life. What results is an inevitable *oscillation* between the two approaches, which reminds us of the humiliating oscillation in the philosophy of mathematics mentioned earlier.

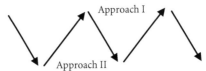

To give a final example, there have been many attempts to reduce the Jewish presence to one sociological category. Yet no simplified solution will do. Who are Jews? Are they only members of the Jewish religion? No, nonreligious Jews also remain Jews. Are they then just a people? No, one can formally convert to Judaism. From the traditional Jewish perspective, Jews form something like a family. Then are Jews just a family? Well, we might answer, Jews are a family with mission. We are faced with either a reduction to one of the general categories or the acknowledgment that there is no proper category and that Jews, as a group, form a specific entity, a *sui generis* category. From Approach I we pass to Approach II. Although this second option is much better, we know that we can't avoid comparisons of this unique group with other religious, national, and ethnic groups. Thus, when considering the problem of who participates in the dialogue—Jews, Judaism, Jewry?—we try to operate on an objective level. We return to using Approach I. When we become dissatisfied with Approach I, we move back to the particularistic view. And so, the dialectic continues.

▨ THE MEANING OF ISRAEL

For a long time the Church claimed that the new Israel replaced the old one. This view has changed among Catholics and many Protestants, although it is debatable to what extent. The Muslims never thought about themselves as Israel, but did believe that they replaced the original Israel. Despite the unpleasant history, Jews should cope with the problem how to take into account the others' belief in being in a special relation with the God of Israel. To take a most daring step, we can ask if they can be seen, in some sense, as Israel? To handle the question requires a specifically Jewish humility, one that relates to the core of Jewish beliefs. The aim is not to compromise them, but rather to open oneself to other religions.

Rambam wrote that those who accept and practice the Noahide laws are worthy to join "all Israel" in the world to come. Theoretically this can apply to everyone. For Rambam it applied to Christians; maybe, comments David Novak, only to Christians. They would be "the only Gentiles who are part of the transcendent trajectory Jews see as the ultimate end of all human striving."[20] This view is limited, not only because non-Christians, specifically Muslims, are not included, but also for another reason. Christians are seen just as an example of a category, and not as a living community of faith. They are treated on our terms. This can be related to the inclusivist theory of truth of religious theses according to which I have the whole truth, and others have only portions of the truth. This makes room for other religions, but they are looked down upon. This is quite common today among Jews, Christians, and others. Although better than denial, and perhaps laudable in former times, it seems to me clearly inadequate in our own time.

The same inadequacy can be seen in the phrase *preparatio messianica*, used by Heschel[21] to describe the attitudes of some rabbis in previous centuries, like Yehuda Halevi, Rambam, Jacob Emden, and others who were open to the value of Christianity. This can be seen as better than the attitude expressed by the traditional Church formula *preparatio evangelica*, because that classical formula denied any essential role for Jews in the Christian era. Heschel's phrase gives Christianity a role. Nevertheless, it is again an expression of readiness to admit that the other is helpful in the process of bringing all of us closer to *my* truth. This means a relatively positive but insufficiently respectful attitude toward the other. It is not good enough for the genuine modern dialogue.

Among more daring contemporary attempts, the one by the already mentioned Irving Greenberg is especially noteworthy. He talks about the plurality of covenants: "Implicit in pluralism is the recognition that there are limits in my truth that leave room for others."[22] He also makes a stronger claim: "When Christians carry on their covenanted mission, are they members of the house of Israel?...only Christians (although possibly also Muslims) may be deemed to be members of the people Israel, even as they practice differing religions than Jewry does."[23] David Rosen has also expressed a similar belief.

Levinas explicitly extends the meaning of Israel. Israel is defined, he says, not ethnically but by having "the dignity of being liberated by God himself."[24] Commenting on the work of Haim of Volozhin, Levinas explains his use of the term *Israel* in a most universalizing way: "the souls of Israel" are "all the souls of humans authentically human." And again: "Humanity already human with unlimited responsibility, called Israel."[25] An even more all-encompassing statement was made by André Chouraqui; according to him, everyone who listens to the word of Biblical God and fulfills it is "from Israel," and the "New Israel" of today embraces not only all Jews, Christians, and Muslims, but also everyone who listens and follows "the will of peace and love."[26] Although obviously nobly motivated, his declaration to include virtually everyone is not supported by theological or philosophical considerations. Whether such considerations will be based on the development of the meaning of covenant, as does Greenberg, or the insight into the status of liberation and the nature of responsibility, as did Levinas, or on other ideas, this work is still to be done.

My own conviction is that Christians are in a distinguished relationship to the God of Israel, which makes them specially related to us Jews. I wish Christians and the Church all the best, though I often feel angry at or threatened by the Church and its people. Yet I believe that Christians are our brethren and can be our allies.[27] I guess and hope that Muslims can be allies too, but my personal experiences are too limited to say this with conviction. It is worthwhile, though, to mention that Jakub Szynkiewicz, mufti of the traditional Polish Muslims who have lived in Poland for several centuries, issued in the 1930s a *fatwa* supporting the Zionist goal of establishing a Jewish state in Palestine. When I mentioned that during our meeting in—of all places—Jerusalem, a Muslim participant in the trialogue, Mustafa Abu Sway, asked if this was what Jews, and I in particular, would expect of other Muslims. I was surprised by the question as I did not refer to this *fatwa* as anything else than a curiosity, though certainly one that extends the realm of what the standard wisdom perceives as compatible with Islam. Although I did not expect anything specific, I certainly would be glad, encouraged, and relieved if Muslims could adopt such opinions.

Christians and Muslims believe in the same God as the Jews do. That is, they respect the revelation that formed the Jewish people and the Jewish tradition. In this sense, they are in a relationship with *Hashem* (English translation, God; literally, the Name). Their own traditions were built upon it, so they have their own revelations, alien to us, that become false statements when transferred to the Jewish framework. In their own frameworks they serve their purpose; they give foundations to Christian and Muslim faith.

Leaving aside, for lack of sufficient familiarity and knowledge, the otherwise key issue of Islam, I have a definite opinion on Christianity. It is a crucial challenge for Jewish thought today to take into more positive account the plurality of religions and especially the role of Christianity. What is the meaning of *Israel*? We Jews and Christians are both chosen—but not in the same way. Jews are Israel—to the extent they participate in the tradition. Christians form another layer of the entity known as Israel. There is still no accepted way of describing this situation;

there are attempts to do better than to use the old Christian term *New Israel,* which has negative associations—for example the "extended" Israel, "second" Israel, "associated Israel" (Michael Wyschogrod's term). Maybe a better term will emerge in the future—not just the term but, I hope, a whole framework and theory making this "extension" possible while avoiding contradictions and allowing for total respect for all the sides involved. I believe this can be done in a way involving the awareness of both the epistemic ignorance and the covenantal certainty.

■ Notes

1. A. J. Heschel, "No Religion Is an Island," in *No Religion Is an Island,* eds. H. Kasimow and B. Sherwin, (Orbis Books, Maryknoll 1991), p. 15.

2. Rae Langton, *Kantian Humility, Our Ignorance of Things in Themselves* (New York: Oxford University Press, 2001). He says, "this humility has its roots in some plausible philosophical beliefs: an empiricist belief in the receptivity of human knowledge and a metaphysical belief in the irreducibility of relational properties."

3. Translation after the Hertz Pentateuch.

4. Joseph Telushkin, *A Code of Jewish Ethics,* vol. 1 (New York: Bell Tower; 2006), p. 210.

5. David Novak in *Christianity in Jewish Terms,* eds. T. Frymer–Kensky, D. Novak, P. Ochs, D. Sandmel, M. Signer (Boulder, CO: Westview Press, 2000), p. 4.

6. David Roskies, in eds. Cohen and Mendes-Flohr, eds., *Contemporary Jewish Religious Thought,* (New York: Free Press), p. 582.

7. These topics are very strongly expressed in Emmanuel Levinas, *Difficile Liberté* (Sean Hand, trans., *Difficult Freedom, Essays on Judaism* (London: The Athlone Press, 1990). Judaism is presented there as especially suited for this kind of maturity.

8. Paul F. Knitter, *Jesus and Other Names* (Oxford, England: Oneworld, 1996), p. 63.

9. Ibid., p. 71.

10. Expression of Fritz Rotschild in his Introduction to Heschel's *Between God and Man,* (New York: Harper and Row, 1959), p. 25.

11. "Judaisme et kénose," in *A l'heure des nations,* (Paris: Les éditions de Minuit, 1988), p. 134.

12. Translation in the Artscroll Chumash, the Stone Edition.

13. I am grateful to Yale Reisner for studying the fragment with me.

14. Alan Morinis, *Everyday Holiness, The Jewish Spiritual Path of Mussar,* (Boston: Trumpeter, 2007), p. 49.

15. Paul F. Knitter, *Jesus,* p. 25.

16. John Hick, *The Fifth Dimension: An Exploration of the Spiritual,* (Oxford, England: Oneworld Publications, 1999).

17. Jacques Dupuis, *Christianity and the Religions: From Confrontation to Dialogue,* (Maryknoll, NY: Orbis Books, 2001). See also his *Toward a Christian Theology of Religious Pluralism,* (Maryknoll, NY: Orbis Books 1997).

18. Irving Greenberg, *For the Sake of Heaven and Earth: The New Encounter Between Judaism and Christianity,* (Philadelphia: Jewish Publication Society, 2004).

19. Marc-Alain Ouaknin, *Mystères de la kabale,* (Paris: Editions Assouline, 2003); I quote after the Polish translation published by Cyklady 2006, pp. 208–210.

20. Novak refers to *Mishne Torah,* Melachim 8.11; see T. Frymer Kensky, D. Novak, P. Ochs, D. Sandmel, M. Signer, eds., *Christianity in Jewish Terms* (Boulder, CO: Westview Press 2000), p. 118.

21. In, H. Kasimow and B. Sherwin, eds., *No Religion Is an Island* (Orbis Books, Maryknoll 1991), p. 19.

22. "Judaism and Christianity: Covenants of Redemption," in T. Frymer Kensky, D. Novak, P. Ochs, D. Sandmel, M. Signer, eds., *Christianity in Jewish Terms* (Boulder, CO: Westview Press, 2000), p. 157.

23. Ibid., 158.

24. Emmanuel Levinas, *Difficile liberté* (Paris : Albin Michel, 1976), p. 112.

25. Emmanuel Levinas, "Judaisme et kénose," in *A l'heure des nations* (Paris:Les éditions de Minuit, 1988), pp. 143 and 146.

26. André Chouraqui, *Les dix commendements aujourd'hui*, (Paris: Robert Lafonts, 2000); the quote (in my translation) is after the Polish version translation of 2002, p. 243.

27. A public expression of this feeling is best seen in the Jewish declaration *Dabru Emet* of September 2000, signed by well over two hundred Jewish intellectuals, including myself. Interestingly, its points were almost entirely anticipated by Abraham Joshua Heschel (see my article "Abraham Joshua Heschel and the Declaration *Dabru Emet*," *Shofar* 26, no 1, 2007: 154–168.)

14   Saving *Dominus Iesus*

Daniel Madigan

My involvement with interreligious dialogue began in a rather indirect way. Since my days as a Jesuit novice I had been looking forward to an academic career in theology. I imagined doing doctoral studies in Europe and returning to Australia to teach. A couple of years before ordination I spent a summer in India, most of the time working with Mother Teresa's brothers taking care of people who suffered from leprosy. A question put to me by one of them just before I left pretty much changed my life. He asked when I would be back. I explained that I probably would not be back – perhaps I could drop in for a visit on my way from Australia to Europe some time, but basically this was "goodbye." That response of mine troubled me for some time, and all the more when people at home started treating my summer experience as though it were a hunting trophy – the booty of a visit to another world. Yet, if my experience had taught me anything, it was that there is only one world and the whole of that world is, in one sense or another, home.

In place of that long dreamed-of career in theology I responded to a request for volunteers to work in Pakistan. Actually I was secretly hoping to avoid the library and student centre which were our main work there, and wanted to find some more leprosy patients to serve. For me that was more a work of the heart than of the mind and appealed to me more. Fortunately for them, virtually no Punjabi (I was in Lahore) suffers from that wretched disease. Inevitably I found myself much more involved in intellectual work – precisely what I had been fleeing when I went to Pakistan – and it was then that I first became involved in interreligious dialogue. After a few years I was supposed to move to China, but at the last minute the Jesuit Superior General asked me to do a doctorate in Islamic studies in order to continue in this field of Muslim-Christian relations. The academic life had caught up with me after all!

Two elements of that story, however, have shaped the way I see my engagement in dialogue. First, there is only one world; our tendency to divide it into separate "worlds" is merely a pretext for treating some people as less than human or at least as irreducibly other. Second, the heart is essential to dialogue. It is not simply an intellectual exercise but has an indispensable affective element.

What have I learned from other religions? I'm not sure I could say. From other *believers*, I've learned great deal. The last 25 years of engagement, mostly with Muslims but also with Jews, have given me a much better grasp of the specificity of Christian faith. It has been their challenges and tough questions that have forced me to take a harder look at those specifically Christian beliefs—original sin, incarnation, crucifixion, trinity—in order to see whether it was possible to develop a personally more convincing understanding of them, or whether they might need to be jettisoned (as some theologians would claim), or at least soft-pedaled.

In my opinion the biggest issue we face is the question of the Other—especially in the case of the dialogue among Jews, Christians and Muslims, because we are contesting the same space and offering broadly divergent readings of the same tradition. It is an old question in some respects, but it has a new urgency at present and it needs to be asked not only in a theological key but at the intersection of theology, politics, economics and anthropology. The struggle is to find a new first-person plural—that is, a new way of saying "we," "us" and "our" that is not predicated on an excluded "they," "them" and "their." At the same time it cannot be simply a first-person plural that denies difference and refuses to acknowledge otherness.

Along with this goes the question of the Third. We have become obsessed with the idea of two "civilizations" facing off against each other, and, though the casualties are many, they are easily enough counted. But in the process we have forgotten that most of the world's daily fatalities—too numerous to count—have nothing to do with that conflict which we think defines our world. The children who die in their thousands every day of hunger and treatable diseases; the seemingly endless victims of civil and ethnic strife that continues unabated. The question is whether we can give up facing off against each other and begin facing up to the more urgent issues.

There have been few ecclesial pronouncements in last 40 years that have received as much attention and provoked as much reaction as the 2000 statement *Dominus Iesus*, "on the unicity and salvific universality of Jesus Christ and the Church." One would have to go back almost the whole of that period to *Humanae Vitae*, published in 1968, to find something so strongly contested. The controversy surrounding *Humanae Vitae* is comprehensible, given the practical importance of the subject matter and the hopes that had been raised for a new and different authoritative word on the issue of contraception. The reaction to *Dominus Iesus*, on the other hand, is more intriguing, especially the reaction from within the Church. In one sense it could be said to have been reassuring news for those on the "inside" that they are indeed on the right track and safe in their salvation. In fact, several groups did welcome its uncompromising affirmations. Yet it did not strike others as being particularly good news.

The statement itself claimed merely to be reaffirming certain fixed points of Christian teaching with regard to other believers in order to allow the necessary theological work on these complex questions to be done within a more secure framework grounded in the tradition. However, various groups found offensive, for subtly different reasons, the apparent claim to exclusivity, or to what seemed at least an overly hegemonic inclusiveness. The responses were not irenic, but neither was the document itself. The originators of *Dominus Iesus* who spoke to the press at its launching made no secret of how offensive they found what they considered to be the relativism and indifferentism of many current theologies of religions.[1]

A detailed analysis of the entirety of *Dominus Iesus* and the difficulties it raises is well beyond the scope of this chapter, and in any case has already been undertaken by many others in the intervening years.[2] Given the context of our project on intellectual humility, this paper focuses on the question of inside and outside, inclusion and exclusion, certainty and doubt. One of the characteristics of the truly learned person is a hesitancy to be restricted by pre-defined limits along with a suspicion of differences too clearly delineated. The more we learn, the more difficult it becomes to define, and to be confined by, clear boundaries—between, for example, cultures, nations, religions, languages, styles. Yet at the same time, there arises the temptation to think oneself universal, to forget one's own rootedness and, therefore, the limitations of one's own viewpoint.

One of the great flaws in much writing on religious pluralism is that it has presumed it is possible to theologize from a point outside the various confessional commitments to which religious people are given. From this vantage point the "truly wise" are able to abstract the essence of all religion and judge particular instances of religious faith against the standard they have devised. Far too many books on the theology of religions trot out the story of the blind men and the elephant, and of course the author poses as the one fully-sighted person, who can enlighten us dullards who are too dim to realize we only have hold of a tail or an ear, and are mistaking it for the whole elephant. When it comes to theology of religions we can only do it from within our particular religious commitments or refusals.

The pluralist theologians criticized by the authors of *Dominus Iesus* are taken to task for the claim some make to be able to discern and abstract the constitutive elements of "religion" from the concrete particular religions, and then to assess individual traditions by these abstracted criteria. This may seem to those theologians a communal exercise in religious humility—de-centering their own and others' traditions—but it takes little account of the inherent difficulty of finding a privileged neutral point from which to undertake this task. The end result of their abstracting is not the Platonic form of religion, but just another particular religious vision that must take its place alongside all the others rather than set itself up in judgment over them.

Many have asked themselves whether *Dominus Iesus* itself is not guilty of the same thing, and so whether this just amounts to an argument between two parties, neither of which has solid ground on which to stand. The difference, however, is that *DI* makes no secret of its prior religious commitment—how could it, coming from the Congregation for the Doctrine of the Faith?—and it makes no claim to stand outside the hurly-burly of competing religious truth claims. The difficulty is that it lends itself, perhaps unwittingly, to that kind of bird's-eye-view reading. As a clearly disciplinary document, it has a certain forthright style which may be judged more or less appropriate for addressing the members of one's own tradition, but which is surely out of place in the very public forum in which the declaration was launched and deliberately disseminated. Though it was addressed in the first place to bishops and theologians, it was made clear in the covering letter to the former that the Congregation did not want this document filtered and thus weakened by the latter before it reached the public. It seems even to have wanted to give to its Catholic public guidelines with which to police theologians on these issues, and to members of other traditions a clear warning that certain trends in theology of religions and ecumenism were not to be taken as "gospel," but rather that they represented only the opinions of theologians, some of whom may have abandoned certain essentials of the Catholic faith.

This paper begins by identifying some elements of the language, presuppositions and methods of the document that together have created such a strong impression of arrogance, and then attempts to re-express some of *DI*'s central concerns in a way that affirms their importance, but with less of what has seemed to some people its confident swagger. The reflection is informed particularly by the experience over the last few years of reading, together with Muslims, Jews and Hindus, the several ecclesial documents (including *Dominus Iesus*) that since the time of the Council have grappled with the question of dialogue and mission. It is an exercise to be recommended. It is not always easy reading our insider documents in the presence of the "outsiders" of whom they speak, but it clarifies many things and teaches us a new hermeneutic.

■ HUMILITY: INTELLECTUAL AND MORAL

Dominus Iesus begins problematically in its very first sentence, choosing as its opening quotation from Scripture the disputed ending of Mark's Gospel, "Go into the whole world and proclaim the Gospel to every creature. He who believes and is baptized will be saved; he who does not believe will be condemned" (Mk 16:15–16). Uncompromising words of dubious authenticity are hardly an auspicious beginning, especially since the key concepts of believing and being saved require, and over the centuries have received, substantial scrutiny in Christian theology. The citation of these verses seems to throw down a gauntlet right from the outset. The quotation from Matthew that followed would have been sufficient for the purpose at hand: "All power in heaven and on earth has been given to me. Go therefore and teach all nations, baptizing them in the name of the Father, and of the Son, and of the Holy Spirit, teaching them to observe all that I have commanded you. And behold, I am with you always, until the end of the world" (Mt 28:18–20).[3]

At the June 2006 meeting of this research group in Cambridge Massachusetts, David Burrell identified the document's Achilles heel as being in paragraph 2. After using the words of the Nicene-Constantinopolitan Creed in paragraph 1 to express the elements of the Christian faith, the authors go straight on to claim, with disarming self-assurance, that "in the course of the centuries, the Church has proclaimed and witnessed with fidelity to the Gospel of Jesus." Proclaimed, yes; but witnessed to with fidelity? If this were true, those past centuries would have been radically different and our own century surely unrecognizable. This is not simply a minor flaw. Ethical humility and intellectual humility are intimately related. Christian theology must always begin, as does Christian worship, with a *mea culpa* and a *Kyrie eleison*. The declaration throughout seems unable to comprehend that the substantial moral failures of the Christian community raise serious questions about the truth claims we make. Had the Christian community, including its officials, a better moral record, we might find a more receptive audience when we speak of the importance of the Church in God's saving plan and activity. Yet this claim to have witnessed faithfully throughout the centuries, so out of touch not only with history but also with present-day reality, only serves to make what follows seem more arrogant and monopolistic.[4]

There is a recent tendency in magisterial documents to draw rather too strong a distinction between the Church and her "children." In the context of John Paul II's famous *nostra culpa* during the Jubilee of 2000 the distinction was insisted upon, lest it be thought that somehow the Church itself were responsible for these sins of the past rather than just individuals who had failed to heed her always sound teaching. This ideal Church is sinless and can never be accused of failure or error.[5] The team that gave us that dubious distinction is the same one that gave us *Dominus Iesus*. They apparently do not realize the extent to which this approach undermines the credibility of the Christian community. Credibility comes not from being perfect but from being honest.

It is true that the greater moral obligation placed on Christians is acknowledged, yet the judgment of which the declaration speaks, quoting *Lumen Gentium par.* 14, seems only to refer to the final judgment: "If [Christians] fail to respond in thought, word, and deed to that grace [of Christ], not only shall they not be saved, but they shall be more severely judged." A severe judgment on the Church is already being made by those who, while seeking God with all good will, are scandalized by the behavior of Christians. The "children of the Church" in the meantime are said to be in an "exalted position" as compared with the "gravely deficient situation" of the members of other religions (*DI, par.* 22).

■ PROPRIETARY LANGUAGE

A sense of monopoly comes through in much of the language that characterizes this area of theological discourse. The discussion of the questions of truth and salvation over the centuries has had the ring of a property dispute about it. Who owns the "territory" of salvation? What do you have to do to get shares in it? If you missed the initial public offering, is there still a chance to buy in? Does one agency have an "exclusive" on it, or can anyone negotiate your purchase? What makes much Christian, especially Catholic, talk about salvation seem so arrogant is that it seems so proprietary: *It's ours. We own it. If you want some, you have to get it from us.* There are several elements in *Dominus Iesus* that reinforce this sense, and there is little explicitly to lessen it, except for some important observations and clarifications made at its presentation.[6] It is unfortunate that these refinements could not have been made explicit in the document itself.

The use of such phrases as "Christian truth" (par. 4), "Christian revelation" (par. 4), and even "Christian salvation" (par. 9) may be just shorthand, but it seems to betray a sense of ownership. Alternatives like "the truth that Christians see expressed in Christ," "the revelation Christians perceive in Christ" and "salvation we believe God has effected in Christ" would maintain a certain respectful distance between Christ and Christians. Christ is not "ours." He is not simply one of us. Christians do not possess or control access to him, though sometimes our language would suggest so. On the contrary, we are his; and what Christians are proclaiming is that all people are Christ's—and that that should be good news for them. What tends to come across, however, is that Christians *have* God, or even that God is *one of us*, and that if any one else also wants contact with God, that person has no choice but to become one of us.

The question is, are the specific and particular claims and offers of Christianity (and of other religions for that matter) necessarily proprietorial or is there another way of reading them? This raises the even more fundamental question of whether it is even possible to make truth claims with humility, or whether they necessarily have to be abandoned as inherently arrogant? These are questions to which we will return.

■ FAITH OR FACT?

Given that it defines itself as a "declaration," perhaps it is not surprising that *Dominus Iesus* is characterized throughout by a markedly declarative style. Yet one must wonder whether such a style is appropriate for the multi-religious readership that was clearly foreseen by the method of the document's publication. Its declarations can seem more like claims of entitlement rather than professions of faith, and in this lies one of its major difficulties. Of course, to the writers they are acts of faith and not simply statements of fact. The word "believe" hovers over the whole document, though it is rarely explicit apart from the disciplinary statements about what is to be *firmly believed* (pars. 5, 7, 10, 11, 13, 14, 16, 20). The weakness of a clear distinction between statements of faith and claims about facts can been seen in a passage from par. 15:

> From the beginning, the community of believers has recognized in Jesus a salvific value such that he alone, as Son of God made man, crucified and risen, by the mission received from the Father and in the power of the Holy Spirit, bestows revelation (cf. *Mt* 11:27) and divine life (cf. *Jn* 1:12; 5:25–26; 17:2) to all humanity and to every person.

So far, so good: the document is enunciating what the community of believers has recognized. The mention of "all humanity" and "every person" indicates that the divine life offered in Christ is for all, not particularly for Christians. However, as the passage proceeds, another kind of language enters in:

> In this sense, one can and must say that Jesus Christ has a significance and a value for the human race and its history, which are unique and singular, proper to him alone, exclusive, universal, and absolute.

What is the meaning of "must" in that sentence? It is a disciplinary statement for Catholic believers, but it can seem as though it is a claim to the logical necessity of what comes after. The piling up of maximalizing adjectives—unique, singular, alone, exclusive, universal, absolute—seems excessive and is certainly not justified by what precedes it. It has the effect of narrowing the universality recognized by the early community of believers even while affirming it. It is a universality now controlled and made exclusive. It confuses things that can only really be known from observation—uniqueness and singularity—with what is affirmed on the basis of faith—universality and absoluteness. The next sentence makes explicit the slide from profession of faith to statement of "fact":

> Jesus is, in fact, the Word of God made man for the salvation of all.

Yet the document then immediately returns to the language of faith:
In expressing this consciousness of faith, the Second Vatican Council teaches:

'The Word of God, through whom all things were made, was made flesh, so that as perfect man he could save all men and sum up all things in himself.'

This slippage between faith and fact characterizes the document overall and arises, perhaps, from a lack of experience on the part of the authors in presenting the Christian faith beyond the Christian community. It may be acceptable for an internal discourse to be declarative and disciplinary, and to use shorthand expressions for those in the know. However, that same kind of discourse when also directed to people of other traditions creates more an impression of pretentious overconfidence, rather than of the love that should characterize any account of the truth that Christians claim to have glimpsed in Christ and of the hope they draw from it.

What we are proposing is not simply "fact" but faith—that is, a particular reading of what we take (also on faith) to be "the facts." The recognition of this is at the basis of the intellectual humility we try to maintain in each other's presence. There is, therefore, a particular grammar and style appropriate to expressing one's faith and the faith of one's community to someone who does not share it. For example, such discourse makes ample use of verbs like "believe" and "perceive" to lead into any declaration that contains the verb "to be."

Apart from its disciplinary tone, *Dominus Iesus* is framed in an insider's language inappropriate for a broader readership. Christian theology, so used to an internal discussion, can often forget that what we proclaim is not simply a kind of rationally-based, natural religion that would require only a few simple logical steps to demonstrate. Though the language of trinity, incarnation, crucifixion, redemption and communion with the divine may be commonplace enough for insiders, we need to remember Paul's warning (1 Cor 1:23) that it can seem to others absurd and even scandalous. More than once Muslims have commented to me that these are concepts not so much of theology as of mysticism. We cannot presume simply to state our faith baldly and expect it to be understood and accepted.[7] The faith we affirm in our creeds and our theologies is not a solution to a knotty theological problem, but a rather a mystery we have committed ourselves to living and exploring.

Gerald O'Collins and the late Jacques Dupuis have already dealt extensively with the weakness of *DI*'s position on "the definitive and complete character of the revelation in Christ." This claim to completeness and absoluteness comes across not just as monopolistic, that is, as a claim to have cornered the market on something of which others stand in need. It also appears a rather rash pretension to have completely appropriated what God has revealed. There seems to be little of the sense, so often underlined in other magisterial documents in recent years, of the long process of grasping and appropriating what God has revealed. The terms "absolute," "complete," "definitive" and "full" can give much too static a sense of revelation as a transaction completed rather than as a relationship established. Other traditions are also seen in a static way. The "rays of truth" and "seeds of the Word" identified there do not seem to be thought of as still living and productive.

Rather they have reached the limits of their usefulness—faded rays, shrivelled seeds—and have stopped short of effecting a real recognition and flowering of the truth of God's Word.

It is true that Christians are not awaiting some further revelation of God not available to us in the Christ event, but we can be helped by the activity of the Spirit beyond the Church, and by the presence of "seeds of the Word" in other traditions to realize ever more fully what has already been expressed in Christ, but not yet fully appropriated. As *DI* insists, there is no separate economy of the Word unrelated to the Word-made-flesh. From this it follows that there will be a resonance between the activity of the Logos in the other religious traditions and what has been revealed in Christ. In those resonances, the Spirit, who Jesus promised would lead his followers into all truth, may be calling Christians through the other religions to a deeper penetration into the mystery of Christ, who we believe reveals for us the mystery of God. In that sense, other religious traditions are not complementary or alternative truths—*DI* strongly rejects such a notion (pars. 14, 21)—but can assist Christians toward a fuller appreciation of the truth. If, as *Gaudium et Spes* par. 16 maintains, other traditions are to be considered a *praeparatio evangelica*, then surely they can also prepare Christians to hear the Gospel more thoroughly.

■ ONE SIZE FITS ALL

Another aspect of the language of *Dominus Iesus* is that it takes a reductionist approach to other religious traditions. There is no recognition at all that these traditions fall into different categories with relation to Christianity, and that in any case each tradition has its own specificity. A great deal of theological writing on religions has the same defect. Generalizations about "religions" too easily lead either to a blanket rejection or to an uncritical affirmation of extremely varied and often mutually incompatible religious visions. *DI*'s most notable failure here was the lack of any acknowledgement at all of the special status of Judaism, given the matrix of biblical religion from which Christianity and rabbinic Judaism both emerged. In fact, there is a rather strange passage in par. 13 in which the document speaks of the way in which the first Christians "encountered the Jewish people"—as if the first Christians were not themselves Jews! Jewish reactions to the way their faith was treated in the declaration were greeted at first with incomprehension, and then with what has seemed to many a compensatory statement published on the front page of *Osservatore Romano* the following December. In it Cardinal Ratzinger affirms that "the faith witnessed to by the Hebrew Bible...is to us not merely another religion, but is the foundation of our own faith."[8]

■ DEFICIENCIES, GRAVE AND OTHERWISE

DI spoke rather bluntly of the deficiencies of other religions, and other ecclesial communities. "Gravely deficient situation" (par. 22) has probably been its most remembered and repeated phrase. Again, although the language seems rather impolite, the point still stands. Religious communities, especially those that see themselves as part of the same family, almost by definition see other faith communities as being in a more or less "gravely deficient situation." Muslims by and large think Christians are in a deficient position because we lack the original Gospel text they believe was given to Jesus, and because our monotheism seems to be severely compromised by Trinitarian faith. Many Christian churches would think that the fact that the Roman Catholic Church does not ordain women, that it has an extremely centralized and hierarchical structure, and that it gives such prominence to Tradition alongside Scripture are all deficiencies. Buddhists are of the opinion that most people are too attached to the illusion of the permanence and stability of their personal identity, so surely any religion that teaches such a notion suffers from a deficiency that is impeding the liberation of its members. The list could go on.

Not all differences are considered deficiencies, of course. However, if we place a high value on something and consider it essential, then we will naturally identify its lack as a deficiency. It is essential that we learn to speak honestly to one another about what we consider important and even fundamental to being human before God, and that we develop the capacity to hear the criticism of what others perceive as our deficiencies. These are two indispensable aspects of dialogue.

The particular problem of *DI* in this matter is that it claimed that those outside the Catholic Church are "objectively speaking" (par. 22) in a deficient situation. The question of objectivity here is surely more complex than the authors presumed. Once we have defined our terms and established our frame of reference, then what we observe and affirm may appear to us to be objective. However, that claim to objectivity ignores the subjective nature of the choice of defining framework. It is not subjective in the sense that it is individualistic, for the faith that underlies it is communal, and is defined within the structure of the believing community. However, even though it is based on communal experience and shared conviction, it is still faith, not simply fact. There is another point at which *DI* speaks of "the Primacy, which, according to the will of God, the Bishop of Rome *objectively* has and exercises over the entire Church" (par. 17, emphasis mine). One has to wonder how the authors could justify the word "objectively" in such a context. Given that they quote in support only two authorities—Vatican I and Vatican II—it is clear that this "objective" affirmation is a statement of Catholic faith not of observable fact.

■ SALVATION AND THE CHURCH—WHERE EXACTLY IS "OUTSIDE"?

In its reaffirmation of fixed points of Catholic doctrine, *Dominus Iesus* was judged by many to be returning to the older discourse of *extra ecclesiam nulla salus*. This may be an unfair judgment, since the declaration is quite explicit in its acceptance of the consensus that has emerged in the Church over recent centuries that visible membership of the Catholic Church is not necessary for salvation.[9] Let us examine briefly the processes by which this change in consensus has come about.

Writing to the Archbishop of Boston in 1949, in the case of Fr. Leonard Feeney, S.J., The Holy Office asserted, "Among those things that the Church has always preached and will never cease to preach is also that infallible pronouncement by which we are taught 'outside the Church there is no salvation.' "[10] Now, there is an old joke that outlines the unmistakeable signs that a novel opinion is on the way to being accepted as official Church teaching—a series of successively stricter warnings and reprimands against the errant opinion is followed eventually by an exemplary condemnation. Then, not too long after, an authoritative statement endorses the novel opinion beginning with the words, "As the Church has always taught...." The Holy Office of the Inquisition, as it was then still called, was not quite so bold. Nonetheless, having reaffirmed the continuing validity of the old adage *extra ecclesiam nulla salus*,[11] it went on to say, "This dogma is, however, to be understood in the sense in which the Church herself understands it" (DzS 3866). Rather ironically, the Holy Office decided that Fr. Feeney had put *himself* outside the Church—he was excommunicated—by insisting on too rigid an interpretation of that formula, and by resisting attempts to make him, if not see the light, at least bow to authority.[12]

We might wonder whether in the end the Catholic Church is not rather like Lewis Carroll's Humpty Dumpty, who claimed to be able to make words mean whatever he wanted them to, "neither more nor less." The formula has never been officially disavowed, yet there is a long history of interpretation and hedging that tries to avoid its obvious meaning. The last forty years have seen a general (though not absolute) hesitancy to use it in official teaching. Indeed it is not difficult at all to find magisterial texts that affirm precisely the reverse: that outside the Church there *is* indeed salvation.

The hesitation seems to have been provoked more by experience than by deduction. The discovery of the New World rather shook the theological certainties of a Europe that had presumed the Gospel had been heard everywhere and that as a result anyone remaining outside the Church had no excuse to offer. The teaching had in any case been first formulated and mostly used not to damn pagans, but to threaten those who had left the communion (and obedience, let it be added) of the Church and also to discourage those who might think of leaving.[13] The discovery of ever more pagans required some more accommodating interpretation of the idea. "Outside" was much bigger than had been imagined.

Furthermore the discovery that beyond the visible boundaries of the Church there were genuinely loving and faith-filled people—not just among other Christians but also beyond the Christian fold—posed an additional challenge to the doctrine. Limbo was beginning to look as though it might have more inhabitants than heaven or hell.

Two elements have long been used to soften the blow and effectively to shrink the "outside" by moving much of it implicitly inside. The first was the idea of "implicit faith" or of an "implicit desire" (*votum*) to enter the Church. Such implicit faith was sufficient to guarantee a kind of honorary membership of the Church. A person can be said to have implicit faith because she explicitly wants to do what God wills. If she were to be aware of God's hope that she recognize in Jesus Christ the truth about God and join the community of those who do the same, then she would surely do so. Again the Holy Office writing in 1949 to the Archbishop of Boston:

> For someone to obtain eternal salvation it is not always demanded that the person be in fact (*reapse*) incorporated as a member of the Church, but what is absolutely required is

that the person should adhere to it by wish and desire. This wish need not always be explicit, as it is in the case of catechumens, but where someone labours under invincible ignorance God also accepts an implicit wish, as it is called, for it is contained in that good disposition of the soul whereby a person wishes to conform his or her will to the will of God (DzS 3870).

Connected with implicit faith, and mentioned here, is the second element that expanded the reach of salvation and shrank the "outside"—invincible ignorance. This is not just a particular obtuseness—but ignorance in the literal sense of not knowing something, and invincible in the sense that through no fault of one's own there is no possibility of coming to know it. Pius IX, a man surely not known for his doctrinal liberalism or a relativistic approach to the truth, cautioned anyone against being so presumptuous as to set limits to what would qualify as invincible ignorance.[14]

Though it has an arrogant ring to it, invincible ignorance seems to me a more important and useful category than we are accustomed to think. Has the Church ever posed with sufficient seriousness the question of how many people are prevented from knowing what Christians perceive to be the truth about God by the shortcomings of those very people who claim to live by that truth? It may even be that with the passage of years and with ease of communication the number of people for whom the Church itself is the stumbling block is, paradoxically, becoming larger rather than smaller. Invincible ignorance means not just that there is no Mother Angelica on the cable TV, and no *Osservatore Romano* to read, but that for all the preaching and writing and broadcasting, in the end the actions and omissions of Christians speak much more loudly than our words. Talk, finally, is cheap, however widely we may publish it. And those actions that speak so loudly can for some, perhaps for many, be an insurmountable barrier to explicit believing.[15]

■ ALTERNATIVE CENTERS

It is often noted that one of the major theological developments given authoritative expression at Vatican II was the shift from an ecclesiocentric to a christocentric view. This de-centring of the Church has not yet been fully achieved—as anyone who lives in Rome can attest. While we have been working on that shift, "pluralist" theologians have encouraged us to take what they claim is the next logical step in the same positive direction and abandon christocentrism for a theocentric approach. To be anything but theocentric in these pluralist days is to be considered eccentric. Christocentrism is seen as only slightly less arrogant and intolerant than ecclesiocentrism, but the way toward peace, we are confidently told, lies in a general move by all religious communities toward a generic theocentrism, or perhaps toward a regnocentrism—a focus on the values of the Reign of God—but again so generically stated as to give the impression that all religions value more or less the same things.

David Tracy has observed that Christianity is, of course, theocentric rather than christocentric, but that it is at the same time inescapably *christomorphic*.[16] That is, the term *theos* is empty without some specification, some content and shape. Christians proclaim their faith not in some generic God, but in the God of Jesus Christ. The creed we profess begins with an affirmation of the one God and then specifies that in terms of Father, Son and Spirit. The elements that give the term God its particular shape in our creed are (1) the "*Abba*" experience of Jesus, into which we are invited and drawn, (2) the experience on the part of the disciples of the presence and activity of God in Jesus, and (3) the early community's experience of the action of God as Spirit within and among those who believed in the risen Jesus.

The shift from christocentrism to a shapeless theocentrism, like the parallel moves in other traditions, would not necessarily be a move toward better interreligious relations. It is a move away from the particularity of each faith. Indeed by tending to reduce all particular traditions to mere examples of a generic religion, the pluralist stream in theology of religions runs the risk of negating the value to particularity and difference, and denying any real significance to the content of believers' affirmations. They are told that, whatever they recount about their experience and whatever they may affirm about the divine, they are "in fact" all experiencing and believing in the same God. For this reason pluralism can easily become exclusive and intolerant. Rather ironically, this style of thinking can lead to the idea that the pluralists have exclusive access to the truth and so to salvation.

■ SALVATIONS

One of the difficulties involved in our talk about religions and salvation is that it tends to presume that salvation is a universal and univocal term. Yet if we attend carefully to what other religious traditions are saying, it is clear that there is a variety of religious ends on offer. Not every community of faith is proposing the same goal or ultimate end. Even those traditions that propose some form of liberating practice understand differently what it is we need to be liberated from—ignorance, perhaps, or sin, or suffering. These are not simply different words for the same thing. We are not in a situation where there is one single salvation and we have to decide which (one or several) among the various religious paths will lead us there. It is quite conceivable that Buddhist practice is a perfectly adequate way of reaching a state of *nirvana*—it delivers what it promises. But it does not pretend to deliver what the Christian tradition would see as salvation. In the Christian understanding, being saved means being incorporated into the divine life through the person of the fully divine, fully human one. This incorporation takes place by the gracious initiative of God, who invites a free human response. Wherever we can discern this response taking place, we are witnessing salvation—even outside the visible confines of the Church. Since none of the other major traditions is based on quite such a concept of salvation, it would make little sense for a Christian to say that there are other ways as good as (or perhaps even better than) Christianity to arrive at the salvation we believe God is offering. Other traditions understand differently what is possible, what is promised, what is on offer. They are not simply commensurable.

The difference in the religious ends on offer seems to me to explain something about the not uncommon phenomenon of "conversion" (let's call it that for want of a better term) to Buddhism in the West. It does not seem to me that people think they have found there a more effective way of "getting to heaven" and so have chosen it over the Christian way. Rather they are convinced that enlightenment and *nirvana* are more convincing or attractive religious ends than "being saved" or "not going to hell" or "getting to heaven."[17] This may be because Christian talk about salvation—and especially the idea that there is no salvation outside the Church—makes it seem as though we are talking about having the right answer on some eschatological exam, and thus that we are talking about something that is entirely in the future. The right name will get you past the door; give the wrong name and you are damned. The way in which Peter's affirmation in Acts 4:12 tends to be used reinforces this sense: "There is no other name under heaven given among men by which we must be saved."

Yet the New Testament word for salvation *soteria*, like its Latin counterpart *salus*, has the connotation not just of final rescue but of health and healing. It has an element of the "already," not only the "not yet." Clearly we do not want to maintain that outside the Church no one is healthy in the fully human sense. We can observe all around us people leading admirably healthy human lives – creative, compassionate, loving, faithful, honest, generous. What makes for a healthy, fully human life, Christians claim, is living at one with God, at home with God, at table with God, sharing in the divine life. This we are enabled to do because of God's initiative in binding himself irreversibly to humanity, something we claim to have witnessed God doing decisively in Jesus Christ. We can see this salvation, this health, being lived out all around us. It may often be lacking within the Church and be in evidence beyond its borders. What is clear is that it is a matter of urgency for our world. That kind of living is a matter of now, not just later.

We find ourselves in a marketplace not only of diverse religious means and methods, but also of quite varied religious ends—"salvations" in the plural. Not everyone sees the healthy life the way that Christians do. Our task is not to try and reduce all these ends to one, and then prove that we possess the best means for achieving it. Neither is it to pretend that the end we are proposing is not particularly unique and so can happily cede its place to any of the others on offer. Our task, rather, is to live toward that end, to live that salvation, and embody it for the world, in the hope, in all humility, that the truth of it will become clear to all and will embrace all.

God's goal, Christians believe, is to create a community—eventually a world community—that consciously lives that relationship of salvation. That is effectively what we mean when we speak of the universal task of evangelization. It is not a matter of getting bigger and bigger numbers, or of spreading the word about the right answer for the final exam. It is about the urgent hope of all of us really being alive now, and from now on.

▨ PROPERTY OR ORIENTATION?

It is difficult to read *extra ecclesiam nulla salus* in a way that does not seem proprietary or territorial. The ideas of implicit faith and an implicit desire to belong to the Church were ways of softening proprietary claims, but they did so by extending implicit membership to people some of whom would surely not have wanted it, and others who may already have explicitly rejected it. Yet in recent developments in Church teaching, that idea of a kind of honorary membership seems to have been quietly dropped in favour of the idea of orientation. The idea was used by Pius XII in his *Mystici Corporis* (DzS 3821), and *Lumen Gentium* par. 13 speaks of people being oriented or ordered toward the Church. The Church itself is oriented toward the Reign of God, and is a kind of seed or instrument of it (*Redemptoris Missio, par.* 18). Again this Reign is for Christians not some generic divine sovereignty but explicitly that kind of reign embodied in Christ.

So we seem no longer to be talking about inside and outside in some kind of territorial way, but rather about direction and orientation. In other places the language of "configuration" is used.[18] There are many ways in which God can succeed in "configuring" or "orienting" people to God's ideal of the human person fully alive—in Christian terms, to Christ. Pius XII, in an often-quoted speech to Italian midwives, affirmed that an act of love on the part of someone not a Christian was sufficient to make up for lack of baptism.[19] Any act of love is a collaboration in God's loving and "configures" the lover to the one whom Christians see as God's love humanly embodied. Another term used is "solidarity."[20]

All this seems to make the question of inside and outside moot. There will be insiders who are not well-oriented to the Reign of God—we all know some of them, and have to admit that at times we ourselves are among them—and there will be outsiders (or non-members) who are admirably oriented to that Reign. Official teaching from the Council onwards recognizes as much, and even before Vatican II there is a long history of reflection leading toward that position.

In *Redemptoris Missio* (pars. 28–29), John Paul II went beyond the Council's positions in *Nostra Aetate, Gaudium et Spes* and *Lumen Gentium* and explicitly affirmed the active role of the Holy Spirit in human hearts and the history of peoples; and that not only in individuals but in the social and structural elements of cultures and religions. This recognition is a very significant step toward grappling with the issue, and it gave rise to an even further step.

In its 1997 document entitled "Christianity and the World Religions," the International Theological Commission affirmed that "the presence of the Holy Spirit in the religions being explicitly recognized [a reference to the advances John Paul had made in this area], it is not possible to exclude that they may *as such* exercise a certain salvific function, that is, despite their ambiguity, they help people achieve their ultimate end." The Commission begins its reflection on other traditions with the observable action of the Holy Spirit in those traditions and so concludes that they can indeed have a salvific function in spite of any ambiguities they might contain. So the "outsiders" whom we recognize as oriented with us toward the Reign of God are so, not by chance, but because of the action of God's Spirit, often in and through their religious traditions.[21]

However, *Dominus Iesus* seems to use this affirmation of the universal action of the Spirit to reduce rather than enhance the significance of positive elements in other religious traditions. The reader is left with the sense that whatever is judged to be a fruit of God's action outside the Church is discounted as somehow second-hand. That action is "but a participation" in the mediation of Christ. Such participated mediations are not actually affirmed; they are only "not excluded" (par. 14).[22] One of *DI*'s central affirmations is that the Church's faith has always been that there is only one economy of salvation (par. 11). That is to say, Christians believe that God has one unified vision for humanity, not several, and one project for realizing that vision, not a series. From that statement, however, two different conclusions could be drawn, depending on the direction we choose to go. The first would be to conclude that nothing outside the Christian dispensation has any value, since God's only project is the Christian project. This has been a long-held position in Christian history and still has its supporters. The alternative deduction that could be drawn would be that everything positive beyond the Christian community is "in some way"[23] part of the same divine project to bring humanity to its fulfilment, and as such has its own inherent value and also a value for Christians. The "seeds of the Word" sown there may be revelatory for us and produce fruit in us. The "rays of truth" found there may show in a fuller light the reality of what God is accomplishing in Jesus Christ.[24]

It might help both to understand better *Dominus Iesus'* thought and to find a clearer, humbler way of presenting it, if we were to make some distinctions with regard to the elements or aspects of God's project for humanity. Christians believe that human beings have been created by God for loving communion not only with one another but with God. Just as creation is one, so, we believe, is God's action in bringing us into communion one. Using a Johannine model and language (see John 1:1–14), we might call this the Word aspect of God's project. I choose this model because it has its roots in John's own Jewish background and also finds ample echo in the Qur'an and in Muslim theological reflection. By God's authoritative Word we are created, and so that Word, that self-expression of God, could be said to be part of our very being and becoming. Yet, strangely, we do not recognize that same Word when it calls to us, and speaks to us of deeper love and fuller life—that is, of our continuing to be created. For some reason we are suspicious of it, and we fear the intimacy with God that it effects. We have taken over the project of our being created and to a greater or lesser extent shut it down. Yet God's Word never ceases to search us out and call us into being. Those rare few of us who do respond to the Word recognize our origin in God and enter peacefully into that primordial relationship with God. It is a relationship like none other, of course, but we can glimpse something of it in the nurturing and tender love of a mother or father and the infinitely trusting and receptive love of a child.

There is something rather otherworldly about this vision of things, and one might well wonder if and where it encounters the concreteness of human living. Christians claim to have experienced this Word fleshed out or, one might say, spoken in "body language" in Jesus of Nazareth (John 1:14). The divine self-expression that invites to and enables communion meets our human resistance head on, and bears the full force of its rejection. The Word is at its most revealing in that moment when it bears without bitterness or vengeance the malice of an unjust and undeserved execution (John 8:28; 12:32 and 19:30). This is the reason the Cross is, more than a symbol, the central motif of Christianity. In the Resurrection it shows itself a Word over which death has no power, an unexpectedly gracious Word—not of punishment or revenge, but a word of forgiveness and a blessing of peace (John 20:19, 21 and 26).

In the Word's preparedness in Jesus to share our vulnerability and to bear as we all do the brunt of human evil, Christians claim to see God's profound solidarity with humanity. If what we have recognized in Jesus about God is true, then we must understand it to be true universally, not just for a limited time or for a restricted group of people. The claim that the Jesus event is unique is not by any means an attempt to limit its universality or control access to it. Rather it is to say the Word is not some empty signifier, but that it is made dramatically and unpredictably specific in the Jesus event. The Word aspect and the Jesus aspect are inseparable from one another in the Christian understanding of God's project for humanity.

Talk of uniqueness in theology tends to make people nervous nowadays, yet there are various senses in which uniqueness is merely an observable fact rather than a monopolistic claim. It is simply the case that no other religious community is proclaiming the same things Christians proclaim. It is simply the case that, even if some other communities see Christ as one among many—many founders, many enlightened ones, saviors, prophets, or ethical teachers—there is no other community that believes about any figure what Christians believe about him. The Buddha and Muhammad are not in competition with him. Their communities claim different things about them, and they themselves play different roles in the configurations of those religions from the role Jesus plays in Christianity. Belief in Krishna as one of the *avataras* of Vishnu is not a simple parallel to Christian belief in the Incarnation of the Word. *DI* does not use the word *originality*, but this is surely the sense in which it refers to the uniqueness of the revelation in Christ. That revelation is not simply a reiteration of a generic message but something quite particular.[25]

In a certain rather obvious sense, it could be said that all religions are unique—though they may have certain elements in common, none of them is the same as any other. Anyone who thinks they are the same has not been paying attention. So there is no need to be embarrassed about a claim to uniqueness; it can be made in all humility. As already pointed out, the uniqueness does not make Christians the proprietors of the salvation revealed here, but rather servants of the message.

What *Dominus Iesus* called attention to—though not in language that always recommended itself for its clarity or, indeed, its charity—was that it makes no sense for a Christian to say that Jesus Christ is not uniquely revealing of who God is, and of how things stand between God and humanity. It is axiomatic that he is. In the same way it is axiomatic for a Muslim that the Qur'an is uniquely revealing, though not because of the novelty of its message but because of the clarity and reliability of its revelation and transmission. Neither for the Christian nor for the Muslim does this imply any limitation on God's activity of revealing. It does mean, however, that what we have recognized as the uniquely revealing event will of necessity be the measure by which we recognize whatever revelation there may be beyond that privileged moment.

Jesus is not all there is to the Word, yet, in the Christian way of seeing things, the fact that we have recognized the Word in Jesus enables us to discern and recognize that same Word wherever it is expressed. We do not believe that the Word will be elsewhere communicating something different from what it has expressed in Jesus. That belief is what defines a Christian. This, it seems to me, is what *DI* is trying to say with its piling on of terms like definitive, complete, and absolute. The Word spoken in Jesus is definitive not in the sense that it is finished and done, but in the sense that it defines for us the characteristics of the divine Word that we are called to recognize and to embrace wherever in God's creation it is found.

■ THE NECESSARY CHURCH?

Dominus Iesus affirms the inseparable unity not only of the Word and Jesus, but also of the Church. However, if it is true that formal belonging is no longer of crucial importance, and if it is now recognized that neither actual membership in the Church, nor even a desire for membership is essential in order for God to orient a person or community toward life in Him, then what need is there for the Church? What remains of centuries of belief if we abandon the proprietary understanding of the Church's relationship to salvation. If there is no outside, in short, then what does it mean to be inside? *DI* sought to stem the tide of this kind of questioning and re-affirm, as indeed earlier documents had from time to time also sought to do, not only the uniqueness of Christ, but also the necessity of the Church for salvation. The question I want to consider now is can these affirmations of *DI* be salvaged from their apparent arrogance? Is there any suitably humble sense in which we can talk of the necessity of the Church?

Again the language is unhelpful. Of course it is true that there is only one community that explicitly points to what God has done in Christ as being decisive for the history not only of humanity but also of God. Therefore the Church is unique as a matter of observable fact. As we have already noted, there are people beyond this community whom we recognize are also in fact oriented to the Reign of God. However, those people do not explicitly link their orientation with Christ, so the uniqueness and importance of the Christian community's explicit witness is not lessened. We have also noted the gradual shift from the idea of the necessity for salvation of membership (whether actual or implicit) in the Church, to the notion of sharing the Church's orientation toward the Reign of God. John Paul II spoke of a grace of Christ "which, while having a mysterious relationship to the Church, does not make [people] formally a part of the Church, but enlightens them in a way which is accommodated to their spiritual and material situation" (*RM.* 10). So how are we now to understand the necessity of the Church for salvation if it doesn't simply mean the necessity of membership?

Let me suggest an answer to that question by asking another question. What would it mean to say we are saved in Christ if there were no community of people who recognized and accepted that renewed relationship with God, lived it out, reflected on it, and found words to express it? If something took place in Christ yet it was not powerful enough to give birth to a community of people that allowed themselves to be changed by it, then we might with some justification say that nothing much really happened. It would make no sense at all to say that God has bound himself to the human family by a bond that can never be broken—as we do, for example, in the liturgy—if there were no human evidence of anything transformative having happened.

In the Christian understanding, the language of God's revelation to us is flesh. It is as the ongoing embodiment of that revelation and the sacrament of that salvation that the Church, the Christian community, is necessary. We are not dealing with God's revealing of some secret knowledge that will help us get through the final test. Rather, when we speak of salvation, we are speaking of God's forming a renewed human family at peace with God and sharing in God's very life. Christians make a commitment to allow themselves to be formed by God into a community animated by the Spirit of Christ, a community that can serve as a nucleus or seed of that new human family—not its gatekeeper or its landlord. Only in that sense is the Church necessary.

We cannot simply dispense with the Christian community in favor of the Reign of God, and *Dominus Iesus* was quick to criticize a vaguely defined kingdom-centeredness as inadequate (par. 19). Without an actual community that tries to embody it, however imperfectly, the Reign of God remains no more than an idea. As a sacrament, the Church points beyond itself to the salvation God is effecting everywhere in the world. It reveals and bears witness to salvation; it does not possess or control it.

Dominus Iesus in a carefully and somewhat puzzlingly worded sentence affirms that the Church has "an indispensable relationship (*imprescindibile relazione*) with the salvation of every human being." Notice that it does not claim that membership of the Church is an indispensable condition for salvation. It is only God's solidarity with us that can save us from falling back into the dust from which we came. That divine solidarity, Christians believe, has been expressed and embodied in Christ, and it is the very *raison d'être* of the Church to be God's instrument of solidarity. If salvation means our accepting the solidarity God offers us, then there is of necessity a relationship of solidarity among all the people who are saved. It is *indispensable* for the Church, the community that explicitly rejoices in this divine solidarity glimpsed in Christ, that it continually place itself in solidarity with all who are oriented to the Reign of God, with all who are *de facto* configured to Christ, whether in their suffering of injustice, in their forgiving, in their gracious generosity, in their humble service, or in their obedience to God.

Jacques Dupuis noted that John Paul II suggested an amendment to the adage we have been considering: *sine ecclesia nulla salus*—without the Church there is no salvation.[26] This has the advantage of avoiding the problematic question of members and outsiders, and it underlines the sense of the necessity of some concrete embodiment of the Reign of God that catalyzes and names what God is doing in the world. However, it does not entirely avoid the likelihood of a too proprietorial reading of the role of the Christian community.

If, as I have been suggesting, *extra ecclesiam nulla salus* is effectively off the books now, where does that leave evangelization? Has it lost all urgency? The urgency lies not in the need to save people from a God who would consign even babies to eternal flames for not having been baptized—as Fr. Feeney maintained. It lies, rather, in the urgent need humanity has to work toward that new way of being human together that we call the Reign of God—that kingdom of justice, love, and peace that is crystallized, as it were, in Christ. We need saving not so much from flames "prepared for the devil and his angels" as from the flames of hatred and violence that we prepare for each other and that threaten to engulf us. Evangelizing consists not in simply *telling* the message but in *being* it, in *embodying* it. It is not the invitation of the real estate agent pushing the acreage with the best prospect. It is not the cry of the barker trying to fill the side-show tent. Rather evangelization is a way of living, a way of *being* the Body of Christ, of embodying the Reign of God, so inviting and so hospitable that it attracts all those who are looking for a fully human life.

■ Notes

1. The speeches of J. Ratzinger, F. Ocàriz, T. Bertone and A. Amato are available (only in Italian) at http://www.vatican.va/roman_curia/congregations/cfaith/doc_doc_index.htm.

2. A very useful volume on the subject is *Sic et Non: Encountering Dominus Iesus*, edited by Stephen J. Pope and Charles Hefling (Maryknoll, NY: Orbis, 2002). As well as providing the text of the declaration, the book documents some of the published reactions of major figures, before going on to twelve articles examining *Dominus Iesus* from various standpoints.

3. The supplementary texts that the declaration cites indicate that the Matthean quotation is more representative of Gospel thought because it has certain echoes not only in Luke/Acts but also in John (*Lk.* 24:46–48; *Jn.* 17:18, 20, 21; *Acts* 1:8).

4. The then Cardinal Ratzinger, in his speech at the presentation of *DI*, indicated briefly that the Church's claim to a unique role in the salvation of all was based neither on some precedence accorded to its members, and certainly not on the basis of what it has succeeded in achieving during its history, but rather on the presence of Christ in the Church and to it.

5. It is interesting to note that in the letter accompanying his *motu proprio* letter *Summorum Pontificum* (7 July, 2007), Benedict XVI seems to acknowledge faults on the part of the Church itself and its leadership: "Looking back over the past, to the divisions, which, in the course of the centuries, have rent the Body of Christ, one continually has the impression that, at critical moments when divisions were coming about, not enough was done by the Church's leaders to maintain or regain reconciliation and unity. One has the impression that omissions on the part of the Church have had their share of blame for the fact that these divisions were able to harden."

6. Fernando Ocàriz concluded his comments at the presentation with this observation: "It is not superfluous to underline that the commitment of Christians to bring to all people the light and strength of the Gospel, is not and cannot be an assertion of ourselves. Rather it is a service we owe to others, being mediators of the truth that saves, a truth of which we are neither the origin nor the owners. Rather we are people who have received it as gift and who are its servants. It is a truth that must always be presented in love and in respect for the freedom of the other (cf. Eph 4:15; Gal 5:13)."

7. Bernard Sesboüé puts it succinctly: "From a Christian point of view, the awareness of the extravagant nature of the conviction that Jesus Christ is the one and only mediator and savior of all humanity should make us particularly humble and modest. Let us never forget that we can also be wrong in the manner in which we make our claim to be right." *Hors de l'Église pas de salut: histoire d'une formule et problèmes d'interprétation* (Paris: Desclée de Brouwer, 2004), p. 301 (my translation).

8. Joseph Cardinal Ratzinger, "The Heritage of Abraham: The Gift of Christmas," in *L'Osservatore Romano* (29 December, 2000): 1.

9. For a recent authoritative discussion of this issue in the context of the question of the fate of unbaptized infants, see the statement of the International Theological Commission entitled "Hope for Salvation" first published in *Origins*, 36.45 (April 26, 2007), pp. 725–46.

10. DzS 3866.

11. For a discussion of the background of this saying, see Jacques Dupuis, *Towards a Christian Theology of Religious Pluralism* (Maryknoll, NY: Orbis, 1997), pp. 86–99. See also G. D'Costa, "'*Extra ecclesiam nulla salus*' Revisited" in ed. Ian Hamnett, *Religious Pluralism and Unbelief: Studies Critical and Comparative* (London: Routledge, 1990), pp. 130–147; and in more detail, the entire study by Francis A. Sullivan, *Salvation Outside the Church: Tracing the history of the Catholic Response* (London: Geoffrey Chapman, 1992). More recently the French theologian Bernard Sesboüé has examined it in his *Hors de l'Église*.

12. See prefatory note to DzS 3866–3873.

13. Sesboüé notes with regret that the adage *extra ecclesiam nulla salus* begins to harden when it is used by Augustine against the Donatists (*Hors de l'Église*, p. 67). However, it is worth remembering that this doctrine, which seems to have such a holier-than-thou air to it was being invoked against the holier-than-thou Donatists, who had separated themselves from a Church they saw as morally and spiritually flawed. Thus, *extra ecclesiam* represents not a preening self-righteousness but the call to a solidarity that does not scorn human weakness.

14. Pius IX, Allocution *Singulari quadam,* December 9, 1854. *Collantes*, 7028.

15. Interestingly John Paul speaks not only of not having the possibility of knowing the Gospel revelation, but also of not having the possibility of accepting it (*Redemptoris Missio*, par. 10).

16. See, for example, his "Augustine's Christomorphic Theocentrism," in eds. G. E. Demacopoulos and A. Papanikolaou *Orthodox Readings of Augustine* (Crestwood, NY: St Vladimir's Seminary Press, 2008), pp. 263–289.

17. Important work on the question of the multiplicity of religions ends has been done by S. Mark Heim in his two books *Salvations: Truth and Difference in Religion* (Maryknoll, NY: Orbis, 1995) and *The Depth of the Riches: a Trinitarian Theology of Religious Ends* (Grand Rapids: Eerdmans, 2001). Heim also comments on *Dominus Iesus* in eds. Pope and Hefling, *Sic et Non*, pp. 68–79.

18. See, for example, "Hope for Salvation," pars. 29 and 66.

19. Pius XII, "Allocution to Italian Midwives," *Acta Apostolicae Sedis*, 43 (1951), p. 841.

20. E.g., in "Hope for Salvation," pars. 88–95.

21. *Dominus Iesus* criticizes the idea that this could be more than a *de facto* matter, but as Gerald O'Collins has pointed out, whatever God does is in a sense *de iure*. G. O'Collins, "Jacques Dupuis, his person and work," in eds., D. Kendall and G. O'Collins, *In Many and Diverse Ways: In Honor of Jacques Dupuis* (Maryknoll, NY: Orbis, 2003), pp. 18–29. In saying this, however, he begs the question of whether the plurality of religious beliefs and expressions is God's doing or ours.

22. Quoting *Lumen Gentium* par. 65, and *Redemptoris Missio* par. 5. There is a marked tendency in Church documents to use the rhetorical figure of litotes when dealing with this argument, attenuating any positive statement by preferring to negate its opposite.

23. "*Quodammodo*" (*Gaudium et Spes*, par. 22), "in a mysterious way" (*Dominus Iesus*, pars. 20 and 21),"in ways known to Himself" (*Ad Gentes*, par. 7).

24. During our discussions in Jerusalem, Elizabeth Groppe raised the very helpful question of how one can put the idea that God has one single project for humanity together with the observation made earlier about the multiplicity of religious ends—"salvations"— being proposed by the various faiths. It seems to me that it is precisely at this point that dialogue becomes meaningful, and urgent. Dialogue is not simply the exchange of travelers'

tales among individuals and groups bound on different journeys. It is the far more serious and demanding discussion about where precisely we are headed together and how best to travel in company. The increasing realization of our interconnectedness and, therefore, our interdependence when it comes to maintaining a healthy physical environment offers us an instructive model. Our being fully alive as human beings is not simply a personal or small-group project. It involves the whole human family. The varied takes people have on what it means to be human have somehow to be reconciled and unified in such a way that we can all flourish together. Such a unification is neither simply the hegemony of the strongest nor a bland lowest-common-denominator social contract. It will be the fruit of a sustained mutual opening to the witness and the questioning of the other—in short, it will be the fruit of dialogue.

25. Both Joseph Ratzinger and Angelo Amato used the term "originalità" in their speeches introducing the declaration. It is unfortunate that the document itself did not dwell on this further, for it might have clarified the use of "uniqueness."

26. Jacques Dupuis, *Christianity and the religions: from confrontation to dialogue* (Maryknoll, NY: Orbis, 2001), p. 205.

15 Between Tradition and Reform: Between Premodern Sufism and the Iranian Reform Movement

Omid Safi

Medieval Muslims were often suspicious of displays of public piety and humility, knowing all too well that God alone sees our hearts, our intentions. How often did they point out that it was Satan (then called *Iblis*) who asserted his own superiority over humanity. In our own age, it seems that the Euro-American world is at times caught up between attitudes of triumphalism and assertions of ethnic/religious/intellectual superiority. I write these words as an American Muslim, struggling to avoid two sets of arrogance.

There are many elements that can easily lead a Muslim who takes the statements of the Qur'an literally to the precipice of arrogance. A main part of Qur'anic teachings is often taken to be that, although the revelations of the previous prophets (in particular that given to Moses and Jesus) are recognized as authentic and divine in origin, a simultaneous part of the Islamic teachings assert that the communities of those same traditions have, in time, distorted, willingly at times, the teachings of the prophets in crucial theological matters such as the divinity of Christ and God's preferential love for the people of Israel. On top of this polemic, there is the additional guarantee, accepted by virtually all Muslims, that God Himself will protect the revelation of the Qur'an from tampering. It is hard to avoid the conclusion that this combination of claims can and often leads many Muslims to theological arrogance.

Where does that leave us today? I would argue that if we ever had a chance to do so, we cannot afford to live parallel existences. We are much more aware these days of the interconnectedness of our lives, our faiths, our fates, and our traditions. This is not to argue that we are merging into—or that we should be merging into—an amorphous blob, which obscures the particularity and distinctiveness of each tradition. What I am speaking of here is what Martin Luther King called the "inescapable network of mutuality."

My own experience is very much a trajectory along these lines. I am a child of the Iranian revolution (1978–1979), where the projection of religion into ideological space eventually led a utopian dream to turn into a dystopia. For many years I stayed away from religion, all religion, until encountering the fervor and passion of evangelical Christians in the South. That led me to examine my own tradition again, starting back with the Sufis of Islam in one hand, and the postcolonial revolutionaries (Malcolm X, Khomeini, Shari'ati, Catholic Liberation Theology) in the other. It took many years before the two would merge together in a more or less harmonious whole. Ironically, the blending of the two powerful streams did not happen for me until a serious spiritual and intellectual encounter with Martin Luther King. In Martin I saw a powerful voice of love, a person who was committed to speaking truth to power, of fulfilling the Biblical legacy of Amos. In Martin I found a figure to embody for self-criticism, as early as his Letter from a Birmingham Jail.

My own trajectory over the last few years has consisted of delving into the rich resources of Islam, and coming back to the loftiest offerings of Christianity, Buddhism, Judaism, and Hindu traditions. I am not going to limit myself to simply denouncing the excesses and violence committed by adherents of these other traditions, and more concerned with the ways in which some of their followers seek to tap into the richest aspects of their own teachings to offer a vision of love, justice, and peace that is directed not just at their own followers, but at the whole of humanity. I recognize the anger of postcolonial Muslims—for whom at times there is no "post" in postcolonialism—but I remain convinced that anger is not a divine quality, whereas love is. All these sentiments are alchemical and transformative, yet only love pulls us higher, toward God.

These days we are told over and over again that Islam is in need of a reformation. My own sense is that Islam's reformation will not be led by a singular Martin Luther—who was, let us recall, a noted Muslim-hater—but rather through a consensus-building communal movement. In the Qur'an we are told that "you" are the best of communities. Today I wonder to whom this "you" refers. Is it the community of Muhammad? Is it Muslims today? Is it the whole of humanity today? Or is it those who follow the call of embodying God's mercy and God's justice, regardless of the faith tradition to which they belong.

I have little patience for the theological arrogance of exceptionalism in traditions that assert God's universal love for all of humanity, and I remain convinced that we all have a great deal to learn from each other. None of us lives alone. The oneness of God we have always known, and we are beginning to realize the goal of the oneness of humanity. The Muslim mystics have long spoken of the "unity of being." It is through this dialogue with the Christian mystics and the Hindu mystics and the Buddhist mystics that I have sought to learn something about the unity of God's love for all of humanity.

One of the exciting aspects of studying contemporary Islam is the sense of witnessing history in the making. Creative processes of engaging tradition (for example, feminist readings of Scripture) are taking place alongside catastrophic branching out that, in many ways, bypass some of the safety mechanisms that have been woven into the fabric of the tradition (calls for *jihad* by demagogues without any religious training). One of the more pressing issues remains: how to balance the call for reform with a thorough, rigorous engagement with the existing tradition.

The case of the Islamic reform movement in Iran offers us important opportunities to engage this pressing issue: Scholars like Abd al-Karim Soroush have called for making distinctions between religion (which is said to be divine in origin and transcendent) and any and all understandings of religion (which are always contingent, historical, and ultimately human). I aim to explore the limits of such distinctions, as flawed as they might be, in order to develop understandings of religion that are simultaneously open to modernity and rooted in a tradition. In particular, I am interested in how some of these critiques end up subverting the absolute forms of authority, whether that of the "rule of the jurist" (*velayat-e faqih*), or that of consensus of religious scholars (*ijma'*).

One of the key questions here seems to be, on the one hand, how to operate in a discursive universe that is humble enough to avoid elevating its own assumptions to an absolutist level while, on the other hand, being critical of dogmatic claims to authority, without falling into the trap of relativism that would eradicate the particularity that offers each of our traditions its own distinctive path to God.

Even more than merely studying descriptively the world of contemporary reform, I am also interested in imagining a role for a vibrant mystical life while trying to avoid both absolution and relativism. After all, premodern Sufis seemed to have worked out an understanding of gradations of certainty that moved from having abstract knowledge of certainty (*'ilm al-yaqin*), to seeing the truth (*'ayn al-yaqin*), to somehow being a part of the truth of certainty (*haqq al-yaqin*). What is particularly appealing to me is that the Sufi premodern tradition did not conceive of anything like absolute relativism to solve the problem of religious dogmatism. Rather, it advocated multiple approaches, from critique of religious scholars and the hypocrisy of other Sufis themselves to a perpetual emphasis on keeping alive the dynamic tension between legal and mystical facets of the faith.

The closer we get to modernity and to whatever the "post" in postmodernity signifies, the more we see many Muslims actively work to exile any and all facets of the spiritual domains of Islam, more or less seeking to create the Enlightenment version of Islam—minus all the critiques that have been made of the Enlightenment since then. My task here is not to offer any definitive pronouncements but simply to explore—and to do so humbly. I do not suggest that the cure for all that ails us today is to be found "back then," either at the time of the Prophet (S)[1] or in the mystical world of premodern Sufis. Nor do I advocate a wholesale abandonment of these rich aesthetic and spiritual traditions. What I seek to explore is merely that of resonance. Can we identify tools in the premodern tradition about locating one's own position vis-à-vis a large spectrum of ideas without giving in to relativism, and about pursuing the "truth of certainty" while remaining on watch against the dogma of asserting one understanding of truth as mandatory for everyone?

Premodern Muslims were fond of ending their opinions by the statement *wa Allahu a'lam*: God knows better, God knows best. God knows better than what we have just offered, although we, too, have our responsibility to seek truth to the best of our abilities. And still, God knows better. *Wa Allahu a'lam*.

■ THE IRANIAN REFORM MOVEMENT: AN INTRODUCTION

In today's political climate, it is a cliché to begin a discourse on Islam and Muslims with the talk of crisis.[2] It is not my intention here to add to that unrelenting barrage of crises. Instead, I assert that the very matrix that has led to great upheavals among transnational Muslim communities has also created a precious opportunity for Muslims who are engaged in processes of reform (*islāh*), renewal (*tajdid*), "new religious thought" (*roshanfekri-ye jadid*), critical examination of Islamic thought, and progressive Islam (to offer some of the more prominent labels). Bruce Lawrence has remarked: "It is the presence of colonialism that linked all Muslim collectivities, throughout the Afro-Eurasian *oikumene*, especially in that heavily populated cosmopolitan area south and east of the Mediterranean."[3] In this chapter I wish to explore the opportunity for one fruitful cross-pollination among two prominent movements in these now linked Muslim collectivities: the premodern world of mystical Islam and the Iranian reform movement.

One of the intriguing characteristics of the discourses on Islamic reform is the extent to which the contestations and cross-pollinations are now taking place at a global level across national and linguistic lines. The cross-pollinations are not without their challenges and controversies. Transnational Muslim conversations are by no means ignored—not in our age of the mushrooming discourse of "global jihadist networks." In other words, many journalists, scholars, and public-policy makers have been interested in mapping out a transnational jihadist or salafi connection.[4] For the purposes of this chapter, however, I wish to explore a more constructive transnational conversation, namely, the possibility that the Iranian reform movement[5] and the premodern world of Islamic mysticism have, in fact, something to contribute to one another, indeed to learn from one another. By the Iranian reform movement I largely mean the works of figures such as Mohammad Khatami, ʿAbd al-Karim Soroush, and the generation of intellectuals who have emerged after Soroush such as Mohsen Kadivar, Mujtahid Shabestari, Hashem Aghajari, Akbar Ganji, Mehrangiz Kar, and of course Shirin Ebadi. In doing so, I am not positing either movement as normative or paradigmatic, but rather I am suggesting that each has investigated some particular areas in greater depth through a sustained engagement. There is now even more indication that some of the leading Iranian reformers are becoming themselves familiar with some premodern Sufis, in particular Rumi. This chapter, then, is an exercise in pushing this conversation forward in a constructive fashion.

This cross-pollination is not merely an academic exercise for me. I am someone who considers himself a participant observer in both movements. The participants in the Iranian reform movements presently have foundational challenges that have to be remedied before each can achieve their potential. I will go through these challenges in detail, but I here, at the outset, as a summary I can say that many modern reformers have yet to develop a sustained methodological approach to the tradition in the broadest sense. I believe that Soroush's explication of the notion of "*ijtihad* of the presuppositions" is a potential methodological breakthrough for those who are drawn to a both reform and the mystical life. As a complement, I will use the insights from the Islamic mystical tradition to argue that the Iranian reform movement has been failing in the area of the mutlivalence of texts and the spiritual core of tradition. I will explore these areas that could benefit from cross-pollination a bit further, but first I offer a brief overview of each movement.

■ WHO ARE THE IRANIAN REFORMERS?

Iran today is in the midst of a paradox. On one hand, the reform movement politically appears to have failed to deliver on its promises, and the new president of Iran, Ahmadinejad, seems to embody a strange combination of anti-Semitism, delusion, torture, and provincialism.[6] In spite of the political failure of the reform movement, Iran is also home to one of the most vital and dynamic critical Islamic debates on issues such as the nature of religious authority, hermeneutics, and the conception of the state, What follows is by no means an exhaustive discussion of significant Iranian reformers; one could easily add other figures to the names that follows. Nevertheless, this list will suffice to give a sense of the dynamic nature of the reform project there, as well as the extent to which this reform process is being discursively pushed on through debate, contention, and engagement.[7] Although Soroush may be the most well known to the Western audience, of the "enlightened religious intellectuals," he is by no means a solitary voice out in the wilderness of Iranian reform of Islam.

Initially, the former president of Iran, Mohammad Khatami, was for most Iranians—especially for youth—the great symbol of the potential of reform. Eventually, however, he became the manifestation of the inability of the reform movement to deliver on its promises. Given the limitations of space, I am not going to discuss here the political troubles of Khatami vis-à-vis hardliners in Iran; instead, I wish to call attention to a few elements of his religious thought. Khatami is a rigorous political philosopher who had spent time in Germany, succeeding Ayatollah Beheshti (d. 1981) in the Hamburg Islamic Center. During this time, he became well acquainted with philosophy. His *Dialogue Among Civilizations: A Paradigm for Peace* contained innovative ideas for intercivilizational encounters, including those between Iran and the United States. The United Nations developed the "Dialogue among civilizations" as their theme in 2001,[8] which was sadly derailed by the horrific tragedy of 9/11 and the subsequent wars in Afghanistan and Iraq.[9]

In seeking a radical departure from Khomeini's characterization of the United States as the "Great Satan," Khatami instead argued that:

> In terms of the dialogue of civilizations, we intend to benefit from the achievements and experiences of all civilizations, Western and non-Western, and to hold dialogue with them. The closer the pillars and essences of these two civilizations are, the easier the dialogue would become. With our revolution, we are experiencing a new phase of reconstruction.... This is why we sense an intellectual affinity with the essence of the American civilization.[10]

President George W. Bush's proclamation of Iran as a member of the "Axis of Evil" certainly did not help promote the project of Iranian-American dialogue.

If Khatami was the political face of the reform movement, Soroush was surely its intellectual and, in many ways, its public face. Almost every analysis of Soroush is obligated to mention that Soroush was one of the biannual recipients of the "Muslim Martin Luther" label used by the American media.[11] 'Abd al-Karim Soroush began his training in pharmacology before taking on the philosophy of science, British rationalism, and then onto Islamics. Soroush is an indefatigable speaker, and many of his lectures have been transcribed as books, resulting in a truly dazzling range of writings. He gained a great level of prominence through his monumental books, *The Theory of Evolution of Religious Knowledge or—Text in*

Context (*Qabz va Bast-e Teoric Shari'at, ya Nazariyeh-ye Takāmol-e Ma'refat-e Dini*), a *tour de force* of 681 pages in the original Persian! His main contribution in this work was to make a fundamental distinction between religion as such and religious knowledge. Whereas religion would be deemed eternal and sacrosanct, all religious knowledge was to be seen as limited and finite expressions of human knowledge.[12] In Soroush's own words:

1. Religion, or revelation for that matter, is silent.
2. The science of religion is relative, that is, relative to presuppositions.
3. The science of religion is age-bound, because presuppositions are.
4. Revealed religion itself may be true and free from contradictions, but the science of religion is not necessarily so.
5. Religion may be perfect or comprehensive, but not so for the science of religion.
6. Religion is divine, but its interpretation is thoroughly human and this-worldly.[13]

An equally controversial, though lesser known, contribution of Soroush has been that of religious pluralism. He began this inquiry with the mischievously titled "Straight Paths" (*Serat-ha-ye mostaqim*). This title pluralizes the last line of Sura Fatiha (the opening chapter) in the Qur'an, where humanity pleads with the Divine to guide us to "the straight path" (*al-sirat al-mustaqim*). In speaking of *serat-ha*, Soroush has already acknowledged that there could be—nay, there *are*—multiple paths to the Divine.[14] Of course this notion is not new to Islamic thought, since it has a long and glorious history in Sufism in particular. However, what is relatively new is Soroush's application of this idea to modern debates on Islamic thought.

The idea introduced by Soroush to which I will return is his new conception of *ijtihad* of presuppositions, which I think pushes the discourse further than it has been so far.

Hashem Aghajari came to international recognition due to his imprisonment and death sentence pronounced on him in November 2002.[15] Although the media coverage has focused on his admonition that one must not follow clerics "like monkeys" and his background as a war veteran, his writings have received far less attention.[16] In his famous speech given in Hamadan, he calls for the renewal of an "Islamic humanism," which he traces to a conception of a *homo islamicus* that trandscends color, nationality, race, class, gender, and religion. Aghajari deliberately and explicitly connects himself to the legacy of Shari'ati, and his Hamadan speech was given on the occasion of the twenty-fifth anniversary of the passing of Shari'ati. Aghajari's reading of the Qur'anic verse "indeed we have honored humanity" leads him to conceptualize humanity's worth as being apart from the designation as Muslim, Iranian, Turk, Kurd, male, or female. He emphasizes that his Islam is based on a "divine humanism" (*umanism-e elahi*), and is the legacy of all the *Bani Adam*, "not just Muslims, not just the shi'a, not just ayatollahs, and not just jurists." The discussion is far from abstract for him, because Aghajari specifically states that it is the utmost of absurdity to torture a human being in the name of religion where religion should be vouchsafing humanity's dignity.[17]

Aghajari also advocates a notion of *protestanism-e islami*, by which he means the transformation of the relationship of lay Shiʻa with the clerics from that of disciples (*murids*) to that of students and seekers of knowledge (*danesh-ju, motaʻallem*). In his paradigm, if or when a student receives knowledge, that student becomes a teacher in his own right, and not bound to remain perpetually a disciple. Aghajari is less clear about whether there is a need/space for the shiʻa clerical institution.[18]

Mohammad Mojtahed Shabestari reached the rank of *ijtihad* in the shiʻi seminary of Qum. Shabestari is a Hojjat al-islam (high ranking Shiʻi cleric) who, at an earlier point, had been invited by the late Ayatollah Beheshti to take his place at the influential Islamic Center of Hamburg. During his tenure in Hamburg, Shabestari became fully conversant with German philosophy, as well as the works of Paul Tillich and Karl Barth.[19] Among contemporary Iranian Muslim intellectuals, he remains one of the most knowledgeable about Christian theology. Indeed, theology as such looms large in Shabestari's thought, and one of his goals is to arrive at a "new theology" (*ʻelm-e kalam-e jadid*) that would entail a dynamic and flowing view of religion through human history.[20]

One of Shabestari's main contributions is the desacralizing of the tradition of Islamic interpretation. Shabestari specifically argues that *sonnat* (Tradition) is not an element of faith or creed (*imani, eʻteqadi*) for Muslims, and that it can be looked at through an *anthropolojik* lens.[21] Furthermore, he argues that, in every age, Muslims have allowed themselves to understand and comment upon the Qurʼan without making the interpretations of the ages before them compulsory upon themselves.[22] He connects this reading to a different notion of time in Islam, not having a "history of salvation" (*tarikh-e nejat*), as does Christianity.[23]

Shabestari is concerned with cultivating a notion of "religious faith" (*iman-e dini*) that is fresh and dynamic, developed in the cradle of personal and social freedom. This religious faith, he argues, cannot take root in an oppressive and totalitarian society. Furthermore, for Shabestari, the true "religious faith" cannot be developed by blindly imitating (*taqlid-e kur*) "people and traditions." Although the notion of "blind imitation" has long been a favorite polemic of many Muslim modernists, it is a radical assertion in the Shiʻa intellectual world that has given such primacy to the notion of *marjaʻtaqlid*, that is, to the necessity of following one supreme *marjaʻ* in legal and creedal matters.[24]

Lastly, he argues that it is imperative for religious faith to be tested and purified in every age. He argues that the "system of beliefs and laws" (*nezam-e eʻteqadi va qanuni*) has to be reconsidered always (*tajdid-e nazar*), so that one can strive for purification, perfection, and reform.[25] Shabestari's latest project is an equally audacious one: exposing official and canonical readings of religion as hermeneutically simplistic—*Naqdi bar Qeraʼat-e Rasmi az Din* (A Critique of Official Reading of Religion).[26]

Like Shabestari, Mohsen Kadivar is another Shiʻa cleric who has been among the most dynamic voices of reform in Iran. Displaying a deft understanding of modernity acquired through Habermas, Kadivar comes to recognize modernity as "an uncompleted project," one that every society should be allowed to pursue as its own destination. Rather than attempting to get an idealized version of Islam to live up to a static version of modernity, Kadivar is more invested in whether certain understandings of Islam can be compatible with certain versions of modernity.[27] His goal, at the end of the day, would be a "critical encounter with modernity— rather than being absorbed in it...."[28]

Kadivar's most important contribution so far has been to demonstrate persuasively that the concept of rule (*velayat*), so essential for any conception of *velayat-e faqih*, has always been a multivalent one in Islamic history. Kadivar meticulously identifies a spectrum of interpretations for the notion of *velayat* in Islamic sources, including linguistic, mystical, theological, juridical, Qur'anic, Sunna-based, shar'i conceptions of the jurist (*faqih*), and those derived from people, before presenting the view of the Islamic republic advocated by Khomeini.[29] In other words, he identifies Khomeini's *velayat-e Faqih* as but one possible interpretation among many, not necessarily a given and transparent conclusion.

In his subsequent writings, Kadivar has been even more explicit about undermining the religious legitimacy of *velayat-e faqih* (rule of the jurist):

> [T]he choice between *velayat-e faqih* and democracy, in the event of unresolved incompatibility between the two, is democracy. Through the discourse in answering the first question, we provided that the difference between *velayat-e Faqih* and democracy is void of any religious requirement, and a matter of rational evaluation. In which case, the alternative that stands to yield the most benefit is the preferred choice. *Velayat-e faqih* has no credible foundation in Islamic jurisprudence. It is a notion that is formed in the minds of a group of honorable jurists through a specific reading of a handful of Islamic passages. Refuting *velayat-e faqih* does not in any way undermine any of the Islamic teachings, requirements or obligations. I believe democracy is the least erroneous approach to the politics of the world. (Please note that least erroneous does not mean perfect, or even error free.)[30]

Kadivar does not idealize democracy; he simply recognizes it as the least imperfect of all the imperfect human political models. As importantly, *velayat-e faqih* is also exposed as merely the product of human juridical opinion, stripped of all its divine claim to authority, and, just as importantly, stripping its claimants of their authority.

Lastly, Kadivar and Soroush have engaged in a rigorous debate about the issue of religious pluralism (*pluralism-e dini*).[31]

Shirin Ebadi is difficult to classify in many ways, as she is an icon, a social activist, a judge, and an intellectual. Displaying a concern for the disenfranchised and the marginalized, her advocacy work has moved between standing up for the rights of children, women, non-Muslim minority, political prisoners, civilian casualties, and so forth. Shirin Ebadi has been the most effective voice in Iran arguing for the compatibility of Islam and international notions of human rights. Her volume *History and Documentation of Human Rights in Iran* provides a detailed juxtaposition of the UN Declaration of Human Rights vis-à-vis the Iranian legal code.[32] She offered a through critique of women's rights in the Islamic Republic in her volume *Women's Rights in the Laws of the Islamic Republic of Iran* (*Hoquq-e zan dar qavanin-e jomhuri-ye Islami-ye Iran*). Furthermore, she also showed how she was keenly aware of the processes of multiple marginalizations that non-Muslim women in Iran suffer.[33]

One of the intriguing aspects of Shirin Ebadi's career is that, eschewing the language of reform itself, she argues that her compatibility of Islam and human rights is nothing other than, indeed nothing short of, a return to the actual real message of Islam. Whereas Soroush, Shabestari, and Kadivar operate in familiar Islamic discourses (philosophy, *kalam*, and *fiqh*, respectively), Ebadi operates more fluidly outside Islamic discourses. It remains to be seen what legacy her work will have for religious reform, as is indeed the case for all the Iranian reformers. One other lasting legacy, no doubt, is that she is the first Muslim woman to have been awarded the Nobel Peace Prize in 2003. Her Nobel acceptance speech was a hallmark of speaking truth to the Powers—both the United States and corrupt Muslim regimes.[34] In her speech, she addressed the global situation of poverty, prison abuses in Guantanamo Bay, and the rights of people to rise up against oppression. It is, perhaps, telling that the most explicit Islamic engagement in her text—aside from a reference to the importance of learning in the Qur'an—is to Sa'di's ubiquitous comment on humanity as the Bani Adam ("children of Adam," that is, all of humanity, above and beyond any tribal, ethnic, or religious affiliations) being created from one essence. Here we see a reference surely to the Iranian Muslim canon, and yet one decidedly outside the discourses of *fiqh* and *kalam* that her male counterparts engage.

■ SHORTCOMINGS AND OPPORTUNITIES FOR CROSS-POLLINATION

The Iranian reform movement is suffering from a number of internal and external shortcomings, which may well prove to derail what has been among the most intellectually rigorous and promising Islamic reform movements worldwide. Although the attention of most Western sources has rightly been on the political tensions that have slowed down and in many cases reversed the accomplishments of the reform movement, I would argue that one of the foundational shortcomings of the Iranian reform movement has been its lack of attention to questions of gender equality. It is not the case that the Iranian example has been lacking in exemplars tackling questions of gender equality. One can begin the conversation for example with the heroic work of Shirin Ebadi and Mehrangiz Kar, among others. The fundamental problem remains that, for many male Iranian reformers who are most explicitly working through religious discourses, the issue of gender equality has been collapsed into "the woman problem." In the work of most male reformists in Iran, women remain the object of Islamic discourse, not its agents and subjects.

This shortcoming has also been pointed out by Iranian feminists such as Ziba Mir-Hosseini: "Yet among these new religious thinkers, no influential man has yet addressed the issue of gender in Islam."[35] Women's right activists in Iran have also critiqued this unforgivable silence on gender issues. One of the first to do so was Mehrangiz Kar in her address to Akbar Ganji, the editor of the weekly *Rah-e Now* (the new way).[36]

For one example of the gender shortcomings of male Iranian reformers, I will analyze Soroush's attempt to engage "the woman problem." He states: "I believe that one of the most important values in the relations between men and women is that a woman should be a woman and a man should be a man."[37] Soroush goes on to state even more explicitly that the nature of manhood and womanhood are fixed and distinct from each other: "The relations between men and women should not impede their attainment of excellence in terms of manhood or womanhood. In other words, these relations must not turn men into women or take women out of the sphere of womanhood." Although Soroush is able to answer what he means by "human," he relies on categories on maleness and femaleness without being able to define or qualify them. He will go so far as to say that the religious law is like a "temporary husk" protecting the values of religion, and that the religious laws involving women are the "weakest link" of gender relations. Yet for Soroush it remains the case that the only reason to change the laws is that they no longer serve our purpose today. There is nothing inherently unjust or patriarchal about them.[38] Here one has to agree with Ziba Mir-Hosseini that even today "gender equality is a notion to which male intellectuals—whether religious or secular in their perspective—still do not subscribe, so they implicitly agree with the gender model embedded in shari'a legal rules. For them, gender is not an issue urgent enough to address, but part of a larger problem, and they hope it will go away when their political vision is realized."[39] In the interest of fairness, Kadivar has recently made some moves in the direction of addressing these shortcomings, but the move as a whole is more a listing of areas of possible inquiry, and not a constructive offering of solutions.[40]

■ IJTIHAD (CREATIVE INTERPRETATION)

It should not come as a surprise that like many modernists before us, Iranian intellectuals, too, have turned to the rich reservoir of *ijtihad*, that is, to the exerting of oneself intellectually to offer religious answers. Muslim intellectuals have utilized the conception of *ijtihad* to justify reform for over a century. Fareed, Muneer Fareed offers a thorough account of the debates on *ijtihad* in legal reform through the ninteenth and early twentieth centuries.[41] In the twentieth century, the call for *ijtihad* has been evident in the various works of Muhammad Iqbal,[42] Muhammad Sa'id al-'Ashmawi,[43] and so many others. A great many of these figures have explicitly justified their efforts by appealing to the famous report in which the Prophet asked Mu'adh ibn Jabal (d. 627) about how he would settle issues confronting him. Mu'adh—to the delight of modernized Muslims[44]—answered first the Book of God, then the *hadith* of the prophet, and if not, then through his own judgment.

Wael Hallaq and others have persuasively argued for a revision of the old myth of the gates of *ijtiahd* having been closed.[45] Today modernists are more likely to side with S.M. Zafar and against 'Ashmawi that the gates of *ijtihad* are not closed, and indeed have never been closed.[46] The conversation is less about whether the gates are open or closed, but rather about what can be done with *ijtihad*, who is qualified to undertake this critical examination, and what aspects and facets of Islam can be subjected to *ijtihad*. Many Muslim (post)modernists today, including the present author, have positioned their endeavor, indeed their intellectual *jihad*, as a form of *ijtihad*. However, before we get to the results of this endeavor, it is important to see first the particular contribution of Soroush, namely, the concept of "*ijtihad* of the presuppositions."

▪ SOROUSH ON "*IJTIHAD* OF THE PRESUPPOSITIONS"

A few elements stand out about Soroush's recent work, *Ijtihad*, which was published in Iran in 1382/2003. This work takes the form of an extended engaged and contentious conversation between and among various reformist and conservative readings of Islam.[47] The background is that Ayatollah H.A. Montazeri had written an article on facets of Islamic law dealing with *jihad*, apostasy, the ritual uncleanliness of infidels, and "commanding the good, and prohibiting the evil" (*amr bi ma'ruf* and *nahy min al-munkar*). In this essay, Montazeri considered the question of whether these interpretations in fact open the door to violent readings of religion, which he answered in the negative.[48] Soroush's essay is an answer to Montazeri's essay. In turn, Soroush's own critique is critiqued by Ja'far Subhani.[49] In addition, other scholars such as Sa'id 'Edalat-Nezhad, Mohammad Mojtahed Shabestari, and Ahmad 'Abedini also share their thoughts on the above critique/countercritique/countercountercritique.

Soroush's discussion begins by acknowledging that there has been a rupture in the fabric of time/tradition, and that we have left "one world," and entered a new world (*'alam-e jadid*). Soroush states some of the rulings of the "old world" would have needed no intellectual defense in their time (the example given is the killing of an apostate), whereas, in today's world, even those who would want to argue for upholding such rulings need to articulate a defense and justification for them. In Montazeri's discourse, the defense of the killing of the apostate is justified using the analogy of a cancerous tumor: "If a person who has been raised in Islam becomes openly an apostate, and starts questioning the sanctity of religious elements, then he is like a cancerous tumor that will gradually spread to the other healthy parts of the body." Soroush problematizes the cancer analogy as applying to non-Muslims, and states that such an analogy is already prefigured for a "cure" of removal of the tumor (or to use the other analogy, the rotting tooth). Utilizing disease/wellness models, Soroush creatively suggests that it is more proper to develop a model whereby hybridity is a sign of strength. In imagining a "society of the religious," Soroush offers the metaphor of a garden in which there can be many grape vines, with some sour cherries. Or, moving the analogy to a textual level, he suggests thinking of a Persian text with a few Arabic words.[50]

Soroush then moves from a discussion of apostasy to a slightly broader interrogation of "individual rights" (*haqq-e fard*). Soroush argues that if an individual is to have the freedom to choose religion, why does one not have the right to be free of religion? In other words, Soroush argues that the freedom of religion doesn't end once a person has chosen a religion. Soroush specifically states that the same religious freedoms that apply to a non-Muslim converting to Islam should be applied to a Muslim who converts to another religion.[51]

In expounding upon the notions of freedom of religion, Soroush states that an individual should have the right to hold religious opinions different from others, even from the majority. Furthermore, an individual should be able to hold different religious opinions than the "lords of power" (*arbab-e qodrat*). Here he is officially taking on the question of who is authorized to offer authoritative opinions on Islam. In doing so he is part of the same broad tradition that Kadivar had begun of critiquing official readings of religion, although he doesn't go so far as Akbar Ganji in calling these official readings "fascist."[52]

Having begun with the issue of religious freedom, Soroush switches to the second of his polemics: the rights, indeed, the human dignity, of non-Muslims. He moves to critique the assertion of certain Ayatollahs that the *mukhalif* (here meaning non-shi'a) have no "respect" (due to them); therefore, it is permissible to engage in talking behind their backs and ridiculing them. In a rare engagement with gender issues for Soroush, Soroush critiques Aytaollahs who believe that it is permissible to shake hands with non-Muslim women since these women lack "human respect," and touching them is akin to touching animals. However, it is still worth noting that even here in Soroush's writings, women figure not as agents and subjects, but merely as objects of Islamic discourse. At this point Soroush returns to the issue of the innate dignity of human beings, regardless of religious affiliation.

Soroush's question is direct and explicit: Do human beings leave the circle of humanity because of their beliefs (*'aqidat*)? Do human rights and social advantages change because of a person belonging to this group or that, or adhering to one view or another? Soroush cites the ubiquitous "There is no compulsion in religion" (*La ikraha fi 'l-din*) verse of the Qur'an, and dismisses the explanations that would abrogate this verse. Soroush postulates that so long as the "*fiqhi* worldview," and in particular its presuppositions (*pish-farzi-ha-ye an*) regarding humanity and intellectual matters do not undergo a thorough rethinking (*tajdid-e nazar-e usuli*), it is inadequate to try simply to deal with contemporary issues in a piecemeal fashion.[53]

Soroush suggests that when we look at the totality of *fiqh* rulings on matters such as the ritual impurity of infidels (*najasat-e kuffar*), the buying and selling of slaves, the killing of apostates, the difference in the rights of slaves and freed people, and the relation between a slave and a master, it becomes clear that "our *fiqh*" is based on a particular view of humanity.[54] He reiterates that until and unless the presuppositions on humanity (*insan-shenasi*) and epistemology are not exposed and laid open to a deep, critical, and explicit critique—something that Soroush alleges the jurists have yet to do—all of the *fatwas* that are related to life and honor and belief and human freedom and social matters and the like will always be problematic and should be viewed with suspicion.[55]

Here are Soroush's challenging conclusions to this section: This is the essence of the *ijtihad* that a *faqih* has to undertake, that is to say, *ijtihad* in the *usul*, not just *ijtihad* in the *furu'*. For Soroush, it is insufficient to merely suspend some of the more problematic rulings of Islamic law, because to do so has not yet "untangled the knot of *fiqh*," and "we have not taken any steps forward."[56] Even if the suspension of such a ruling is justified on the basis of the public good (*maslaha*), that darling of modernist Muslims, for Soroush it remains the case that the apostate still remains a human being without the full dignity of being human. Soroush specifically states that the greatest *maslaha* would be the

rethinking of our presuppositions and a return to the original sources, the foun-
tainheads (*sar-chashma-ha*). The use of the word *fountainhead* is significant, I
believe, because although containing the notion of origin and access to an ever-
renewable source, it also has the sense of producing a dynamic current that
flows through time and space.

■ COMPARING SOROUSH WITH TARIQ RAMADAN

The issue of suspension of the problematic *ahkam* (legal rulings) is one that has
been in the news a great deal recently. When Muslim intellectuals have brought
the discussion of these topics to the community, they have often been accused of
giving in to the forces of westernization, or even attempting to destroy Islam
within. A particularly noteworthy example has been both the praise and the damnation[57] that Tariq Ramadan received when he called for a moratorium on the
hudud (Islamic penal code). The original call issued on March 30th, 2005 came out
in "An International call for Moratorium on Corporal Punishment, Stoning and
the Death Penalty in the Islamic World."[58] The item was quickly picked up by many
international news agencies, such as the BBC, which ran a story on it the very same
day.[59] In Muslim sources in the West, the reception was far from enthusiastic, even
in usually more liberal sources such as altmuslim.com.[60]

Tariq Ramadan's argument is based on working within the parameters of the
existing tradition to argue for the nonapplicability of that same system:

> The majority of the *ulamâ'*, historically and today, are of the opinion that these penalties
> are on the whole Islamic but that the conditions under which they should be imple-
> mented are nearly impossible to reestablish. Conditions for the application of these pun-
> ishments are not met.[61]

In other words, Ramadan does not deny the ongoing relevance of the *hudud*, nor
does he consider the practices inherently problematic. Rather, his argument is
based on the fact that the conditions that the *hudud* call for are difficult to realize
justly in today's society, and as a result the enforcement of the *hudud* must be
suspended. Ramadan particularly highlights the injustice of the disproportionate
application of the *hudud* to the marginalized of society: women, poor, prison
inmates, and so on:

> A still more grave injustice is that these penalties are applied almost exclusively to
> women and the poor, the doubly victimized, never to the wealthy, the powerful, or the
> oppressors. Furthermore, hundreds of prisoners have no access to anything that could
> even remotely be called defense counsel.[62]

The somewhat ubiquitous Al-Azhar Legal Research Commission (*lajna Al-buhûth
Al-fiqhiyya*) issued a statement critiquing Ramadan's statement on April 28, 2005:
The Commission primarily advances three arguments in its official statement:

1. The statement raises the initial point: "Whoever denies the *hudûd* (Islamic
   penal code) recognized as revealed and confirmed or who demands that
   they be cancelled or suspended, despite final and indisputable evidence, is to

be regarded as somebody who has forsaken a recognized element which forms the basis of the religion." One of the Members of the Commission, Dr. Mustapha ash-Shuk'a affirms that "the *hudûd* are a part of the religion, they are Qu'ranic and they can be neither subject to debate nor discussion."

2. The point is then raised: "The *hudûd* are known and Tariq Ramadan is demanding that they be stopped because it is hurting the message of Islam: this is a refuted matter."

3. Finally, on the example of Umar ibn Al-Khattab (may peace be upon him), Dr. ash-Shuk'a affirms that "during given periods of time, the Caliph suspended the punishment in instances of war, and then it was re-applied. We are not today in a situation of war which would enable us to suspend these applications. One could suspend the application of *hudûd* in Iraq, because it is a country at war, but this punishment cannot be suspended in Egypt or in other Islamic countries.[63]

In turn, Ramadan offered his own countercritique of the al-Azhar critique.[64]

What stands out in Tariq Ramadan's view on the *hudud*? He is quite careful to affirm that the *hudud* have been and continue to be a part of the shari'a corpus. There is, in other words, nothing fundamentally unjust about the idea of the *hudud* for Ramadan. The only problem for Ramadan, at least in terms of how he articulates the vision, is that the conditions mandated by the *hudud* can no longer be justly realized, thus the practice must be "suspended" in the interest of *maslaha*. Soroush on the other hand, living under a regime that is actually likely to apply and enforce corporal punishment and torture against dissidents, wants to use such rulings to expose and problematize the very presuppositions of such rulings. He then argues for the construction of a new Islamic paradigm that is built upon a humanistic foundation. I propose that in the long run, this perspective is likely to have a much more meaningful constructive contribution to the project of *ijtihad*, both in Iran and in the global audience.

■ CONCLUSION

Perhaps the most exciting part of the new emerging global Muslim identity is that Muslim figures everywhere are seeking one another out, reading each other's work, collaborating with one another's organizations. This is a fruitful process of cross-pollination. One can point to the influence that Shari'ati has had on South African Muslims, or the impact the Palestinian struggle has had on South East Asian progressives. Today, we are witnessing the emergence of Iranian intellectuals who are fluent in English, German, French, in addition to the expected Arabic. One can only hope that at least some portion of the global Muslim reform audience will learn Persian to engage their imaginative and daring project.[65]

Much of this contact is taking place via e-mail, and in English. Both Soroush and Kadivar, for example, maintain extensive web sites.[66] We may well already be in the midst of a generation for whom the serious global conversation on Islamic reform takes place in English more than any other language.[67] We are clearly in the initial stages of this formulation. It is an exciting process that has the promise of ushering in a real paradigm shift in the relationship of Muslims to both Islam and modernity.

■ SUFISM'S CONTRIBUTION TO CONTEMPORARY ISLAMIC THOUGHT: PREMODERN TOOLS FOR A POSTMODERN PRAXIS

Muslims have encountered nonscriptural sources of wisdom and knowledge before, in their repeated encounters with Greek philosophy, Persian medicine, Indian mathematics, and so on. Perhaps the most successful interaction was the centuries-long absorption, internalization, and commentary on the legacy of Aristotelian and Neo-platonic thought by Muslim sages. In the last two centuries, Muslims have confronted the challenge of modernity. This is a challenge that some have taken head on, others in more subtle ways, and yet others in confrontational ways. The responses have not always been fully articulated, yet the engagement is surely one of the more urgent struggles for Islamic thought in the past two centuries.

One of the important developments in the reform movement of Iran has been to recall that religion is always multifaceted, speaking through multiple theological, philosophical, legal, moral, poetic, and ethical voices. In particular they have found that the mystical voice of Islam offers them great resources. In pursuing these decidedly modern and even—gasp!—postmodern commitments, it might seem strange to turn back to a figure who lived about a thousand years ago. To make matters worse, this is not one of the enshrined immortals, nor a member of the pantheon of great mystics and philosophers universally known across the Islamic world (al-Ghazali, Avicenna, Ibn 'Arabi, Mulla Sadra, Rumi, or Averroes). The mystic I will talk about is the little known, but much beloved, rebellious mystic 'Ayn al-Qudat Hamadani (1098–1131). As is the case with far too many coura-geous souls of the past and present, he was exiled, persecuted, convicted in a hope-less juridical system, and eventually brutally killed in front of the university in which he taught. Unlike many other premodern Muslim luminaries, 'Ayn al-Qudat has no shrine, because we are told he was burned and had his ashes scattered to prevent the possibilities of a cult developing around his tomb.

Why turn to such a premodern persecuted soul? I suggest that for those of us who wish to be on the frontlines of a double engagement with Islam and moder-nity, it is vital to preserve a sense of continuity with the full spectrum of what has come before us in the Islamic tradition—not just Qur'an and *hadith*, but the full expanse of theological, mystical, legal, commentary, poetic, and other traditions. We must explore this full spectrum to see if we can find tools and resources that aid us in affirming the God-given dignity of all of humankind, Muslim and non-Muslim, male and female, queer and straight, rich and poor, privileged and mar-ginalized. When we find such resources, we must bring them back to the foreground and highlight them in today's context. At the same time, we must have the honesty to admit that we will not always find such resources. From time to time, it will become necessary for us to throw our hands up and say that the entire discourse about a certain subject can no longer offer such sufficient moral and ethical guidance. A prime example is the medieval discourse, surely a part of discussions of Islamic law, about slavery. As a human being living today, my conscience no longer allows me to believe that it is possible for one human being to own possession over another. However, in many other matters—perhaps most—I would propose that we are likely to find tools and resources, voices from both the mainstream of the Islamic tradition and also out on the blessed margins, that are likely to resonate with our own projects. It is in that light that ʿAyn al-Qudat's work is invaluable.

The great secular humanist, that already much missed voice of resistance and criticism Edward Said, used to say that one of the results of imperialism is that none of us today is single and pure, but all are "hybrid, heterogeneous, extraordinarily differentiated, and unmonolithic." Said rightly connected this to the fracturing experience of imperialism and colonialism, and to that extend we might be surprised to find a premodern Muslim in the eleventh century also reject the sirens of authenticity and tradition. Yet this is precisely what ʿAyn al-Qudat did. In a letter to a beloved disciple, he stated: "Everyone today claims to be following the paradigm of the Prophet (*Sunna*). But we are all far from the Sunna. I am not saying that *they* are far from it. I see many heretical innovations in my own self!"

It is unthinkable for many modern Muslims to conceive of premodern Muslim sages who are so willing to recognize innovation and hybridity in their own self. Yet it is vital for us to document them, to point out that such traits are not the unique gifts of modernity. As the late Marshall G.S. Hodgson—arguably the greatest historian of Islamdom in the twentieth century—used to say about the "best thinkers" of the medieval periods: "They were not simply working the consequences of the particular insights of their own immediate tradition, as often before, but now come frankly and honestly to grapple with the best insights that any accessible tradition could offer."[68] That is a great example for us to follow today, in this age of hybridity and multiple, fractured identities.

This freedom to learn from all sources of wisdom is a hard lesson for many in the religious communities of all traditions to appreciate. And yet we are not without examples. In the United States the legacy of social justice in the Christian tradition in the twentieth century is permanently intertwined with the legacy of Martin Luther King, Jr. King freely acknowledged his own debt to Gandhi's teachings on nonviolence. His Holiness the Dalai Lama of the Tibetan Buddhist tradition has written frequently about the need to evaluate mystical knowledge in light of contemporary scientific evidence. Muslims today likewise would do well to recall that the freedom to drink deeply from all founts of knowledge and compassion has been a part of the Islamic legacy, embodied in the ʿAyn al-Qudats of the past and the present.

One of the conventional Muslim strategies of dealing with other religious traditions has been to affirm that, in the beginning, these previous divine dispensations presented an authentic revelation from God. However, we are told, in time the people came to distort it, to forget the true message, until the next cycle. In a sense, this hermeneutical move provided a tantalizingly powerful—even if, by itself, incomplete—step toward the pluralism of acknowledging the value of other religious traditions. That insistence has often been coupled with what one might call Muslim theological triumphalism, an unquestioned faith in that God Himself would uniquely preserve the sanctity of the Qur'an, and perhaps the entire tradition. Here again we see 'Ayn al-Qudat break rank with the majority, and admit that like all other traditions, the whole of Islamic practices (*Musalmani*) can also become worn out bit by bit, unless it is revived in each generation and each person by a direct experience of God. It is not sufficient to simply pass on that which has come down to us, but each of us has the awesome cosmic task of realizing the Divine Presence here and now, and to relive the majestic task of being human here and now. That approach is fully resonant with the Qur'an's own revolutionary emphasis that it is indeed the pagans of the world who practice something simply because they found their forefathers doing the same. This connection with the past with the insistence on moving forward leads 'Ayn al-Qudat to a bold assertion that if the previous religious masters such as Shafi'i and Hanafi were alive today, they, too, would be following 'Ayn al-Qudat's teachings on human-divine love.

Recall that Said identifies the *sine qua non* of being a social critic as being oppositional. For Said, "it is not practicing criticism either to validate the status quo or to join up with a priestly caste of acolyte and dogmatic metaphysicians." Without needing to project back all of Said's notions of secular criticism and contrapuntal reading (reading against the grain of dominant discourses and hegemonies), we can find the tool of speaking "truth to power" already manifest in 'Ayn al-Qudat's being. Here we have a premodern Muslim who takes on all the "priestly castes" of his time: the ruling sultans, the court administrators, the military, the theologians, the legal scholars, and even the group that he himself is most closely associated with, the mystics. This oppositional style is most manifest when he discusses the injustices of the ruling dynasty of his time: he calls the sultans nothing more than "scoundrel emperors," and talks about their system of land-grant (the most common way of paying the military) nothing more than "plunder."

He likewise carries the critique of the "priestly caste" by blasting the scholars who associate with the unjust rulers by contrasting them with the religious scholars who have come before:

> In the past ages, the caliphs of Islam would seek after the scholars of faith, and the scholars would run the other way. Now for the sake of a hundred pissy gold coins and fifty forbidden ones, the scholars associate day and night with scoundrel emperors. The scholars go to greet them ten times, each time being drunk, and so excited—like someone who releases semen in sleep!

There is a profound distrust of military and political power here, with an insistence that the task of religious leaders is, not to assume political power and not to legitimize political powers that be, but to act as their watchdogs and voices of conscience, to speak truth to the powers. That is a lesson that Muslim spiritual leaders today would also do well to heed, in places like Iran and Saudi Arabia, and also in the United States and Europe.

Yet 'Ayn al-Qudat was more than a premodern postmodern, an anachronistic Marxist well ahead of his time. He was a luminous mystic soul, one who sought the ultimate mysteries of what it means to be human—and what it means to be divine—through subtle teachings of love. In a charming usage and subversion of the discourse of religious law, he redefines the whole realm of "religious obligations" to mean none other than love:

> If you cannot attain to the love of the Creator, at least attain to the love of creatures…Oh my precious one, arriving at God is a religious obligation. That which delivers humanity to the Divine is love. So in this light, love has become a religious obligation on the path to God![69]

The heart of 'Ayn al-Qudat's masterpiece, the *Tamhidat*, is a wonderful lengthy chapter on the reality and spiritual states of being in love.

In a typical 'Ayn al-Qudatian way, he wanted to reinterpret all known religious dogmas through the majestic lens of love. Whatever had been set up as forbidden and taboo by the religious scholars was reinterpreted by him to correspond to some state of love: Heaven? A prison in which true lovers are kept away from the real presence of God. Hell? The fire of love. Satan, the accursed tempter of humanity? None other than the only true lover of God, the one who loved God so much that he refused to love one other than God, namely humanity. And so it goes, in the most bold, original, and daring of all the Islamic narratives of love ever conceived.

There is much to adore and admire, even to emulate, in 'Ayn al-Qudat's courage and compassion, wit and rigor. Yet the greatest injustice to him would be to read him as somehow timeless and eternal. All of us are situated beings. As the Sufis say, it is in this very breath—between the inhale and the exhale—that we truly and *only* live. 'Ayn al-Qudat inspires because he was *timely*, and we, too, must be timely in our own age. The greatest injustice that we can commit toward 'Ayn al-Qudat would be to turn him into an icon—nay, an idol—and admire the level of courage and sophistication that a premodern Muslim had achieved, and perhaps lament that we don't have more 'Ayn al-Qudats today. To do that is to forget that the waters of mercy are always flowing and are never static. The question is not "what would 'Ayn al-Qudat do," anymore than it is "what would Jesus (or Muhammad or Buddha) do." The question of our day is what are we doing? What am I doing? What are you doing? What are we doing together to bring healing into this oft-broken world? What are we doing to help all of us realize the full extent of what it means to be human?

Ours is a majestic, brilliant, frightened, and fragmented age. We have majestic heights of modern marvels and tens of millions suffering from HIV/AIDS. We have reached possibilities of advancement in medicine and technology and computers that would not have been imagined two generations ago, even as we have a fifth of the world's population that starves on a dollar a day. What are we doing?

Our world shares something with that of 'Ayn al-Qudat: the madmen in power continue to rule, deceiving the world by their promises of "order" and "security." Will we rise up, 'Ayn al-Qudat like, and speak truth to powers, to the leaders of the East and West, regardless of nationality, wealth, or religion? Will we challenge the religious bigotry of the conservative mullahs in Iran, the Wahhabis in Saudi Arabia, the Hindu BJPs in India, the right-wing Likuds in Israel, and the Christian fanatics in the United States? Will we insist that religion and the name of God will not be used to divide humanity against humanity, but rather to bring all of us together in the recognition of what that Christian Sufi, Martin Luther King, so beautifully articulated as the awareness that "all life is interrelated, and we are all caught in an inescapable network of humanity, tied into a single garment of destiny"?[70]

The tools that 'Ayn al-Qudat offers us is that of realizing not just the possibility, but the necessity of linking together a vital spiritual life with concrete and righteous acts of social justice in the world. Sufism meets Jewish Tikkun. Liberation theology on board with secular humanism. Let all the great lovers of humanity strive forward in this caravan of justice. That ecumenical move toward the praxis of pluralism and justice is perhaps the best way to honor the legacy of this premodern rebellious mystic.

■ Notes

1. The addition of an "S" after mentioning the Prophet is a way of offering honor, and means "peace be upon him."

2. Among others, one could mention Bernard Lewis, *The Crisis of Islam: Holy War and Unholy Terror*, (New York: Random House, 2003); Bassam Tibi, *The Crisis of Modern Islam: A Preindustrial Culture in the Scientific-Technological Age*, (Salt Lake City: University of Utah Press, 1988); Mahmoud Ayoub, *The Crisis in Muslim History*, (Oxford: Oneworld, 2003); etc.

3. Bruce Lawrence, *Shattering the Myth: Islam Beyond Violence* (Princeton University Press, 1998), p. 25.

4. For one example, see Marcia Hermansen's essay "How to Put the Genie Back in the Bottle: 'Identity' Islam and Muslim Youth Cultures in America," in Omid Safi, ed., *Progressive Muslims*, (Oxford, England: Oneworld Publications, 2003) in which she gives as an examples the impact of Wahhabi organizations on the American Muslim Student Association organizations starting in the 1960s.

5. For a broad overview of the reform movement in Iran, see Said Amir Arjomand, "The Reform Movement and the Debate on Modernity and Tradition in Contemporary Iran," *International Journal of Middle East Studies* 34 (2002): 719–731.

6. See Ahmadinejad's speech on the "Holocaust as a myth": http://www.cnn.com/2005/ WORLD/meast/12/14/iran.israel/index.html. For the Persian original, see *http://www. sharghnewspaper.coms/840924/html/index.htm*.

7. Indeed one Iranian reformist, Akbar Ganji, has stated that it is only through debate and dialogue, and indeed contention, that the various positions of reformists can be clarified.

8. http://www.unesco.org/dialogue2001/en/khatami.htm: "The General Assembly of the United Nations has only recently endorsed the proposal of the Islamic Republic of Iran for dialogue among civilizations and cultures."

9. http://www.un.org/Dialogue/.

10. Khatami interview with Christiane Amanpour, January 7, 1998 on CNN: http:// www.cnn.com/WORLD/9801/07/iran/interview.html.

11. Robin Wright, "An Iranian Luther Shakes the Foundations of Islam." *The Guardian*. Feb.1, 1995. Subsequent "receipts" include Khaled Abou El Fadl, Abdullahi an-Na'im, and Asra Nomani.

12. For a good English translation of this essay in a mercifully abbreviated format, see Charles Kurzman, ed., *Liberal Islam: A Sourcebook* (New York: Oxford University Press, 1998), pp. 244–254.

13. Soroush, "The Evolution and Devolution of Religious Knowledge," in Kurzman, *Liberal Islam*, pp. 245–246.

14. Soroush, *Sirat-ha-ye mustaqim* [Straight Paths] (Tehran: Sirat, 1998).

15. http://news.bbc.co.uk/2/hi/middle_east/3053075.stm.

16. Purya Hajizadeh and Pardis Hajizadeh, *Aqajari* [Including the complete text of the Hamadan speech, etc.] Tehran, Jama-daran, 1382/2003.

17. Aghajari, "Hamadan speech," in Hajizadeh, pp. 38–39.

18. Aghajari, p. 36.

19. Sadri, "Sacral Defense of Secularism: The Political Theologies of Soroush, Shabestari, and Kadivar," *International Journal of Politics, Culture and Society,* 15/2 (Winter, 2001): 260.

20. Shabestari, *Iman va Azadi,* (Tehran: *Tarh-e No,* 1376/1999), p. 95.

21. Ibid., p. 100.

22. Ibid., pp. 104–105.

23. While Shabestari does not specify this, he seems to have *Heilsgeschichte* in mind.

24. For an earlier attempt to draw this distinction, see Bazaran, "Religion and Liberty," in Kurzman, *Liberal Islam,* p. 79.

25. Shabestari, *Iman va Azadi,* pp. 7–8.

26. Shabestari, *Naqdi bar Qera'at-e Rasmi az Din* (A critique of official Reading of Religion), (Tehran: Tarh-e No, 2000).

27. Kadivar, "The Principles of Compatibility of Islam and Modernity," p. 1. Available: http://kadivar.com/Index.asp?DocId=831&AC=1&AF=1&ASB=1&AGM=1&AL=1&DT=dtv

28. Ibid., p. 9.

29. Kadivar, *Hokumat-e Velayi.* (Tehran: Nashr-e Ney, 1377/1998).

30. Kadivar, "Velayat-e Faqih and Democracy," p. 14. Available at: http://kadivar.com/Index.asp?DocId=834&AC=1&AF=1&ASB=1&AGM=1&AL=1&DT=dtv

31. *Monzara-ye Dr. 'Abdalkarim Soroush va Hojjat al-Islam Mohsen Kadivar dar bara-ye Dluralism-e Dini.* (Tehran: Nashr-e-Nay, 1378/1999).

32. Ebadi, *Tarikh-che va asnad-e hoquq-e bashar dar Iran,* (Tehran: Roshangaran, 1373/1994). The English work which appeared as *History and Documentation of Human Rights in Iran,* (New York: Bibliotheca Persica Press, 2000), is an abbreviation of the massive 350 page Persian original.

33. Ebadi, *Hoquq-e zan dar qavanin-e jomhuri-ye Islami-ye Iran,* (Tehran: Ganj-e Danesh, 1381/2002), pp. 160–163.

34. For the Persian original, see: http://nobelprize.org/peace/laureates/2003/ebadi-lecture-fa.pdf. For an English translation, see: http://nobelprize.org/peace/laureates/2003/ebadi-lecture-e.html.

35. Ziba Mir-Hosseini, "Religious Modernists and the 'Woman Question': Challenges and Complicities, in Eric Hooglund, ed., *Twenty Years of Islamic Revolution: Political and Social Transition in Iran since* 1979, Syracuse University Press, 2002, pp. 74–95.

36. Mehrangiz Kar, "Roshanfekri-ye dini va Mas'ala-ye 'Zanan'" ("Religious Intellectuals and the 'Woman Problem'"), *Rah-e Now* 1/16 (17 Mordad 1377 [August 1998]): 32–33. Cited in Ziba Mir-Hosseini, "Religious Modernists." If one were to adopt a progressive self-critique and offer a critique of Mehrangiz Kar's own project, it would be the naïve way in which she has become affiliated with Benador Associates, a public relations think tank for some of the leading neoconservatives and Islamophobes of the day, including Charles Krauthammer, Michael A. Ledeen, Richard Perle, Walid Phares, Richard Pipes, David Pryce-Jones, and James Woolsey. Although there is no questioning Mehrangiz Kar's own commitment to women's rights in Iran, when women's rights advocates align themselves with such ideologically triumphalist advocates, it does expose many in the gender-equality movement to the charge of being pawns of the Empire. Benador has quite wisely surrounded

their neoconservative members with liberal Muslims who critique the patriarchy and corruption of Muslim regimes—but never that of the American regime, or, of course, Israel. For another example, see their inclusion of Saad Ed Din Ebrahim.

37. Soroush, "Contraction and Expansion of Women's Rights," available through http://www.drsoroush.com/English/Interviews/E-INT-20000200-Contraction_and_Expansion_of_Womens_Rights.html.

38. Ibid.:

> It may be the case that our laws are imposing severe social constraints on women, but I believe that they are the weakest links in the chains restraining women. I think that the main issue we need to concern ourselves with is the basic principle of womanhood and manhood. The social contradictions are staring us in the face now and they make it clear that these regulations and commands do not correspond to our social needs and the roles that men and women have taken on in society; in other words, these laws do not meet the needs of the current relations between men and woman.

39. Mir-Hosseini, "Religious Modernists," p.17. In addition, in Mir-Hosseini, *Islam and Gender: The Religious Debate in Contemporary Iran,* (Princeton: Princeton University Press, 1999), see "Challenges and Complicities: Abdolkarim Sorush and Gender" pp. 217–46.

40. Kadivar, "Hoquq-e zanan dar islam-e mo'aser az zaviye-ye digar" (Women's Right in Contemporary Islam from Another Angle). See http://kadivar.com/Index.asp?DocId=1&AF=1&ASB=1&AGM=1&A:=1&DT=dtv.

41. Muneer Goolam Fareed, *Legal Reform in the Muslim World: The Anatomy of a Scholarly Dispute in the 19th and the Early 20th Centuries on the Usage of Ijtihād as a Legal Tool* (Bethesda, MD: Austin and Winfield, 1996).

42. Muhammad Iqbal, "The Principle of Movement in the Structure of Islam," in Charles Kurzman, *Liberal Islam,* pp. 256–257.

43. Muhammad Sa'id al-'Ashmawi, in Charles Kurzman, *Liberal Islam,* p. 55.

44. To recall Sherman Jackson's new term.

45. Wael Hallaq, "Was the gate of *ijtihad* closed?" *International Journal of Middle East Studies* 16/1: 3–41; Wael Hallaq., "On the origins of the controversy about the existence of *mujtahids* and the gate of *ijtihad,*" *Studia Islamica,* 63: 129–141.

46. Charles Kurzman, *Liberal Islam,* pp. 55 and 67–72.

47. For an American observer such as myself, the level of the discourse and the critique and the countercritique and the counter-countercritique is simply dazzling, and a painful reminder that in the North American there are no or at least few comparable sustained engagements across ideological lines outside cyberspace.

48. Hussein-'Ali Montazeri, "Dar bab-e Tazahum," *Majalla-yi Kiyan* 45 (1377/1998): 150–151. Quoted in Soroush, *Ijtihad,* (Tehran: Tarh-e Nau, 2003), 14.

49. Ja'far Subhani, "Falsafa-ye Fiqh," in Soroush, *Ijtihad,* pp. 65–78.

50. The analogy here, of course, is an ironic reminder of the attempts under Reza Shah to purge Persia of all the Arabic vocabulary, a failed endeavor. In a way, Soroush is ironically comparing Reza Shah's nationalist linguistic *'asabiyya* to the Ayatollah's religious intolerance. One issue does remain that in both the garden metaphor and the textual one, one element (grapevine and Persian, respectively) is hegemonic.

51. Soroush, *Ijtihad,* p. 17.

52. Akbar Ganji, *Talaqqi-yi fashisti az din va hukumat. (The Fascist Interpretation of Religion and Government),* (Tehran: Tarh-I Naw, 2000).

53. Soroush, *Ijtihad,* pp. 21–22.

54. Ibid., p. 22.

55. Ibid.

56. Ibid., p. 23.

57. http://www.tariqramadan.com/article.php3?id_article=0277&lang=en.

58. Ibid.

59. http://news.bbc.co.uk/1/hi/world/middle_east/4394863.stm.

60. http://www.altmuslim.com/perm.php?id=1424_0_24_0_M.

61. http://www.tariqramadan.com/article.php3?id_article=0264&lang=en.

62. http://www.tariqramadan.com/article.php3?id_article=0264&lang=en.

63. Cited in http://www.tariqramadan.com/article.php3?id_article=0308&lang=en.

64. http://www.tariqramadan.com/article.php3?id_article=0308&lang=en.

65. I would argue that had Soroush and company been writing in Arabic—or German (!)—there would already be dozens of dissertations on their project.

66. Kadivar's web site, kadivar.com, has been accessed 150,000 times. One of Soroush's sites, Drsoroush.com, has 240,000 hits (both as of January 2006).

67. The primacy of English as the language of cyberspace cannot be overstated here.

68. Marshall G.S. Hodgson, *The Venture of Islam: Conscience and History in A World Civilization,* Vol. 2, (Chicago: University of Chicago Press, 1974), p. 154.

69. Both the previous and this quotation are from a manuscript presently being translated by the author for publication in the Paulist Press series on the *Classics of Western Spirituality*.

70. Edited by James M. Washington. *A Testament of Hope: The Essential Writings and Speeches of Martin Luther King, Jr.* (Harper San Francisco, 1986, 1991), p. 254.

Epilogue: The Purpose of Interreligious Dialogue[1]

Reuven Firestone, James Heft, and Omid Safi

■ JAMES HEFT

On the last day of our conversations in Jerusalem, one participant raised the question: "What does your religious tradition give for reasons for interreligious dialogue?" It was, in one sense, an obvious question, but in another sense, it immediately evoked a moment of reflective silence from the group—a group that had had no trouble until then filling the time with heartfelt words. Indeed, the question goes to the heart of what we had been engaged in for three days, but had not explicitly reflected upon.

A variety of responses to the question were given. One person said simply, "So that those in power don't kill us." "In today's world, it is dialogue or die," another added grimly. Although agreeing, another participant suggested that the reasons for interreligious dialogue had to go deeper than political and personal survival: they have to deal with the spiritual and theological dimensions of life. One participant worried that the centers of power in our religious traditions did not promote self-correction sufficiently. But self-correction, responded another, is rarely as effective and accurate as the corrections that come from an informed person of another faith.

Should we not, asked another, paraphrase the poet, John Donne, and say that "no religion is an island"? In fact, added another, it is a mistake to think that our three religious traditions were ever only single, even though they appeared at different points in history. Abraham Heschel, someone else reminded the group, once said that we enter dialogue to help one another reveal the living God. Through such dialogue, this person believed that we deepen the brotherhood and sisterhood of religious believers. In the light of Heschel's comment, might we not imagine, he continued, that at this point in global history God is inviting all of us to know each other better?

One participant put the question into the immediate context of our theme: learned ignorance. He reminded the group that no religious tradition possesses an adequate understanding of God. It was then asked, are we not committed Jews, Christians, and Muslims because we believe what our respective religious traditions affirm, however inadequately? Don't we remain committed Jews and Christians and Muslims because we find the claims of our respective traditions more true than those of the other religious traditions, however much we may respect those other traditions and love their followers?

We realized at the end of this day that we were able to raise such questions better than we were able to answer them. Now that some time has elapsed since those blessed days in Jerusalem, we three editors of this volume wish to add a few further comments on the purpose of interreligious dialogue. And we wish to make our remarks also in the form of a dialogue among the three of us.

Speaking now for myself, I was struck with something David Burrell, a member of this trialogue, wrote later concerning the insistence of the Vatican not just to aim at better mutual understanding in interreligious dialogue, but also to proclaim the truth of one's own faith. Burrell questions any stark contrast between "dialogue" and "proclamation," which can suggest that dialogue alone is radically insufficient for believers. He asks:

> But what would it be to proclaim the truth? Would it be to make an assertion and then to insist that it was true; or as one wag put it: to stamp one's foot? In fact, of course, any properly formed assertion, actually stated, intends what is the case. Grammar is inherently ethical, which is why lying—deliberately stating what is not the case—is inherently wrong. Yet we know that one's acceptance of what another says is often conditioned by the moral probity or veracity of the speaker. So, "proclaiming the truth" of one's faith is better done than said, as the Amish in Pennsylvania demonstrated to America by forgiving their children's killer. Merely stating one's faith convictions cannot in fact count as proclamation. What counts is witness; and while the fact of dialogue may give telling witness in certain situations, like Israel/Palestine, the intellectual endeavor of dialogue can at best be a means of sorting out awkward from promising ways of stating what we believe.[2]

Burrell's comments suggest to me three things of importance in trying to understand the purpose of interreligious dialogue. First, fruitful interreligious dialogue presupposes persons who are deeply rooted in the faith of their own religious tradition. Moreover, dialogue depends, not only on words spoken, but also on the adequacy of the words; that is to say, does the person who is speaking give an informed and adequate representation of his or her tradition. If not, the dialogue falters.

Second, any form of coercion—stamping one's foot—has no place in interreligious dialogue. When I am in conversation with Jews and Muslims, I presume that they are committed to their religious traditions because they believe them to be more true than other religious traditions. Why should this offend me? I also believe the same thing about my religious tradition, Christianity, though just what that "same thing" is needs careful description. Otherwise, my position could be misinterpreted as one that claims, wrongly, that I possess all the truth and people from other religious traditions are simply lost. Of course, it is possible that very well-versed believers in one tradition, though identifying themselves as members of that tradition, simply abstain from taking such a position. That is to say, they bracket the issue of whether one tradition is truer than another. What is affirmed is that one's own religious tradition is true for the believer. I do not think such a stance is that helpful in interreligious dialogue, for it does not represent what most religious believers actually affirm of themselves, nor does it engage the difficult question of what I believe to be true about God.

I was struck by the honesty of one Jewish scholar who, writing to a fellow believer, recently said the following:

> I think the Christian story about the incarnation and resurrection is an out and out falsehood, and is a travesty when imposed on my Hebrew Bible. Yet, I have read Augustine, Aquinas, Teresa of Avila, *The Cloud of Unknowing*, and, yes, passages in the Greek Bible, which I have found profoundly moving in their spiritual sensitivity and love of God. That is the basis of my respect and even love (for some forms) of Christianity. Indeed, as you know, in our tradition if a holy book falls to the ground, when picking it up one is to kiss it. Well, once I was at a place where I saw a New Testament lying on the ground. I picked it up and instinctively kissed it.[3]

What is most moving for me in this observation, and what brings out for me a third and final valuable insight suggested by Burrell, is the importance of witness. I feel drawn to talk with this Jew whom I have just quoted. He is deeply informed, not only about his own tradition, but also about mine, and sympathetically about mine. What's more, he witnesses to his faith with an extraordinary example—kissing a book not considered as revelatory to him, but nonetheless "instinctively" kissing it out of a deep respect, which he learned in his own tradition.

So, I'd suggest to Reuven and Omid that the purpose of interreligious dialogue is, not only better mutual understanding (which includes self-correction and finding "less awkward" ways of expressing our beliefs), but also trying, however inadequately, to embody the truths that we affirm.

Question from Omid to Jim Heft: *I was in agreement with everything in your piece, but had this lingering question about this phrase: "First, fruitful interreligious dialogue presupposes persons who are deeply rooted in the faith of their own religious tradition." I do understand that a pluralistic trialogue presupposes faithful participants. But I am wondering if that dynamic may not lead to a "narcissism of small differences," while forgetting about the fact that all three religious communities are part of a worldwide community where faith can at times be seen as a luxury, as irrelevant to the "material" realities that many have to live under. In other words, how do we as faithful members of a trialogue continue talking, while being mindful of the fact that all of us are confronted with similar challenges external to the trialogue conversation?*

Jim's response to Omid: Your reference, Omid, to the "narcissism of small differences" reminds me of a comment by C. S. Lewis who, in the preface to his classic *Mere Christianity*, a series of talks he gave over the BBC during the Second World War, wrote that one of the things Christians are in disagreement about is the importance of their disagreements.

> When two Christians of different denominations start arguing, it is usually not long before one asks whether such-and-such a point 'really matters' and the other replies: 'Matter? Why, it's absolutely essential.'

In dialogues among Christians of different denominations, the participants have wisely begun with the major issues on which they believe they will likely agree before turning to the likely points of disagreements, which also could be major. The more deeply persons are rooted in their faith traditions (as I understand that phrase), the more likely it is that they will be able to distinguish the major from the minor issues. Even more important, if they are deeply rooted, then they will have a historical sense of their tradition, and be more likely to understand how even major issues might be expressed in a variety of ways, none ever fully adequate.

But you've also raised a second issue—the critical need for "academics" not to be just "academics," by which I think you mean, being privileged people oblivious to the sufferings and deprivations of many of their co-religionists throughout the world. To be quite honest, I have often wondered whether I have sufficiently acted on what I believe and effectively witnessed to what I have been privileged to learn through study and interreligious dialogues. I have had periods in my life when I have desired to be a monk and then other times when I'd like to be out in the streets protesting. Perhaps my calling is to locate myself somewhere in between. I think our major religious doctrines are very important, but I also believe that if they do not move us to love and risk for others, especially those less fortunate, much of our life remains, sadly—even scandalously—only "academic."

Question from Reuven to Jim Heft: *You reiterated a question that was brought up in our dialogue and then you rephrased it as follows: "Don't' we remain committed Jews and Christians and Muslims because we find the claims of our respective traditions more true than those of the other religious traditions, however much we may respect those other traditions and love their followers?" I have two related question linked to the assumption that seems to be imbedded in the question: (1) If you were to arrive at the position that the claims of Judaism or Islam were as true as yours for Christianity, would you no longer be a committed Christian? Can one ever arrive at a true understanding and truly respectful view of the religious other if one insists that one's own religious tradition is truer?*

Jim's response to Reuven: I've wrestled for years with how to express this issue of how to think about what I, as a Christian, believe as the truth of God's revelation, especially when in conversation with members of other religions. Over twenty years ago, I wrote a short essay for Catholic high school religion teachers in which I outlined four possible positions to take with regard to other religions. The first two I quickly dismissed: absolutism (we have all the truth and everyone else is lost) and relativism (all the religions are basically the same). The remaining two I described as "confessional systematic" and "confessional dialogic" (forgive the awkward phrases). By "confessional" I meant saying basically what one believes to be true; that is, "confessing" one's faith. By connecting the word confessional to "systematic," I meant that after confessing my own faith, I would then proceed to evaluate the other's religious tradition in the light of my own. I explained that, in my view, the "confessional systematic" position is premature and inappropriate—premature because serious interreligious dialogue has only begun in the last few decades, and inappropriate because such a position sets one up as an all-knowing judge of another religious tradition. After all, it is hard enough to get a good grasp of one's own religious tradition; in fact, acquiring an adequate grasp of one's religious tradition is a life-long challenge. Instead, I recommended that the proper stance for interreligious dialogue was to confess one's faith and do one's best to learn from and to dialogue with the other. Obviously, one will inevitably be formulating various judgments during a dialogue, not only of what the other believes, but also of how one understands and formulates one's own beliefs.

You also asked, Reuven, whether, if I came to the conclusion that the claims of Judaism or Islam were as true as my own, I would no longer be a committed Christian. I have difficulty imagining how, at this point, I could come to the position you describe in your question. I say this because one of the major differences between us is the claim we Christians make that the Word became flesh, that is, the Incarnation. The radical character of this claim is well brought out by the chapter in our volume contributed by Olivier-Thomas Venard. Though I tend to think that many Christians on the practical level are theists rather than Christians (that is, they really believe in God more than a trinity or put a central importance on Jesus as God's son), I also believe, speaking quite personally and as a Catholic that Jesus and the Eucharist influence deeply how I think and live. Although I have learned (again, through interreligious dialogue) that there are some parallels to a palpable sense of God's presence in both Judaism and Islam, I do not think Jews or Muslims will be able to embrace my belief in Jesus and the Eucharist, unless they become Christians, and, indeed, Catholic Christians. Hence, I cannot quite picture myself getting to the point where I would see the claims of Judaism and Islam and Christian as equally true, at least with regard to the Incarnation and, therefore, the trinity.

One last point: Can I truly respect Jews and Muslims who believe differently than I do on these central issues? I think I actually do, and not in a patronizing way—as if I were to be saying to you, "You're a good person but you just don't get it (fully)." Oddly enough, I feel closer to some Jews and Muslims than I do to some fellow Catholics. How can that be when I just said that key Christian beliefs are central to my faith and life? Really, I am not sure. But what I do know is that my respect for you is deep and genuine. I think we both agree that friendship and living our respective faiths are crucial, and that friendship and respect can be very deep indeed.

In thinking about all this, where we might differ is the extent to which we believe that our respective religious beliefs are different and central to who we are and how we live.

■ OMID SAFI

I think that interreligious dialogue is both socially and politically necessary, and theologically vital. Let me address them separately. We are becoming more and more aware of our interconnectedness as members of one human race. Some of this awareness is coming from the environmental crisis, where we are becoming more mindful that the CO_2 gasses produced in the United States and China contribute to the melting of the Polar ice caps, which results in the shifting of jet streams and eventual rising of ocean levels, and that all this will have catastrophic consequences for places like New Orleans and Bangladesh. Our actions have consequences, and we are caught up in this same network together. Interfaith dialogue is part of this connection, part of what Martin Luther King called the "inescapable network of mutuality." There can truly be no peace among humanity until and unless there is peace among the religions of humanity. That peace cannot emerge without profound dialogue, exchange, humility, and learning from one another.

The other point is more theological. Up until now we have spoken of the "truth" of our own religious traditions, and the relationship that has to interfaith dialogue. I would suggest that for me, as a Muslim who is committed to inter – and intrafaith work (the second often being much harder, and as urgent), it is not only difficult but also maybe idolatrous to speak of the "truth" of my own tradition in an absolute sense. The reason is simple: In the Islamic tradition, only God as such may be called *Haqq*, Truth. It is God alone who is Absolute Truth, Absolutely Real. Religious traditions cannot be called "Truth" in that sense, for that would be putting them on the same level as God, and thus a challenge to God's absolute Unity. I would suggest that Muslims look at different religions as paths, acknowledging that God has designed multiple paths for the multiplicity of humanity, while, God willing, hoping that these paths lead us to the same destination.

So why engage in interfaith dialogue? Because for me, as a Muslim, God is greater than any one path leading to God. Any path, by definition, is limited and particular. God is not. Let me be more specific by offering a concrete example: It was not until I studied the Taoist tradition that I really came to learn about the reality of the natural realm as a manifestation of the Sacred, and of the virtue of living harmoniously with the natural realm and the cosmos as a great human spiritual trait. It was after learning that lesson that I returned to my own tradition as a Muslim and came to realize that when the Qur'an refers to the natural cosmos as an "aya," a Sign of God, that meaning has been there as well, but I needed to see it first in another tradition, to cultivate a spiritual "taste" for it, and to open up a new set of eyes to see a beauty that had been there in my own tradition all along.

I do remain convinced that neither I nor my own traditions has a monopoly on truth, because in reality we belong to the Truth (God), not Truth to us. If God is ultimately our beloved, I learn something new from each adoration, though I remain on my own path. This is not an argument for relativism; it is an adamant insistence on the Absoluteness of God, and recognition of our own limitedness before an awesome God.

Jim's Question to Omid: *Does not "learned ignorance" enable believers to affirm the truth of their own religious tradition without any claim to full comprehension of it, or making any assertion that is presumed to be "absolute"?*

Omid's Response to Jim: Not surprisingly, Muslims have tended to have internal debates about the issue of how to affirm the truth of one's own tradition in a pluralistic world. Historically, most Muslims have looked to verses of the Qur'an, such as 5:3, which states: "This day have I perfected your religion for you, completed My favor upon you, and have chosen for you Islam as your religion." For many Muslims, that verse is sufficient and conclusive reason to conclude that God has blessed Muslims by blessing them with Islam, which represents a "complete and perfect" favor. Furthermore, many Muslims have also developed complicated systems that attempt to explain how all teachings that deviate from Islamic doctrines must represent the willful or mistaken developments in previous traditions.

At the same time, other Muslims, particularly of the mystical orientation, have tended to view religious traditions as paths, not destinations. In other words, they have been and remained mindful that the same One God has sent numerous messengers and prophets, and not even the Prophet Muhammad has been told about all of them. Furthermore, there are numerous Qur'anic warnings about not favoring one messenger over another, such as Qur'an 2:285: "The Messenger believes in what was sent down to him from his Lord, and the believers; each one believes in God and His angels, and in His Books and His Messengers; we make no division between any one of His Messengers." Furthermore, there are also verses that address how all peoples have been sent a prophetic figure. For these types of approaches, it would seem that the best approach is to exercise spiritual and intellectual humility by acknowledging both the particularity and the shared Divine origin of all revelation.

For this second group of Muslims, it seems that whatever path, including Islam, that brings humanity to the Divine, is a worthy path. My own position is more in line with the second approach. Echoing Gandhi, I am less concerned with asserting the final truth of my own path and more interested in seeing whether the paths we are collectively pursuing transform us into kinder, more compassionate, and more just human beings.

Reuven's question to Omid: *I am moved by your suggestion that study of Taoist tradition enabled you to learn something new to you about God's manifestation in nature. After engaging with the Tao, you returned to your own religious tradition, enabled to discover something of the same within it as well. Engaging in another religion can deepen and enrich your experience and appreciation of your own. This leads me to a question: is it necessary for your own religion to validate the significance of what you learned from another? What if you find something very moving in another religious tradition for which you find no parallel in your own? Does it remain valid even if foreign?*

Omid's response to Reuven: In many cases I have found that exploring another religious tradition allows me to detect the presence of similar themes in more implicit forms in my own tradition. However, in some cases that has not been the case. The fact that a teaching or practice does not exist—yet—in my own tradition does not take away its truth or beauty in my eyes, and this for a number of reasons. First and foremost, I see religious traditions as paths to the Divine, and by definition the Divine is broader, larger, more encompassing than any one path—even my own. Indeed, it would be shocking from this perspective if all the wisdom, all the beauty, all the magic of religion, was exhausted in any one tradition. This is at least one meaning of Qur'an 6: 103, where it is stated: "No vision can grasp God, but God's grasp is over all visions." Therefore, it does not surprise me that each tradition might have worked out an area of emphasis on particular teaching, which, in some ways, may surpass that of others. So in the example we have been talking about, I have no problem stating that all traditions call us to live humbly and harmoniously with the natural cosmos, but that the Taoist path has stated this most clearly. In the same way, I might state that all traditions talk about the need to balance love and justice, but I find the clearest articulation of this balance in Islam. To paraphrase Edward Said, no tradition has a monopoly on goodness or beauty.

Secondly, I think it is good and beautiful to add that teachings that one finds lovely in another tradition may not—yet—exist in one's own tradition, because that way we can come to think of all traditions, including one's own, not as fossilized in the past, but as part of what W. C. Smith used to call "cumulative traditions."

If we use, not a fossil analogy, but a river analogy, may it be that with the flow of time, each tradition comes to pick up beautiful elements, and incorporate them into its own fabric.

■ REUVEN FIRESTONE

The British Anglican theologian, Alan Race, has proposed a helpful typology of encounter between religions.[4] He observes three basic approaches in interreligious encounter. The first is *Exclusivism*, which characterizes the view that only through one's own faith can God's authentic truth be found. This is a declaration, a theological verdict, and it is not conducive to real dialogue and understanding of the "religious other." Needless to say, such an approach would not epitomize the kind of openness that we have sought out in our dialogue, and although one might honestly arrive at the exclusivist conclusion through humble study, participants in our dialogue would agree that it could not be one of deep charitable and religious humility.

Race's second approach to religious encounter is *Inclusivism*, which balances the poles of particularity and universality imbedded in religion and God by affirming that the truth of one's own religion can also be found, in one form or another, within *other* religions. It allows for the redemptive value of other religions, but only because their essence reflects the truth of one's own. He cites the official Catholic encyclical, *Redemptoris Missio* as an example of this approach. I include only the core of his citation:

> [M]any people do not have an opportunity to come to know or accept the Gospel revelation or to enter the Church. The social and cultural conditions in which they live do not permit this, and frequently they have been brought up in other religious traditions. For such people salvation in Christ is accessible by virtue of a grace which, while having a mysterious relationship to the Church, does not make them formally part of the Church but enlightens them in a way which is accommodated to their spiritual and material situation. This grace comes from Christ...[5]

This approach, too, would appear to fail our "test of humility." On the one hand, it is patronizing, because it assumes an implicit desire among the un-churched to enter the Church. They would if they could, or if they only knew more about it. Most believers in other religions would resent such an assessment of their faith and practice. This approach refuses to accept the possibility of a true, unique, and independent relationship with God that derives from a different religious experience.

The third approach Race calls pluralism, which he suggests is far more than the simplistic proposition that because many religions worship and believe in the same God, their religious differences and philosophical/theological clashes are irrelevant. He acknowledges that differences are important, but insists that they need not cancel or annul the value or even the truth of a religion that is different from one's own. In fact, thinking about the differences can help us to better understand our own religious ideas as well as the ideas of other religions. Race cites John Hick's articulation of the notion:

If salvation is taking place, and taking place to about the same extent, within the religious systems presided over by these various deities and absolutes, this suggests that they are different manifestations to humanity of a yet more ultimate ground of all salvific transformation. . . . If, then, we proceed inductively from the phenomenon of religious experience around the world, adopting a religious as distinguished from a naturalistic interpretation of it, we are likely to find ourselves making two moves. The first is to postulate an ultimate transcendent divine reality (which I have been referring to as the Real) which, being beyond the scope of our human concepts, cannot be directly experienced by us as it is in itself, but only as it appears through our various human thought-forms. And the second is to identify the thought-and-experienced deities and absolutes as different manifestations of the Real within different historical forms of human consciousness.[6]

Hick's formulation here, to my mind, tends toward a bland and impersonal, universal deism. God to me is not just an idea, an ultimate transcendent divine reality, but a real something or someone with whom we can communicate, cry to, entreat, and argue with. Yet this approach fully acknowledges the validity of my faith tradition.

There are, of course, thoughtful arguments in support of each of these three approaches, as well as thoughtful critiques. From the perspective of "learned ignorance," however, only something like the last approach exemplifies the religious and theological values that we in the group have cherished during our period together in interfaith encounter. An ultimate, transcendent divine reality *must* lie behind the grand and extraordinary wisdom that we have encountered through dialogue with religions not our own.

How we grapple with the tension that we tend to assume between the particularity of our own religious experience and the universality of the transcendent divine reality has become more than simply an interesting problem for theologians. The tension, which appears to be irresolvable on a universal scale, has not only been expressed in history through the writing of treatises, but also through public disputations, religious persecutions, and bloody wars. That tension may never be fully relieved, but as we move onward in history it is of utmost consequence for leaders in religion to engage in the process of dialogue with, if not a realization of learned ignorance, at least one of intellectual and personal humility.

Jim's question to Reuven: *I think I understand well how our theme of "learned ignorance" should prevent dialogue partners from claiming superiority over the other. However, as a believing Jew, do you run the risk as a pluralist of saying that my Christian tradition is just as—well, just as "good" as yours?*

Reuven's response to Jim: I have been taught through my tradition that there is an absolute truth about God. If God is real, which we accept as axiomatic, then that reality has aspects that must be true. Additionally, because there is such significant disagreement between people over the nature of God, there must also be views and opinions among them that are false. Therefore, there is, indeed, something that can be called truth, and we as religious individuals are encouraged to seek it out. But I have also been taught through my religious tradition that the real truth about these things is so elusive that it is often described simply as *sod*, "secret." There is a truth out there, but we must recognize that we will not ever fully grasp it. The entire enterprise of *midrash* or interpretive investigation of Scripture is based upon the premise that we are obligated to engage in the process of striving toward that truth and living in relationship to God. At the same time, we recognize that that truth is so complex that we should never be satisfied that we have arrived at it.

In the second- to third-century Talmudic handbook for rabbinical scholars and judges known as *Chapters of the Ancestors* (*pirkey avot*), there is a statement: *lo hamidrash hu ha`ikar ela hama`aseh*—"the essence is not the interpretation but rather, deeds."[7] Judaism places greater emphasis on striving to achieve proper behavior than striving to find the truth of God. For me, therefore, I will judge my dialogical partner ultimately on the value of that person's behavior far beyond the value of that person's truth claims. In fact (and this is also basic to my tradition), the acts of a person are perhaps the best articulation of their relationship with God. As Daniel Madigan wrote in his chapter for this collection, "[I]n the end, the actions and omissions of Christians speak much more loudly than our words." Is your Christian tradition just as "good" as my Jewish tradition? In terms of theology I will never know, but the question is really not of great concern to me as I deepen my understanding of God, humanity, and religion from my dialogical partners. However, in terms of behaviors expected or taught formally or even informally by a religion that is different from my own, I feel free to make a judgment.

Omid's question to Reuven: *I very much like these distinctions between inclusivism, exclusivism, and the gradations of pluralism. I also appreciate the notion of particularity of each religious manifestation and the ultimate, transcendent Divine reality. All fair enough. But it seems to me that in this pluralistic trialogue, we have to do more than simply affirm the particularity of each of our traditions: How do we come to grapple with the particularization of that absolute divine reality? How do we read/engage/challenge the process whereby the absolute reality has become connected to particular historical manifestations (be it the experience of the children of Israel, the theophany in Christ, or the revelatory experience of Muhammad)?*

Reuven's response to Omid: I am reading your question in two parts. On the one hand, I understand your question as directed to the particular religious truth claims of revelation that serve as the authoritative pillars supporting each of our three religious traditions. On the other, I understand your question as one directed to the particularity of religious institutions. Regarding the first, it is impossible for me to prove or disprove the authenticity of any divine revelation. There is no apparatus that would allow me to do so in an objective manner. In each of the three religions represented in this dialogue, the particularity of revelation is different (though they share aspects as well) and the record of revelation is recorded only within the specific religious literatures of each. No contemporary writings or archaeological findings have been found to confirm or disprove them. I, therefore, have no choice but to accept the possibility of each revelation being true and authentic. Because of my own particular history I feel more comfortable with my own religious tradition and intuitively tend to have more faith in its truths, but I consider myself open to the reality of the others as well.

Regarding the particularity of religious institutions, I agree with you not only that religious traditions cannot be called "Truth," but I would go a step further to suggest that religious traditions develop out of human interaction with and interpretation of the reality that is God. I consider religious institutions to be human creations, human organizational responses to the Ultimate. And here we can observe common trends (or even laws of institutional behavior) that influence relations among religious institutions. To give one example related to your question, religious institutions announce an end to revelation by canonizing Scripture. Any revelation that postdates that canonization is considered by the religion-as-institution to be false. That is not an objective assessment, to say the least. On the other hand, revelations that precede it are considered true but somehow flawed, therefore, opening the way to their own revelation. This consistent trend might be called a law of religious institutional relationship. Thus, Judaism as a religious institution cannot accept the revelation of either Christianity or Islam, but Islam as religious institution must accept the revelations of Judaism and Christianity, even if they are regarded as flawed. Christianity is positioned in the middle, accepting the "Old Testament" as incomplete but rejecting the Qur'an. Likewise, Islam cannot accept revelation that occurred after the canonization of the Qur'an. Baha'i revelation, for example, is, therefore, rejected.

This attitude is institutional and it reflects the politics of institutional religion. Pious Jews, Christians, and Muslims can transcend the polemics of institutional politics, but this is often quite difficult. As dialogicians, I believe we are obligated to work toward influencing our religious institutions to become more open to the *actual truth* of the religious other. We are likely not to be convinced, but I do not consider this to be problematic in the slightest. Being a believer and yet truly and honestly open to the possibility of another's truth claims is the essence of humility and, to my mind, theological maturity. History has proven how religion has been an effective means for motivating large numbers of people to engage in extraordinary behaviors, sometimes good, sometimes evil. We must assume responsibility today to move the equation of religious history to the balance of the good.

■ CONCLUSION

Jim Heft writes: It should be evident from this exchange that, although there is one important convergence in this epilogue—namely, that none of the writers believes that his religious tradition contains in an adequately articulated way all the wisdom of God—there remain differences that are not insignificant. As a member of the Catholic Christian community, I am part of a tradition that has a clear central authority capable of making, under strictly limited conditions, binding statements of faith for all its members. Neither Judaism nor Islam has such a central authority. At the same time, all three traditions have histories of interpretation, debates both within and beyond their communities, which have led to clarifications of fundamental teachings and the performance of practices deemed obligatory. By staying at the table of dialogue, these three great religions can continue to clarify their self-understandings, reduce misunderstandings of each other, and be a positive force for justice and peace in our troubled world. Serious interreligious dialogue remains a privileged vehicle for furthering strengthening this positive force.

Notes

1. This epilogue has a different structure than this book. Here, the three editors have written short essays about what they think is the purpose of interreligious dialogue. After each short essay, the other two editors pose questions to the author of the essay, who then responds to each question. The Epilogue ends with a conclusion written by James Heft.

2. David Burrell, C.S.C., "Dialogue Between Muslims and Christians as Mutually Transformative Speech," in ed. Catherine Cornille, *Criteria of Discernment in Interreligious Dialogue* (Eugene OR: Wipf & Stock, 2009), p. 90.

3. Yehuda Gellman (this striking statement is found in an e-mail sent to Professor Michael Signer, who was a member of this trialogue).

4. Alan Race, *Christians and Religious Pluralism,* 2nd ed. (London: SCM Press, 1993); Alan Race, *Interfaith Encounter* (London: SCM Press, 2001).

5. Race, *Interfaith Encounter*, p. 26.

6. Ibid., p. 30. Race cites the following works for further reading: John Hick, *An Interpretation of Religious: Human Responses to the Transcendent* (Basingstoke: Macmillan, 1989); John Hick, *The Rainbow of Faiths: Critical Dialogues on Religious Pluralism* (London: SCM Press, 1995), published in the United States as *A Christian Theology of Religions* (Louisville: Westminster/John Knox, 1995).

7. *Pirkey avot* 1:17.

INDEX

veneration of, 78
Christian beliefs, 257
  faith, in the Qur'an, 131
  fanatics in the United States, 295
  dialogue, intellectual humility and, 25
Christiani, Pablo, 151
Christianity and the Religions
    [Dupuis], 251
Christianity
  as a new religion, 117
  Biblical Israel and, 121
  considered idolatry, 138
  core belief, 130
  critical of other relgions, 117
  dogmatic side of, 130
  importance of chosenness in, 121
  in Jewish terms, 59
  other-worldliness of, 81
  the world religions and, 270
Christians
  as a minority in, 24
  as living community of faith, 253
  as members of the house of Israel, 253
  bloodstained history of, 210
  claims of, 304
  considered pagans, 138
  evangelical, 278
  first encountered [other] Jews, 264
  God of Israel and, 254
  in interreligious dialogue, 130
  Jewish theology of, 250
  learned from Islamic traditions, 46
  millen, 212
  mission of, 253
  more theist than Christian, 303
  New Testament, 27
  nonviolence of, 205
  salvation of as in the Qur'an, 121
  Syriac-speaking, 75
  world mission of, 27
Christology, the first, 131
  idolatry and, 132
  interpretation of, 251
  learned ignorance and, 41
  "low," 138
Church of the Holy Sepulcher in
    Jerusalem, 197, 199, 202, 226
church, 96
  all mankind and, 274
  and her "children," 261

as mystery, 95
as necessary, 273
as pilgrim, 96
hierarchy of, 95
members of, 95
membership, inside and outside, 265, 270
nature of, 91–5
proprietary claims of, 269
protested by Muslims, 73
salvation outside, 266
self-critical, 211
teachings, some are infallible, 96
Chysostom, John, on Jews, 200
Cicero, influence on Augustine, 193
circumcision and Passover, 153
citizenship, regardless of religion, 226
civilizations, clash of, 68, 138, 228
  revivers of, 81
  two, 258
clashes, interreligious, irrelevant, 307
classics of the ancient world, 75
classroom, dialogue in, 59
Clearchus of Soli, 116
Clement of Alexandria, on humility, 192
coercion, no place in dialogue, 301
Cohen, Hermann, 161
coincidence, iconographic, 59
coincident theology, 35
Cologne
  massacres in, 199
  synagogue of, 198
colonialism
  Greek, of Asia, 123
  Muslim collectivities and, 281
  perpetuates human suffering, 228
  Western, 183, 228
Columbus's voyage, 28
columns, as symbols of religions, 251
commandments, revelation and, 244
  truth and, 244
commitment, call to, 178
  faith, differences in, 29
common good of humanity [maslaha], 83
common ground, 68
Common Word project, 67
commonalities, bonds of, 29
  discovering, 72
  eliminating, 226
  of human beings, 69
  points of, 228

Printed in the USA/Agawam, MA
November 21, 2011

0 1341 1366904 5